REINVENTING THE WHEEL

SUNY series in Philosophy and Biology
David Edward Shaner, editor

REINVENTING
THE
WHEEL

A Buddhist Response
to the Information Age

Peter D. Hershock

STATE UNIVERSITY OF NEW YORK PRESS

Published by
State University of New York Press, Albany

For information, address State University of New York Press,
State University Plaza, Albany, N.Y., 12246

Production by Cathleen Collins
Marketing by Anne Valentine

Library of Congress Cataloging-in-Publication Data

Hershock, Peter D.
    Reinventing the wheel : a Buddhist response to the information age
/ Peter D. Hershock.
        p.   cm. — (SUNY series in philosophy and biology)
    Includes bibliographical references and index.
    ISBN 0-7914-4231-4 (alk. paper). — ISBN 0-7914-4232-2 (pbk. :
alk. paper)
    1. Information technology—Religious aspects—Buddhism.
2. Buddhism—Social aspects. 3. Buddhism—Doctrines. I. Title.
II. Series.
BQ4570.I55H47   1999
294.3'375—dc21   98–46706
                                                          CIP

10 9 8 7 6 5 4 3 2 1

For Supin

Contents

Part Two
Practicing the Unprecedented:
A Buddhist Intermission

Part Three
The Wheel of Dramatic Impoverishment:
The Crisis of Community in the Information Age

Introduction

This conversation began a couple of summers ago in Honolulu at a faculty development institute on infusing Asian content into the core undergraduate curriculum. A professor from a minority-serving college in New York City asked what I thought of the new information technologies. In particular, she wanted to know whether I thought television, distance learning, the Internet, and CD-ROMs could be used to effectively preserve and even encourage respect for cultural diversity.

I had just returned from a surf trip to Indonesia where, even in remote seaside and mountain villages, I had repeatedly been mistaken for the American television character, McGyver. This was not necessarily a bad thing. McGyver, after all, was an ingenious, morally earnest character with whom I was also quite familiar even though I had never watched the show and had, in fact, never owned a television in my entire adult life. But it was shocking that a ten-year-old girl living on the slopes of Bali's sacred Mount Agung would not only know of the character, but be able to rehearse one after another of his exploits. When I asked her what she knew about the heroic acts of Arjuna in the Ramayana—the most widely performed dramatic work in South and Southeast Asia for the last two millennia—she shrugged, smiled, and asked if I wanted to buy a bottle of Coke from her brother.

After relating this tale, I had simply raised my eyebrows and asked, "What do you think?" That day, the conversation got only so far as to establish that there were indeed serious political, economic, and social reasons to be wary of the claims that the new information technologies—at least as currently put to use—were likely to foster real cultural diversity. But as I continued working through the factors conditioning the relationship especially between mass media such as television and radio and the new technologies behind the spreading Internet and World Wide Web, it struck me that focusing on the explicit images and narratives conveyed by these media was like assuming the visible tip of an iceberg was all you had to worry about navigating around. I came to see that the global spread of high-tech media is only the visible and highly equivocal tip of a process I now refer to as the "colonization of consciousness"—a process informed by values shared by many of our most cherished political, societal, and religious institutions and inseparable from the corporate globalization of the economy. To play out the metaphor, I've been swimming ever since.

In what follows, I want to argue that the rapid spread of high-tech media is adversely related to the ideal of cultural diversity, not because of their explicit content or the varied intentions directing their use, but rather because of the way in which they tacitly reconfigure our awareness as such. Used ubiquitously enough, the media and the technologies on which they depend "invisibly" alter the structure of personhood in ways that erode the differences on which viable cultural diversity—and so harmony—finally depend. More generally and just as "invisibly," our technological lineage as a whole is conducive to patterns of attention that deplete our lives of the dramatic or narrative resources needed if we are going to meaningfully—and not merely factually—resolve our problems. In short, the more we are technically enabled to attain what we want, the more we are being left wanting.

Curiously and tragically, we apparently would not have it any other way. Because the values being expressed and focused by our technological lineage and the ongoing colonization of consciousness are also integral to our economic and political ideals and the way in which we understand what it means to be a person, we take this new form of colonization as our inalienable right. And so, under the rubric of "informing" ourselves and "bettering" our lot through technology, we have not only been earnestly placing true cultural diversity in deep jeopardy, we have practically committed ourselves to what amounts to a canonization of ignorance—a willfully entered, almost ritual neglect of our thorough and dramatic interdependence with all things. In consequence, we are not only eradicating species and cultures at an unprecedented rate, we are rapidly silencing those that remain—rendering them incapable of truly contributing to our meaningful narration. It is this ignorance that lies at the roots of our postmodern compulsion to read all things as mere signs and our increasingly cavalier embrace of and justifications for both narcissism and nihilism.

This, no doubt, is a lot to swallow. Our prejudice is that while the world we've realized as a result of technological "progress" might not be perfect, it is certainly better than what came before. After all, the successes of the women's and human rights movements can arguably be tied to changes in education, labor, and communication practices directly conditioned by technological advances over the past century. But so can the breakdown of the family and the epidemic rise of violent crime, substance abuse, and clinical depression. With high-tech medicine, catastrophic illness has come under almost miraculous control. At the same time, chronic illnesses have not only eluded effective treatment, they have become increasingly widespread and virulent. The absence of direct causal links between these phenomena is, of course, taken to be sufficient reason to dismiss their correlation as "irrelevant." But is our faith in this method of evaluation well placed? If our technological lineage has developed on the basis of a rigorous application of causal analysis and the experimental verification of controlled intervention in linear causal processes, do we not lapse into a blind and vicious circularity?

Most fundamentally, if we are to critically evaluate the claims of technological progress and the promises of the information age, we must first question the extent to which our technologies express the prejudices of our critical faculties as such—the extent to which they not only promote certain values, but tacitly block out others, effectively excluding truly contrary perspectives or ways of being human. This is no simple or easy task. A deep critique of our technological tradition necessarily entails interrogating both how and who we have come to be. And that, we all know, is never comfortable.

Reinventing our relationship with the media and technology finally means re-imagining ourselves as well—entering into a world where our customary habits and stances no longer seem natural and in which many of our oldest and most cherished beliefs are seen as presuppositions bereft of any claim to universality. Thus re-imagining ourselves is—to borrow a phrase from William Blake and made (in)famous by Aldous Huxley—a process of cleansing the doors of our perception. But it is also a profoundly countercultural act—an entry into a new modes of conduct or narrative movement that challenge us to evaluate our values as such and the societal institutions they have come to sponsor. Perhaps less paradoxically than might be supposed, unbinding our imagination in this way also marks a first step along the way of authentically embracing cultural diversity and improvising a new and truly harmonious world order.

As a way of facilitating this resituating and re-imagining of ourselves and so opening up the possibility of critically evaluating our technological lineage, substantial recourse will be made here to Buddhist concepts and teachings. The Buddhist understanding of personhood—based as it is on the realization that we have no essential self, no universal nature, no permanent identities, and no legitimate and nonviolent claim to either individuality or autonomy—is perhaps as far removed as possible from that of the mainstream of Western thinking about who we are. Most importantly, these teachings are not mere theories, but practices. That is, they establish concrete possibilities for reorienting both our technological and ideological biases—our views of what ways of being human are ideal and how to go about realizing them.

Of particular importance will be the teachings of co-origination and karma. Together, these teachings prohibit taking *the* world to be an objective reality that we can know without altering, but rather as always *our* world—a function of our own values and conduct. Eschewing both realist and idealist metaphysics, these teachings insist on our seeing relationships as more basic than the 'things' we take as 'being related', and values as ontologically prior to facts and existence. That is, they direct us to see ourselves as living in a world wherein all things are dramatically (and not merely factually) interdependent, and wherein all boundaries and identities are horizontal—a function of perspective—and never naturally given. Granted this, conflicts in the world of our experience must be seen as conflicts among our own values, not objective problems caused by something or someone "out there." Since technologies are responses to particular problems, they should be seen as modes of conduct aimed at resolving conflicts among particular competing values.

In critically evaluating the claims of our technological lineage, we cannot begin, then, by reducing technologies (patterns of conduct) to tools (instrumental artifacts) and then appealing to linear chains of causation to determine if these tools factually perform as intended. To the contrary, what we must investigate are the values these technologies express, the patterns of conduct in which they are dramatically articulated, and whether these constitute meaningful resolutions of our problems or if they in fact only contribute to the further generation of problems that are, at bottom, axiological and not factual. In short, the merits of a technology must be seen as pivoting on the ways in which it alters the meaning of being human—the meaning of our interdependence with all things—and whether this alteration constitutes a liberation from conflict and want and the realization of what might be termed fulfillment.

From such a perspective, the exponential growth of technology over the past several centuries in the West should not be seen as a mark of success and progress, but of a deepening entrenchment of conflicted values. Consider, for example, the way widespread antibiotic treatment of disease brings about both new and more virulent strains of disease agents in a population and a weakening of individual immune system response capabilities. Or consider the way in which technological development conditions economic growth, itself proposed as a cure for existing inequities in standards of living around the world, a way of redressing both individual and national poverty, when in actuality, such growth has led to a greater, not lesser, gap between the rich and poor. A major part of our task in what follows will be to flesh out the structural logic of such forms of axiological entrenchment and the conditions of their arising.

An immediate rejoinder to this approach, of course, is to ask why—if our technologies are apparently so fundamentally flawed and self-defeating—

have they been so avidly adopted throughout the world? If they represent only one set of culturally specific values, what is the reason for their virtually ubiquitous appeal? Is it not more reasonable to simply admit that our technological lineage properly articulates universal values that may not have been indigenous to all the world's cultures, but that quite clearly must be if we are all to share similar levels of command over our environments, physical and otherwise? The answer to these questions is a long one, but it begins with evaluating the effects of colonialism on indigenous value systems and the possibility that certain values—while well suited to one set of physical, cultural, and spiritual circumstances—can be violently infectious as free radicals.

Thus, the free export of values like 'individuality' and 'autonomy' through, for example, the spread of information technologies throughout the world is seen as unproblematic in the context of mainstream Western constructions of personhood, political democracy, economic benefit, human rights, and so on. But in much the same way that germs relatively harmless among the European sailors reaching the Hawaiian islands killed off four out of every five native Hawaiians in a matter of a generation or two, such values—so crucial to what "we" mean by "cultural diversity"—might well contribute to its very rapid demise.

Thus, the technologically induced compromise of cultural diversity and the homogenization of personhood need not be seen as due to any particularly nefarious intentions on our behalf, but simply because the kinds of personhood supported by our dominant technologies and the values they express stand in such diametric opposition to those prevailing in cultures where appreciative contribution—and not control—is taken as the nexus of all technical values; where relationship—and not individuality—is understood and valued as irreducible; where communication is not the successful exchange of information, but the harmonious sharing of a common perspective; and where our most basic "right" is not to be left alone in self-sufficient integrity, but rather to realize horizonless and meaningful intimacy.

And it is in this that lies, I believe, the best justification for making extensive use of Buddhist concepts like co-origination and karma in evaluating our technological lineage. In isolation and in a particular context, each of the above "opposing" values makes sense—they are meaningful ways of disambiguating a conflicted situation and bringing it to some form of resolution. Indeed, our actual lives as members of contemporary societies are always a more or less adaptive and creative complex system of such values. But values are not identifiably bounded things that one can—like a tool—set aside in a closet at will. Rather, they are ambient or insubstantial phenomena that combine with remarkable freedom and generate new modes of conduct, new expressions of what it means to be human. Ignorance of the consequences of combining certain values—an ignorance sedimented by a disposition to see situations objectively and as comprising individual objects or ideas—should be seen as grounds for the greatest caution.

   This said, it is not my intention to call for some kind of "back to basics" return to a romantically conceived "pretechnological" age. That, as virtually everyone who thinks about such matters insists, is simply not an option. Once adopted, technologies become part of who we are, and it is very seldom indeed that we simply discard some parts of ourselves, though we often spend a great deal of time trying our best to "improve" them. Nor is it my intention to mount an absolute and so indiscriminate condemnation of our entire technological lineage and the values it expresses. From a Buddhist perspective, all absolute views are, by virtue of their absoluteness, an expression of some form of deeply sedimented ignorance. Our technological lineage has done remarkably well at solving the problems with which we've found ourselves confronted. That much must be granted. But as will hopefully become apparent, precisely because of its overwhelming bias toward control, our technologies have also been responsible for generating the majority of these problems and will continue doing so in spite of its myriad individual "successes." We are in no better position to "jump off" the technological juggernaut than is the hapless fellow in the Indian folk tale of jumping off the tiger on whose back he is riding.

   Fortunately, as the Buddha pointed out nearly twenty-five hundred years ago, nothing stays the same. Across the entire scale of phenomena from the most minute to the most grand, nothing is finally permanent: not the mountains or the sea, not the sun or stars, not our selves or the cultures they uniquely express. This teaching has typically been understood as underscoring the ephemeral nature of all that would give us joy and ease. But, the impermanence of all things also guarantees that no situation, no matter how terrible or overwhelming, should be seen as intractable. Everything is always in motion, and if the world we live in is indeed karmic, that movement is always dramatic or meaningful. What is most important is not the way things *are*, but the way they are going. Meaningful changes in the direction of our conduct—our narrative movement, our world—are always possible from exactly where we have come to be, at this time, in this place. The only prerequisite is that we cultivate an ever-greater awareness of our own habits of thought, speech, and deed, and earnestly dissolve them by continuously relinquishing our horizons for what we consider relevant, what we take as our responsibility, and what we are ready to offer. That can be a very great deal, but it is never too much.

   As indirectly evidenced by much of the above, I've drawn a great deal of my inspiration for what follows from my own long-term Buddhist practice—first in the relatively traditional Kwan Um Zen School of Son Master Seung Sahn, and then in Dharma Master Ji Kwang's explicitly innovative

Lotus School of Social Buddhism. But while I've written *as* a practicing Buddhist and have appealed to various core Buddhist teachings as has seemed appropriate, I've made no attempt to summarize Buddhist history, theory or practice. Nor have I recommended the general adoption of any particular system of Buddhist techniques for dissolving habits or embarking on the path of relinquishing the limits of our own virtuosity. That, it seems, would run the danger of debunking one ideology—one set of explicit conclusions and implicit assumptions—only to promote another.

At the same time, I've also elected not to include a summary of Western philosophical or political critiques of technology. There are many such critiques, stretching back at least to Plato's *Republic*, and they provide valuable insights into the inner workings of our technological lineage and commitment. But because these insights were developed in complex and dynamic correlation with our technological tradition, they represent that tradition from deeply internal or intrinsic perspectives. That is, they may be very good for goading our tradition into more rapid or slightly reoriented change, but not for articulating a true alternative.

More importantly, it seems to me that explicitly concerning ourselves with the historical and present range of thinking about technology—whether in the East or the West—would be conducive to a compromise of our potential for intimately engaging the issues raised and taking them in the most deeply vulnerable and personal way possible. That, far from being an advantage, would mean being distracted from precisely where we must be if we are to actively reorient our dramatic interdependence in the most liberating ways possible.

Part One

The Axis of Factual Success:
From Controlling Circumstances
to Colonizing Consciousness

Chapter 1

Technology and the Biasing of Conduct

Establishing the Grammar of Our Narrative

Balance is hard to maintain. Things are never "just right" for long. For most of us, these are lessons learned very early on in life. The succor we took from our mother's breast was only temporary. The vibrant clarity of our awareness upon awakening from a nap gradually and yet invariably diminished, replaced by an unsettling discomfort—sometimes a dull lethargy and at others a buzzing impatience. In fact, nothing in our circumstances lasts forever. Like it or not, things change.

By and large, this means trouble. No matter how hard we work at reaching a point of satisfaction, something inevitably interrupts, our satisfaction dissolves. The state of things being "just right" is quite delicate— hard to attain and very easily disturbed. In a very general sense, technologies are value-laden patterns of conduct oriented in such a way as to successfully correct or forestall trouble. That is, technologies are meant to insure an easier time of achieving and maintaining balance, helping us keep things as close as possible to being "just right." The liberation rhetoric used to market new technologies is thus not entirely gratuitous. Technology is supposed to free us from some measure of worldly exigency, supplying us with tools for intervening in the process of the world on our own behalf. At the very least, technology should hold disruptions at bay and grant us some advantage in recovering from those that it cannot. How a technology does this will depend on the presuppositions of its basic orientation.

In general, our conduct can effectively be seen as oriented either socially or societally—either toward improvisation with an aim of realizing difference-maintaining harmony, or toward regulation with an aim of realizing universal, difference-eliding agreement. On the one hand, our communal narration—the dramatic dimensions of our interdependence—will shift in the direction of intimacy and the unexpected, and on the other hand in the

3

direction of institutions and certainty. Likewise for our technologies. Socially constituted technologies orient us toward an increased sensitivity for
relational nuances and an enhanced capacity for improvisationally and creatively responding with environmental uncertainty. By contrast, societally
constituted technologies will orient us toward the increasingly precise manipulation of objects and an enhanced ability to dictate the terms of our
environments. As a shorthand, we can characterize these respectively as
technologies of contribution and technologies of control.

Quite clearly, these disparate types of technical development not only reinforce incompatible conceptions of order, they work toward sedimenting
quite definite and disparate attitudes about the nature and attainment of freedom and the ideal human life. In fact, technology provides a highly reliable
index to a given society's understanding of freedom and personhood and, because of that, an insight into the organization of its world. All technologies
are thus deeply political. As systems of value that are definitive of unique
worlds, they are also cosmogonic, even religious. Like every religion, a technology is the cultivation of a particular and overtly ideal way of intercourse
with the world. But unlike religions, technologies present this ideal in its raw
and unjustified form. They are entirely obvious—so much so that it is often
easiest to see what values they promote by attending to the broader contexts
in which they are rooted, and in which they are either decaying or thriving. In
the same way that we need to look into the furthest distance to see the color
of the air surrounding us, we need to take a very broad and deep view in order to see how our technologies color our narration, our lives.

I'd like to do that in what follows over the next several chapters. This
will mean combining some specific examples with some very sweeping gen-
eralizations—so sweeping, in fact, that at times they will border on carica-
tures. If my greatest concern lay in "being right," this would be disastrous.
Recalling the dictum that the only thing worse than making gross general-
izations is failing to do so, I'll be more than happy if we just manage "turning right."

PRIMORDIAL TECHNOLOGY IN THE DRAMA
OF CHILDHOOD

It seems reasonable that a culture's most basic values and its root presuppositions about personhood are likely to show up with greatest clarity in the
practices surrounding the care and education of infants and the very young.
And so, I'd like to begin investigating the technical prejudices of our understanding of freedom and personhood by unpacking two typical (albeit "fic-
titious") domestic vignettes involving a two-year-old child, her mother, and
a new rubber ball.

Nearly horizontal rays from a late afternoon sun are shining through the aluminum railing bordering the outer curve of a high-rise apartment balcony. The uprights cast shadows that angle across the outdoor carpet and then make a sharp turn up the wall. Sitting among the shadows are a toddler and her mother. From behind her back, the mother produces a new ball. Its bright colors seem to pick up the glories of the coming sunset and hold them captive. "What is this?" she asks her daughter, who replies by stretching out her hands. Holding the ball closer to her breasts, the mother instructs her daughter to say "ball." This takes a while, but finally the daughter complies. Rolling the toy through the bands of dark and light toward her daughter, Mother says, "Now you roll it back to me." This simple game continues for a minute or two with much squealing and bubbly laughter from the little girl who then suddenly stands up with the ball and hides it behind her back. Mother asks her to roll it back, but the girl shakes her head, slowly at first and then as her mother repeats her request, even more demonstratively. When her mother tries sneaking a hand behind her daughter's back to steal the ball, the girl shrieks and runs to stand beside the rail, her smile full of mischief. When her mother advances, she turns and throws the ball over the railing and without watching to see where it lands, runs past her mother to stand against the sliding doors leading into the family room, both her hands hidden behind her back, squirming with delight.

What happens next? If the mother is a typical American, chances are the first words out of her mouth will include "no" (most likely repeated two or three times), "that wasn't nice," and "now look what you've done." The new ball is lost. Depending on the mother's mood and temperament, she may slap her daughter's wrist while directing the girl's attention over the rail and down into the parking lot below. "You could have hurt someone," she informs her. She may even add that her daughter was "a bad girl" for throwing away the ball. Their playing has stopped being fun. The daughter may cry. The mother reminds her that she is the one who threw the ball away and that it's gone forever now. "I hope you learn something from that," she adds, pulling her daughter close to stroke her hair down over her heaving shoulders. "Maybe if you promise to be a good girl, I'll get you another ball tomorrow."

In a traditionally East Asian family—let's say Japanese—the scene plays rather differently. To begin with, when the mother produces the ball, she holds it up to the westering light and admires its colors. Bringing it back down, she extends it toward her daughter with one hand supported by the other—a gesture of offering. If her daughter understands the ritual context, she will receive the ball with a complementary gesture and say "thank you." The mother will ask for the ball in return and also say, "thank you" when it's returned.

This is a deceptively casual exchange. In fact, it encapsulates one of the most important and basic differences between traditional East Asian and

American cultures. In learning language, what is prioritized in America is vocabulary—being able to name things. By contrast, for example, what comes first in Japan is instruction in the social grammar of communication. Names are subordinated to verbal exchanges that announce changes in and nuances of relationship. In short, words are not first and foremost *about things*, but *specific ways of ordering conduct*. Thus, when Confucius, the most famous and revered East Asian teacher, was asked by his students to tell them the meaning of authoritative personhood or *jen*—the conceptual pivot of his entire philosophy—he refrained from ever giving them a definition. In diametric opposition to the Platonic insistence on defining essences, Confucius related paradigmatic stories. Knowing what a word means is not knowing *what it signifies*, but *how to conduct oneself* in situations where it is used. When the Japanese mother asks her daughter to roll the ball back, the emphasis will be on how the ball connects them through play—not on the ball as an independent thing, but as a facet of their relationship.

When the daughter tosses the ball over the rail and escapes to the doors, the mother pauses. Staring over the edge of the rail to see if she can locate the ball, our Japanese mother takes her time responding to her daughter's conduct. Consciously or unconsciously, she is looking for their lost connection. Finding the brightly colored toy at rest in the grass surrounding a flower bed on the edge of the parking area, she motions her daughter over and directs her attention below. The ball is now what allows them to stand side by side and contemplate the space separating them not just from the ball itself, but from the play that it had been mediating. Perhaps the mother picks up a feather from the carpet and tickles her daughter's nose with it before holding it ceremoniously over the edge of the rail and dropping it. Mother and daughter follow the winding, spiraling path the feather takes until it too rests in the grass far below.

Japanese children are not routinely told "no." While we assume that saying "no" to our children is necessary if they are ever going to learn 'right' from 'wrong', the Japanese believe that telling a child "no" will only train him or her to say "no" back—often with absolutely no discrimination or understanding of how it changes the relationship they are interrupting with it. So the Japanese tend to elide "no" from their child-educating vocabulary. Instead, they say "yes" to their children as often as possible, granting most wishes, and carefully guiding the attention of their children on to what can be granted when they ask for something they cannot have. This is believed to train children in the art of generosity and respectful compliance or social flexibility.

The American mother emphasizes what is "lost forever"—the ball as a *thing*, playing as a *state* of happy distraction. The Japanese mother stresses the continuity of her relationship with her daughter. Nothing is broken irreparably by the distancing of the ball even though a change occurs in the quality and orientation of the conduct through which mother and daughter are articulating who they are with and for one another. The communicative model on the American balcony is that of discourse—literally a "flowing apart" of mother, daughter, and ball. The daughter realizes her separation and difference from the ball, which is a thing that can be "lost forever." She also realizes a difference from her mother who has chastised her behavior and shown disapproval, repeatedly uttering "no" and even punctuating the finality of the word with a raw physical contact. The hair-stroking lets the daughter know that she is still loved, but also that the pain and loss she is feeling are part of her mother's will. 'Right' and 'wrong' hurt.

By contrast, the communicative model on the Japanese balcony is one of concourse or "flowing together." As in the American situation, there is a hierarchy, but there is no contest of wills. Neither the world at large nor the things and people in it are placed in an adversarial role. The American daughter may beg to go down the elevator to retrieve the ball, but the mother is likely to say "no" as a way of making "the consequences" clear and as a way of asserting her place as the one in control—the arbiter of moral reward and punishment. This, after all, is the only way her daughter will learn to act like a "good girl." The Japanese mother works hard to avoid the conflict and loss of intimacy that comes with opposing or divergent wills. She stresses the pattern of her relationship with her daughter as something ritually performed. What matters most is not individuating wills and responsibilities and consequences, but deepening and extending their partnership.

It is, of course, possible to object that with modernization and the growth of worldwide mass mediation, the "Japanese" version of the above vignette might not play so disparately. Contemporary Japan is a consumer society like no other, and that this will have had an effect on the Japanese family is unquestionable. However, as evidenced in Tobin and Davidson's, *Preschool in Three Cultures* (New Haven: Yale University Press, 1989), in broad outline, the communicative presuppositions proper to traditional Japan are still very much applicable. Using case-study comparisons of early education in the People's Republic of China, Japan, and the United States, Tobin and Davidson highlight the extent to which the primary function of early education in each of these cultures can effectively be seen as a modeling of culturally approved strategies for problem solution, conflict resolution, and character development. But more importantly, their studies evidence the extent to which there are radically divergent assumptions about what it means to be a 'teacher' or a 'student' in these three cultures. And so, while all preschool training can be described as "character-building" activity, there is much less commonality about what "character" consists of than we are likely to have ever imagined. Gertrude Stein's remark about roses notwithstanding, a person is not always a person.

As evidenced in the raging debates about abortion rights, the American view is that we are born persons. That is, our humanity is contemporaneous with our entry into the world. That we are embroiled in a mortal debate about when this "entry" occurs—at conception, at quickening, with viability, at twelve weeks or upon delivery—reflects our belief that humanity and personhood are basically inherent. East Asian cultures do not share this view and it is one of the principal reasons that human rights conversations with them are so difficult. In these and indeed many of the world's cultures, our personhood and even our humanity are not given, but acquired. That is, we become persons, and in particular human persons. Personhood is not a minimal fact, but an achievement—a mark of some degree of excellence in conduct. Child-rearing practices in American and East Asian cultures reflect this divergence in how personhood is conceived—as an inviolable 'state' or as a particular quality of 'relationship'.

Inevitably, a profound resonance obtains between how we are conceived as persons, our understanding of freedom, and the kinds of technology we develop and maintain. When persons are seen as distinct, manifestly isolated biological/factual events rather than as lifelong and irreducibly relational processes, it is only natural that freedom be constituted as a status—a particular standing we possess. The antipathy of nature and nurture that is so much a part of our ways of grappling with differences in our identities is a function of the same basic values that associate personhood with individuality and freedom with choice. They also underlie our broad predilections in politics, religion, and technology.

In many societies—and as illustrated in the Japanese mother-daughter narrative—the primary value-orienting conduct is that of cooperation or mutual contribution. Personal training—that is, training in the art of conducting ourselves as persons—emphasizes attention and appreciation. In practice, this means a valorization of virtuosity or the capacity for sensitive improvisation. By contrast, conduct in most Western societies is predominantly oriented by an intense valuation of regulation or control. Instead of personal training focusing on qualities of attention, it emphasizes will and the management of activity and experience. While often quite subtle, the disparity has immense ramifications.

FREEDOM AS A DIALECTIC OF PROJECTING SELF AND OBJECTING WORLD

While a newborn is typically considered a person in a minimal sense in the West, it's popularly understood that a child begins developing a distinct personality roughly between the ages of twelve and twenty-four months. This is usually referred to as entering "the terrible twos"—an attainment synchronous with the child's rapid acquisition of a "will of his or her own." As the popular phrase suggests, it is a trying period, a time when children first learn to vehemently and verbally disagree with and consciously try to control their environment—and so their parents, caretakers, and siblings. It is when children begin saying "no"—loudly and clearly distinguishing themselves from the wills and ways of others and the world at large.

This "no" is in fact the outward manifestation of an assertion of self over and apart from other. It is the birth of a sense of independence. Socialization consists of learning to properly contextualize this independence—to put brakes on the assertion of egoistic will. There is from the beginning, then, a sense in our tradition that actual (as opposed to ideal) freedom occurs as a dialectic between self and other, between will and resistance, between the absolute and relative.

I would like to suggest that this fundamentally adversarial relationship is crucial not only to the awakening of the "Western" personality, but to the identity of our preferred technologies, political systems, economies, and religious systems. In a word, it focuses a set of values that is pervasive in our cultural tradition and that manifests in the virtual synonymity of freedom, independence, and willful control over circumstance. There is, of course, no way to provide anything like an exhaustive proof of this claim in the scope of a single chapter or even a single book. To begin with, our tradition is not a lineage in any literal sense, but a quilting of many traditions taken up in whole or part. Very often, the roots of Western civilization are said to lie predominantly in Greece and its flowering in the emergence of a Christian Europe, but that is a vast oversimplification. Not only did Egyptian and Semitic elements go into the making of Greek and early Christian thought and practice, but the course of our culture's evolution has throughout been dialogic. Thus, the medieval period saw the incorporation of numerous pagan beliefs and ideals into Christianity, and the birth of modern science can be traced in large part to the Indian invention of the zero and the work of Andalusian Muslims and Jews working with Greek and Arabic texts not widely available in the rest of Europe. Nevertheless, there is a remarkable consistency in the kinds of fabric that have been incorporated in the quilt of the "Western world"—a distinctive conceptual aesthetic, especially in the portrayal of freedom.

For example, it has almost unilaterally been supposed in the dominant European/Western traditions that freedom entails perfecting of our independence. Philosophically, this can be traced back at least as far as the Platonic valorization of a personal inquiry into and revelation of Beauty and the Good—an ascent of the soul from the obscurity and confusion of sensed particulars to a direct apprehension of the eternal and universal ideas of which they are but pale renditions. As the famous myth of the cave illustrates, we are imprisoned in our "natural" estate, living in an impoverishing realm of shadowy forgetfulness. Freedom means rejecting our immersion in and dispersion among the myriad things of nature and so recovering from the multiplicity and dependency into which they've driven us. This ideal has evolved over the millennia, but has remained remarkably consistent in its broad outlines.

Thus, the evolution first of "natural philosophy" and then scientific inquiry has run parallel to a movement away from systems of correspondence—and so continued embeddedness in the world—to the isolation of universal laws and a statistical analysis of worldly events. Indeed, the ideal vantage adopted by science so attenuated the importance of our own worldliness that until the unsettling implications of quantum theory began to be understood, it was widely supposed that we could enjoy a "view from nowhere" and (given sufficient knowledge of initial conditions) rationally calculate the shape of the future. Even where the possibility of success in this venture has been systematically denied—as in some of the virulent, contemporary strains of relativism—the *ideal* of independence in and from circumstances remains. The relativist may deny the possibility of some realizable absolute truth, but freedom is no less a function of the independence of the individual than in Platonic eschatology—even if it only comes down to independence from the opinions of others.

Religiously, the association of freedom and some level of independence is already present in the biblical account of the "fall of man" where Adam is said to have chosen wrongly, eating the forbidden fruit in pursuit of his own ends. Since then, religious eschatology has pivoted on choice or the freedom of our will. But, whereas the Judaic understanding was that the tribes of Israel were the locus of independence and so of freedom as well, quite early in its development—and no doubt in part due to the infiltration of Greek ideals—the Christian view of salvation became explicitly individualistic. Divinely guaranteed that we enjoy an absence of any ultimate bodily or spiritual constraints on our choosing either salvation or damnation, each one of us came to be understood as individually deciding the fate of our soul. Though we might be sorely tempted to forfeit our integrity and give in to circumstance, as Job's unwavering steadfastness illustrates, even in the most extreme cases, the choice remains finally our own. In short, the historical articulation of the Judeo-Christian-Muslim "lineage" marks a shift from communal to individual salvation—from a saving relationship articulated between a temperamental Yahweh and his chosen people, to one established through Jesus the Christ as the Son of God and a sincere penitent, and finally to an "immediate" relationship given in an individual's willing submission (*islam*) to Allah. The Protestant Reformation—coming at a time when Western technology was being driven by new scientific advances from a long, relatively unproductive slumber—was more than anything else a movement to free the individual from the mediation and machinations of the Roman Catholic Church, taking back what was perceived as a cleverly usurped responsibility for our own, private destinies.

Politically, the evolution of the ideal of freedom has likewise progressed from the independence of a tribe or people—classically, a monarchic state where the king (or queen) is the "head of the family" and hierarchic relations are the norm—to the radical independence of each citizen. That is, a "progression" is evident from seeing the nature of independence as contingent on our actual place within our society to seeing it as a universal characteristic possessed equally by all, irrespective of place or position. Not coincidentally, the ideal of universal participatory democracy only began taking firm root in our cultural heritage when our technologies made practical cooperation between the royal and nonroyal members of a state decidedly less crucial. Arguably, the notion of individual rights earned widespread acceptance only with the advent of technologies that decentralized power enough that the will of any individual had to be given serious and due consideration. Dovetailing with the Enlightenment ideal of the independent inquirer so trenchantly exemplified by Descartes, political freedom came to be epitomized by our right to vote anonymously and without coercion. In this sense, our right to either directly (as in referendum) or indirectly (through the election of representatives) choose or decide our societal and political destiny expresses in the mundane world the same guarantee understood to prevail in the spiritual. The free citizen is a soul in the body politic.

Finally, and as might be expected, our way of talking about and understanding who we are as persons has shifted from communal/mythical to psychological narrative. Whereas mythic heroes achieved their status by superlative efforts benefiting all who lived in community with them, modern "heroes" manifest their "success" in how much fame, money, and influence they amass. As played out in personal narrative, the valorization of freedom as independence from and control over circumstances has led to the glorification of "self-made persons"—individuals who, against the odds resisting their will, manage to advantageously leverage the world and accomplish what they want. In a contemporary sense, being complete as a man or woman means being self-sufficient.

In keeping with this popular transformation, the seminal psychological theories of both Freud and Jung appealed to the language of independence. Each in its own way exemplified the bias that personal maturation should be understood explicitly in terms of individuation—as a kind of psychological continuation and culmination of the biological process highlighted by parturition, weaning, entering adolescence, and finally leaving the family home to fully enter adulthood. That is, instead of personal maturation and freedom being seen as pivoting on the deepening of our relationships as such, modern psychology has almost unilaterally insisted that it involves developing an identity embedded in and yet essentially apart from these relationships—the constitution of a self abstracted from the various wombs of our communal setting. If childhood means living in dependence, maturity is realizing our independence—the ability and inclination to choose our lives for ourselves.

Ideally, then, whether philosophically, politically, religiously, or psychologically, the articulation of freedom in the dominant Western tradition has played out historically as the progressive cultivation of an absence of both internal and external constraints on our ability to do what we want, when we want. From the first stirring of humanity in the mythic Garden of Eden onward, freedom has been understood as pivoting on choice. As fortune would have it, however, the world has never been a particularly ideal place. In fact, our day-by-day circumstances seem at times to quite strenuously resist our intentions. We want to lift a stone and find it too heavy. We want to stop a war and cannot. We want someone to love us, but he or she is unmoved by our own emotions and efforts. At a purely physical level, the world apparently runs according to laws not subject to our private whims, according to a caprice impervious to our wishes, impelled by forces of momentum so great as to entirely dwarf our individual wills. It has been the ongoing business of technology to close the gap between this 'reality' and our ever-refining ideal of independence. That is, in much the same way that Socrates described his philosophizing as a kind of midwifery for the soul, technology has helped us bring into full flower our embryonic freedom to project our wishes and shout down the world's objections.

The prevailing tendency of overt technical development in our tradition has thus been to increase the effective range and specificity of our choices. Importantly, while much of this increase is realized reactively—that is, as an ability to bring errant situations back into order—an ever more significant trend has been for cultivating prescriptive control. The ideal of such technologies is not just dealing with trouble when it arises, but so configuring our circumstances that trouble can't even get its foot in the proverbial door. This means not only securing ourselves from unnamed threats, but actively endeavoring to identify them as such in advance. The fascination we have with 'things' of every sort—be these atoms, animals, gods, persons, or what have you—and our desire to break them down into as small and manageable components as possible is not purely a function of intellectual curiosity. To the contrary, it is part of a project of developing an effective taxonomy of objective resistance to our wills—a project of identifying exactly what can or is already proving recalcitrant or intractable. Science seeks out immutable laws and entities—a search that at once isolates what contradicts our will and establishes a clear grasp of what we can use as "fulcrums" in the technical leveraging of the world.

As might be expected, technologies geared toward controlling our circumstances are energy-intensive. It requires no small expenditure of effort and energy to break up the obdurate continuities of the natural world into manageable units more consistent with the realization of our wishes. An example of this is the refining process by means of which inert stone is first broken down into a slurry of waste and a remainder of useable ore that is then further purified by heating to produce workable metal. The metal is "released" from the stone by subjecting the latter to great enough stresses that it gives up its confused integrity, yielding those more basic and 'finer' elements comprised in its structure. Similar processes of "refining" occur when we isolate biological exemplars of preferred traits and breed them to produce superior animals or grains, or when we successfully cook pine sap to make first tar and then turpentine. But such processes, by breaking down established relationships or forms—essentially stable patterns of stored energy—can also release more energy than they consume. Ultimately, the principle lying behind the use of either fossil fuels or atomic fission is that of creating a kind of situational "vacuum" into which an otherwise inert form will be dispersed and to then harness the resulting movement for the purpose of refiguring the world.

We can say in general, then, that such technical processes rely not only on better leveraging our physical or mental powers, but on marshaling or gaining useable access to previously unavailable or contrary forces. Until our ability to break down natural forms (patterns of energy) reached a critical turning point, the vast majority of our technical advances were oriented toward growing and storing food and toward harnessing the energy of other beings. The techniques of animal husbandry, harness and cart manufacture, and so on are thus the relatively "benign" forebears to the technical identification and utilization of energy as such. More literally sanguine and yet often more effective in the long run than husbanding animal labor were techniques for marshaling (or less euphemistically, enslaving) human energy—basically superior weaponry and military strategies. In all such cases, the point was making previously inaccessible amounts of energy available to our individual wills. With the advent of means for practically accessing the energy of fossil fuels through combustion, a great leap forward occurred in technical development because the energy requirements of living, organic forms could be factored out of the equation. Slavery died out not so much for political or so-called humanitarian reasons as because the mechanical capture of the energy stored in fossil fuels and running water made possible both large-scale urban industrialization and rural mechanization. Quite simply, owning and maintaining slaves became unnecessary, if not an outright liability. It was not altruism, but energy and economics that ended the practice of keeping human chattel.

This technical process of breaking down natural forms to identify or create more useable, generically combinable elements and the parallel endeavor of marshaling the energy of relational disintegration can (not altogether metaphorically) be thought of as stealing the memories of things or robbing nature's graves. Natural forms are places where relationships are in relative stasis, where the disruptive forces of change and the integrative forces of adaptation have come into singular balance. The Native American conviction that mining is a form of desecration is in this sense less a "primitive animism" than it is a recognition that natural forms embody the history of the world—a history that is finally the womb of all our own narratives. Taking what nature has not given is ultimately stealing from ourselves, stealing our own pasts. And while the future is constantly being renewed, once our past has been "refined" and "refashioned" it cannot be renewed or replaced. Erasing our past by clear-cutting forests, by leveling mountains to mine various mineral ores, or by damming rivers to turn electricity-generating turbines is no less dangerous than cutting ourselves off from our families and the wisdom embodied by our elders and our traditions. In short, we condemn ourselves to entirely fashionable lives.

As technologies of ostensive control have become not just more prevalent but more powerful or energy-intensive, our experience of temporality itself has taken on an increasingly interrogative quality. In our own myths about the origins of culture, it is generally agreed that at the dawn of human community people had a basically propitiatory relationship to things. So-called primitive peoples felt—and even today persist in feeling—that it was necessary to ask the elk for the right to use its horns, or the stone if it could be moved in order to build a wall. Natural forces, we say, were perceived as deities that had to be placated. Our epistemic and technical evolution has shifted us from this propitiatory mode of conduct to a proprietary one. Accordingly, our experience of time is now more than ever before based on asking and answering for ourselves whether we want or don't want what is happening. Do we approve or disapprove of our present situation and that toward which it would seem to lead us? If we disapprove— if we don't want it as is—to what extent can we change it? How much time will that take? And at what cost? Time has become a kind of commodity broken down into tradable units. Think of the way, for instance, that information costs are coming to be measured as a function of on-line charges. What we are buying is not data as such, but time on the Net, so many hours of access at such and such a rate. Increasingly, time is becoming money— the most direct measure of how much of our attention-energy is being consumed and how systematically.

By associating freedom with both choice and independence, and by increasing our ability to marshal the world's ambient energy for our individual purposes, we have also unavoidably associated freedom with discrimination and dictation. Most elementally, this manifests in our virtually incessant assertions of "yes" or "no" to the events in our lives. Accepting or rejecting has become so much a part of our experience of time and timeliness that we are typically unaware of our standing in judgment of the world. If at all, we notice this and its potential liability only when the conflict between another's will and our own is both chronic and skewed to the other's benefit—typically because he or she enjoys access to greater technical mediation and so greater power over circumstances than we do. In this light, political dictators must be seen as a threat to freedom not because they categorically limit what we mean by the word, but because they have gathered too much of it to themselves. That is, dictators do not so much pervert (or turn aside from) our traditional ideals about freedom as they invert them—tipping them as fully as possible to their own, private account.

Given all the above and as might have been expected, such techniques as have been developed in our tradition for insuring the absence of internal (as opposed to ostensive) limits on our freedom have centered on safeguarding or shoring up our ability to make and maintain the right choices. This is clearest in the sphere of the religious, where what is at stake is the freedom of our ownmost selves—our souls. According to the root myths of the Judeo-Christian-Muslim tradition, it was only at the point where the alternatives of salvation and damnation were made evident that we were granted genuine independence. That is, freedom primordially appeared as the divinely ordained opportunity to decide the nature of our path—the status of our individual eternity. From that point on, since the alternatives are only two and since they are in fact quite clear, the only relevant direction of technical expertise—expertise geared toward supporting or augmenting our independence—would be that of perfecting and controlling our will. The choices being evident, what we need is the power of choosing rightly.

In the dominant, Western religious traditions, damnation is a linear result of sinning—of knowingly doing what is wrong, a conscious perversion or turning away. The fact that sin originated with Adam—the "first man"—and has since then colored each and every one of our souls means at the very least that knowing what is right is always enough of a given that our salvation ultimately depends on how well we're able to act on this knowledge. It is this presupposition that warrants the central place that has been accorded to the rhetoric of temptation in the Judeo-Christian-Muslim lineage. It is not our lack of understanding that waylays us on our journey toward our salvation, but deficiencies in our will—our ability to confront and control temptation. The importance of the technique of prayer is thus not epistemo-logical—a means of developing our ability to better perceive the good—but hinges precisely on its role in functionally reinforcing our will.

And so, while Christian theologians, for example, have long debated the ramifications of the fallibility of human understanding, popular Christianity has consistently moved in a conative direction. Temptation came increasingly to be understood in terms of an explicit contest of wills and salvation as the triumph of our own—even if at times only through our faith in or submission to the will of "our Creator." It would be interesting in this light to analyze the tragic history of Lucifer's transformation from an impetuous angel suffering from jealously and "a big mouth" into the personification of evil temptation itself—a history that really only got into full swing during the late medieval and early modern periods when science and then technologies of ostensive control began evolving at unprecedented rates. At any rate, even a cursory glance at the Star Wars film series or at George Bush's denunciations of Saddam Hussein during the Gulf War shows that the basic image of a moral contest of wills framed in explicitly individualistic and confrontational terms is still with us. We are embroiled in a Manichean battle of the forces of Good and the forces of Evil. And salvation, when it comes, is clearly seen as a triumph, a victory.

In sum, then, Western religious technology has focused on insuring our ability to willfully take the path of salvation. Likewise, much of modern psychotherapy is geared toward revelation—the exposure of those emotional, behavioral, ideational, or obsessive complexes that constrain our ability to choose a "well-integrated" life. In psychiatric circles emphasizing the biochemical basis of "mental illness" or the inability to cope with the world in consensually approved and understood fashions, drugs replace conscious revelations as the means of regaining the ability to choose freely and independently. That is, nonreligious inner freedom is understood in terms of insuring or regaining (even surrogate) control of our epistemic or biochemical circumstances.

In the secular domain as well, choice and will have remained explicitly crucial in articulating our sense of intensive freedom. But whereas the religious sphere admitted little in the way of human engineering—after all, the Creator of the universe set the terms of the battle as well as the nature of the spoils—our worldly circumstances are clearly much more open to reconfiguration. Unlike the deep moral structure of the universe, which seemed to have been fired in the kiln of divine will, the world of day-to-day commerce is still quite malleable. In result, we have not been limited to strengthening our wills in an effort to augment or secure our freedom. To the contrary, we have dedicated ourselves and much of our life-energies to extending, generation-by-generation, the range of our choices in shaping our circumstances. To this end, we have managed to take control over that with which Satan once tried bribing us—good crops, better health, the easing of pain and suffering, the longevity of our offspring. And against the "evils" of fascism or communism threatening our soils and livelihoods, technology has been no less effective—in fact, it has been our best and most proven weapon.

Because our model of freedom has been so much shaped by its intimate association with independence and control, both as a cultural tradition and as individuals we have given very little consideration to the larger narrative ramifications of our brand of technical evolution. In a sense, it is an association that blinds us to the advisability of considering whether the control our technologies afford us is ultimately for the best. We simply continue changing the world, matching it ever more precisely and immediately to our individual needs and 'desires' and feeling all the freer for it.

In spite of the scientific admission that the natural world is ecologically—that is, interdependently—organized, this valorization of control has remained basically unchallenged. In fact, one of the reasons it is so difficult to successfully lobby for ecologically sensitive legislation is the unspoken belief that we no longer need to fear nature as we once did. Even if we screw things up, we can always fix them. In classical Greece, it was not uncommon for children of the victorious to be educated by slaves drawn from among the most highly educated and even martially adept of their parents' enemies. Likewise, what willingness we have shown in setting aside tracts of wilderness for the benefit of future generations can be traced to the extent to which we believe we have vanquished the wilds. For the most part, we are only inclined to preserve nature because we are convinced we could destroy her. It is no longer her moods that determine our fates, but our dispositions that determine hers. Or so we think. Of nature's greatest contradictions of our will, perhaps only death remains out of reach.

Seen through the lenses of our technical success, the future of the technotopian West looks an awful lot like Disney's EPCOT center or the inside of the Starship Enterprise. It is a future in which the face of time is, for all intents and purposes, ours not only to cosmetically alter, but actually redesign. With the advent of sufficiently sophisticated virtual reality technologies, the distinction between inner and outer environments or circumstances may well blur to the extent that very little point will be seen in maintaining the wild spirit of the nonelectronic cosmos. Regular, predictable, and secure, a world in which novelty is manufactured for the sake of priming our interest, technotopia is societality taken to its logical extreme—a world in which worry and the disagreeable have been vanquished.

That, however, is a still imaginary future. And while there are good reasons to be concerned about what we imagine, such a future is much less relevant than where we are at present and how we have come to be here. Right now, we already have a greater apparent capacity for choosing to do what we want than ever before. Indeed, we are often compelled to make choices. But what if Ch'an master Pai-chang was right in insisting that we see the principle of liberation as "not selecting anything," not making any choices? What if increasing our choices actually means sacrificing our freedom?

Chapter 2

The Canons of Freedom
and Moral Transparency
In Technology and the Media We Trust

The media are everywhere. They are the connective tissue of our society. I'm not referring here only to the so-called mass media—television, radio, print and music publications, the Internet, films, and so on. In addition, there are relatively private and small circulation media like news services, stock market dailies, corporate interoffice networks, voice mail systems, and pagers. Broadly construed, the media include all those institutions that allow us to inform or be informed. Even in these first years of the information age, electronic media already allow us to contact practically anyone, anywhere, whenever we want. We can acquire or distribute any information we please at the speed of light. In cyberspace, there is no friction, there are no borders. If freedom is seen as measurable by degrees of choice, access to the media represents a virtually ideal form of empowerment.

This is very familiar rhetoric. To a degree not shared by other technologies, the information technologies give us the ability to choose what we want. That is, they are essentially neutral with respect to our wishes, and in this sense, value-free. Of course, we can decide to use them for good or ill—either to find a life-saving supply of a rare blood type in a matter of seconds or to electronically distribute child pornography. For this reason, the frontiers opened up by the media are at once perfect and terrible. As such, they constitute a uniquely appropriate place to begin critically evaluating our technological lineage as a whole and the kind of freedom toward which it is disposed.

THE IMAGINED NEUTRALITY OF TECHNOLOGY

The belief that technologies are value-neutral has long been widespread. According to it, for example, the Cold War was not caused by nuclear weapon technology, but by seemingly atomic and antagonistic ideologies. Since nuclear energy can be used for peaceful purposes like generating electricity and treating cancerous tumors, this belief seems almost commonsense. The same commonsense reasoning allows us to denounce Hitler's propagandistic use of television and radio in engineering the Holocaust while praising the entertainment and education programming on public radio and television. Aside from the fact that commonsense beliefs are typically held without any critical examination and tend therefore to be prejudicial, there are other reasons to be suspicious.

Tools versus Technologies

A tacit, but quite crucial precedent for believing in the neutrality of our technologies is that we perceive them in terms of the tools they generate. When asked to consider the effects of technology on our everyday lives, we think of computer terminals and televisions, the automobile we have parked at the curb, and the answering machine in the kitchen. This conflation of tools and technologies is far from innocuous. Indeed, it has had the effect of masking a great deal of the impact of technology on our lives. It has also made it quite easy to dismiss looking into and evaluating that impact as one of the impractical preoccupations of an ivory-towered elite.

The premises of the argument for open possession of firearms is a classic instance of such a reduction blindness: "Guns don't kill, people do." While some people may abuse the power a firearm (or a television station or computer terminal) places at the tip of their fingers, this is no reason to bar everyone from access to that same power. Guns can also be used to hunt, to protect our families, to defend our nation. The conclusion to the argument is obviously that "bearing firearms is and should be an inalienable right supporting our need to protect ourselves." Indeed, the Constitution of the United States, now over two hundred years old, insists on as much. Phrased in terms of the media, the argument is that: "Since it's not the media as such, but only their content that have the potential to disrupt or pervert society, free access to the media is and should be an inalienable part of our need and right to inform ourselves." If you don't want to watch certain programs or visit certain World Wide Web sites, you don't have to; you can even refuse to own a television or computer altogether.

Pistols and televisions are tools. Tools are extensions of our body-mind. They are designed and manufactured in order to extend our natural capacities for sensation and movement. For example, while we can use our teeth to peel a mango or husk a coconut, a knife allows us to do this faster and with greater precision. Most generally defined, a tool is a limited instrument that enables us to extend our individual wills in quite specific ways. In using tools, our focus is not on the tool itself, but on what we want to accomplish, our goal. A tool focuses our desire. This is true whether the tool is an ax, a wheelbarrow, a television, or a computer.

A tool is something we control directly. We buy tools, use them, loan them, and hopefully maintain them. And quite clearly, if a tool does not help us do what we want, we feel cheated. I can remember buying a pry-bar when I started restoring my sister's 1920s' vintage home and having it bend like some kind of children's toy the first time I tried pulling apart some framing timbers. I can remember as well the satisfaction with which I later bent it into an S-curve and dropped it on the counter at the hardware store along with my receipt, a dirty look, and a demand for a refund. The simple moral is, tools must make good on their promises. If not, we give them away, put them into storage, or cannibalize them to make tools that do.

Technologies are quite different. Technologies are not limited objects present for control by individual wills. Instead, they consist of patterns of conduct through which particular desires are literally incorporated and made manifest. In this sense, a technology is a set of dynamic orientations, a way of biasing the movement of natural resources, labor, capital, and so on. The "existential" status of technologies is not entitative, but relational. In the vernacular, technologies are not things. To the contrary, technologies have much the same status as the cultural, political, or economic institutions that so definitively shape our day-to-day lives. Just as a school or a bank is not a building or a particular inventory of desks, computers, telephones, and so on, but a purposeful patterning of goods, services, people, and their interactions, a technology is a way of making things happen. And just as our political and social institutions do, technologies express and inculcate sets of values crucial to both the actual and ideal development of our individual and communal identities—regardless of whether or not we are able to articulate or even specify these values. In this sense, technologies are perhaps best seen as practices.

Seen as a tool, a television is something we can put away in the closet or disassemble for parts. We can refrain from using it—a thing directly subject to our decisions. By contrast, seen as technology, television—the distance transmission and reception of visual and auditory information—marks a significant and unique change in *how we do things*. Specifically, it transforms how we communicate with and entertain one another. It involves not just the cameras, transmitters, satellites, and cables needed to electronically mediate our experience, but the factories that build these, the people working in those factories and the families they support, the producers and directors of the programs offered us, the editors and set builders, the reporters and advertisers. Involved as well are the conversations we have about soap opera characters, the music videos our teenagers consume with almost religious fervor, the toys modeled after TV puppets that we buy for our toddlers and the way these change the patterns of our play. As technology—as a purposed transformation of our conduct—television cannot simply be unplugged and given away to the Salvation Army.

As stated above, tools are individually controlled, and because of this we are in a position as individuals to effectively assess their utility. Deciding whether it's worthwhile changing from my old wood-handled, Craftsman hammer to a fully integral, all steel Estwing is up to me. I don't need to consult you or the rest of the neighborhood. After all, what hammer I use has no significant effect on how you remodel your bathroom—even if I happen to be helping. The locus of responsibility for choosing and using tools is individual, and the range of considerations need go no further than the specific utilities involved in the task individually in mind. In short, the horizons for relevance in evaluating a tool can be quite constrained.

This is not true of a technology. As practices or value-driven and value-producing patterns of conduct—and so unlike tool-using behavior—technologies are not liable to purely individual evaluation. Conduct literally means being "led together," and I use it in this context to stress that what is at issue is not our individual actions as such, but the pattern of our relationship—the movement of *our* narration, *our* story. Conceiving of technology as a patterning of conduct has two important benefits. First, it becomes clear that *deciding whether a technology lives up to its promises must be undertaken by communities*, not isolated individuals or interest groups. At the same time, precisely because technologies exist between us as the patterning of our conduct, like all other institutions they are practically invisible or ambient—part of the very atmosphere of our lives. As such, they easily escape evaluative scrutiny. This is, in fact, one of the reasons why it is so easy to ignore the presence of technology and why we tend to concentrate our critical attention on tools instead—thereby lending substantial "credibility" to the advertised neutrality of technology in general and of the information technologies in particular.

Secondly, because conduct consists of the movement of our narration—the dynamic and inherently dramatic (or to use the Buddhist term, karmic) process of our interdependence—it is clear that *no technology can be value-free*. In short, every new technology amounts to a novel biasing or conditioning of the quality of our interdependence. As such, it must be evaluated in terms of the broadest possible horizons for relevance, and not just with respect to its efficiency.

Because tools allow us to realize our individual intentions, we quite naturally place them on the line of causation proceeding from not-having (the thing, situation, power) that we want to having it. If the tool doesn't complete that line, it has failed us. How good a tool is can be seen, then, as a function of how efficiently it closes the gap between our intention and our goal. One of the consequences of serving in this capacity is that tools are often considered an extension of ourselves and any criticism of them is taken as criticism of us and our intentions. But seeing technical matters in terms of such a linear model of causation reinforces our confusion of tools and technologies because it is simply incapable of representing the role of the latter.

Simply put, linear causality does not apply to technologies. The reason we find it so hard to establish any direct causal link between, for example, television programming and random acts of violence is that technologies transform conduct, and not behavior. To put this another way, technologies operate according to the logic of interdependence. They do not exist on a line of causes and effects proceeding from any one of us to some altered state of affairs. To the contrary, they help shape the overall context in which both our intentions and actions take place. And so, what is most crucial in evaluating a technology is a consideration of its axiological—and not merely its factual—impact on our relationships. We must ask how it affects the *manner* in which we live, the way we perceive the world and ourselves, the *quality* of our reciprocity and community.

Now, if we see technologies as systems of envaluation—that is, as modes of projecting values definitive of a world and so our conduct and experience within it—they are most likely to be developed and proliferate to the point of virtual ambiance when the biases they embody and enact resonate with those otherwise obtaining in a given society or culture. That's quite a mouthful and it bears a bit of teasing out. If a new technology projects values widely disparate from those already indigenous, it will either be felt as a source of conflict or its benefits will seem so elusive as to be held nonexistent. As stated above, technologies arise as institution-like transformations in the patterning of our conduct. To the extent that a new patterning will augment, improve upon, or reinforce those already obtaining, it will be readily, almost thoughtlessly adopted and developed. Only if the new pattern of orientations contrasts too markedly from those already prevailing will a novel technology be subjected to caution. Consider, for instance, the difficulty with which acupuncture has become an accepted medical practice in the West.

Thus, while every new technology is a transformation of our conduct, when a lineage of values is being maintained or improved upon, this transformation is seen as evolutionary, as progressive—a good. Another way of putting this is to say that technologies always appear as answers to problems, as solutions to adaptational crises. And in this sense, it is hardly mysterious that new technologies are advertised as "saviors." Each technical innovation in fact ensures the continued viability of our basic assumptions about the world and our place within it.

Nor is it particularly mysterious that while we frequently discard our tools, we very seldom ever discard a technology. Once initiated, a technological lineage involves a co-evolution of useable and useful tools and patterns of wanting. Perfecting a technology is thus a way of perfecting—bringing to completion—a style of valuation, a particular fashioning of likes and dislikes. Because they are not things but forms of relationship, by changing our conduct, technologies necessarily take part in transforming not just what we desire, but who we are in our desiring.

This difference is crucial. While we can discard a tool with little impact on our sense of who we are—our identity—the same cannot be said of a technology. Criticizing a technology—and not just proceeding with its "perfection"—is in fact a criticism of ourselves, of our assumptions, our prejudices. Seen as tools, the printing press, televisions, computers, and even firearms are clearly innocuous. We can take them or leave them. For now, we take them and realize some individual gain in doing so. They augment our will. What is not typically appreciated is that making such an "innocent" choice conceals the communal costs of supporting the spread of print media, television, computer, and weapons-related technologies. That is, the price of seeing a technology in terms of either the products or the tools it generates is a narrowing of the focus of our concern to the point that the technology itself entirely eludes assessment. Quite simply, we will be incapable of attending to it. To the extent that this is true, Western individualism—the promotion of autonomous selfhood—is conducive to technological blindness.

Moral Transparency as Cultural Artifact

The claimed neutrality of firearms and the media is in part a function of our ignoring the overall patterns of conduct from which they—as tools—result as simple products. But it is also a function of establishing a particular, ostensive relationship with both these patterns and their products—a way of identifying ourselves over and against them as creatively empowered beings. We are moral agents. Technologies and their products are morally transparent objects that only become 'good' or 'bad' through our use of them. The moral universe pivots on our human will.

This is a familiar and profoundly anthropocentric view of considerable antiquity—one that has perhaps found its most pristine expression in the biblical narrative regarding the Garden of Eden. According to the story that has come down to us in the Book of Genesis, Eden was the perfect setting for the jewels of Yahweh's creative efforts. By any estimation, Eden was a gloriously well-knit world-within-a-world—a place into which evil (and for that matter good) had never been introduced. In Eden, there was originally neither morality nor its lack. All this changed with Adam's assertion of his freedom of choice. His act of eating the fruit of the tree of knowledge—an act individually undertaken even if seductively invited by Eve and the serpent—marks the birth not only of good and evil, but of passion and guilt, of selfishness and tragedy and grace. In short, it was an intentional, human act that introduced moral directions into the world. And it is at this point that human beings are "given" dominion over all the birds and beasts and plants of the world—to name and act as steward over them.

The subtext of the story is clear: it is by objectively identifying things and discriminating among them that we are able to subject them to our will and know that we literally exist or "stand apart" from them. That is, our position as sole moral agents in the world is first established by ignoring the values inherent to the living patterns of interdependence among all things. Afterward, it is maintained through the systematic crafting of things in accordance with our own needs. The agricultural revolution—perhaps the greatest technological "advance" in human history—is a perfect example of this process by means of which we at once take responsibility for our own good and arrogantly deny the world any capacity for creative moral partnership with us. From this moment on, we are free to choose either 'good' or 'evil'—to do what we want—and the things surrounding and supporting us can have only instrumental value.

It is to such a mythic and yet quite consequential moment that one can trace the notoriously persistent difficulties encountered by those who argue that plant and animal species being endangered by human activity are intrinsically valuable and so deserving of moral consideration. In the mainstream of Western thinking and praxis, precisely because plants and animals—as part of the natural, "God-given" world—have been seen as living instinctively or without the freedom of choice, they have been thought of as morally transparent and so "legitimately" excluded from any calculus of communal needs. That is, these species matter—have value—only through their relationship to we humans who are at once blessed with and cursed by the freedom of choice. Having no will of their own, they are presumed rightly subject to ours. The extent to which we are entitled to use them to serve our own purposes is thus held to be a practical, economic, and perhaps eco-scientific matter, not a dramatic or moral one.

There are, of course, other cultural narratives. For instance, within the Vedic tradition of India, plants and animals have long been understood as being subject to the same laws of karma or moral retribution as humans.

That is, the specifics of any incarnation—human or otherwise—are seen as a matter of past intentional activity (karma), a function of choices made, of values first projected and eventually embodied. Moving through a cycle of births as an insect and then as a reptile and then as a human and perhaps back again is at every step a journey of our own making. Thus, all beings exist on the same moral continuum. For the Vedic Indian, the entire cosmos—and not just the humanly mediated portion—is thoroughly moral.

Now, while the Vedic model of moral significance foregoes any restriction of free choice to humans and so allows all sentient beings to be considered morally charged, it does pivot on the individuality of choice. That is, while each sentient being enjoys the fruit of its choice and so possesses a distinctly moral dimension, each being has its own karma, its own lineage of moral expression and experience. No less than moral failure, moral success and spiritual salvation are understood to be both individual and individuating. Contrary to the Vedic model and even further removed from our own, Buddhism takes up the theme of karma and its implications for morality and combines them with the insight that all things are empty—that is, interdependent as opposed to independent and so self-existent. Especially in its East Asian forms, Buddhism has thus tended to stress the communal nature of all responsibility and so a definite skepticism regarding not just the possibility of moral transparency, but the concepts of individual choice and destiny. According to a well-known passage in the sayings of Ch'an master Ma-tsu, "Enlighten one, and the ten thousand [the myriad beings of the entire world] are enlightened; delude one and a thousand follow."

What is interesting about the Buddhist formulation is that while intention remains crucial in the conception of morality, it is neither reduced to choice nor strictly localized. Responsibility is understood as always and intimately shared. That is, if we are born into a world in which people take up guns in anger or greed and commit conscienceless murder, it is not simply *their* karma, but necessarily *ours*. Were we free from implication in such acts, we would have been born in a world where they quite literally did not occur. In this sense, it is simply foolish to insist that guns are morally transparent. The presence and need for firearms in a society speak volumes about the karmic and so moral natures of everyone involved. More importantly, far from being neutral elements in the make-up of this society, firearms are part of the conditions under which robberies, rapes, and murders come to pass. In a word, guns are as morally blemished as those who make conscienceless use of them. They do not simply reflect our values, but quite literally embody them.

I am not concerned at this point to debate the superiority of these views, but simply to encourage an admission that moral transparency—whether of various species or various technologies—is an artifact and by no means a universally supported one. Granted this, it becomes incumbent upon us to question to what extent we can dissociate ourselves from responsibility for the havoc wreaked by firearms or strip mining or international advertising. It becomes necessary to ask whether a given technology works because it enables us to effectively "cut the world at its joints," or because it is part of that disambiguating projection of values symptomatic of our personal and cultural karma.

These are admittedly very fine philosophical hairs to split at this or any other juncture. But appreciating their implications for how we construe multiculturalism, personhood, and the role of the media technologies is absolutely critical. If moral transparency pivots on an association of freedom with unconstrained and individual choice, projects aimed at globalizing media technologies on the basis of their supposed neutrality do not promote cultural diversity, but rather cultural imperialism. Bluntly stated, they eventuate a hegemonic subordination of interdependence to independence, of intimacy-with to integrity-in-the-face-of all things.

INDIVIDUAL FREEDOM AND THE OBDURATE, OBJECTING WORLD

In a world where moral transparency obtains, what is basic are individuals acting on one another, either for themselves or for others, but always *as* individuals. Perhaps the boldest articulation of the consequences of this view are found in Leibnitz's monadology according to which each of us is literally an impregnable atom, each reflecting the same universe and interacting with one another through it while remaining absolutely closed to one another. We are together, and yet irreducibly held apart by the very mode of that finally generic togetherness. In such a world, action or individually generated behavior is obviously prior to conduct or the movement of our narration, our intimacy with one another. At bottom, this means that if freedom, safety, and happiness are not simply illusions, we will discover them first within, in our own experience, individually if not always privately.

Of course, we don't need to venture into the thin air of seventeenth-century German metaphysics to find illustrations of the extent to which freedom and individuality have become practically inseparable in the American mind. Not long after my son entered preschool—at about age three—he suddenly developed an acute sense of his rights. In situations where it became clear that he was not going to get his way, he would first try to ignore the currently disagreeable imperative. When this failed to cause his problem to disappear—either me or his mother and our "unfair" demands—he would question our authority, politely and yet with always (to us) surprising vehemence. Listening to our probably incomprehensible reasons, he would meet our gaze steadily and silently as tears welled up in his eyes and his lower lip began very endearingly to quiver. And then, just at the moment we reached out to gather him up in parenting arms and kiss his tears away, he would solemnly protest—"But I'm still my own person."

What lies behind this vignette of contemporary family life is a long history of deepening associations between personhood and individuality, and so between our understanding of who we are and an acute awareness of resistances to our will. It has become commonplace to assert that maturation is itself a process of individuation, of learning the boundary conditions of societal acceptance, and at the same time not allowing the submergence of what is my very own—my wants, my dreams, my likes and dislikes—in the collective consciousness of the family or peer group or community. The discovery of the contemporary Western self is thus inseparable from articulating the limits of immediate control. And in this sense, my three-year-old behaved as a model child—sure of himself, of his own feelings and inalienable integrity, even when his tender heart was bruised to the point of bursting. But that his personhood at age three was already consciously bound up in recognizing the limits of what he could *control*—and not, for example, what he could *contribute*—is a profound revelation of the extent to which our identity and freedom are wrapped up with our isolation, our existence or "standing-apart" from one another.

To caricature the situation, we have a contrast between on one hand a world in which independence is seen as an irreducible good standing in contrast with its perversion as either unilateral dependence or pathological codependence, and on the other hand a world in which each of these is seen as a limiting abstraction from what is in fact always present and prior—our exceptionless interdependence. In the former, freedom can be characterized as fundamentally assertive. That is, freedom pivots on an absence of constraints on individual choices and actions—being able to state the exact terms of our existence. In the latter world, freedom is understood as fluency in conduct, as the quality of appropriate and unobstructed relationship or concurrence. In this sense, freedom is not seen as mine or yours, but ours. It is not understood as the state of an individually initiated act, but the quality of our narrative movement; not as successful protest, but rather virtuosic response. Understood in this way, freedom implies community—the mutuality of living not only with, but in a very real sense for and even as one another.

Seen in terms of virtuosic harmony—the mutual nurturing of what remains irreducibly unique or different—freedom does not imply any kind of necessary status or circumstances. It does not even imply the presence of multiple choices, of apparent and concrete options among which we can select the one or ones that accord best with our needs or desires. To the contrary, the presence of choices must quite literally be understood as marking an at least temporary forfeiture of freedom since standing at a crossroads trying to decide which way to proceed is an interruption of our fluid virtuosity. In short, an awareness of choices implies the abstraction of a deciding, if not always decisive, ego or self. In the midst of truly improvised and hence unprecedented responding, no choices are being entertained or made.

By contrast, whenever freedom is construed in terms of the absence of unnecessary constraints, we will always be concerned with establishing—even if only ideally—some kind of difference-eliding identity or equality of each of us with every other. In the long run, you and I can only be free if our differences are rendered effectively incidental. If instead our differences place me—through no direct choice of my own—at some kind of marked disadvantage, it is not only my behavior that is unduly constrained but my freedom as such. At a minimum, freedom entails not being placed under any unique and galling constraints, and this means in the end that each of us must enjoy the same basic perspectives and prospects as everyone else—the same initial conditions with respect to all crucial resources, be these material, educational, political, social, or what have you. Quite literally, we must possess substantially the same choices; and the more, the merrier.

That such equality is simply an ideal is by most of us quite readily admitted. But even as an ideal, it deeply informs our attitudes and aspirations. On our city streets and increasingly in the halls of our schools, guns are referred to as "equalizers." They render differences in strength, speed, and rhetorical genius practically irrelevant. Similarly, a great part of the seductiveness of the media is their promise of placing each of us equally "on the scene." Television has allowed all of us to watch the same football games, to sit in the living rooms of the same sitcom families, to receive identical, up-to-the-minute news briefings from around the globe. With the breakthrough into cyberspace, the reality of each and every one of us being effectively equidistant from all the relevant information and virtual leverage needed to realize our particular aims seems finally within reach. In cyberspace, we can choose not only to go where we want when we want, we can, to a previously unimaginable degree, determine who we travel as. As the burgeoning discourse on cyberspace-mediated relationships makes evident, this newest technological advance makes it possible to maximally attenuate not only our physical location, but the constraints of our physicality itself. In cyberspace, we can choose our gender, our past, our persona and 'body' type. In short, our choices—at least in terms of access to information and mediate contact with other parts of the world—are becoming virtually limitless.

Some of us may have concerns, even fears, about the latent dangers of electronic mediation. But for most of us, the immediate benefits of eliding the effects of actual proximity or its lack are nothing short of intoxicating. The new media would seem to have the power not only of extending and refining our dreams, but of raising them through the layered realms of the merely possible until they are finally able to come true. As some prophets of the cybernetic age put it, this will liberate us not only from the parochialism of the neighborhood and the nation-state, but of the body itself and the narrowness of a mind bound by its strictures. The new media are not just entertaining us or informing us. They are engineering our freedom.

If the foregoing analysis is accepted, however, even the possibility of wielding this power would seem to have come about only at the very definite cost of having prioritized individuality over community, action over conduct, integrity over intimacy, rights over responsiveness. Wielding it in blind enthusiasm promises to only further intensify these priorities. Granted this, it should come as no shock that there is a notable correlation of the maturing and spread of mass mediation and, for example, both rampant consumerism and the painful individuation marking the contemporary demise of the extended family and its replacement in turn by the so-called nuclear and single-parent families. This is not to say that mass mediation caused these broad social trends, but rather that such trends are both encouraged by and encourage the virtual universality of mediate experience. In Buddhism, this kind of relationship is referred to as *pratitya-samutpada* or codependent origination. It is not that the spread of mass media determines the disintegration of the family or vice versa, but rather that they have arisen in mutual dependence or support of one another. Their relationship is in this sense intrinsic or symbiotic. Unavoidably, if we have reason to lament the latter, we have equal reason to be chary of the former.

There are, of course, a myriad of possible ways of explaining away this and other unsavory correlations. Our lives are complex enough that by foregrounding certain facts and sending others into the background, it's possible to construct alternative and internally consistent histories that conserve those values we hold most sacred. In short, because of the virtually infinite richness of our individual and communal lives, it's possible to claim that the apparent interdependence of mass mediation and say the demise of the extended family is ultimately a historical accident, a mere coincidence. For example, it is clear that other conditions than mass mediation have played a significant role in the atrophy of the family. The rise of industrialism, the specialization of labor and production, and so the separation of the workplace and homeplace have profoundly contributed to the dilution of the family across an increasingly compartmentalized or rationalized life-world. This is, no doubt, true enough. But, it takes nothing away from the interdependence of mass mediation and these other trends as well.

By relying on a clever if largely unconscious employment of counterfactuals—claims made about what would have obtained had things been more or less different than they were—such arguments implicitly rely on our adopting a linear view of causality. That is, our premise—that we can isolate causes and imagine what world would have resulted were we able to simply cut them out of the picture—is in and of itself a refusal to admit the priority of interdependence. By directing our thinking along linear-causal lines in the service of carefully analyzing our history and its possible alternatives, we are effectively stacking the deck in favor of preserving those cultural assumptions that fuel not just our enthusiastic hopes for the media, but our sense of what it means to be free as autonomous individuals. In a word, far from grounding a neutral assessment of our situation, the appeal to counterfactuals should be seen as a means of enshrining a bias that may be long-standing in the dominant cultural traditions of the West, but one that is hardly universal.

All such biases are at root conservative—a resistance to change in the service of preserving integrity or identity. It is immaterial whether the rhetoric of defense is drawn from the revolutionary vocabulary of the liberal left extolling the need for free media, for the continued 'anarchy' of the Internet, or from the religious fervor of the capital-inspired, censorship-endorsing right. In both cases, the same construction of selfhood and freedom obtains and the supposedly inherent neutrality of mass media is a given. The association of freedom and autonomous choice is taken as irreproachable. And beneath all of this is the belief that one thing leads to another (action is basic) and not that all things are guiding and guided by each other (conduct is basic). As understood in the Ch'an Buddhist tradition, when most honestly appraised, this disposition must be seen as a selfish indulgence in and enforcement of dualism—either that or a preamble to the assertion of one or another monism that is just a dualism infected with and blinded by pride.

In sum, the neutrality of the media is integral to our seduction by a particular conception of both selfhood and freedom. Because it's a conception that—in both its dualistic and monistic versions—denies our basic interdependence, it is a conception that fosters our continued discourse, equalizing us at the cost of generic isolation. The virulence of our defense of the media's positive potential—like the adamant disbelief of one who has been manipulated in love—reflects not just our severely misplaced hopes, but the stubbornness of our refusal to admit our ignorance in the affair. When other people, other cultures, are similarly seduced and end up wanting what we have wanted, we take a kind of pride in having been first—the first to see the beauty of conceiving freedom in terms of choice and selfhood in terms of autonomy; the first to invent technologies allowing these conceptions to be realized as rapidly as possible; the first to feel the purported inevitability of the changes on which we are so amazingly embarked.

Criticizing the root values that have informed the arising of the media and that they have in turn further empowered is to call into question our own genealogy. But more than this, it is also calling into question our tele-ology, our purposes—that for the sake of which we live and learn. Needless to say, this is to enter very heavy waters indeed.

JUST SAYING NO TO THE LOGIC OF CHOICE

Roughly fifteen hundred years ago, the Indian Buddhist philosopher and practitioner Nagarjuna declared that the Buddha taught for the purpose of our relinquishing *all* views. His opponents, much like the advocates of me-dia neutrality, pointed out that it couldn't be the case that the Buddha sought the dissolution of all views because his own Four Noble Truths and the Eightfold Path by means of which they could be realized are in fact con-stitutive of a particular view. Clearly forgetting that the Buddha described his own teachings as a raft that it would at some point be necessary to dis-card, these opponents, much like those of us inclined to preserve a belief in the moral transparency of the media, argued that the point of Buddhism was divesting ourselves not of *all* views, but only those that are found to be false or impractical. In short, they insisted that it could not be views as such that the Buddha maintained were necessarily troubling, but only the contents proper to certain views or the ways they were put to use. For absolutists, this meant that our task must consist of discerning the right or ultimate view, the Truth with a capital T. For relativists, it meant cultivating a plethora of views to avoid the narrowness of slavish adherence to only one or a small set of limited perspectives as universally right or true. Nagarjuna disagreed. And in the case of media and their relationship to enlightening virtuosity, so must we.

A Buddhist understanding of media drives us to the same conclusions regarding their purported neutrality as Nagarjuna reached in his analysis of the structure of having views: media entice conduct away from improvised harmony and propel us toward institutionally regulated agreement. In fact, the structure of mediation disposes us toward a fragmenting of conduct into individual behaviors comprising equally individual actions and intents. That is, mediation encourages a fissuring of our narration into what is 'me' and 'mine' and what is 'you' and 'yours'. And so—just as the Buddha insisted with respect to views—media distance us from realizing an unchecked readi-ness for liberating intimacy. Instead, they foster dispositions toward accept-ing as natural, relationships that are not only binding, but with increasing frequency both generic and merely virtual. In other words, media foster a so-cietal and not a truly social orientation of our presence with one another. They promote not our lively and ultimately unprecedented concourse, but a discourse by means of which our differences are initially recognized only to be turned eventually into homogenizing, tradable commodities. And this is not because of the content of the media, but the manner in which they structure our awareness as such.

Importantly for us, by undertaking a Buddhism-informed reflection on media, it should become possible to recontextualize the debate about cultural diversity in such a way that a more viable middle path may be articulated between the isolationism practiced by, for example, certain fundamentalist Islamic/Arabic nations, and the uncensored cultural consumerism now running rampant in much of the electronically mediated world. It will also mean accepting a responsible role in either the proliferation or voluntary simplification of the technological umbrella out from under which contemporary society is finding it increasingly difficult to venture. If we are to preserve not just *our* freedoms, but those endorsed by cultures other than our own—if we are to stop being willing accomplices in our own colonization—we may paradoxically find it necessary to limit our choices and question the univocality of progress.

Chapter 3

Technology as Savior

It's Getting Better, Better All the Time

Precedents for a notion of progress in the West can arguably be traced back to Aristotle. Whereas most of his predecessors in the Greek philosophical tradition tended to dismiss change as ontologically suspect, Aristotle made it absolutely integral to his understanding of reality. This was not, of course, an entirely new idea. The notion of a return to the promised land, so much a part of the Hebrew cultural narrative and worldview, implicitly affirmed the reality and central importance of change and time. Plato, too, had made frequent appeals to psychologically experienced change as a part of the process of the soul's return to the eternal and unchanging eidetic realm and an eventually direct, nonsensory and atemporal apprehension of the Good. But in these systems—or, for that matter, in the cyclic cosmology of the Vedas—change was allowed as provisionally real, but essentially meaningless. Change was real and important only in the sense of a repatriation—a return to the source of all originations.

Aristotle broke radically with this circular understanding of change and with the metaphysical conundrums it spawned by seeing change and motion as linear vectors. Set into original motion by the activity of an "unmoved Mover," the universe and everything in it are not just going, but going somewhere quite definite. Time and change are the unfolding of purpose, a movement toward final completion or perfection. Far from being a metaphysically pointless and unjustifiable circulation, change over time *is* the point. Things are getting better, all the time.

For Aristotle, an immediate implication of such a view is that not only past conditions and present circumstances have to be seen as causally significant, but also the future. In concrete terms, one of the "causes" of an acorn is the oak tree it will become; one of the "causes" of the child is the adult he or she will grow up to be. This strictly teleological conception of the universe and the reciprocating model of causation it required underwent sufficient conceptual erosion that by the end of the medieval period the notion of causality came to be restricted to a 'forward'-moving influence over time and the meaning of perfection exported from the potentiality of things themselves to the intentions of the Creator of all things. But the prejudice for seeing the world as turning out "the way it ought to" is still very much with us.

In part, this is a function of a superimposition of Aristotle's secular assumption of an "unmoved Mover" and the Judeo-Christian, religious assumption of a divine and concerned Creator. According to the resultant image, not only did the universe begin with a particular intent, it is evolving toward a definitely ordained climax. In Einstein's pregnant phrase, God is not playing dice. But there is also a logical/scientific gene in our conception of progress, perhaps best expressed in the nineteenth-century works of Hegel—in whose dialectically structured universe, all of history is the purposeful mounting of Spirit (*Geist*) through itself, to itself, knowing itself as itself—and those of Darwin, who proposed that species were not transcendently created but arise out of progressive adaptation to changing circumstances with only the fittest, and so best, surviving.

Though we may know better, in our popular consciousness, we still exhibit a decided tendency for believing that what is happening now is not just things as they are, but things as they ought to and even must be. For example, we not only see *Homo sapiens* as the current pinnacle of terrestrial evolution, we assume that our vantage is the highest our planet has ever witnessed. We tend as well to see the kind of societies, governments, religions, and aesthetic sensibilities we now enjoy as being equally at the crest of a perpetually rising tide of progress. The way things are now are the best they have ever been—and necessarily so.

As might be expected, our ever-accelerating development of new technologies is not viewed as just a fact, but as a kind of manifest destiny. Our knowledge of the world and the technologies through which this knowledge is most powerfully expressed are seen as better and better mirroring nature and so as warranting that we're on the right track. And should proof be needed, we simply point to the ever-increasing control we have over our various internal and external environments. If our technical developments were not in sympathy with the ways the world is organized and evolving, how could they be so evidently successful? How could we literally have moved mountains, traveled to the moon, or learned to map and tailor our own genetic material? Granted that divinity entails being able to translate ideas into reality more or less at will, technological development seems to have enabled us to climb out of animal subjection to instinct and necessity toward an increasingly divinized relationship to the world about us. The history of technology is a secular history of salvation.

Glancing over the way new technologies have been represented and marketed in the past century, it's clear that the messianic role of technology has been no secret. To the contrary, the advertised benefits of technical advance have quite explicitly included increased cleanliness, efficiency, ease, safety, security, leisure, beauty, and power—a litany that adds up to "a better world," a "paradise on earth." Technology allows us to get up out of the dirt of material existence and toil and enjoy the things around us, satisfying our every want. It frees us from the physical dimensions of labor and makes it possible to simply say the word for a task to be quickly and accurately carried out. And this is not because we lord some authority over other men, women, or children, but because we have largely mastered the laws of nature. The only limits to what we can do are the limits of our imagination.

We are all familiar with this rhetoric: we began some thousands of years in brute subjection to the objects of the world, but through technological progress we have come to a point where we can heed the world's objections or not as we please. We have become the masters of our circumstances. What most of us have not done is admit that this rhetoric is at all plausible only because of a collusion of values proper to our religious and philosophical heritage and those proper to our dominant technological lineage. In fact, it is this collusion that has driven the canonization of "progress." Far from being a culture-neutral term, "progress" is at root a religious imperative— the directive to be truly adamant in realizing our independence from things, our capacity for ignoring or stewarding them at will.

Objections might well be made that there are many within our Graeco-Judeo-Christian traditions who have been suspicious of the inherent goodness of our increasingly technology-laden way of life. Indeed, there have always been "angry prophets" who have seen "progress" as a prelude to the end. For some, today's high-tech society is founded on an arrogance that will lead to the end of the world, even the end of time. But even these marginal voices buy into the basic prejudice that our present—perverse though it may be—is at the apex of an overarching historical process and is inexorably heading us toward some ordained climax. Whether this process has us moving first into Armageddon and then paradise rather than through a continual evolution of relative paradises toward some absolute consummation is less important than our belief that we are where we ought to be given where we are headed. Likewise, whether this destiny is sacred or secular—a function of creation or evolution—is less important than that it is assumed in the first place.

Granted this, any criticism of the foundations of progress will feel like an attack both on what makes us who we are and why. Questioning technology—like questioning the authority of scripture—is a blasphemous act. It is tantamount to an attack on what structures our world and ensures that it is a true *universe*, not just a pointless assembly of accidental events. The crisis of confidence in our religious foundations that was articulated with particularly original force by Nietzsche—a crisis that found successively more pointed and thorough expression in the existential tradition running through Heidegger, Sartre, and Camus—has been for this reason a crisis in our confidence in technology as well. Our lives, Camus decided, are basically absurd. And absurdity makes a mockery not just of divinely ordained destiny, but technological predestination as well. The interlocking of lost faith in the Creator and lost faith in our own technological creations and creativity manifestly underscores the extent to which our religions and our technologies have shared a set of common assumptions about causality, meaning, and temporality—assumptions from which we can hardly imagine disentangling ourselves without losing faith in ourselves as well.

Not all cultures have traditionally shared these assumptions. Many of them have already been eradicated and many more are on the verge of extinction. Under the persuasion of our prejudice, this is quite often seen as simple due process. There is tragedy in the demise of a culture, but justice as well: a culture disappears because it was incapable of adapting to and competing in an ever-changing world, because it lacked the idea and ideal of progress. Cultural Darwinism of this sort is rampant not so much as a consciously held position, of course, but as presumed absence of alternatives. We are sorry that the aboriginal inhabitants of "the Americas" were forced to change so rapidly, with so little preparation. But after all it has ultimately been for their 'good'. They have lost a tradition to modernity first and now to postmodernity, but have gained much in return. At any rate, we are inclined to state with grave finality that the process is inevitable—you cannot, perhaps must not, stand in the way of progress.

Like all prejudices, this view is not fully and rationally defensible. But being a prejudice, that doesn't matter as much as we might imagine. Even for those who feel aboriginal cultures should be actively preserved, this typically does not mean forfeiting our technologically mediated destiny, but rather making room within that destiny for aboriginal peoples to persist if not flourish. Just as we have taken to creating wilderness preserves to protect the planet's biodiversity, we think of creating aboriginal reserves to protect cultural diversity. In both cases, the basic premise is that preservation depends on segregation. To save wilderness—whether cultural or biological—we marginalize it, make it other. And we do so because we assume that, failing this, our present way of life will simply overrun the wilds.

Mildly put, what this amounts to is a domestication of wilderness, a domestication of aboriginal culture. If these are to persevere, they will do so in our home, according to the logic of *our* way of life, *our* economy. More pointedly, preserving cultures and endangered species means cutting them off from the conditions of their growth, the risk-filled domains in which their unique forms of creativity might flourish. Preserved fruit will never produce a tree, and preserved cultures—like preserved species—exist in a similar limbo between growth and decay.

Dualisms, precisely because they allow us to assert 'this' over 'that', are conducive to the most altruistic forms of arrogance. It was in the spirit of having clearly seen this that the Buddha declared that 'is' and 'is-not' are the twin barbs on which humankind is impaled. And it is also why he denied that our world had some definite beginning, that it is informed by a singular purpose or intent, that its history is essentially and necessarily progressive. The segregation of progress and regress or the domestic and the wild—like all segregation—is ultimately an act of impoverishment and mutual destruction. Among other things, the Buddha's refusal to take a stand on either 'this' or 'that' provides us with a method for beginning to question our conviction that the world we happen to inhabit lies at the summit of all cultural and technical evolution. Far from signaling a skeptical disengagement from the world, this refusal aims at inaugurating an ethics of resisting our habits of valuation and conduct—a concerted return to the virtuosity of truly horizonless intimacy.

TECHNOLOGY: THE ORIGINAL BROKEN PROMISE

Thus far, our conversation has been quite theoretical and abstract. Advocates of technological progress often excuse themselves from such conversations with the statement that technologies are about practice, not theories. It is one thing to look at conceptual precedents and potential contradictions at the level of "pure values," but technology takes place in the marketplace, in the factory, in the home. And it is there that we must take account of it. If technology is our savior, it is one that answers our needs without questions asked or terms demanded. In other words, what salvation means is up to us.

This is the moral transparency argument all over again and we should strenuously resist it. But there is some merit in taking technology at its word. After all, the internal history of technology is rife with high expectations. Each breakthrough is attended by promises of remarkably less work, more luxury, more freedom, a revolution in our quality of life, the realization of a New Eden. Because new technologies are consolidated through a feedback-mediated distribution of tools designed to have immediate, individual benefits for their users, and because success tends to narrow rather than dilate our horizons for evaluative relevance, these promises have typically been seen as honored.

Even when a technical "advance"—say, transportation systems based on the internal combustion of fossil fuels—proves to have unadvertised and massively negative side effects, its past success weighs so heavily that we typically see them as "unintended consequences." In a recent book, *Why Things Bite Back: Technology and the Revenge of Unintended Consequences* (1996), Edward Tenner almost apologetically categorizes and catalogues a host of such "revenge" effects. But like most of us, Tenner remains steadfast in regarding the technologies he reviews as essentially "innocent." Revenge is taken, not by the technologies themselves in some display of maliciousness or mischief, but by the world at large, which proves to be more complexly resistant to control than we'd anticipated. The values expressed by the technologies themselves are never seriously questioned. We remain essentially loyal to a technology until a new one takes up the essence of the original promise and goes one "better" for us with newer, "cleaner," and even more "user-friendly" tools.

Immediately apparent individual gain, however, is not all there is to our readiness to ride the technological juggernaut wherever it happens to lead us. There is also a kind of intoxication that comes with appropriating a new technology—an intoxication combining the thrill of vicarious invention with the immediately sensed power of clearly increased control. In part, this is natural and good. Appropriating a new technology is a form of learning, and learning is exciting—a way of quite literally raising our level of realized interdependence. Each time we learn a new skill or so familiarize ourselves with a field of inquiry that we can improvise within it, we effectively expand the dimensions of our world. Since every increase in the subtlety of our possible modes of perception and response opens up a novel intimacy between us and the rest of our world, and since this intimacy—like that which dawns with a new love affair—always announces the limitlessness of its possibilities, we are naturally moved by them to a kind of joy. Whether this thrilling is short-lived or not takes nothing away from its reality. Witness, for instance, the astounding, practically overnight popularity of internet and world-wide-web "surfing." It is not at all rare for subscribers to spend ten or twenty hours a week logged on and exploring cyberspace. Every major "news" magazine in the United States has (in the early fall of 1996) run feature articles on the cyber-revolution. And in these magazines, computer manufacturers touting their multimedia support systems have been running not just full-page, but up to eight-page, full-color ads. This is not a "dry" or dutiful involvement with the technology, but a consuming national—and all too soon, I'm afraid, world—passion.

Immediate, typically quantitative, tool-mediated gains in our ability to satisfy our wants, when combined with the quite visceral thrill of acquiring new ranges of individual potency and skill make the resistance of technology a very hard ethic to sell. Even if Western technology is seen as a system of values that deeply alters the modes of our conduct, and even allowing that its spread means the subversion of the indigenous values of other cultural traditions, this is not usually enough to convince us that these changes are not progressive. We may admit that while each new technology resolves some previously existing problems, it often raises entirely new ones in their place. But this does not mean that we are willing to admit the failure of the technical enterprise as such. We persist in believing that the promise of technology is for the most part being honored, and that it is just a matter of time before any problems ensuing from new technical advances will be solved—by further and continuous technical advance. Technotopia is a dream coming true faster and more surely every day. In practice, that is our deepest and most universal faith.

Unfortunately, it is also a particularly dangerous form of ignorance. Especially for the last two and a half centuries, the dominant Western cultures have indulged in an almost obsessive fascination with technical 'evolution.' Tired of waiting for a divinely realized heaven on earth, matters were taken definitively into our own hands. Previous generations may have been content to wait for the arrival of the future kingdom of heaven on earth, but their patience bore far too little fruit, far too slowly. And so it was tacitly decided that if paradise was not going to fall from heaven, it would simply have to be fashioned here in our midst. The question we should be asking—that we should have been asking all along—is whether or not the future we have been so zealously and faithfully building from scratch is the one we've been promising ourselves.

This, however, is dreadfully hard. Familiarizing ourselves with a new technology is not just a matter of external acquaintance. Even as using our tools changes them—directly through wear and tear or indirectly and over time through practice-informed modification—through their use, our tools and the technologies that spawn them are changing us, continually and profoundly. When we play with a new tool, it is just a novelty. But real familiarity means quite literally an adoption of the tool as part of ourselves. The tool becomes family. And we, in turn, become members of the clan of its originating technologies. Asking ourselves to seriously criticize the arsenal of tools gathered in the emergency room of any major hospital or to denounce the electronic gateways to the world that we have enshrined in our living rooms and bedrooms—that is asking us to criticize our own assumptions about the purpose of the good life, to denounce our own families, and so our own identities.

We should make the effort. Viewed dispassionately, technology has *not* lived up to its promises. It has not done so thus far, and we have no evidence suggesting that it ever will. For all its apparent, individual benefits, technology has quite literally been a waste of our time. Consider the following.

Subsistence versus High-tech Living: The Case of the Hawaiian Islands

The first human inhabitants of the 132 islands comprised in the Hawaiian archipelago sailed up from either the Marquesas or Tahitian islands some 1,200 to 1,500 years ago. According to estimates based on the likely growth rates of an initial settling party of 50 to 80 persons, the population on the eight islands inhabited at the time of European contact in 1778 would have grown to about three hundred thousand. Estimates based on first hand descriptions by Captain Cook and others in the first wave of European visitors would place the population somewhere between eight hundred thousand and one million. Conservatively, we can say that the Hawaiian Islands were home to about half a million persons.

This population was entirely self-sufficient. There were no imported foods, fuels, clothing, tools, or sources of energy. Even though they were "limited" to tools fashioned out of volcanic stone, sufficiently extensive terracing, irrigation, and aquaculture enabled the Hawaiian people to produce regular and significant food surpluses and enjoy a robustness that would be the envy of any present-day Western nation.

As recorded in chant and hula (ceremonial dance), native Hawaiian life was profoundly spiritual. Founded upon a direct appreciation of the cosmos as family, Hawaiian society was organized in such a way that relationship was stressed over individuality, cooperation over selfish gain. So deep was this appreciation of relationality that all illness was seen as rooted in social disease. The traditional healing arts required not only a treatment—primarily through herbs and massage—of the afflicted person's body, but a balancing and reinvigoration of their relationships with others. Referred to as *ho'oponopono*, this comprehensive treatment required the presence of every member of the extended family and an airing and settling of all grievances and perceived wrongs. Health was understood as social; healing as the process of repairing tears in the fabric of our narration, in the continuity and complementarity of our life stories.

Observations by the first European visitors report that the Hawaiian people were not overly "industrious." Like most so-called aboriginal peoples—a term that for us connotes immaturity and lack of sophistication—the native Hawaiians spent much time in the communal celebration of ritual, in social visiting, in play, and in rest. They did a lot of what in local Hawaiian culture is now referred to as "talking story." That is, daily life was not only inherently meaningful, it was narratively structured meaning—a meaning that remains personal at every level rather than becoming arcane or abstract. In both work and leisure, emphasis was placed on realizing and appreciating health.

That life and culture no longer exist in full flower. Within fifty years of European contact, the Hawaiian population had plummeted to barely fifty thousand. At present, native Hawaiians represent roughly 10 percent of the population. Like native peoples throughout the United States, and in sharp contrast to their former estate, they enjoy the lowest levels of income, the shortest expected life spans, the worst health, the highest rates of crime and alcoholism and the most nutritionally bankrupt diet in the state. A culture that had spawned and nurtured self-sufficient, narratively and spiritually rich communities for at least a thousand years lies in virtual tatters. Meanwhile, the major islands have become home for some of the most affluent people on the planet and a favorite vacation land for millions of tourists each year—all of which can be traced to the prevalence of safe and rapid mass transportation of goods and people. For the Hawaiian Islands, as everywhere, technological "progress" has been a Janus-faced affair.

The disruption and eventual destruction of native Hawaiian culture is to my heart and mind nothing short of criminal. And marketing colorful remnants of this culture as tourist draws only adds galling insult to an already crippling injury. But my point in offering this description of pre-contact Hawai'i and sketching its postcolonial fate is not to stimulate either sympathy or outrage. Rather, I'd like to use the contrast between pre- and post-contact Hawai'i to assess the process by means of which one was traumatically transformed into the other. In particular, I want to critically review the promises made by technology—promises crucial in supporting the common view that what happened in the Hawaiian Islands represents an inevitable fallout of that globally altruistic (if sometimes locally tragic) phenomenon we call "progress."

As the received story goes, the Hawaiians—like many indigenous peoples—may have enjoyed a profound harmony with their natural surroundings, but it was a precarious and naive harmony. The coming of Western-style progress meant an end to the Hawaiian "age of innocence," but this can hardly be seen as entirely a loss. After all, native Hawaiian culture endorsed a deeply ritualistic life and a rigidly structured society in which individual rights were wholly subordinate. In pre-Cook Hawai'i, vertical movement in society was practically prohibited. Commoners could not own land. Conflicts between the members of the ruling class were often bloody and human sacrifices were apparently offered in propitiation of the native gods. Diseases and injuries that are easily treated by modern medicine claimed uncounted lives.

Was pre-Cook Hawai'i a paradise? Would we want to live there? Probably not. The death of as many as 750,000 people in half a century cannot but be mourned. But according to the received view, this was an accident that could not have been avoided—not at the time, at least. And it may be that on the whole, the Hawaiian people—or at least people of the Hawaiian Islands—are now in definite and quantifiable ways better off than if the archipelago had never been colonized up into the twentieth century.

Maybe. If the promises of technology have indeed been realized, the state of Hawai'i should be more of a paradise than the island chain happened upon by Captain Cook. But is it? Our prejudice is surely that it is. For all that most residents of the Islands might complain about traffic and noise and increasing crime, few would trade their cars and refrigerators, their electric lights and televisions, for the canoes and taro of the native Hawaiians. To the contrary, what they seek are better technical solutions—geothermal energy production, mass transit, the conversion of garbage into electricity, and linking up to worldwide electronic networks to create a more viable, international economic base. Current affairs might not be perfect, but making them better is almost invariably understood, not as requiring a deep reevaluation, but increased investment—of time, money, energy—in the way things are already being done. In a word, what is needed is more progress. As for the tourists who visit the Islands in the number of about 6 million per year, they would not be very likely to show such enthusiasm were they required to sleep on woven mats and forego their favorite liquors, snacks, and climate-controlling devices. "Roughing it" is not a typically favored idea of vacation—the current popularity of "eco-tourism" notwithstanding.

The current, very ethnically diverse population of the islands is just under a million—roughly the high estimate for pre-contact Hawai'i. According to the promises of technological advance, the lives of these million people should be maintained better and with less effort than those of the Hawaiians living in the Islands prior to the arrival of Captain Cook. There should be on the average less expenditure of energy to meet the basic requirements of life, more leisure, better health, and a more harmonious and vigorous community. But there is not.

Pre–European contact Hawai'i was a largely vernacular society. As used by Ivan Illich, the vernacular is that domain where sustenance occurs through reciprocity patterns rather than by way of formalized exchange and the hierarchically structured distribution of commodities. By contrast, ours is a commodity-intensive society. Technologically dense, it is characterized by limited access to the use-value of our environment—the commons. That is, the means of sustaining our lives and lifestyles are not readily accessible. We have to "trade" something valuable for them—our attention in the form of either money, tangible resources, labor, or simple time.

We have been taught to believe that life in vernacular societies is hard and uncertain. Toil is constant and the results spotty. There are few professionals and correspondingly little expertise in controlling disease, the production of food and clothing, the building of reliable shelter and modes of transportation. The vernacular world is one of poverty and scarcity. We have also been taught that ours is a society of plenty, of relative ease and leisure. We have entrusted much of the orientation of our activities to experts—doctors, lawyers, politicians, agricultural specialists, therapists, corporate presidents, accountants, and so on—but in return, we enjoy a satisfyingly regular and safe life. When catastrophes do occur, there are experts trained and authorized to handle them with maximum efficiency. In short, we have been taught that, in balance, life is as good as it has ever been.

A few facts stand in the way of endorsing these beliefs. Early in the nineteenth century—not long after the arrival of Europeans in Hawai'i—it was estimated that the average working day was four hours in length and that the number of days spent working amounted to something between 160 and 200 days a year. In other words, nobody worked more than part-time, part of the year and yet everyone had food and shelter in plenty. This was not an isolated miracle we can chalk up to the lush, tropical environment of the Islands. Hopis farming the desert in the American Southwest, Bushmen in Central Africa, the Inuit in the far Arctic Circle—these peoples and many more have traditionally worked similar numbers of hours in sustaining themselves. And lest it be thought that in such societies the woman's work—which in our culture is commonly admitted to "never be done"—must have taken up the slack, the distribution of labor is remarkably equitable. Women often work throughout the day, but less continuously than their male counterparts, and on average only about 10 percent more hours in the course of a year. According to Marshall Sahlins, whose *Stone Age Economics* (1972) is an eye-opening classic, the average work week in Hawaiian and most other so-called "Stone Age" cultures is about twenty-five hours.

In the 1990s, an average professional in Hawai'i—as in most of the industrialized West—works about 50–55 hours a week, 48–50 weeks out of each year. Blue-collar workers often have shorter weekly schedules but less vacation and often supplement their regular salaries with part-time employment or cash-economy "side-jobs." Compared to the horrific conditions prevailing at the dawn of the industrial age in New England and Britain, this is an undeniable improvement. Gone for most of us are the sixteen-hour days, the complete absence of health or vacation benefits, and the dangerous working conditions. But, compared to the original inhabitants of Hawai'i—or for that matter, pre-industrial Europe where the work year averaged only 180–220 days—we are still slaving away.

Matters look much worse when we take into account that the estimates for work among our technologically "disadvantaged" predecessors include not just gathering or hunting food, but carrying out agricultural duties, making and repairing tools, clothing, and shelter, and preparing daily meals. In other words, this is the sum total of effort spent in "making ends meet." The average citizen in Hawai'i now spends a great portion of his or her nominally "free" time working in what Illich (1981) has called the "shadow economy"—the hemisphere of unpaid, unacknowledged labor, often performed disproportionately by women, which supports the hemisphere of formal, paid labor. Shopping for food, household goods and clothing, repairing and maintaining the family automobiles, taking care of cleaning and maintaining the house, washing clothes, preparing meals, paying bills, balancing the checkbook, and so on—these are not luxury activities, but part of our daily subsistence. They amount to a "second job" for which we are not paid and which does not factor into our economic analyses.

Shockingly for us, Sahlins asserts that "the amount of hunger increases relatively and absolutely with the evolution of cultures" (1972, 36). In short, the evolution of the economy is at once enriching and impoverishing. Today, one fourth of the world's population is chronically malnourished, in spite of "scientific" farming and worldwide distribution networks. Homelessness is becoming increasingly common even in the most developed countries. The claim that high technology can be associated with relative ease and freedom from uncertainties about food and shelter is purely mythic.

When it comes to energy and resource consumption, it is clear that the more advanced a nation is, the more per capita energy and resources are expended in sustaining its population. The standard figure is that 20 percent of the world's population in the most "advanced" nations uses 80 percent of the planet's total resources. We assume that the quality of our life explains and justifies our increasingly high rates of energy consumption. But does it? In vernacular societies like that of the Hawaiians or Inuit, there is some burning of fuels for cooking and heating, but none for translation into mechanical "advantage." Native Hawaiians not only imported no food or clothing, they imported no energy. Present-day inhabitants of the Islands are obliged to consume incredible quantities of imported energy—both directly and indirectly—much of it simply to get to and from work.

The standard claim is that our energy and resources are well spent since we enjoy a higher "standard of living" than ever before. That, however, is very debatable, pivoting as it does on our definition of "higher" and what exactly we're measuring. To be sure, we have more perceived "needs" than ever before, an increased sense of being left wanting. Indeed, this will become an important focus in chapters to come. What is not open to question is that the way we perceive the world around us is radically altered by our dependence on consuming fossil or other fuels for the purpose of satisfying our day-to-day needs. Our energy dependence not only exacts definite costs on our labor, our environments, and our health, it places us at enough distance from our world that we are no longer aware of its sacredness. Unlike native Hawaiians and other native peoples for whom the land is quite literally part of the family—something truly loved and revered—we can no longer be taught by our land. Separated from it by our machines, we no longer understand the language of the winds and rain, of the insects and trees. We are unaware of the song of the seasons and can no longer read or appreciate that most intimate poetry written in the lines of our grandparents' or parents' faces.

Losing Touch with What Matters

Our dependence on using huge amounts of energy to sustain and entertain ourselves through electronic and mechanical leveraging has made us unobservant bystanders in natural process. In result, we realize our own "impotence" and enter into a successively more acute dependence on external sources of energy and expertise to manage our affairs. Using outside energy sources to satisfy our daily needs means we are no longer in direct contact with what nourishes us. Instead of caring for the plants that offer us our fruit—caring in this way for us—we care about our car that allows us to go shopping, our refrigerators that allow us to eat fruits and meat shipped from halfway around the planet. Our energy consumption is part and parcel of our loss of intimacy with the communities that support us.

With a single exception—the short-lived Luddite revolt in nineteenth-century England—there has been no significant ethics of resistance to technical 'evolution' in the West. Like partners in a classic, codependent relationship who will cling to one another with utmost tenacity, not in spite of but almost in celebration of their mutual pain, we have refused to countenance the possibility that we have gone basically wrong. Instead, we have committed an ever-increasing portion of our personal and communal resources to the relationship.

At the most rudimentary level, tools allow us to carry out individual tasks faster, with more precision, greater force, and so on. That is a large part of the incentive of inventing them. They are supposed to save time, effort, and worry. New tools mark a quantitative change in our work, analogous to what happens when we add "another mouth to feed" in our family. To be sure, more needs will have to be met, but eventually more work will also be done, and it is hoped—especially by the poor of the world—that the account will eventually shift from deficit to profit, from increased expense to increased benefit or gain. More, it is hoped, will eventually mean better.

That this is not typically true is perhaps relatively self-evident. But for the most part, we have not taken the time to reflect on the equation, preferring instead the convenience of believing that 'more' and 'better' share the same roots, that they are at bottom synonymous values. Put so bluntly, of course, objections will ring out all around. Few of us are so crass as to admit a belief that quality can be reduced to quantity or even that the two are expressions of a common root value. And yet, asked to explain why this is so, we are likely to discover that the distinction is not as clear for us as we might be comfortable thinking. Our conduct betrays this lack of clarity most notably in our readiness to embrace technologies on the basis of their "improving the quality" of our lives when in fact they do no more than improve the speed and accuracy with which our wants are satisfied.

The cant is that improving the rate and precision of our consumption—whether of ores, food, works of art, information, or what have you—is indeed an improvement of our standard of living. But what seems to actually occur with increasing the speed and accuracy of the satisfaction of our "desires" is a retarding of the maturation process they would otherwise undergo. In vernacular cultures where our connection with the varied climates and communities of our environing world has yet to be severed by the interposition of technically mediated control, it is understood that desires change over the course of a lifetime. This change is seen as evolutionary, as a deepening and broadening of our relationship with others and the world we narrate through our conduct. Among other things, this has included cultivating a caring readiness to allow the fruit of our labors, the consummation of our desires, to be deferred—until later in our own lives, until our children are grown, even until the sons and daughters of our grandchildren are born. Maturation meant widening the horizons of our desire.

What we have seen in the last century of the industrial and now information revolutions is a slowing of this maturation process. While our manufacturing, transportation, and information technologies have afforded us undreamed control in determining when and how our wants will be satisfied, this control has also undermined the temporal and narrative context crucial for relinquishing their limiting horizons. We are given time to want more, but not to cultivate a qualitatively new kind of wanting. We joke that forty-year-old men are more and more acting like teenagers with hormones out of control, that teenagers armed with guns are killing each other with no more sense of the ethical ramifications of their actions than their toddler brothers and sisters display in striking a playmate who won't yield up the toy they want.

We joke, but we are disturbed as well, and for good reason. Often spoken of as a kind of liberation, technology has contributed to a prolongation of the lives enjoyed by the motivating values of our infancies, our childhoods, and adolescence. And because the gratifications come faster and more accurately than ever before, there is no time for these values to grow. Growth—and here I mean primarily personal evolution—occurs only with discomfort, with the sense that old patterns of behavior and conduct will no longer do. Especially in terms of our moral and spiritual development, growing is always outgrowing as well—not just forgetting or discarding as fashion dictates, but both deepening and extending the range of our interdependence with our world and all that is dramatically related within it. It is precisely this process that uncritical technological proliferation retards.

As an example of how technology, desire and attention interrelate, I'd like to take a look at the construction "industry." In vernacular societies, building is a communal, not a commercial activity. Based on patterns of reciprocity, such societies build for use, not for profit. At the same time, far from being merely utilitarian in design, vernacular structures tend to closely express the values of the community. That is, they are buildings imbued with significance, focusing an ambient dimension of meaning. Buildings are in this sense not just things, but sacred modes of conduct—modes of conduct through which the spirit of a people is directly and joyously expressed. Moreover, because the tools used are both few and "primitive," there is little hierarchic division of labor. Often, the fashioning of tools is seen as part of the work of building itself, not a separate activity. What is most important throughout is coordination—the ability to work together, to mesh efforts, accomplishing as a community what no individual could.

This changes as sophisticated tools and their associated technologies come into play. Building technologies lead to a specialization of labor, to a separation of tool making and tool using, a disjunction of designing and constructing. Technologies of control individuate effort. As exemplified in the communal barn-raising practiced in American society until relatively recently, fairly sophisticated tools are not wholly incompatible with communal effort. But the tendency is for such tools to promote a division of various aspects of building—an analysis of conduct—and a loss of the meaning dimension once possessed by the structures themselves.

This can be made clearer by examining what has happened with the introduction of power tools. Around the turn of the century, all the work done in the building trades was directly a result of applied muscular force. Trade work was for the most part truly manual labor. Speed came about only as quickly as precision skills because the feedback between, for example, a carpenter's hands and eyes and the movement of his saw through an oak plank was minimally mediated. Trying to make faster cuts without being able to see and feel more precisely the graining of the wood, the flexing of the saw, the grab of its teeth, and the angle it is being held at would only lead to wasted lumber at best. Increasing the speed of a cut meant a continuous fine-tuning of arm, hand, and of course the movement of attention so that the saw, wood, and carpenter could cooperate smoothly. While this entailed a continuous and personal commitment to carpentry, it included as well observing masters in action, asking immediately relevant questions of them, and absorbing their ways of material and conscious attunement.

It is this cooperation—and the gracefulness that can come about through its refinement—that has been largely lost with the introduction of power tools in the building trades. With electric saws, routers, drills, and so on, speed no longer requires the kind of attention to either the wood itself or one's own body that an old-style carpenter had to muster. That is, will is not only imposed more directly on the material, it is imposed with a minimum of practice. In result, the material is effectively silenced—simply not given the time to speak.

An electric plane, for instance, can work in any direction on a plank while a hand plane will work properly only if used with the grain. With power, it's simply not necessary to attend to the voice of the wood—its grain, the record of its growth, its flush times, and its lean. Electricity erases the importance of the wood's memory. Dimensional lumber—lumber milled to precise specification at a factory rather than by a tradesperson on the job site—was not only made possible by power tools, it reflects the tradesperson's growing lack of concern for the individuality of his materials, the uniqueness of each piece of wood, and the trees from which they've been fashioned. The relationship between carpenter and wood becomes increasingly generic as the focus on speed of production intensifies. And as the materials become standard, so does the work they occasion.

In result, rewards now come not for how creative a solution to a woodworking problem you come up with, but for how many tasks you can carry out in a given amount of time. Since the cooperative relationship between builder and material has been intensively mediated by powered tools, the care involved in working wood has gradually been supplanted by a 'desire' to simply move as quickly through a job as possible. What matters is not the quality or virtuosity of our conduct—that which alone can imbue a structure with meaning—but the quantity of our products.

Maybe things didn't have to turn out this way. But they did. And I think they always have and always will. There are a few craftspersons working wood now who eschew power tools, preferring to enter into deeper communication with their material and through it with themselves. There are also a limited number of craftspersons using power tools who produce work of amazingly high quality. But both are exceptions. According to the rule of technology, it is "clear" that even if more cannot always be equated with better, less will almost invariably fare much worse. And so, the average home—like the average store or church or train depot—is built with tragically less quality in terms of both material and labor than a hundred years ago.

It would be easy to say that the drop in material quality is unavoidable—a result of depleted supplies of lumber-producing forest and so on. Just the sheer numbers of homes needing to be built—well, that also places constraints on quality. There is too much demand to take more time, which means more money. Rationalizations abound on the more and less of it all. But none of these arguments get at the core interdependence of attention, labor, and material. When attention becomes generic—speed is what matters most—so do labor and material. Houses are built much faster today than ever before. In new suburban developments, a tract house can be framed in a couple of days and finished in two or three weeks including paint and carpet. A house built a hundred years ago and that is still standing today probably took ten or twenty times as much time to complete by the same number of workers.

The relationship between the builder and the house, like that between lover and beloved, is partly a function of time. An affair of a day or two's duration, even of a couple of weeks', will most likely not change us, will not stimulate us to really stretch and grow. We leave before the tension requisite for real growth has had a chance to build. In the same way, carpenters do not develop a real relationship with a job they work on only for a day or two, and nothing substantial in one they finish in a couple of weeks. It is only by living with our work that we develop a deep relationship with it. And so, not only is the quality lower in our tract house—the feeling it is imbued with—so is its meaning, its history. Made of such low-quality materials and with so little care that it will fall apart in a matter of a decade or two, the average tract house is quite naturally deemed hardly worth fixing—even by its owner. Such homes are better off bulldozed and replaced. The generic trend intensifies.

In short, an emphasis on speed produces not only more stuff in less time, it produces more generic stuff in less time—stuff with which we develop no lasting relationship at any point. Speed distances us from our work and so from ourselves by denying our interdependence with all things. This is not to say we should work slowly simply to work slowly, but that we should work at whatever pace is compatible with our attention shaping itself according to our work even as our work is shaped according to our attention. That is, we should work at a pace where we are being taught by our materials even as we are instructing them with new forms.

Just as a new child in the family soon changes much more than just how much food is eaten and how much cleaning has to (or even can) be done, as soon as the tool has become familiarized, it also begins transforming the nature of our work. That is, by virtue of our intimacy with them, tools take on limited, but quite real personalities. Our children reflect who we are and in mirroring us amplify our character—for both good and ill. They show us who we are, often most intensely before they are even able to speak in sentences. Likewise for our tools—a different kind of progeny.

The Frankenstein story is, of course, a vision of what this might mean if taken to an extreme. We could mention in a quite different vein Robert

Heinlein's novel, *The Moon Is a Harsh Mistress*, in which a computer gains—in this case an ultimately benevolent—self-consciousness and personality. But anyone who has owned and eventually named a car or who has used the same hammer for fifteen years has experienced some level of this process whereby a tool becomes a character in our life narrative, an extension of our selves. But our children are more than mirrors. They have their own natures irreducible to ours, and in the end they manage to profoundly change us by their presence beside us as we discover together what it means to be a family and what our work is in this life we share. In time, the relationship we have with our tools also brings about a new definition of task and with it a new definition of our selves. Not only how we work, but what work we choose to do and why will have changed dramatically and for the most part both unpredictably and irreversibly.

TOWARD AN ETHICS OF RESISTANCE

In classical Chinese, the written character for harmony—*ho*—includes within it the characters for "mouth" and "growing (not harvested or cooked) grain." That is, harmony implies the mutual nurturance of two communities—the human and the plant. Without our care, the grain would not prosper. Without the grain's offering, we would not prosper. Harmony is working together, not in spite of differences, but precisely because of them. By using mechanically and electronically transformed energy to satisfy our needs, we break down the basic relationships out of which harmony emerges. It was for this reason that Lao-tzu said (in the 6th century BCE) that the ideal society is one in which carts exist, but no one uses them; in which high technology is possible, but no one bothers. In such a deeply vernacular society, harmony occurs without expert intervention and sleep is contented.

This would be merely entertaining if it was only the musing of an isolated mystic from China, but it is not. Resonating perfectly with Lao-tzu's Taoist analysis of technology, Illich has written extensively about the "counter-productivity" of progress—the fact that we spend more and more time and energy to get less and less in return. In a study of transportation technologies and travel time, he discovered an apparent paradox: the faster we travel on the average, the more time we spend traveling. More precisely, the breakoff point is at 19 mph—roughly the speed of a brisk bike ride. As technologies are developed that allow the average vehicular speed in a society to rise above this point, increasing amounts of time will be spent per person, per day just getting around. Because we can go faster, we go more—so much more that we find ourselves spending 300 to 500 percent more time transporting ourselves than people who are limited to horse-drawn carts and bicycles (Illich, 1973).

It should be clear that the reason for this is not because any individual trip takes longer in a car than on a bike. It is not the automobile as a *tool* that increases the time we spend in travel, but the effect of automotive *technology* on our conduct—the dynamic, narrative aspect of our community. Our towns and cities change shape and size. Workspace and homespace become increasingly separated. We begin thinking differently about travel, about time and distance. What is proximate may no longer be what is intimate. What was once too far away to bother wanting may well become a current rage— something we will not live without, simply because we need not.

The results of Illich's studies of the relationships between technology and our transportation, education, and medical practices can be generalized as a rule that in each technology, there exists a threshold of utility beyond which the technology becomes an end in itself. Later, we will undertake a karmic explanation for this seeming paradox that more can often lead to less. At this juncture it is enough if Illich's findings cast some doubt on our tendency to claim that trade-offs are always unavoidable, a corollary of the *necessity* of progress. If native Hawaiians, living on the same limited land mass as present-day inhabitants of the Islands and with roughly equivalent population density archipelago-wide, were able to contentedly get along without commuting two hours a day and working 60 to 70 hours a week, why are we insisting on doing so?

To have more things than ever before? To live on average a bit longer? We also spend less time with our families and friends, less time articulating the intimate details of our shared time and space. We do spend more time, however, in fear of crime, and worrying about the shape of the economy, the status of our jobs, our security in old age, and our souls in whatever may or may not lie beyond. Most inhabitants of the "first world" do not own their own homes or die with substantial holdings. For the most part, we borrow all our "possessions"—our homes, our tools, our space. We eat and sleep and procreate as people have always done, coming into life empty-handed and departing equally empty-handed.

But unlike our preindustrial ancestors, we inhabitants of the "developed" world each effectively burn the equivalent of several tons of coal each year and work at least twice or three times more than they did to meet our basic needs, *as a matter of course*. In recent years, major corporations and all levels of government have undergone massive downsizing or "rightsizing" in order to trim the waste from our business and public services. But the average worker's salary in real dollars has gone down, not up. Benefit packages have eroded or been eliminated. So where are the savings going? In the corporate pocket and back into that of the taxpaying citizen, yes. But what does that mean, really? Are we supporting our harmony with others in this extra work we do, or are we supporting precisely those structures or patterns of conduct—those technologies—that hold us apart from them? Does the "quality" of our lives make up for what we have given up for it? Is television programming really higher quality than the stories of our uncles and aunties, the smiles of our children, the satisfaction of singing and dancing with our neighbors? Is dying in a nursing home or a hospital bed higher quality than passing slowly from this world to the next in the company of those we love, in our own beds, in our own time? We have access to the "best" health care in the history of the world, and yet do we feel whole, at one with our world and all those sharing with us in its celebration?

Questions like these could be argued over for a long, long time. At bottom, we know that our lives are not perfect, that we live in increasing isolation in spite of our ever more extensive, media-provided knowledge of the world about us. Are we happier? More content? Wiser? Often, that is hard for us to say—one way or the other. We have a hard time knowing our own minds on the matter. But when we ask indigenous peoples around the world if they want our style of technology, our development, our knowledge, our stories, we often find they really and truly do not. According to Jerry Mander (1991), native peoples have had the opportunity to see what we are offering, not as people brought up in the prejudice of technological evolution and the ideal of freedom through control, but as people who value harmony with their environments and their neighbors. They see us as only people outside the purview of our prejudices and assumptions can. And by and large they perceive our technically mediated world as a place of death. If we look into our own hearts, we may well find ourselves nodding in agreement.

Chapter 4

The Direction of Technical Evolution
A Different Kind of Caveat

We have not yet been saved. The progressive development of our technological lineage has not delivered us from want. If anything, the opposite seems to be true. The more technologically advanced we have become, the greater our per capita consumption of energy and our per capita expenditure of effort. We have typically excused by noting that life is much more complex than it was in pre-Cook Hawai'i or pre-industrial Europe. In a word, the comparison is "unfair." But this excuse begs the child's question of "which came first, the chicken or the egg?" Are we consuming more energy because our lives are more complex, or are our lives more complex because we have gotten in the habit of spending more and more time and energy making ends meet? Do we need technology because our lives are so complex we wouldn't be able to manage without it, or are our lives so complex because we've taken our technologies so far across the thresholds of their utility that we spend more time servicing their ends than we do our own?

Seen from a Buddhist perspective, since all things are finally interdependent and not independent, answering which "came first" is ultimately beside the point. All beginnings are conventional—monuments we have erected to symbolize the finality of the horizons we have set for inquiry and relevance. What matters is the meaning of the relationship among complexity, energy consumption, and the advance of technology. Put in the form of a query: Where are all our efforts and energy really going? Who or what are they actually supporting?

CULTIVATING DISCONTENT: ADVANTAGING
EXISTENCE—LIVING APART AND AT A DISTANCE

We are not a particularly contented generation. In fact, discontent seems to be less an exception than the norm, ambient enough that we no longer find it remarkable. More to the point, we typically feel that there isn't really anything we can do about "things." We shrug our shoulders and concentrate on "getting by." Although it is dangerously easy to romanticize other cultures, people living in more vernacular societies appear to be less dissatisfied with their lot than we. Even if this is only our perception, it is one that is very natural for us and that thus speaks volumes about how we view our own lives and the extent to which we feel we have been losing something important.

An indisputable difference, however, is that whereas our inclination is to see circumstances as being largely out of our own hands and in those hidden away inside impersonal and inattentive institutions, vernacular peoples commonly understand their "fates" as being immediately tractable. A season of poor hunting is understood as a function of past overzealousness or of some disrespect shown to the hunted or its totems. Even where deities of one sort or another are invoked as partial causes of calamity or triumph, it is understood that they are part of the local community. Vernacular gods are not transcendent beings, but members of a spatially and temporally extended family. Quite literally, they are seen as ancestors who may guide with sometimes gentle and sometimes strict hands, but they do not simply dictate our fates. Autocratic gods are of relatively recent mint in human history, as are the notions of irreversible fate, blind chance, and the association of freedom with free or uncontested will. Vernacular peoples do not claim control over their environment, but do typically assume that they have voices that are heard and worthy of response.

Perhaps in large part because the cosmos is not seen as transcendently centered, in spite of a relative paucity—from our point of view—of novel experiences and material possessions, people living technologically simple, vernacularly intense lives do not seem inclined to seek out experiential release. Even in the midst of what we would take as great privation or suffering, life is understood as inherently full. It is we—bombarded at every moment of the day with demands on our attention—who feel that we are missing something, that life is not quite complete or whole. It is not the bodies of vernacular peoples that are distorted with physical, emotional, and intellectual stress, but ours.

What these contrasts suggest is that while we work longer and expend more energy in our consumption of a greater variety and perhaps greater quantity of things and experiences, we are getting less and less in return. In short, as the number and variety of things we have and do goes up, their quality—the extent to which they are conducive to our sense of wholeness—goes down. In short, we are caught in a cycle of diminishing returns. Although technical "progress" promises us control and hence freedom from both chance and fate, it does so by placing us at sufficient distance from the rest of the world that we can—with the appropriate tools—leverage its 'parts' into a more satisfying configuration. Unfortunately, from such a distance, we no longer feel meaningfully connected, existing instead in an axiological vacuum that the sheer variety of our factual experiences does little to assuage.

The Buddha talked about there being four kinds of "food": food that we incorporate through eating; food we incorporate through breathing; food that we incorporate through sense perception; and, finally, food we incorporate through conception. These four foods sustain us in all that we do, and their relative qualities are an index of the quality of our karma—the dramatic or meaningful dimension of our intentional activity or conduct. A sense of wholeness means being properly nourished by our intake of all four kinds of food. If we are consuming more than ever before and finding ourselves less satisfied—less physically, emotionally, intellectually, and spiritually whole—then the quality of our "foods" must be waning. Granted that we are putting more energy than ever before into the production of these foods that stock our refrigerators and enter us via our newspapers, televisions, and universities, it must be that the energy and effort are going somewhere else. If we have not been benefiting in any substantive way, who or what has?

It is arguable that no one has. There is no doubt that in addition to consuming more energy to navigate from birth to death than in any previous generation on earth, we are also producing more garbage than ever before. A great deal of our energy is simply lost in pollution or waste of one form or another—literally more and more experiences meaning less and less. Contrasting a vernacular culture like that of the Inuit with a technically advanced one like that of the Canadians of European descent who are now sharing the Inuit's aboriginal lands, it is clear that only the Inuit utilize virtually everything they take from their environment. They lose a bit of smoke from burning seal or whale fat, but other than this, very little is disposed of as waste. A glance at the curbsides of any American city on refuse pickup day drives home the point that we have become expert at wasting.

The Inuit have dozens of words for what we generically refer to as "snow." Snow is crucial to their mode of subsistence. So ubiquitous and important is waste in our lives that we've identified dozens of different species of waste—hazardous, recyclable, non-replaceable, biodegradable, suitable for landfill or ocean dumping, incinerator-bound, things that are garbage (useless) or simply junk (possibly useful to someone, sometime). We study waste at the university, write books about it, and manage it. Most of all, though, we produce it. Waste is a kind of contemporary raw data in which are deeply inscribed our habits of wanting and satisfaction, the temporality of our discontent. It is thus particularly fitting that the main characters of Don DeLillo's great American novel, *Underworld*, are a baseball that's no longer in use, an artist who paints abandoned B-52 bombers in the New Mexican desert, and a corporate everyman involved in waste handling and waste trading—a "cosmologist of waste" for whom "waste is a religious thing."

But as great as our polluting is, it cannot account for the incredible disparity between the amount of energy we consume and the amount used by vernacular peoples. A significant part of the problem is no doubt due to the complexity of our systems of supply and demand. If we see both labor and capital in terms of energy, what is most striking about the contrast of vernacular and technologically rich societies is the distance energy is transmitted in accomplishing a given task—say, placing a dozen ears of corn on the table for dinner. In a vernacular society, the energy involved remains very much local. For the Hopi who farm the desert in the Four Corners region of the American Southwest, the reach of the entire cycle is that of a single growing season and a distance of perhaps a dozen miles. In the entire process from selecting seed to planting, nurturing, harvesting, setting aside the next season's seed, storing the harvest, cooking, and finally sitting down to eat the season's first corn, there are perhaps a dozen hands involved, typically all members of the same family. Even the water used is quite local since the Hopi do not irrigate over long distances.

By contrast, getting a similar dozen ears of corn onto my table involves not just my hands in choosing and cooking the corn, but the stock clerk at the grocery, the drivers who brought the corn from the port to the local distributors, the shipping company, the truckers who got the corn to the mainland distributor, the agri-business growing the corn, the company from which the seed was purchased, and those by whom it was perhaps genetically engineered. In all, hundreds of hands spread out over thousands of miles. And this is typical of everything we eat and use in our day-to-day lives.

Consider what this really means. Seen in terms of energy, and knowing the laws of thermodynamics, it is no wonder that something gets lost along the way. "Transmission line" losses are quite real. We cannot involve hundreds of people spread out over thousands of miles and mediated by hundreds of machines all burning one type or another of fuel and not expect some very tangible losses. The theory about mass production is that since the individual hands and machines involved spend so little time in contact with our energy as it cycles out of our hands as money, into the economic/industrial system, and finally back into our hands as corn, that not much is lost.

I'm not so sure. There is great evidence to suggest that our cost of living is as relatively affordable as it is only because long-term costs to environmental, communal, and personal health are *not* included in the economic calculus (see, for example, Daly and Cobb, 1994), and because payment on that debt is being routinely and strenuously deferred. At any rate, what is quite certain is that—as Illich has pointed out with personal transportation—once we cross a technology's threshold of utility, what was once only 'possible' becomes 'necessary'. We would like to think this is not so, but all evidence is to the contrary. Locally grown produce becomes a luxury not because it is harder to bring corn from a small farm just outside the city into the marketplace, but because it runs counter to the slippery slope of corporate profit-making established by our agricultural and marketing technologies (Krebs, 1992).

The analysis of production—breaking it down into atomic components like growing, storing, shipping, marketing, and consuming—encourages efficiency, specialization, precision, and reliability. At the same time, it means an atrophy of personalized interdependence—that sense of shared drama and so a common life that are at the heart of any true community. In this sense, economic globalization—impossible without the technically mediated analysis of our productive and consumptive conduct—severs us from the root conditions of a deeply and spontaneously meaningful life. Meaning, too, becomes something marketable, a commodity like any other.

Mass-Marketing and the Impoverishment of Place

The ecology movement has over the last several decades been championing the concept of bioregionalism as a political and social alternative to both the parochialism of state centralism and the homogeneous universalism of globalization. And as far as the idea goes, it is a good and useful one—a return to a more balanced relationship with issues of scale. But a bioregion is not the same thing as a locale. What is lost in our technically mediated lives is not just energy or an immediate apprehension of our factual interconnectedness, but a *felt* relationship with our place. The technologies of mass mediation especially encourage a conviction that we are "citizens of the world" for whom our physical site is at most a matter of relative convenience. Most of us simply have no sense of belonging—literally "going completely along with"—where we are. That we have an address, a "location" is clear. But this is a relationship of existence, of subtly standing apart from our place as if our homes and workplaces were simply variables in Cartesian three-dimensional space.

The Hopi not only knows everyone involved in bringing tonight's corn to the table, but understands and feels the manner in which the corn focuses his or her efforts and care, the unique way it transforms sunshine and earth, wind and rain. Partaking of the offering of the corn, the Hopi becomes aware of the circulation of energy through the heavens and earth, through the human and plant communities. There is nothing of this celebration of interconnectedness in our grocery store world—the sense of our personal and not merely abstract interdependence. What is most satisfying to those of us even now fortunate enough to live—as I do—in the Hawaiian Islands is the sense of locale that still obtains. Each island, each valley, each reef is for many still felt as having a unique signature of *mana* or spiritual energy, just as do the customs of the people caring for and cared for by these places. There is no greater honor than to be told by those born and raised in the Islands that you are "local." It means that you have understood the spirit of the place and its many peoples—some human and some not. In a very real sense, you have become an expression of the land itself as human, a *kama'aina*.

Far from being mere island-life romanticism, this felt sense of place is possible for all of us. Urban neighborhoods too, had something of this even just a generation ago. But enjoying such a meaningfully full relationship with where we are means resisting the technically compelled urge to dictate our convenience and instead listening for and responding with the clarifying voice of our place. It means forfeiting unconsidered, individuating assertion for realized harmony and communal celebration. That entails, of course, our willingness to refine our ability to attend to and care for everything that helps constitute our home—a refusal to distance ourselves enough to readily and in "good faith" leverage our situation to our own, privatizing advantage. It requires as well cultivating a disposition for seeing the quality of our circumstances as our personal responsibility—that is, refusing to see the relevant factors as either "too big" or "too much a matter of chance" for us to think we might contribute to much more than our own life or the life of our immediate family.

In an apparent paradox, from the most mundane levels on up, this means making an effort to keep our energy circulating locally enough to retain our sense of belonging—not in order to hoard or unduly concentrate it, but in order to conserve the dramatic quality of our place *and* the quality of its connections to all other locales. For example, on the Kona coast of the Big Island of Hawai'i, there has been a rash of development by multinational discount marketers or superstores. Ostensibly, this is good for the local population. People there have been paying "premium" prices at "mom and pop" stores for all their clothing, groceries, and so on, and superstores change that. They bring in bulk goods at prices "too hard to resist." Everything from produce to meat, from tools to toiletries, costs so much less than usual that people simply stop spending their income elsewhere. It would be "foolish" not to do so. Plus, superstores create "new" jobs and hire quite a few local people to fill them. According to the mythic American dream, this is good for the economy. And what's good for the economy is good for us.

Or is it? It is quite true that there are immediate and substantial up-front savings for Kona residents shopping at Costco or Walmart. But these corporations are not in business to do anyone favors. They are in the business of making money, and specifically making more money each year. They do so by coming as close as possible to monopolizing the market in a given locale, using bulk-discounted pricing to entice sales away from existing local merchants incapable of buying in competitive quantities or chasing global markets. The result is that a very sizable portion of Kona's expenditures for household goods and groceries is deposited in a corporate bank account somewhere on the U.S. mainland. Money that once directly supported local families now circulates a great deal further and only a fraction of it ever returns.

The numbers cannot lie. In order to be financially viable, superstores—like any other business—must take more out of any local economy than they return by way of salaries, local property taxes, and so on. But unlike local merchants who cycle large portions of their income back into the local community, using local mechanics, carpenters, groceries, repair shops, legal and medical services, and so on, large corporations permanently siphon off this money for investment elsewhere. Multinational corporations zealously apply this simple logic worldwide.

The market strategy of bulk retailers is quite simple. A minimal amount of capital is used to prime the local economy through building a warehouse-style store that offers goods at "irresistibly low" prices. Drawing on a market size determined by locally perceived ease of automobile access, the store then acts as a kind of monetary well or siphon. Once started, the process continues almost without friction until there is no longer enough local pressure—remaining, free income—to force money through the store at a profitable rate. Should this occur, it is in the corporate interest to simply pull up stakes, allowing any local employees to go on unemployment and fall back on their now depleted local resources to get them through the resulting hard times. People will say the local economy is in a slump. In fact, it has been pumped dry. Corporations make a profitable science of impoverishing locally scaled economies.

THE CORPORATION AS TECHNOLOGY

Corporate structure filters the family out of business. That's good for rapid "economic growth," but bad for nurturing the dynamic ties that bind us into locally more meaningful community. Still, we might be inclined to discount the overall impact and importance of the contemporary corporation on our lives, arguing that it evolved out of economic necessity and does exactly what it is supposed to do. This, however, is to reduce the corporation as technology—as an instrumental pattern of conduct that is effectively ambient throughout a society and that expresses a particular set of values—to individual businesses seen as tools for maximizing returns on investment. The difference is crucial.

As a way of disentangling the two perspectives, we can see the corporation as an organizational pattern useful in taking controlled advantage of the flow of goods, services, and capital through an economy. Seen as energy, the rate at which goods, labor, and capital flow is just as important as how much flows; and control over the direction and rate of that flow generates not just economic, but political and societal power. Since corporate structure is designed to maximize its own growth and profit—rather than, say communal contentment as in a vernacular economy—the further and deeper its "gravitational" field and the more precisely focused its center, the better. That is, the more energy that can eventually be made to flow through the smallest number of hands, the greater the velocity at which it will be moving and the greater the control it will afford. In the same way that a car handles best in a turn when you're able to accelerate through it, a business responds best to market dynamics when it can effectively accelerate the flow of capital and labor with the least amount of advance notice. Thus, a corporation drawing energy from around the world (especially if through somewhat diversified industries) and funneling it through a small decision-making board will have an incredible potential for placing profitable "spins" on the market. In this sense, global information gathering is as much a must for corporate success as is global marketing.

Since energy drawn through a corporate structure from an increasingly global market is hierarchically and systematically redistributed, this will mean great profit for a few and relative impoverishment for many. This is colonialism in a new guise. Corporate structure—as a technology—allows tremendous amounts of energy to be gathered and channeled at will. Of course, as recent banking scandals evidence, the centralization encouraged by corporate structure also means a potential for more spectacular failures. Successful corporate decision-makers—like champion racecar drivers—must possess a special talent for concentration under extreme duress.

Analyzed in this way, the evolution of corporate structure can be seen as entailing on the one hand a centralization of highly informed decision-making and on the other an intense diversification of both products and markets. Information transfer and analysis technologies are the primary means of insuring the former. Multinational corporations are clearly unthinkable in a world limited to postal transmission of information, hard currency, and card-file databases. Whereas the average homeowner can get along perfectly well without a personal computer, a modem and a fax machine, there is not a single multinational corporation that could claim the same thing. We are often told that personal computers will make each of our lives simpler and easier, but the fact is that the real beneficiaries of computer technologies are corporations that could not operate without the "global nervous system" they provide.

The diversification of products and markets required for the proliferation of corporate structure pivots on both an analysis of vernacular, subsistence practices into components liable to technical mediation and improvement and a conversion of common, environmental resources into marketable commodities. That is, a life-world practice like farming is "rationalized" or broken down into distinct activities like land clearing, fertilizing, planting, harvesting, storage, transportation, and marketing. Each of these phases is segregated from the others by specialized tools, knowledge, and personnel, and so accomplished with greater precision and efficiency. Whereas vernacular, subsistence practices are often carried out by one person or a group of intimately cooperating persons, rationalized practices for raising food, providing clothing, shelter, entertainment, education, and so on are devoid of the personal dimension. It's not just that different aspects of the task are carried out by different people, but that these people are not in a caring relationship with one another. The practice itself is thus stripped of those qualities associated with care. The corporation promotes economic anonymity.

Vernacular practices are not abstractly constituted patterns of individual behavior. They are not necessarily even "sensible" or rationally efficient. To the contrary, they are forms of conduct—forms of our being led together in mutual and always dramatic interdependence. Vernacular practices are like story forms, plotlines, or verse patterns. They organize our narration, orienting our conduct in ways that strengthen our community and the meaningfulness of our efforts and attention. By transforming vernacular practices into commercial activities, corporate structure promotes autonomy rather than community, efficiency rather than intimacy, novelty rather than dramatic unpredictability.

At the same time that the analysis of vernacular practices elides their narrative dimension, it leads to a functionally similar atrophy of inherent meaning in the materials on which those practices depend. Thus, the river that is diverted to irrigate the village paddies ceases being seen as a living and contributing member of the community's healthy narration. It becomes a source of water or power. The trees used in building canoes lose their aura of sacredness, their spirit, and become sources of timber and then generic, standard-dimensioned lumber. Rational production means not only mass-produced end commodities, but the commodification of basic material resources as well.

Today, the earth has been commodified via the mining, agriculture, and tourist industries. Water is no longer free, and I would suspect that very soon there will be taxes paid for using/preserving air quality. We have already begun speaking of buying or leasing space and time as such—office or storage space and clerical or internet access time, for example. And as the resource components of our productive activity are commodified, so are the products of our activity. Plants and animals have been commodified as 'food' to such an extent that they are being genetically altered to make their harvesting, transportation, and marketing most efficient. Bodily and psychological health have been commodified through the interventions—now considered standard and unquestionably expert—of the medical and therapeutic service industries. The arts, education, and even death are all being packaged for maximum marketability and being rendered both increasingly expensive and productive. With the advent of a worldwide system for multimedia communication, even the values on which our cultures are based are being turned into commodities and subjected to the market demands of fashion. Think of the explosion recently of 'natural' foods, fibers, and lifestyles. Marketed as an elite fashion, even living unadulterated lives turns out to be quite an investment. 'Nature' has become expensive.

Commodification focuses our attention on products rather than on conduct, on things rather than relationships. Systems that resist commodification—for example, a rainforest as such—are either excluded from corporate purview or broken down into commodifiable integers. In the case of a rainforest, breaking it down into arable land, grazing potential, board-feet of lumber, a holding basin for a hydroelectric dam, and so on, will make an otherwise "useless" tract of land productive. Like ecosystems, cultures are not readily commodified and must first be broken into component parts that are amenable to marketing—Thai cuisine, Nigerian Ju-ju music, Navaho weaving, and so on.

Because corporations function as "engines" for maximizing profits, their spread and intensification depend on much more than a commodification of our life-world, our life-narration. In addition, there must be continual increase in the investment of energy expended in the corporate movement and exchange of commodities. Otherwise, the flow of energy in even the greatest marketing network would eventually stagnate. The bottom line, then, must be a continual cultivation of 'desires,' which, when acted out, will funnel otherwise "unproductive" energy down the "gravitational" well of corporate structure. Without this, growth ceases and that, according to corporately construed economics, is a fate worse than death.

Thus, at the most elemental level, what corporations must do is attract attention, and the more the better. We are all familiar with the direct cultivation of new 'desires' in each individual through, for example, mass-mediated advertising and lifestyle marketing in music videos, films, and television programming. That is, our attention is diverted away from contentment and sufficiency and oriented toward an ever-changing manifestation of dissatisfaction. There is only one way this cultivation of felt incompleteness can be successful in the long run. The activities and tools that we're convinced will help overcome our lacks must be the very things that impoverish us. We must be convinced that our sense of incompleteness is a result of not committing enough of our energy to the project. So, we try harder—working longer to buy more, to take more exotic vacations, wear more fashionable clothes, and sculpt more attractive bodies. It's as if we are being sucked into a whirlpool caused by the very energy we expend in trying to swim out of it. The harder we stroke, the more powerfully we are pulled into a downward spiral. Like all technologies, the corporation has a threshold of utility.

Granted the standard measurements of economic health, this is not obvious. Herman Daly (1996) and Clifford Cobb along with Ted Halstead (1996) have done wonderfully succinct jobs of explaining why and arguing for alternative standards. For example, according to Cobb and Halstead, using the Gross Domestic Product to measure economic health and progress puts us in the position of making the breakdown of families and communities—as reflected in the legal fees associated with divorce, moving costs, the necessity of setting up separate households, the provision of therapeutic services, and even the building of prisons—good for national economic health.

Through the intensification of individual wants, corporate commodification enhances and is in turn enhanced by a disintegration of community. Quite simply, since the quantity of wanting or 'desire' in a society—and so the size of the total market—can very effectively be increased by opening up more loci or sites of 'desire', in "lean times" there is an economic imperative to do so.

In an ideally vernacular society, sharing is emphasized as a communal value par excellence. Difficult times are occasions to pull together, to contribute more than usual to mutually sustaining conduct. This applies not just to sharing food and shelter, but everything from tools to understanding. The idea of private possession is maximally attenuated. By contrast, as a society moves toward a commodity-based economy, not just goods, but services and finally information—impersonalized and so depersonalizing knowledge—all come to be understood in proprietary terms as having definite exchange values. When this attenuation of inherent (rather than exchange) value is combined with a valorization of the individual—as through the dominant Western religious, political, and societal institutions—a profound feedback loop is established. Privatization is good for business, but privation is even better.

The disruption of clans into extended, biologically related families means at the very least that instead of everyone in an entire clan sharing certain tools and responsibilities, each extended family must do so. Each must now have a house, vehicles for transportation, provisions for storing goods, tools for repairing and building, and so on. Further atomization will, of course, prove even more conducive to corporate technology. As the extended family is broken down into separate generations and finally into atomic or nuclear families, the redundancy of necessary goods and services increases. At its most deeply established levels of feedback, commodification, the corporate funneling of energy, the cultivation of 'desire', and technological mediation split the nuclear family. Single parent families, the advent of children's clothes, children's television and books, the eruption of short-lived, teen cultures—these are all part of the same process by means of which attention and so economic power is "liberated" from our communities.

It should be clear from even a casual glance at what has been happening in those communities caught up first in the industrial and now the information revolution that this description is historically apt. It should also be clear that these transformations of our narration cannot be pinned on the machinations of politicians or business moguls intent on taking excess advantage of unsuspecting populations. Such individuals have and do exist, but they are symptoms of a restructuring of our lives that is not individually intended. To the contrary, this restructuring is a function of the meaning of our technologies—the values and hence the reorientations of conduct they promote. At the same time, it should be stressed that the relationship between the dissolution of the family and the advancement of Western technology is not one of linear causation. Rather, the fracturing of community into ideal individuals sponsors technical development even as technical development fuels that splintering. They are interdependent.

Corporate structure is a managerial technology. It is a technology that arises especially in codependence with transportation, communication, and information-processing technologies. As they advance, so corporate structure advances. In this sense, the industrial and information revolutions do indeed mark a significant break with the rest of human history in the sense that the flow of energy through our societies is no longer geared toward particularly divine, planetary, natural/ecological, or even individual human ends. Some of this flow is indeed diverted into the production of waste and into transmission losses. But, for the most part, it would seem that our energy is primarily being channeled into the cultivation and maintenance of corporate technology and the computer networks, fiber-optic systems, and databases on which it is crucially dependent. In short, our energy is being funneled into the embodiment of technical values—toward the ends of technology itself.

Chapter 5

The New Colonialism

From an Ignoble Past to an Invisible Future

It has been pointed out by many that there is a striking and "disquieting continuity" between the colonial era and its values and the present era of development (see, for example, Goldsmith, 1996). This continuity can be read as pivoting on a shared commitment to exploitative economic growth through an engineered and crippling dependence of local markets on global patterns of commerce established by and for the benefit of a relatively small number of players. But it can also be seen as expressing a shared commitment to realizing a particular sort of 'freedom'—the expression of a shared lineage of values that makes such engineering not only possible, but apparently and 'positively' inevitable. That is, the continuity of the eras of colonialism and development can be seen as a function of their shared technologies of success.

There is no denying that classic forms of colonial exploitation and contemporary development initiatives rely equally on technological dissemination. However, our faith in the moral transparency of technology is such that we are not disposed to see our technologies as in any way culpable. To the contrary, we firmly believe and are regularly reminded that the free dissemination of technology is the only viable alternative to the reprehensibly selfish engineering of dependence. It is, we believe, not our technological lineage, but greedy individuals—whether individual nations or heads of transnational corporations—who are to blame for the economics of exploitation today, just as it was nations like Great Britain and colonists like Cecil Rhodes who were responsible for the last great wave of classic, material colonization. But what if we are wrong? What if our technological lineage and the institutionalization of greed—like the proverbial chicken and egg—actually share a common genealogy?

EXTENDING CONTROL THROUGH CULTIVATING
DEPENDENCE: THE COLONIAL METHOD

Colonialism of the sort practiced by the major European naval powers from especially the early seventeenth through mid-twentieth centuries is no longer fashionable. It was, however, absolutely crucial to our transition from a world in which vernacularly structured local economies were more or less loosely and incidentally linked through long-distance trade and in which wealth was relatively evenly distributed, to one wherein the global market practically dictates the function of local economies and where wealth is more unevenly distributed than ever before. That is, the birth of the contemporary world can be traced to the maturation of colonial intentions. As will hopefully become clear in the remainder of this chapter, the contemporary world is in turn now giving birth to a new form of colonialism in which the traditionally sharp line between colonized and colonizer is effectively being erased, and in which our increasingly virtual independence marks our ever more deeply sedimented and practical dependence.

Classical or material colonization can be defined as wantonly diverting the material resources and physical labor of another culture or community away from the realization and maintenance of its own values and intentions toward those of the colonial power. Material colonization is not fundamentally about acquiring land either for the purpose of simple territorial expansion or for securing strategically useful buffer zones. Nor is it about entering into a dynamic and mutually enriching relationship with other cultures— attaining a greater and more flexible health or wholeness by encouraging lively diversification. To the contrary, material colonization is about establishing axiological and economic hegemony.

Unlike a military dictatorship that subjugates a people by ostensive violence and perhaps enforces some system of formal tribute, material colonization relies on a passive-aggressive strategy for control. Instead of openly forcing colonized peoples to do their bidding, colonial powers have traditionally achieved effective and relatively cheap domination by altering and then replacing the values of the indigenous population. Once accomplished, the colonized actually *choose* a subservient role—having been convinced not only of the desirability of what the colonial power offers in return, but often of their own material and spiritual poverty.

Among the most effective tactics employed in this process is the use of the colonist's native language in all important business and social transactions. Unlike simple utterances or individual expressions of surprise, fear, or ecstatic joy, languages arise with the sedimentation of values. That is, language is the dynamic record of the ways—and so how and why—a people relate. Languages emerge from consistencies in the conduct of a people much as a volcanic island gradually takes on the particular topography it has as a result of customary patterns of wind and waves. Out of all the possible island landscapes, only one is realized. Of course, once wind and rain have begun shaping an island, the island more and more particularly begins shaping the paths of wind and rain. Likewise, the individual actions of members of a language community, arise in interdependence with the layered values of the community. The imposition of a colonial tongue thus amounts to a forced and accelerated erosion of traditional lifeways and modes of personhood and the emergence of new ones perhaps only tenuously related to the local environment and ecology. Old patterns of commerce and conservation are undermined; the movement of goods and services can not only be redirected, but greatly accelerated. Such changes can be (or at least can seem) exhilarating, even liberating.

This breakdown of cultures and vernacular patterns of commerce liberates economic energy and labor much as the breakdown of coal or oil "frees" previously only potential energy that can be used to run a locomotive, operate an industrial loom, or light a city. However, one of the concomitants of the colonial diversion of resources and labor is a steady atrophy—more or less rapid—of the traditions and unique aspirations of the colonized. Importing new tools and so new forms of labor thus eventually means a discarding of those forms of conduct through which are ritually established and maintained the mutually nurturing patterns of response relating a people and their place. The eventual result is the total dependence of previously self-sustaining communities on the goods, expertise, and narrative orientations of a colonial other.

Interestingly, the term *colonization* derives originally from the Latin *colonus* or "farmer" and so implies an apparently beneficent activity by means of which a land and its people are cultivated. Colonizing means taming what is wild, ordering what is chaotic, seeding and tending what is fertile, but not yet truly productive. Seen in this way, colonization is open to moral justification as an aspect of practical, evangelical humanism. Thus interpreted, colonialism is a way of saving what has until now and would otherwise continue "going to waste." The consistent accompaniment of colonists by missionaries served to ensure that not only the land, but the peoples of a colony would be effectively cultivated. While Christian missionaries were busy convincing an indigenous people that they had souls in need of salvation, Christian farmers and colonial administrators were convincingly demonstrating an almost magical power of control over what people had previously seen as worthy of respectful and ritually prescribed cooperation. In both cases, patterns of interdependence dramatically relating a people, their deities, and the spirits of nature were actively replaced by induced allegiance to a transcendent authority.

It is vitally important to recognize that such colonial "salvation" is always carried on—at least initially and in significant degree—with the tacit approval of the colonized. Far from being a form of piracy (the violently imposed surrender of resources) or outright slavery (the violently guaranteed extraction of labor from a population), the relational structure of material colonization is one of honored—if steeply biased—promises. In its African colonies, for instance, England offered tribal peoples the opportunity to enter the Empire with all the benefits that would accrue therefrom. In return, they would be obliged to perform certain services for which they would be (well) compensated. And to this bargain, various peoples by and large agreed. They did so, not because they wished to sacrifice themselves to forms of progress they neither understood nor desired, but because that seemed the best way of retaining some measure of control over their own destinies—a way of getting what they wanted.

As intimated above, behind an indigenous people's acceptance of the colonial power's economically savvy, formal promises is their guided perception of their own inherent want or lack. In short, the success of colonization hinges on nurturing a sense of things going to waste mixed with a desire for change, for more. Colonialism as such is inconceivable in the absence of effecting an awareness of intrinsic lack, the impression of an unnecessary and hence ever-deflating poverty or privation. In the absence of this wanting and the awareness on which it is based, the native population would simply laugh at the promise tendered. After all, the system of values on which their lives had hitherto been based had always been sufficient. If another people did have some resources or skills that they lacked themselves, these could always be traded for or stolen or acquired as spoils in war. What an effective colonial power offers—whether spiritually or materially—must be something that cannot be negotiated for in the old ways.

The history of colonialism is the history of corrupted desire. More specifically, it is the history of the erosion of native desires and their reconstitution as intimacy-compromising wants and satisfactions. Although the life of a colonized people continues, it increasingly does so only through the individual lives of its members.

The basic rule of all forms of colonialism is: no matter how much 'you' and 'I' prosper, *we* are in steady decline toward greater poverty. Colonialism is not explicitly a violence against individuals, but communities. In fact, colonialism has often promoted individual welfare—a promotion that succeeds in direct proportion to the compromise of communal vitality. That is, the individually enjoyed benefits of colonization are purchased with the responsive virtuosity of the people as a whole. And so, while colonialism raises the future into wholly unprecedented prominence, it is never really *our* future, but rather a future into which we are swept up and eventually dissolved.

Colonies are not naturally occurring entities, but rather artifacts. So obvious is this that we seldom consider its full implications. Among other things, like any other artifact—say, a camera or satellite dish—the factual existence of the colony may not be understood in the same way by the colonized and the colonizer. That is, the identity of the colony may be relatively mysterious, even invisible, to those living in and sacrificed to it. A common component in this sacrifice is the reduction of diverse local communities to a single, relatively homogenous entity—for example, Britain's invention of "the Hindu," the surrogate creation of a "Hawaiian" monarchy, or the contemporary fashioning of a distinctive "Generation X." It is this virtual self or colonial identity that is then "defended" and "benefited" by the colonizing power.

Now, because material colonization operated under the severe temporal and spatial constraints of moving personnel and goods to and from "remote" locales, it was not possible to establish a new identity for each person in the colony directly—an identity based on their being "impoverished" and in need of "salvation." Instead, initial inroads were typically made through prominent intermediaries. Far from lavishing every local inhabitant with the kind of attention needed to inculcate 'useful' wants, this attention was directed largely at the local, ruling elite. And where this elite did not exist, the first order of business was necessarily its immediate creation (see, for example, Fieldhouse, 1984).

By selectively acknowledging or in some cases instituting a people's identity, and by establishing a small, ruling elite, the colonial power vastly simplified the task of effectively translating its intentions into local patterns of conduct. Indeed, the severity of disproportion in benefits received by the elite and the common people provided a relatively reliable index of a colony's "health" as an investment. Such a method of exerting control over a colony was not, of course, without risk. To the extent that imported technologies allowed local elites to abusively command and exploit the common people, indigenous values that had originally funded their authority could deteriorate to the point that no fulcrum remained for relatively nonviolent leveraging of the people's conduct. Conversely, too weak or too equitable a distribution of the benefits of colonization throughout the colony as a whole was liable to result in immediately lower returns on investment and a failure to develop sufficient and efficiently purchased control over local conduct. In either case, the cost of extracting and managing native resources and labor could easily become impracticably high.

As long as the general, colonized population had no direct encounter with the luxuries of the colonist's lifestyle, they could be effectively discounted. In fact, the general population only mattered in any significant sense if it somehow assumed a politically dangerous stance—that is, if and when it threatened to alter the slope of colonial advantage in commerce. Since the benefits of colonialism were perceived as necessarily scarce—only so many tools, pieces of cloth, furniture, and weapons being imported at any given time—and since they were distributed along traditional or familiar lines of power and authority, the general population experienced no fundamentally novel forms of discontent. As long as the day-to-day lives of those who most directly benefited from the arrangement could be screened off from the masses, the lives of the latter would continue for the most part status quo. Not surprisingly, then, such intermediaries were encouraged to think of themselves and live as if they were truly members of the colonial power—its local heads, arms, and legs. In a word, they were encouraged to forfeit their own values for those proper to the colonizer. In result, colonialism could be practiced openly and with a certain measure of satisfaction.

Since colonization acts as a catalyst for the atrophy of indigenous values and since as well this atrophy is structurally tied to a privileging of local 'authority', it follows that active coercion—and so the "costs" of colonization—are held to a minimum. With the breakdown of traditional patterns of governance, commerce, and education comes as well a breakdown in the traditional organization of the family and, more generally, in the web of relationships within—and as a function of—which traditional forms of personal identity are articulated. Because this breakdown is catalytically triggered—that is, unnaturally accelerated—the indigenous culture and people don't have the time, the capacity and leisure, to evolve new and yet still properly indigenous patterns of conduct. In short, they lose their ability to effectively resist being bound and so controlled by their colonial circumstances. This means a steadily decreasing sense of community and ultimately a sterilization of a culture's grounds for creative intimacy. Any attempts to resist the meaning or direction of colonial values are for this reason likely to be weak and sporadic, marked by a glaring and condemning absence of solidarity or the spirit of cooperation.

Put somewhat differently, because the values defining a culture's way of life enable its members to participate in one another's identities, the dissolution of these values marks a shift toward their living and acting as autonomous individuals. Instead of a unified and creative response to colonial aggression, efforts to throw off the imported values of a colonial power typically foil themselves. At one extreme, they end in internal, factional disputes, and at the other in mob actions of a sort that prove their undesirability to all concerned—colonizer and colonized alike.

Of course, it follows from this that the tools and technologies used to advance the colonial intent must be fully compatible with the institutionalization of generic individuality—the realization of merely virtual independence. Indeed, just such a compatibility is responsible for the remarkable and seemingly "inevitable" success of the material colonialism practiced by the post-Enlightenment West. It was precisely through effectively and even "righteously" spreading the technological values of 'independence' and 'controlled autonomy'—values central as well to the dominant streams of European political, religious, and social culture—that the colonial venture insured its own success.

Not surprisingly, Gandhi's ability to effectively generate a viable home-rule movement in India was in large part a function of his embodiment of the most traditional Hindu values and his charismatic ability to gather "disciples" willing to discard British-instilled notions of freedom as implying individual autonomy and violently confrontational protest. In particular, his weaving of native cloth on a handloom—while symbolic of a rejection of British-made cloth and the economics of dependence—perfectly illustrates the need to reject not only the dominant political values of the colonial power, but its technical values as well. Only thus can a colonized people begin the dual process of at once reclaiming their own traditions and history and improvising with them to realize a set of new and yet deeply shared values, entering thereby into responsive and truly effective and creative conduct.

On the basis of such an example and others that might be cited, it might be argued—as historians often have—that the disintegration of Europe's colonial empires in this century have been due in part to the charismatic rallying of nonsectarian, communal spirit; in part to shifting economic and political fortunes resulting from the so-called world wars; in part due to a reawakening of ethnic sensibilities and so an interest in indigenous value systems; and finally due in part to the creation of novel communities centered on imported systems of value like Marxism. I would like to suggest instead that these conditions, while important, are in fact secondary to the internal factors contributing to the demise of material colonization. What ended the era of material colonialism was its practically unmitigated success.

THE EVOLUTION OF COLONIAL INTENT INTO THE DEVELOPMENT OBJECTIVE AND BEYOND

Material colonization was from the outset limited in its effectiveness on two counts. On one hand, there was the necessity of physically transporting the resources and productively translated labor of the colonized population back home. This required not just a sophisticated transportation system covering both land and sea, but well-developed infrastructures for both bulk transport and energy transmission in the colony itself and security both there and along any transit routes. Especially in the early days of colonialism, losses due to weather and piracy were much more frequent and real than we might be inclined to imagine today, and the absence of refrigeration and other sophisticated storage technologies rendered the long land and sea transits involved much more than mere inconveniences.

On the other hand, there was the necessity of sending appropriately maintained administrative, military, economic, and cultural emissaries to the colonized locale. This involved providing adequate housing, medical care, support staff, and education not only for the immediate representatives of the colonial power, but for their families as well. And because colonial assignments were clearly long on the exotic but short on immediate comfort and the rewards of status at home, the most qualified candidates for administering the colonies were seldom interested or interested for long.

In short, maintaining a high level of appropriate and loyal expertise at the local levels of colonial administration was far from easy. A balance had to be struck between a colonial administration committed to following directions from "home" and one decisive and strong enough to act with relative autonomy. In the latter case, independence often led to excessive graft or locally motivated, globally disastrous wielding of authority that—in "worst case" scenarios like the American colonies—led to outright revolution. But where the colonial center continued controlling the periphery directly over great enough distances, the slow pace of travel and so written and personal communication made effective responses almost impossible. In the same way that dinosaurs are believed to have stopped their drive into gigantism when signals from the brain simply took too long to reach the extremities for size alone to be sufficient compensation for slow response time, in the absence of technical solutions like the wireless telegraph, the limits of colonial expansion might have been reached long before colonialism had fully reached its prime.

Instead, by the latter part of the nineteenth century, the technically mediated control of conduct throughout a colony had pressed this equation of risk to its limit. As new communication technologies became more and more ubiquitously essential to managing colonies, the ease of reporting exploitation within and between colonies also increased and along with it challenges to the authority of the elite. Moreover, the efficiency of extraction, transportation, and production technologies had reached a point where colonies had to function not just as sources of raw material and labor, but as markets for manufactured goods from colonizing nations. As intimated above, however, since the benefits of colonization had traditionally been restricted to small elites, and since colonial peoples had been sufficiently impoverished by the breakdown of local patterns of commerce, most colonies proved to be very poor consumer markets. If the colonial system had not effectively collapsed over the years between the Great Crash and the end of World War II, it would have had to be dismantled as an impediment to realizing its own deeply technological aims.

With the mercurial growth of both the world economy and population in the late nineteenth and early twentieth centuries, a ceiling came into view for how much power could be redistributed given the restrictions of a mechanically based technology for mediation. Beyond this ceiling, the cost of controlling the selective redistribution of wealth was simply greater than the value of that wealth itself. By the end of the third decade of the twentieth century, this ceiling—largely a function of the turn around time on invested capital—had effectively been reached.

Whether material colonization could have been stabilized at the then current level of global coverage had all other things remained relatively equal is a moot point. Things did not remain equal. The trajectory and accelerating pace of those technological developments that had made possible the great success of colonialism were at this same time freeing our technological lineage itself from the gravity of specific national interests and the confinement of their colonial orbits. That is, the technologies crucial to colonialism were reaching their respective thresholds of utility and becoming proper ends in themselves.

The resulting abundance of goods was in substantial conflict with the continued withholding of the benefits of colonial economics from the colonized. In addition, the technologies of communication that had made practical the European colonization of 85 percent of the Earth's surface by 1914 began subverting existing colonial interests by making the facts of exploitation increasingly easy to disseminate in and between colonies. Finally, a structural adjustment was unavoidable. The Great Crash occurred not because of excessive speculation in the world market, but because efficient production and distribution technologies had brought about an unanticipated scarcity of markets and because the colonial politics of poverty had come into technically mediated conflict with the economics of exploitation.

Following the Crash came a decade in which various attempts were made to control and balance production against consumption. The apparently competing rhetorics of federalism, fascism, market capitalism, communism, and remnant colonialism in fact shared a common aim: a reassertion of control over the dynamics of what had already become a global economy, seen but imperfectly through the outmoded lens of "spheres of influence." In both the European and Pacific theaters of the Second World War, there played out the tragic end of colonialism as it had existed for nearly three centuries. Today, we are still only partially aware of the extent to which this heralded as well the end of the reign of national as opposed to properly transnational interests—the realization of economic codependency.

Ironically, among the spin-offs of the war effort aimed at retaining viable national autonomy were commercially viable means of electronically augmenting the transfer of goods and resources that eventually did away with the need for physically transporting wealth in order to manipulate and accumulate it. The long-term effect of these technologies—quite in keeping with the overall logic of individualism and the technologically embodied conception of freedom as autonomy—has been to undermine the viability of nationalism as such. Borders have effectively been rendered porous in all but the crudest sense—a process that is reaching its perfection in the Internet-mediated realization of what has been called a "casino economy" in which billions of dollars of capital can profitably exchange hands thousands of times in a single hour.

In such a virtual geography, centering interests in a nation as such is neither necessary for realizing monopolies of power nor useful in the profitable manipulation of market interests. The postmodern world of the Internet is decentered and functionally borderless, but hardly conducive to true diversity. The development of radar, radio, television, cybernetic guidance, electronic computation, and data storage—these conspired not only to end classic forms of material colonialism in a paroxysm of success, they ushered in a new age of transnationally profitable development. Altruistically motivated changes of heart played no part in the dismantling of the colonial world.

Thus, while the rhetoric of development that replaced explicitly colonial management of world trade can be traced back well into the nineteenth century, it was formally christened only in 1944 at the famous Bretton Woods conference. There, the World Bank and the International Monetary Fund were created, and the foundation laid for the General Agreement on Tariffs and Trade (GATT), the primary legal instrument of "free trade" as we now know it. Since then, world economic growth has meant cultivating new markets—whole new classes of people in want—in substantial disregard of old political, commercial, and social borders.

Development became a plausible and then necessary alternative to colonialism because the latter had been too good at exploiting the colonies and not good enough at inculcating in them a usefully extensive and sophisticated set of wants. The problem, in fact, was an economic "catch-22" of sorts. On the one hand, while a ruling elite could be efficiently converted toward colonial ends in the absence of an extensive infrastructure for distributing and marketing consumer goods and luxuries, the same could not be said of the common people. On the other hand, while an elite could effectively be persuaded toward colonial ends by knowledge—that is, access to the history, literature, religious rituals, science, and technology of the colonial power—illiterate commoners nonconversant in the colonial language were impossible to move in this way. Building the infrastructure to create a wanting populace of consumers was too expensive. Less expensive was providing universal education, but this ran substantial risks of providing the intellectual and organizational tools needed for crafting a revolt against the institution of colonialism itself.

With the postwar spread of especially electronic mass media (radio, television, and, now, the Internet) the most restrictive temporal, spatial, and social barriers to the colonial creation of markets were virtually eliminated and the catch-22 effectively dissolved. To begin with, the advent of television rendered literacy—and so formal education and the infrastructure that it requires—much less than absolutely necessary. Just as importantly, the relatively refined and potentially dangerous enticements of knowledge, which included profound critical and historical elements—especially the sciences and political philosophy—could be replaced with more immediate and universally or "popularly" appealing gratification and entertainment. Markets with extremely wide ranges of wants for a "new life" could be created, not through critically disciplined formal education, but through pleasurable diversion.

The beauty of this as a tool for colonization is almost breathtaking. Fully co-opting a ruling elite runs the risk that suitably educated and "socialized" members of that elite will at some point catch on to what is being perpetrated in the name of mutual beneficence. Especially when this education occurs in the colonial "homeland," it can actually constitute an irreplaceable resource for effective rebellion. In the case of India, many of the most influential voices of the home-rule movement were as young men granted insight into Britain's elite power structures by attending her best universities. The success of Gandhi's campaign owed much to his charisma, but perhaps just as much to his firsthand experience of what it meant to be British. Knowing the enemy intimately is a decided advantage in defeating him.

With the proliferation of mass media, this advantage can be maximally attenuated. Whereas an elite education necessarily appeals to and develops some form of critical awareness, entertainment can induce nonnative values in the complete absence of critical engagement. By pitching itself to the lowest common denominators in a population, mass-mediated entertainment can both guide and reinforce axiological change with a minimum of resistance. That is, with the least possible risk of losing indispensable ideological or technological leverage, entertainment inculcates and nurtures profitable wants in an entire population. And this can be done without discriminating on the basis of indigenous divisions of gender, class, age, and so on.

Among other things, this means that a youth audience can be targeted that has not yet been fully initiated into traditional values and lifeways and is therefore both profoundly malleable and naively selfish. Thus, the colonial power can "fairly" and yet very efficiently cultivate a generation whose wants or 'desires' have been stripped entirely of communal meaning—a generation whose attention is not disposed toward intimacy-refining conduct, but toward increasingly isolated and episodically pleasurable individual be-havior and private experience. In the colonization of consciousness, the "elite" consists of the autonomously fashionable ego—the beneficiary, for instance, of self-help regimens, of technologically sophisticated health care, of designer label clothing, and health club membership—a virtual self by means of which all other aspects of who we are as persons and as commu-nities are leveraged into generically profitable action.

Of course, while the electronic media can be thus portrayed as perfect tools for furthering the selfish intentions behind traditional forms of mate-rial colonization, we might nevertheless be tempted to conclude that the media are only accidentally tools of cultural hegemony. That is, we might be tempted to invoke the moral transparency argument that "the media don't colonize, greedy nations or transnational corporations do." Accord-ing to this view, if consciousness is being colonized through mass media, the blame must be laid at the feet of those who are directing and in effect abus-ing the media. In some ways, it would be nice if this were true. If the moral opacity of the media were a function of individually selfish intent, if colo-nialism were perpetrated via the messages conveyed through the media and not by the media themselves and as such, we would be in a position to proactively legislate against our colonization. The actual situation is much more dire.

No one is in charge of the colonization of consciousness. It is not you, or I, or even the ever-troublesome "they" who are to blame, but that which selectively mediates and so segregates us. Marshall McCluhan said thirty years ago that the medium is the message. But it is also true that the message is the medium—that what we value and want to inform others about is in-creasingly expressive of the structure of the media that have occasioned our functional equidistance from every point of information space and disposed our attention almost exclusively toward the iconic and generic. It is not just we who speak through the media, but the media that speak through us. And what we 'desire' is more and more exactly what the media want.

Information technologies have rendered possible for the first time in hu-man history the translation of knowledge into information, reducing it thereby to a tradable and so context-independent commodity. In place of material colonization, they have ushered in—behind the screen of globaliz-ing the economy for the good of all, and much more silently than any rail-road or truckline or aircraft could have—a new form of colonization whose principle players enjoy just as deep and righteous a conviction of manifest destiny as any colonial missionary of the past. Only it is no longer lands that are colonized, but consciousness itself; no longer material resources that are exported, but attention itself. Paraphrasing an old pop song, in the new colonialism, it is the hunter who has been captured by his game.

THE COLONIZATION OF CONSCIOUSNESS

The colonization of consciousness is a function of axiological incest. Understandably, perhaps, we are not inclined to admit this or evaluate the conditions of its possibility. It is a form of colonialism that is deeply closeted. But that this new form of colonization has been diligently at work without being acknowledged as such is not proof of any conspiracy to keep it secret, but rather of its decentered or ambient nature. Among the most important characteristics of the colonization of consciousness is the fact that it occurs in the absence of any clearly centralized destination for exported 'resources'. As in material colonization, the diversion of resources and energy from the interests of the colonized to those of the colonizers—in this case, technologies as such, primarily in the form of transnational corporations—is tragically welcome. But unlike material colonization, which took place in a space liable to measuring and mapping and which skewed this space in easily observed ways, the colonization of consciousness is not something we can literally view from without. Instead, it transpires in what is ostensibly a completely private domain—that of individual experience as such.

The colonization of consciousness is an outgrowth of the technical triumph over the kinds of physical and temporal constraint that led to the stalling and even reversal of colonial expansion in a purely material sense. Simply put, the technological advances that might have solved the problems involved in mounting a truly profitable, material colonization of the so-called third and fourth worlds also rendered the project outdated and finally irrelevant. They not only cut free the goal of gathering wealth from the limitations of actually transporting physical commodities like precious metals and stones, they made it possible for corporations to carry out essentially colonial projects without any need to appeal to the authority of an imperial or national center. In short, the colonial nation gives way to the multinational corporation, which can operate with startling clarity of purpose precisely because it has no explicit and public involvement in politics, no responsibility for considering communal (as opposed to corporate) welfare. Corporations are free from the need to maintain any military presence since their "battles" are purely strategic—a warfare that dispenses with physical troops and weapons and is waged entirely through the distillation and rapid dissemination of information.

Effected through globalized electronic media—primarily radio, television, film, and the computer-mediated transmission of a virtually infinite array of information—the ubiquity and economy of the colonization of consciousness is without historical precedent. In fact, wealth has come to mean not the possession of valuable things, but the holding of attention as such. Witness the importance of the Nielson ratings, the way political campaigns work, the effectiveness of advertising and credit-based consumption. Wealth—or what is more salient, power—is redistributed and concentrated almost magically. Expertise is available almost instantaneously. And so, to the extent that the media have quite literally become part of the very atmosphere of contemporary life, it can be said that our colonization proceeds quite invisibly. It has even become a design value for the tools of our mediation to recede into virtual absence—always present, but not directly *to* our awareness since at their most successful they function iconically and simply pass our attention on to where it will serve as a "good" or commodity in the greater scheme of things.

Since the dawn of the mechanistic, industrial age, inventors have dreamed of developing a perpetual motion machine—a mechanical system that could be set in operation with a minimal amount of energy and continue working by itself, with no further energy investment. The key to realizing this dream, of course, would be the defeat of friction, the reduction to zero of energy (and so potential work) lost in transit or the movements of the system itself. While global, electronic media are not technically frictionless, they have so reduced transmission losses that wealth can be redistributed at literally lightning speeds. By way of the stock market, I can "move" pork futures from Raleigh to New York to Taipei in less time than it takes to drink a cup of coffee and make a cool million dollars along the way.

All of which makes the colonization of consciousness very exciting. It plays into our dreams of perpetual motion, our dreams of instantaneous control, of freedom from constraint not only physically, but psychically. And the cost is unbelievably low—nothing more than our attention—something so readily available and apparently replaceable that we seem to be getting access to almost everything for practically nothing. Not unexpectedly, even if our attention is drawn to the colonization process, the recursion typically leaves us simply clamoring for more, oblivious to the possibility that we are in fact losing much more than we ever stand to gain.

As it happens, we are particularly susceptible to the promises of mass mediation and the colonization of our own consciousness because these promises reiterate so many of our basic assumptions about both the viability of technological salvation and the inherently autonomous nature of the self and its proper freedom. Every junior high school student learns that with a lever long enough and an appropriate fulcrum, it's possible for even a young boy or girl to move (and so control the placement of) the earth itself. According to the myth we are in the process of telling one another, the fulcrum is increasingly starting to look like our multimedia home computer terminal and the lever like the vastness of the fiber-optic web that links our terminal with every other. At once democratic and heroic, the possibilities and potencies of the media speak to us where we have traditionally been most tender, most often bruised. And as this vulnerability is further reinforced by the media's encouragement of our nearly epidemic flight from the challenges of actual rather than merely virtual intimacy, we have more and more reason to look to the media for salvation. In effect, we are increasingly inclined to accept an *iconic* mode of life—a mode of life wherein we accept signs as substitutions for what ultimately eludes all signification; a life wherein symbols are accepted as the truest realities.

Much is made of the 'externalization of costs' by critics of the global economy. The commodities we consume each day are as relatively cheap as they are only because their purchase price does not include payment to repair damage to the environment, to our cities, to our societal and personal health. What we pay with our charge cards at the checkout counter does not include the vast costs of collectively subsidizing transportation and energy systems worldwide or the increased burdens placed on local systems of welfare. But to date, no voices are being raised to protest the externalization of costs related to the mining and export of attention as such.

In preview of a longer treatment to follow, imagine a child learning the meaning of happiness in a home where most of his or her understanding about the world and its ways comes from watching television, listening to the radio, and "surfing the Net." If fully immediate interactions with his or her parents are limited to an hour or two a week—now a relatively average situation in American households—instead of being regularly exposed to and drawn bodily into the confluence of relational qualities that are implied in actual and so active happiness, such a child quite naturally takes as his or her inspirations the dynamics of a sitcom family in which happiness is acted out—not lived, but presented through carefully chosen and aurally or visually perceptible marks. And so, absent is the changed quality of the air around a happy man or woman, the tingling thrill carried by the subtle modulations of their energy, the unblocked nature of the time they share, the utterly unique and healing potency of their touch. Happiness (and for that matter, sadness, love, hate, loneliness, contentment, and so on) will in all likelihood seem not to be the fruition of an entire life of sharing with others, but the prize won at the end of a thirty-minute minidrama. Formally accurate, perhaps, such an iconic experience of happiness is ultimately impoverishing. In a particularly harsh and yet still partial critique, we might argue that if mediated life is imitating an art, it is the art of cartooning or caricature.

This is perhaps sad enough. But that only scratches the surface of the poverty to which the colonization of consciousness subjects us. When our consumption of mediate experience is almost unbroken from morning to night, can we really claim our minds belong to us? Consider the facts that the average American now watches 22,000 commercials a year and that

75 percent of network advertising time is paid for by the 100 largest corporations among the 450,000 currently registered in the United States (Mander, 1996b). In total dollars, corporate advertising just in the United States would allow us to increase by 50 percent the amount spent on primary and secondary education in the country. Worldwide, the amount of money invested in corporate advertising exceeds the total spent on education at all levels in all countries combined. The costs of indirect advertising through the global film and television industry are, of course, astronomically higher. The investment of such vast sums in advertising—both direct and indirect—is clearly profitable. But to whom and why? Who owns the attention of a child so immersed in a videogame or a tape of a Disney movie or the broadcast antics of the Morphin Rangers that he or she neglects eating, refuses offers to play outside, and even ignores threats of corporal punishment? If we pay attention to the media more than we do to each other, who benefits? Who loses? If our attention isn't literally our own, what is?

As the principle process by means of which the colonization of consciousness is carried out, regular investment in mass-mediated forms of advertising, information, news, and entertainment is profitable not because it directly results in the purchase of corporate-produced commodities. Rather, it is profitable for much the same reason that the colonial disintegration of indigenous values and patterns of commerce were for the colonial power— because the breakdown of these relationships, like the breakdown of the relationships between the molecules in a load of coal, releases a great deal more energy than is required to execute the breakdown itself. Since the freeing up of this energy is effected through a dissolution of guiding values for conduct or the movement of energy in a community, it can be directed more or less at will. Likewise, attention freed from our immediate circumstances—from our dramatic interdependence as such—is placed into open circulation where it can serve a multitude of ends, where it can be profitably directed by any nearby icons.

Objections can, of course, be made to such a reading of the way the information revolution effects change and who it benefits. It may well be that the institutionalization of iconic modes of attention quite literally channels our energy away from attending to the world's natural rhythms, from nurturing the continuously responsive pulse of a truly viable and local community. But—or so the argument goes—we are in return able to process a much greater variety of stimuli in a great deal less time. At the same time that the media increase our choices, they undermine our parochialism. Think of a family living in some Appalachian valley an hour's drive from the nearest town. Miles from the nearest human neighbor, their world is profoundly closed, comfortable perhaps, but uneventful. Think now of the incredible diversity that enters their lives along with cable television! Instantly, not only do the candied offerings of Hollywood grace the family's home, but music from the concert halls of London, nature scenes from the Australian outback, university classes from Richmond or Chapel Hill. In a word, what the media open up is the possibility of an ostensibly multicultural environment anywhere at any time. If this is "colonization," perhaps it is not too bad.

Such reasoning underlies much of the popular cant on the subject and we will have much more and decisively critical things to say about it in chapters to come. At this point, I'd simply like to suggest that what is actually promoted with the incursion of, for example, cable TV, is not a subtlety-encouraging diversification of awareness as such. Rather, awareness is trained into adopting a yes-no attitude, a dualistic stance that—because of its crudeness—reinforces an iconic reading of our experience. Either we switch stations or stay, turn the program on or off. If an Internet bulletin board interests us, we can log on as participants; if not, we can remain mere voyeurs free to move, opinions unchallenged and unexpressed, as we please. There is a shifting here away from analogic subtlety, from indeterminacy, from ambiguity, toward the absolute decisiveness of the digital. There is liking and disliking, staying or not, and precious little in between. The media train us to discriminate with the crudest and most immature movement of attention and will—mere acceptance or rejection. Sacrificed for 'good' or 'ill' is the infinite variability, the almost acrobatic flexibility, of awareness unconstrained by the dictates of excluding the middle.

Among researchers interested in defining intelligence—admittedly an odd lot—there is consensus that creative intelligence is correlated with an ability to see familiar things or situations in new ways. Stated so straightforwardly, this seems almost tautological, an obvious truism. But I find it profoundly telling because it suggests that the key to creative conduct is an ability to forego seeing things in rigid terms of 'is' or 'is not', and engaging instead in unprecedented *seeing as*. That is, creative intelligence emerges precisely when we refrain from excluding the middle, when we resist the biasing of experience toward the harsh dualisms of being and not-being, of right and wrong, liked or disliked. Such an understanding of creative intelligence echoes precisely the Buddha's claim that, at the very least, enlightenment means relinquishing both 'is' and 'is not' and responding freely to the shifting interdependence of things as needed. By supporting an iconic relationship to our own experience, the media discourage creativity—not because of poor programming or a reduction of choice, but because they encourage an impatience with ambiguity and indetermination.

I can recall with great immediacy the shock of my first interview with the Korean Zen master Seung Sahn. A recent graduate in philosophy from Yale, schooled in the best and deepest of the Western tradition, I entered the interview anticipating a clarification of the meaning of enlightenment. I had attended Seung Sahn's public talk the night before and had been completely taken aback. Relating one teaching tale after another, he had woven a narrative context in which every question posed by members of the audience—my silent queries included—were already answered. No professor had ever managed this and I fully expected to be let in on the "secret" in the course of the three-day meditation retreat I immediately decided to attend.

After the initial, ritual greeting of student and master, Dae Soen Sa Nim (Seung Sahn's Buddhist title) asked what I wanted. Because I felt it was the thing to do, I said I wanted to attain enlightenment. Screwing his face up as if surprised by a vulgar smell, he asked, "Why?"

I was stumped. The last thing I expected was a Zen master who couldn't understand my wanting to be enlightened. Wondering how to express myself more clearly in light of Dae Soen Sa Nim's limited command of English, my mind had just slipped into high gear when he shoved his zen stick into the pit of my stomach and growled. "If you don't know, *only don't know*." This teaching phrase hit me like a silent train on a starless night. Responding with creative virtuosity to the needs of the situation in which we find ourselves depends on *not* being certain of anything in advance, not acting on the precedent of what 'is' or 'is not'.

Fourteen years later, it strikes me that among other things, this Buddhist teaching gives us a wonderfully succinct way of pointing toward the central dangers of the new colonialism and the so-called digital revolution that has made it possible. We are being trained by the media to adopt the mode of 'accepting or rejecting' as basic to how we entertain and inform ourselves. We not only sediment a view of freedom that is deeply bound up with choosing and the satisfaction of wants, we establish the habit of relating to our world as experts. We know what we like and what we dislike, what we want and what we don't. As sophisticated and critical a thinker as Jürgen Habermas (1984)—in complete conformity with the dispositions of our technical lineage—has argued that communicative action pivots on uncoerced agreement and the possibility of free and autonomous disagreement. Communication itself, on such a model, comes down to conduct oriented toward either assent or dissent—a digital process in an increasingly digital world in which criticism perpetuates the roots of what is being criticized.

Seated before our cable-fed television or our home computer and the myriad destinations they afford us, we may act as autocratically as we please. The media are in principle democratic. Given sufficient technological investment, they are open and available to all. But in practice, we grant our audience as we will. Within the range of choices before us—a range that increasingly seems subject only to technical limitation—we can control our experience with astounding power and precision. If we like, we can simply turn the world or any of its parts 'on' or 'off'. In sedimenting such conduct, we reduce our tolerance for ambiguity. We sacrifice what Zen teachers often refer to as our "beginner's mind"—a mind that doesn't take a stand on either 'is' or 'is not', and so remains capable of doing the wholly unexpected and yet wholly appropriate. It is only such a mind that has the flexibility to "accord with the situation, responding as needed"—a classic expression of enlightened, and so enlightening, conduct.

When the world is attended primarily through electronic and print intermediaries, it is quite naturally taken to be *given*, not something underdetermined and limitlessly responsive, but a thing that *is*. Moreover, it is a world that mediates or stands between each one of us and all others even as it connects us. Far from being seen as that irreducible field of relations out of which 'you' and 'I' are only contingently or conventionally abstracted, the mediate world is that ever-present, if inconstant, "other" by means of which we most familiarly locate and safely identify our 'selves'. But because the mediate world is what we have in common, it is also a primary condition in the generic constitution of who we are.

Far from preserving cultural diversity, the media-driven colonization of consciousness contributes to its demise by cultivating a functionally singular perspective to be shared by all. In place of the possibility of creative harmony—implying at the very least a diversity of perspectives—we are increasingly being disposed toward realizing a sterilizing agreement in the construction of our "global village." In the process of building our always brave new world—a world whose face changes as a reflection of public values or the movements of mass-mediated attention—we are carrying out an unwitting neutering of indigenous values that eliminates their potential to radically and unpredictably reorient our conduct and so engender for us truly new lives, new stories. In the end, "cultural diversity" becomes but one commodity no less subject to the fortunes of fashion as any other.

Chapter 6

Pluralism versus the Commodification of Values

One of the claims made by advocates of the media is that they promote a less provincial mindset, a more open-minded, informed attitude about the world and the tremendous diversity it sponsors in everything from bodily form to cultural values. Especially with the apparent (although not actual) breakdown of the network monopolies and the proliferation of small presses, cable stations, and web sites, it is argued that the media are helping to bring about a positive acceptance of the relativity of our own dispositions. By making virtually present a vast array of possible lifestyles, political agendas, and aesthetic and spiritual sensibilities, the media open a much larger door than ever before realized to what we might refer to as axiological commerce—the exchange of basic human values. In this sense, the growing ubiquity of mass mediation can be seen as particularly serendipitous for those hoping to foster our movement toward a truly multicultural world community. The idealization of difference is "a good thing."

That, at least, is the prevailing orthodoxy. So say the purveyors of corporate commodities and the pundits of postmodernity. According to this dispensation, what we have been disparaging as the colonization of consciousness is in fact nothing short of our liberation from the biases to which we have historically been quite individually and often selfishly liable. Just as the "unsophisticated" minds of a colonized people are "opened up" and newly vitalized by the influx of foreign goods and values, those of us living in the dawn of the information age are having the doors of our perception thrown wide open. What is not so clear is whether the result is any different now than it was a hundred years ago in the lands of Central and South Africa, in Hawai'i, or in Central America. Are our minds being opened in an expansion of our humanity, or are they being left gaping in order to facilitate their ready plundering?

It is far from obvious that the benefits of mediately transmitting cultural values can be found in any worlds but those that are strictly virtual. For example, it may well be that by watching a program on the pygmies of Central Africa we find our horizons interestingly stretched. But since our exposure comes without the opportunity for those pygmies to watch, speak with, and perhaps reach out and touch us, its importance remains largely subjective even where we are stimulated to campaign for the preservation of the native forests of the pygmy peoples.

What is glaringly absent from any mass-mediated contact with other cultures and the alternatives they provide for the construal of reality is the immediately dramatic interweaving of our life stories with those of others. We may become quite familiar, say, with a particular pygmy family that a documentary film maker lived with for six months and whose lives are the subject of a twelve-hour series on pygmy culture. The names and dispositions of these family members may even become as common in our conversations as those of our own local friends. But we are not friends. When the youngest child of this family dies after a tragically brief bout with cholera, we do not send flowers or grieve alongside the gathered uncles and aunties. No one in the village will recount our names among the relations who came in support and sorrow. None of our own children will cry themselves to sleep in tearful remembrance of smiles and gestures they will never see again. In short, we are not part of that family's story and they in turn are not truly part of ours.

There is no doubt a special kind of familiarity that we develop with this family so different in basic beliefs and lifestyles from our own. We can almost guess how the father will react to his youngest child's playful antics over their meal or how the eldest daughter will smile when mention is made of a particular young man whom she has begun dreaming about each night. But if this constitutes an intimacy with them, it is an intimacy that is strictly virtual. We are given profiles of the family's life together—views taken from the perspective of the filmmaker and film editor. And as with any view, there is necessarily a foregrounding that takes place and a complementary placing into the background. A view is in this sense always an evaluation. This would be just as true if we were the ones living for a time with the family. Our encounter would still be partial. But our partiality would then be taking place in and so woven into their world, not our own. That is, our prejudices, our judgments, our likes and dislikes, our appreciations or lack thereof would all be taking place in a non-native context. They would no longer be indigenous and, like the proverbial sore thumb, would stick out loudly and clearly. We would be forced into some level of consciousness about our presuppositions.

Now, it is crucial that this takes place only when intimacy is no longer merely virtual or abstract—something occurring across only a limited number of the dimensions of our conduct. Implied here is not just time spent in the same place together, but time spent getting along. Living with a family for six months is not like sleeping in a five-star hotel and rubbing elbows with the locals only in and out of taxis, trains, restaurants, and so on. When it is successful, living with someone is an improvisation of domesticity or homeliness in the most positive possible senses of that word. It is realizing a very real sense of being an "us" that is not subordinate to "you" or "I," but rather superordinate. Entering into the life of a family always feels like finding our own source, the place out of which our individuality has been flowing, perhaps unnoticed or ignored, but flowing nonetheless. It is realizing that each one of us truly has his or her origin in community.

What the media promote, however, is not community, but collectivity. The homogenizing effect of programming that reaches millions and at times billions of people at practically the same time guarantees that in some sense we share experiences to an extent previously unknown. But in fact we are not living with one another, but simply coexisting. That is, we stand beside one another, but always apart. The media connect us but cannot put us in real touch. Through it, we share memories, but we are no less strangers to one another for this common past. If anything, we are more estranged since the stories we share—the ones gathered from the news, from novels and sitcoms and films—do not include us even if we do include and claim them as our own. There is, in short, no narrative reciprocity.

What this means practically speaking is, of course, that it is not just the pygmy family that remains at a distance from us or the people of Bosnia, but the families of our neighbors and our caretakers, those who build our homes and—for that matter—those who wreck them. Because we think of knowledge as being a function of verifiable beliefs, we have the impression that by hearing *about* other cultures, other times and places, that we know more than before. We have access to information about Chinese peasants, Peruvian ranchers, Parisian models, and Maori feminists. And yet we must admit that these people have a merely iconic status in our lives. We are not telling a life story together. Were knowledge construed as responding appropriately in a situation, we would see things rather differently. To begin with, we would realize that the kind of private comprehension afforded by the media is not yet knowledge. Knowledge implies community—and that means not a static, formal organization of individuals, but a dynamically continuous pattern of conduct whereby part and whole are in full interpenetration.

Most importantly, for the colonized consciousness this breakdown of active interdependence is not experienced as a failure of any sort. To the contrary, it is understood to be a 'natural' concomitant of a life of increasing objectivity and rationality. As Thomas Nagel (1987) so graphically illustrates in his valorization of the so-called "view from nowhere," ours is an age in which individuality and individual rights are on the one hand elevated to the highest possible stature while on the other hand personal perspective is roundly distrusted. That is, we must be staunchly autonomous in our individuality and yet free of all unique biases. The ideal knower is not someone born in Las Vegas, raised Roman Catholic, and now actively practicing Korean Zen. To the contrary, the ideal knower is radically individual without being at all personal—a kind of epistemological Everyman.

The dilemma here runs deep enough to be traced at least as far back as the discrediting of rhetoricians in Platonic Greece. While our theories of knowledge since then have almost invariably maintained that personality and uniqueness are maximally discountable, and that it is only individually verified universality (or at least generality) that is to be at once trusted and striven for, our politics and the metaphysics that underlie them have insisted on the sacredness of precisely such personality. Briefly put, the dilemma is that we feel compelled to at once maintain a belief in the intrinsic value of individual experience while distrusting anything like a truly unique perspective. And so, for the last twenty-five hundred years in the dominant Western tradition, individuality and universality have been unlikely but insistent bedfellows. And not surprisingly, the fruit of their joint labors—the ideal knower—looks a lot like the Spock character in the Star Trek series. Logical, precise, only half human and with an absence of attachment to any place or person, Spock is able to simply assess the available data and dispassionately decide what is what. There may be times when he is undone by his genius and it is the emotion-rich perspective of a Captain Kirk that finally saves the day, but this is the "mystery of being human." That this mystery plays such a prominent role in the series is a credit to the sensibilities of the writers. That it is a mystery in the first place stands in telling evidence of the depth of our colonization.

The media allow us to maintain individual experience as such. That is, they foster a retreat from the kind of joint experience that naturally arises with immediate encounters with one another while at the same time determining that all such experience will be channeled along a very limited range of perspectives. Only thus can we effectively manage both maximum autonomy and maximum homogeneity. At times, as many as half a billion people all over the planet are "enjoying" exactly the same perspective on some event—be it the Super Bowl, the World Cup matches, the Olympics, or the latest CNN report on the shelling of Baghdad. And in the end, the very fact that we are *not* intimately implicated in the stories we share via the media is taken as support for the legitimacy of the perspectives they articulate.

It is of course arguable that the tension between individuality and universality on the one hand and personality and uniqueness on the other is hardly new or peculiar to our age. While it is clearly the case that a mythopoetic cosmogony includes a people in the story of the universe in a fashion that a scientifically objective cosmology explicitly eschews, it is nevertheless the case that both act as a subtle form of mediation. Both tend to at least subsume and potentially to simply omit all personally unique perspectives from active consideration. A cosmogonic account—for example the world genealogy chanted by pre–European contact Hawaiians—may leave room for acknowledging and appreciating the unique aspects of our own day-to-day lives, but it nevertheless also orients each one of us toward a common set or system of values/perspectives. The scientific account may take this to a logical, if perhaps only asymptotic, extreme, but the difference may well be one of degree and not kind.

This is plausible enough. One of the side effects of our colonization is that we sometimes develop an inordinately romantic view of aboriginal cultures and equally sophisticated but alternative traditions. My feeling is that all mass mediation is destructive of our truly folk traditions—those cultural lineages based on the person-by-person evolution of a system of values conducive to our spontaneous and harmonious community. Media almost invariably center the deepest and most far-reaching meanings of our lives well beyond us—somewhere that we, as irreducibly unique persons, do not and perhaps cannot abide. In the mass-mediated world, it is not you and I who are the indispensable founts of the cosmos' manifest creativity, but always someone else, somewhere else. Our role is simply to receive and either accept or reject.

A folk tradition is a system of explicitly nonuniversal values. Like other organic systems, folk traditions grow at all points at once. It is not, for example, that the head grows and then the neck and shoulders, internal organs, and so on follow. Also like other organic systems, a folk tradition is not hierarchically ordered. Instead, all its elements depend on and are depended upon by all the others. In this sense, a folk tradition—like a human being—is a unique configuring of interdependence.

Mass media, because they transmit profiles or perspectives, cannot transmit whole systems of values. No matter how extensive a documentation is prepared, it cannot be held as a substitute for the multidimensional, continually changing world or narration that it purports to represent or to which it promises us access. To the contrary, what the media afford us is access to individual values or lineages of value. It is not the *system* of values, but *select components* of that system to which we are exposed and with which we may come to have some familiarity by way of mass mediation.

Now, because the West's dominant metaphysical assumption has been that individual, independent existence is at some level irreducible, the abstraction of particular values for media transmission has not typically been thought of as inherently problematic. In the absence of such an assumption, this is either incredibly naive or unapologetic arrogance. We may record the music of the rainforest pygmies and market its unique sensibilities regarding tone, harmony, and rhythm, but we are not conveying the system of values out of which such music grows and on which it is nurtured. An office worker in Los Angeles may buy a CD of pygmy chants, but, cut off from the rest of the life values—the narration-orienting dispositions—of the pygmy peoples, he is not likely to change his own way of living. In fact, by this summer, his fascination with pygmy vocals will likely have been replaced by Norwegian folk singing accompanied by jazz saxophone, and by winter creole choruses from French Polynesia.

The point here is not just that cultural values are turned into individually marketed commodities, but that these commodities will necessarily enjoy only a very limited lifetime. They will be as subject to fashion and obsolescence as any other product of the marketplace. In part, the limited life of these values is a function of the drives of a market economy for novel stimulations. But much more importantly, it is because as commodities these values are severed from their systems of support and their own meaning as contributors to those systems. In effect, they are sterilized—turned into the axiological equivalent of mules that can serve us for a season or two and then pass away.

In and of itself, isolating for export certain of the more widely palatable values in a culture is relatively harmless. Values, after all, are not like material resources that can be harvested or mined into scarcity and then extinction. In some cases, the imported values may even trigger off relatively long-lasting changes in the terrain of popular culture. The ultimate value of such changes can be left for experts to decide; the variety they provide is itself a kind of immediate benefit. But when combined with a destabilization of the value system of the host culture, the importation of "competing" values raises the possibility of a kind of cultural imperialism whereby seemingly innocuous values act as "viruses" that deeply undermine the integrity of the host system. That is the kind of claim made in many Asian countries, for example, regarding Hollywood's exportation of American values regarding sexuality and moral integrity.

As evidenced by similar concerns in America regarding the effect of media violence on actual behavior—especially in children and adolescents—the relationship between importing virtually presented values and setting off long-term and perhaps irreversible changes in actual values is far from linear. In fact, this nonlinearity is often used by proponents of market-driven programming as a kind of evidence that the content of the media simply isn't that influential when it comes to actual behavior. Analysts of advertising, of course, might argue otherwise. At any rate, the disruption that occurs through spreading individual axiological "viruses" strikes me as insignificant compared to that conditioned by the spread of media as such.

As long as troubling values are situated at the level of the content of mass mediation, they can be identified as such and resisted. In what we have been calling the colonization of consciousness, by the time we have begun questioning the positive or negative effects of this or that value, it is already too late. Our colonization is so advanced that we are in effect just comparing the relative costs of market-delivered apples and oranges, not determining to grow our own and stop buying altogether.

This kind of claim suggests that I would have us move in the direction of cultural isolation and rigidly enforced conservatism. In one sense, this is true. In raising my son, I realized early on that—contrary to my previous belief that all censorship was evil—someone had to safeguard my child's creativity from the threat of axiological viruses until he was old enough to do so for himself. I decided that I would rather that this "someone" be me or his mother and not the head of Disney Enterprises or Big Bird and his cohorts on Sesame Street. Until the age of seven, he led an "unplugged" life, and I think he is stronger and freer in partial consequence thereof.

But I am far from conservative if that means holding a belief that there are individual cultural values that are so universal and unmitigatedly positive that they should be preserved at all costs. To the contrary, my worries about the relationship between mass mediation, the colonization of consciousness, and the possibility of true multiculturalism are related not to conserving any individual values, but rather systems of value—cultures as such. More specifically, I would conserve the capacity such systems have for creative evolution, their suppleness and spontaneity.

The media encourage a proliferation of free-standing values—values abstracted from the systems by virtue of which they have developed their unique characters. The increasing availability of such alternative values is in turn connected with an increase in the range of choices we have in organizing and managing our lives. More choices being associated with more freedom, this seems like an incontestable good—rather like adding new colors to a painter's palette. We aren't obliged to make use of these alternatives, but should we desire doing so, they are ready and waiting.

This reasoning, however, deserves close scrutiny. Values are a shorthand for strategies in the movement of our narration, our conduct. As such, values precede being. They evoke reality—meaning here not a substantial bottom line, an objectivity opposed to our subjectivity, but an ability or relationship whereby crises can be appropriated and resolved. Values are in this sense the birthsites of all meaning. They establish the basic topographies of our worlds, the contours of our experience. When values fully complement or harmonize with one another, the topology of our world is such that things naturally take care of each other. We see this in the vitality and resilience of an ecosystem and in the conduct of a set of improvising musicians who are exquisitely attentive to one another. Systems of value are like families or species. Their wholeness depends on articulating diversity in such a way that offering outshines acquiring and community is augmented and not undermined by personal innovation. A culture is a world-making aesthetic—not an entity, but a way, a *tao*.

IS THERE A UNIVERSAL TECHNOLOGICAL PATH?

Every technology focuses some set of values and promotes their ready diffusion throughout a society—whether this is a family, a clan, a city, a nation, or an entire civilization. Put somewhat differently, technologies not only allow us to more efficiently attain what we want, they circulate a hierarchy of importances that crucially inform our further understanding of what is "desirable" and what stands between us and the satisfaction of our wants. Properly read, a technology is not only an index to a society's interpretation of freedom, but to its understanding of purpose.

For this reason, it's quite interesting to look at the world's major cultural traditions and ask: first, what it means that technological innovation exploded with such logarithmic intensity only in the post-Enlightenment West; and, secondly, why it is from the West that colonialism initially and most successfully spread and flourished. It has been argued that most of the world's cultures have not enjoyed the intellectual or scientific sophistication of the West and for that reason were simply not in a position to initiate or sustain intense technical evolution. According to such a view, the advent of explosive technological growth is a mark of "cultural maturity." Perhaps that's so. Although patronizing in the extreme, such a claim is at least plausible if applied to aboriginal peoples living as hunter/gatherers. But even allowing the conceit underlying the argument to go unchallenged in these cases, what then explains the decidedly nontechnical quality of the cultures of imperial China or Mogul India? Here we have cultures that are just as literate and philosophically sophisticated as the European West at the time of Descartes. And even after contact with the West, these cultures hardly picked up the technological banner to march side by side with Europe into a brave new world of human manufacture. The Chinese, for example, remained a steadfastly agrarian society well into the twentieth century. If it is the pressures of population and scarcity that spur cultures with sufficiently sophisticated conceptual resources to leap into technical proliferation, surely China and India—the world's most populous nations—would long ago have done so. At the very least, we would expect them to have done so soon after their initial contacts with the technical wonders of the West.

This did not happen, however. To the contrary, while even the most refined cultures around the world allowed the West to export various tools into them and readily made use of these, none took on the mantle of technological genius and entered into real competition with the European West—at least not until the early twentieth century when Japan loudly proclaimed its right to membership in the circle of colonial powers. That is, these cultures neglected to fully adopt as their own the lineage of values for which modern Western technology has come to serve as savior. But contrary to the speculation of historians of technology and science like Joseph Needham (1954), these cultures did not fail to become full players in the advancement of technology along European lines because they lacked the material or intellectual resources to do so, but because of an absence of axiological resonance—an absence of sufficiently shared purposes and presuppositions

Of course, even allowing the importation of tools—because of the interrelationship of tools, desires, and technologies—can eventually trigger a quite real alteration of an indigenous way of life. The success of technologically spurred and mediated colonization depends in large part on the strength of these connections among tools, technologies, and values. In general, successful colonial domination has always begun with the skillful diversion of attention from indigenous, communal values to purely individual values through a selective distribution of tools—not only material, of course, but managerial, political, and intellectual. More specifically, a colonial power introduces new tools that can be assessed on the basis of their ability to save individual time, money, labor, and so on. Since tools are used individually, and their effectiveness judged on the basis of individual gain, the colonial power effects a shift of the native culture's center of axiological gravity from the good of the community to *my* good, *my* benefit.

That is, colonialism taps into the individual's existing biases toward convenience and self-gratification—the values underlying greed—and provides positive feedback for their reinforcement. And because an appeal is thus being made to what amounts to a lowest common denominator in human nature, this process is viably advertised and gains support as a promotion of universal good. In short, a tool-effected bias toward individualism allows the rhetoric of universal values to take root and choke out those lineages of excellence unique to a given time, place, and people.

The effect of all this is the dissolution of those systems of indigenous values that might retard or advert the acceptance of colonially expedient patterns of conduct. By shifting a population from communal to predominantly individual values, the range of evaluative considerations is narrowed enough to make quite likely the uncritical adoption of new forms of technology and so new and previously discordant systems of value and conduct—systems favorably disposed to furthering the evolution of the colonial power's axis of concern. Moreover, the breakdown of local systems of value through a biasing of concern toward individual benefits will eventually encourage the development of generically applied institutions for social, political, and economic regulation.

Since all this is carried out under the rubric of leading the colonized people out of Stone-Age subsistence or feudalism or ritually prescribed simplicity, it is done with a relatively clear conscience. By helping indigenous peoples to see themselves as individuals first and as members of a community only secondarily, the reinforcement of ego values contributes to their "maturation" and eventual readiness to enter "democratic" relations with others in the world market. In this sense, colonialism is profoundly patronizing. The native people are "children" who must undergo—just as our psychological theorists tell us we must ourselves—a process of individuation before they can fully realize who they are. In our tradition, both freedom and maturity imply autonomy.

It can be concluded, of course, that since the colony's indigenous values were inhospitable to Euro-American-style technical development—this much the history of the culture demonstrates—and since even in their atrophied form they are likely to remain so, to the precise extent to which these values are preserved, the colony will be forced into the role of playing catch up. If the colonized are to enjoy any of the individually assessed benefits of the imported technologies, they must either jettison their remaining, uniquely indigenous values, "universalize" their nature, and vault themselves into technical competition, or continue bartering themselves for these benefits.

That is good for the colonial power. Even long after the end of any political responsibility for the colony, it is guaranteed a ready market for its own goods and services. In a sense, the colony pays twice, as long as it tries to maintain its own traditions. A disproportionate amount of its natural and human resources are siphoned off to support the values of the colonial power, and then what remaining resources exist are used to purchase the new tools the colony is told they must have if they are ever to extricate themselves from this dependence and become a leader in the evolutionary march of technology—a classic catch-22. And this, I would suggest, is the result of the colonized peoples' having failed to see the tools offered them as intimately connected to technologies having impacts far in excess of the identifiable and individual gains afforded by using the tools proffered.

In the period of classic, material colonialism, there were no exceptions to this pattern of taking basically self-sufficient peoples and transforming them into parasitic consumers of foreign goods and values. And since then, not a single ex-colony has catapulted itself into the league of "First World" nations. Even as unique and successful a long-term and now former colony as Hong Kong remains somewhere between the core economies of the First World and the Third World periphery. In fact, it is arguable that until now there has been only a single exception to the Euro-American domination of technical culture. Japan alone has managed to become more than a subsidiary of Western corporate technologies, not only equaling but in many ways surpassing its European and American forebears in certain industries. The so-called "mini-dragons"—rapidly growing, but relatively small (compared to Japan or China) economies like Singapore and Korea—have undergone tremendous growth in the last two or three decades, but they are still "semi-peripheral" countries subject to the capital and techniques of the West. Witness the current financial crises that only an IMF bailout—actually a buy-out—can "resolve." Such countries have managed to garner a significant slice of the manufacturing pie, but are still doing the "dirty work" of the West rather than acting as an equal in technical innovation and market orientation.

Japan—The Rule-Proving Exception

What made the Japanese case so different? Like all the other major cultures in Asia, Africa, the Americas, and the Pacific, traditional Japanese culture was by European standards nontechnological. More specifically, their technologies tended to be organic/agrarian rather than mechanistic/industrial, social rather than commercial, 'aesthetic' rather than 'logical'. Also like these other cultures, Japan initially welcomed contact with emissaries from Europe and even developed a taste for various European cultural artifacts. During the Tokugawa shogunate (1600–1868), however, Japan reversed its welcoming stance and effectively closed it ports. This act has been variously understood, and in the West not infrequently been interpreted as a power play carried out for the benefit of the ruling elite. Most generally, however, the closure of Japan to the West was an act of purification aimed at conserving traditional Japanese culture.

This closed door policy lasted for roughly two centuries—centuries in which Europe left behind forever its agrarian roots. But in the middle of the nineteenth century, this policy was openly rescinded in the so-called Meiji Restoration. It might be thought that the Japanese had finally come around to seeing the value of European culture. But insofar as the Japanese had enjoyed more than a century of commerce with the West—economic, aesthetic, and religious—before they closed their ports, this seems rather unlikely. In fact, it is arguable that the major impetus behind the restoration of visitation rights to the nations of Europe and the United States was not some newfound appreciation of the technical and cultural achievements of the West, but the appearance of advanced technology warships in Japanese waters. Quite simply, the imperial Meiji court was prescient enough to realize that unless they opened their ports and made a concerted effort to rival the West's technological expertise, Japan would be destroyed—something the Chinese should have been able to see as well and did not until much too late. The Japanese quite consciously undertook industrialization and a cultivation of the particular technological spirit that goes along with it in an act of self-preservation—because they had no interest in becoming a colony.

What distinguished the Meiji period Japanese from their Tokugawa forebears is that the latter had felt secure enough to expel all foreigners. That is, their sense of self-sufficiency and military strength was great enough to feel that they could afford to be bad hosts. They could lock their doors and know that their house would remain safe. With the appearance of technically advanced American warships in their ports, this confidence evaporated. Japan had never—not even once—been conquered in more than a thousand continuous years of its imperial heritage. China's several attempted invasions had ended each time in failure. Korea had never been a real threat. The ocean surrounding the Japanese archipelago was simply too unpredictable, too rough, too much an ally for the islands. The ocean *kami* or spirit powers were too much on Japan's side. But by the mid-1800s, it was clear that this invulnerability had somehow been dissolved. The culprit was not any shortcoming on the part of Japanese culture or an explicitly changed relationship with the *kami* (spirits), but Western innovations in the technologies of naval transport, navigation, and artillery.

It would be interesting to explore in depth what has happened to Japan and Japanese culture in the century and a half since the Meiji Restoration, especially in light of Japan's eventual colonial aspirations and her alliance with Nazi Germany. That, however, would take us very far afield. What is important for us in Japan's re-opening to the West is that it marked an explicitly Faustian bargain in which Japan was banking on the resilience of her own native values to carry the day. It was not that the goals and glories of Western Europe and the United States had suddenly revealed themselves to the Japanese as the natural pinnacle of human development. To the contrary, it was to eventually safeguard themselves from the patterns of these values that the Japanese opened their ports and began sending their brightest young men to study in the West. In short, they banked on being able to ferret out from their enemy's house what they needed in order to preserve their own. Whether they have actually succeeded or have instead been co-opted or colonized by the values underlying Western technology is arguable. What is clear is that traditional Japan no longer exists and that corporate Japan—for all the unique traits it brings to management and the bargaining table—has an overwhelming family resemblance to corporate Germany, corporate America, and so on. The simple fact that "Japaneseness" has become something to preserve—and among young people just one fashion among many others—suggests that Japan's bid for retaining its unique freedom has proven no more successful than Faust's.

The importance of all this for our conversation is that it forces us to allow—contrary to both the prejudices and rhetoric of our own tradition—that the kind of rampant technological proliferation seen in the West since the 1700s (and since the early twentieth century throughout much of the rest of the world) is *not* a function of natural, environmental pressures. Nor is an overwhelming focus on technological development a natural or spontaneous function of human evolution generally—something that occurs whenever cultures reach a sufficient level of sophistication. While the uncritical familiarity we have with our own lifestyles makes it hard to admit, there is nothing necessary about the kind of technological advances on which these lifestyles so largely depend. Instead, the proliferation of Western technologies is crucial only to the triumph of the view—the system of values—that says increasing independence from and control of our environments promises increasing personal and societal freedom.

The burgeoning interest throughout most of the "developing" world in high-tech manufacturing and communications is not proof of their inevitability or inherently positive and progressive nature. To the contrary, this interest is a function of the extent to which the proliferation of Western, individually beneficial tools has insinuated into virtually every culture on the planet a bias toward values proper to the Western traditions of autonomous selfhood and freedom through prescriptive control. Unchecked, this will mean the extinction of forms of conduct that have supported viable, aesthetically rich and creative communities for thousands of years. Seen strictly in terms of their artifacts rather than as unique patternings of conduct or communal narration, these cultures may well "survive"—preserved as tourist draws and through museum exhibits—but they will no longer be truly viable.

INDEPENDENT VALUES, THE VALUE OF INDEPENDENCE, AND THE EROSION OF TRADITIONS

When a value is abstracted from the culture in which it originated, it will not typically maintain its original meaning. That is, values put into circulation in an axiological economy do not necessarily carry along with them their ability to meaningfully orient the movement of our narration. To the contrary, as a free radical, even the value of familial relationships may serve to undermine rather than enhance communal health—as is arguably the case with the rampant trade in so-called family values or the independent value of "choice" in contemporary American political discourse. Indeed, such independent values may serve to distract attention from the cultural context into which they are being imported in a quite dysfunctional way, with the result that the traditional system of values expressing and expressed by a particular cultural orientation is itself no longer properly nurtured and suffers a loss of both suppleness and vitality. Such an erosion of traditions of value has become epidemic in the media-rich environments of the "postmodern" world where attention has become the single most important commodity in the global market.

There are, of course, cases in which independent values are absorbed by a culture and come to a positive role therein. But such cases are, by and large, quite rare and not the result of mass mediation. Again, mass media encourage a commodification of values, transforming precedents for the meaningful orientation of conduct into simple goods that are traded and relativized much like any other products of the fashion industry—an industry that conditions everything from what we eat to what we wear and what we read, from whom we claim as heroes or denounce as villains to whom we vote for or dream of marrying. Because the circulation of such values is useful only when maximum attention is funneled through a minimal "space," there is a kind of resistance to system-building, to long-term coordination and resonance. In short, such values typically discourage concerted practice in favor of immediate gratification. Trying to increase the overall resilience and creative responsiveness of a system of values by randomly importing abstracted alternatives is like trying to increase our flexibility through random stretching. What works for our bodies is a daily, systematic practice like Hatha yoga or T'ai Chi Ch'üan. Our communities and cultures are no different. We might like to imagine that improvisational virtuosity comes about through random activity, but this is simply not so.

With the weakening of our indigenous systems of value, media-advertised alternatives often start looking better and better. It is no accident that it is in the most intensely mass-mediated societies that the appeal of the so-called new religions has been most widespread. Whether the system is a take on fundamentalist Christianity like the Branch Davidians, or on Hindu-Buddhist ideology like Om Shinri Kyo, or encounter group psychology like est or Scientology, it allows people whose native systems of value have been disrupted to acquire the means of rendering their worlds coherent. The selling points vary from system to system, but it is coherence that all these point toward—the sense of things falling into place.

On the face of it, unless we're willing to set up some hierarchy of value-systems whereby we can discriminate worthy ones from unworthy ones, this proliferation of not just freestanding values but alternative value-systems would seem to be a good thing. At the very least, it would seem to promote a kind of pluralism; perhaps even a sort of multiculturalism. It would, that is, except for the fact that the condition of this proliferation is an increasing monopoly on attention by the value of the media and our technological lineage as such, independent of their program content and ultimate purpose.

We can say, then, that the commodification of values itself expresses a value—that of individually centered control over the content of our experience. It renders both economically and politically expedient the disengagement of values from the patterns of meaningful interdependence to which they were originally native—patterns not only among the various members of a community, but between that community and its human and other-than-human contexts. As commodities, values can be readily preserved, but only because they have been rendered dramatically sterile—incapable of taking part in the improvisation of meaning.

Among the independent values now in general circulation, none has a greater potential for cultural destruction than the value of 'independence'. That is hard for us to accept, given that independence is one of the seminal values of our tradition. And that is precisely why we are so naive when it comes to the effect it has on cultures where it has never been prominent. Our technological lineage is geared to increasing our capacity to control our circumstances, to individually dictate the terms of our experience. The media may be practically ubiquitous, but because the technologies on which they depend assert the value of individual control, we do not have the impression that this ubiquity in any way causes a "leveling down" of our capacities for attention and personal satisfaction. To the contrary, we think of ourselves as making independent use of the media to "inform" ourselves, to make contacts, to keep abreast of things, to preserve our basic rights and freedoms.

But consuming values that have been preserved for free circulation in the global economy is not the same as engaging in the development or cultivation of meaning. For this reason, the colonization of consciousness is very good for business. Because it depletes our resources for meaningful engagement with our immediate context, the colonization of consciousness taking place primarily through our addiction to mass media leaves us very hungry. And the hungrier we are, the less discriminating our "cultural palate." We will simply take what is given. In the end, the media benefit by our attention, our time, regardless of what we are attending through them. In this case, it's not what we read or listen to or watch or "surf" the Internet in search of that provides the leverage for our colonization, but simply how much time we dedicate to doing so. Pluralism is at bottom simply beside the point.

How legitimate, then, can we consider the claims that media foster multiculturalism? Because mediated knowledge is not so much nurtured and grown as simply consumed, the mediately imported values of other cultures change us only incidentally. We can, for instance, eat rice on a daily basis without ever undergoing the kind of cultural transformation that the Chinese and Japanese each did with their importation of wet-field rice cultivation. Their lives changed dramatically and with them their values, their arts, and the structure of their communality. As mere consumers of rice, we are not so moved. The meaning of a life is never altered by what is consumed in its support, but only by what is nurtured and hence related with in full interdependence. It is caring for the rice that altered the Japanese and Chinese, not just eating it.

Because the structure of mass mediation biases our awareness in an iconic direction—that is, away from actual things and toward mere representations or signs—it powerfully and yet "invisibly" prejudices us against truly caring. Far from promoting a marriage of cultures, the media promote only the factual juxtaposition of abstractly preserved cultural values among which we can choose as freely as we want precisely because they are dramatically weightless. It should be no wonder, really, that the colonization of consciousness brings about an increasing orientation of our awareness and conduct away from intimate appreciation toward the decisiveness of control. As we shall see in coming chapters, the consequences of this are dire enough—the depletion of what it takes to meaningfully, and not just factually, resolve our conflicts and troubles. But more tragically still, we are at the same time being depleted of the capacity for even noting the loss.

Part Two

Practicing the Unprecedented:
A Buddhist Intermission

Chapter 7

Appreciative Virtuosity

The Buddhist Alternative to
Control and Independence

Thus far, we have been taking a rather long view of our technological lineage and its consanguinity on one hand with the dominant streams of Western thinking about the nature of personhood, freedom, and salvation, and on the other with the precedents for and practice of colonialism. Such a perspective, by rewriting the history of the future toward which we are apparently accelerating, is useful in bringing about a realization that our narratives regarding technology have been deeply prescriptive—as much a function of our prejudices and presuppositions as of what we refer to as "facts" about "the way things are."

But, it is the nature of long views to tend toward the abstractly general and away from the immediate—that is, to be more theoretical than practical in nature. In the second half of our conversation, we will be looking much more specifically at the ways in which our preferred technologies affect the structure of our awareness and our manner of community. As a way of bridging the gap between our more abstract and our more immediate concerns, I would like here to explicitly consider the relevance of the Buddhist middle way both as an ethics of resistance to the colonization of consciousness and as a source of concepts particularly suited to evaluating the extent of our present complicity in the market-driven canonization of ignorance and its most tragic consequence—the institutionalized replacement of meaningful resolutions of conflict and suffering by merely factual ones.

LIBERATING INTIMACY:
A NEW COPERNICAN REVOLUTION

Along with the Four Noble Truths, the Eightfold Path, and the teaching of *paṭicca-samuppāda* or interdependence, the teaching of the three marks or *lakṣaṇa* has been considered to be of critical importance in every Buddhist tradition of teaching and practice for the past twenty-five hundred years. It also provides a particularly fruitful point of entry for articulating an explicit and responsibly Buddhist understanding of the proper orientation of technology.

According to the teaching of the three marks, all things—all *dhamma*—can be characterized as impermanent (*anicca*), as absent of any fixed essence or self (*anatta*), and as troubled or troubling (*dukkha*). These "marks" should not, however, be understood in existential or ontological terms. That, after all, would put us in the self-contradicting position of asserting that while all things are without any fixed nature (*anatta*), they are inherently and necessarily 'impermanent', 'troubled', and 'self-less'. Hence the Buddha's frequent insistence that he does not take a stand on either 'is' or 'is-not' (*Saṃyutta Nikāya*, V. 752–53), these constituting the twin barbs on which all humankind is impaled. Far from making ontological or existential assertions, the teaching of the three marks directs us to see things *as* impermanent, self-less, and troubling. That is, it instructs us to flexibly alter the scale, perspective, and horizons of our perceptions in such a way as to free things from our conventional and largely uncritical identification of them as definitively either 'this' or 'that'.

At the same time, resisting our own habitual modes of perception is to stop taking a stand on whether things *are* good or bad or indifferent and to recognize our irrevocable intimacy with all things. Freeing things from our habitual views of them is to free ourselves from these very same views—a liberation from the twin barbs of 'me' and 'not-me', 'self' and 'other'. Because consciousness and so attention are seen in Buddhism as irreducibly relational, freeing ourselves from our habitual ways of attending is to free ourselves from the kinds of relationship constitutive of who we have been—a way of liberating ourselves from our previous and often fixed identities. To liberate others is to liberate ourselves.

The teaching of the three marks, like the Four Noble Truths—which at once include and are included by the Eightfold Path—must be seen, then, as at once theoretical and practical, both heuristic and healing. For instance, seeing all things as impermanent does on the one hand alert us to the ephemeral nature of all pleasure, the fragility of all security, and the provisional nature of all knowledge. But it also enables us to realize that no situation is intractable, that no barrier is absolute. Recognizing and appreciating the impermanence of all things is to attend as fully as possible to their fathomless dynamism. It means consciously making an effort to sense things from different perspectives and on different scales. After all, a mountain and the rock it comprises can seem permanent if seen through a sufficiently restricted temporal window or from a sufficiently great distance. Likewise, a diamond can seem unchanging if we abstract it from both its molecular dynamism and way in which the quality of its "fire" changes as light passes through it at different angles. At a deeper level, however, seeing all things as impermanent is also to see that no relationships are fixed and that the very process of their transformation involves the continuous release of energy—a ceaseless radiance of potency. Granted this, there can be no lack of energy immediately available for redirecting the meaning or movement of our narration, for reorienting the dramatic nature of our interrelatedness.

Attending to the selflessness of all things means realizing that no 'thing' (including impermanence or change itself) is either universal or independent. If all things are without any abiding essence, there can be no such thing as truly eternal laws—something modern cosmologists are only beginning to be ready to admit. For the Buddhist, selflessness means that nothing really exists—that is, nothing stands alone and apart, self-defining and self-subsisting. All things support and condition each other. So thorough is this participation of each thing in all other things that the notion of identity becomes highly problematic—a matter of convention.

A mango tree, for instance, is not just the trunk, limbs, leaves, and fruit that we see before us. It includes also the roots sunk deep into the surrounding earth, and that earth itself since this is drawn up into the roots along with water to create bark and chlorophyll and sap. A mango tree also embodies sunlight and wind and rain. It expresses gravity since without it the differentiation of trunk and branch would make no sense. And because the gravity in which it grows is a function of the entire planet's curvature of space-time, a tree also focuses the mass of Earth and its relationship with the Sun, the Moon, and the other eight planets and their satellites. From this very spot on the island of O'ahu to the furthest galaxies, there is no hard and fast line where the mango tree ends. In attending to the selflessness of this mango tree, we must also recognize that it is not only boundary-less in space, but in time. It includes not only the fruit just beginning to ripen on its limbs, but the generations that will spring from it and those to which its genetic makeup give tangible expression. No tree is truly restricted to the present or to this or that location. Ultimately, each mango tree gives expression to all things. And yet, precisely because of their emptiness, no two things—or even the same thing at different times—can be the same. Uniqueness is irreducible and yet completely unfixed. There is no ground zero, no substance underlying all change.

Finally, the teaching of the three marks enjoins us to appreciate that all this, right here and now, can be characterized by *dukkha* or what I have translated as "trouble." *Dukkha* is a Sanskrit term that has typically been translated into English as "suffering"—a highly unfortunate choice that has led many to assume that Buddhism is fatalistic and negative. In fact, the root meaning of *dukkha* is simply a wheel with an off-center axle hole. Since a cart with an off-center wheel will continually and at times even violently bounce us, even on the smoothest road, a more vernacular alternative to "suffering" would be "a pain in the ass." Saying that all things are marked by *dukkha* is actually saying that they are always going out of kilter, always jolting us, always insisting on our attention. In this sense, all things can be seen as troubling—a word deriving from the same root as "turbulence"— because they tend to interrupt our chosen narratives in unpredictable and surprising ways.

But seeing all things as troubling means as well relinquishing our habitual horizons for relevance in order to become increasingly and compassionately aware of the full "costs" of our pleasurable experiences—say, eating a chicken sandwich from McDonald's or vacationing among the indigenous people of a South Pacific island. It is entirely too easy, through ignorance of our interdependence with all things, to think that 'pleasure' or 'happiness' is something definite and pure and obvious to one and all. For the chicken slaughtered for the sake of our sandwiches or the islanders whose subsistence lifeways have been destroyed by commercialism, our 'pleasure' is far from pleasant. Seeing all things as *dukkha* is not, then, to indulge in unmitigated pessimism, but simply to become critically apprised of the intimate connections between our individual experiences and the full range of conditions sponsoring them.

According to the teaching of the three marks, the turbulent quality of life—its propensity for turning troublesome—has no ultimate or world-transcending basis. Although it is not purely random, change has no set, permanent pattern. It is not teleological—evolutionary in the sense of leading to some particular culmination. Nor is it a function of some original first cause—the playing out of the will or intent of an original Unmoved Mover. Not only is there no destined 'end' of all things, there is no 'beginning.' From the Buddhist perspective, seeing this is good. It means realizing that any inquiry that seeks a final—and so necessarily abstract—solution to our problems is ultimately pointless. But it also means that we cannot assign blame for the suffering we undergo or that which we witness all around us. Like all things, suffering arises in complex interdependence with everything else. Our connection with it should, therefore, always be seen as intimate, involving a responsibility we can disown only at the cost of sedimenting the very conditions of suffering.

Understood as a practice, the teaching of the three marks makes it clear that both the apparent permanence and identity of things and our isolation among them cannot be dissociated from how we attend to them. At bottom, it is a teaching intended to powerfully direct us toward deepening responsibility for our own experience and so for realizing that our interdependence with all things is not simply factual, but irreducibly dramatic. Seeing all things as *anatta* means accepting that they are not inherently 'good' or 'bad', 'salutary' or 'unsalutary', 'important' or 'trivial'. That is, the perceived 'natures' of things—what we take to be their simply manifest identities—are a function of horizons we have established for determining what they 'are'. It is for this reason that Nagarjuna claimed that realizing the emptiness (*śūnyatā*) of all things means relinquishing all fixed perspectives or views (*Mūlamadhyamakakārikā* 13.8). In the context of such a realization, there are no horizons for relevance (*Mūlamadhyamakakārikā* 24.14), and so no limit to our intimacy with and responsibility for all beings.

At the very least, taking seriously the emptiness and interdependence of all things requires us to eschew the extremes of both idealism and realism. It means refraining from seeing relationships as secondary to the individuals, entities, concepts, or qualities "brought into" relationship. Practicing emptiness commits us to seeing all identities or distinctions—whether that of 'self' and 'other' or 'idea' and 'reality'—as more or less purposeful abstractions, not as "atomic" building blocks. The existence of things—their standing apart from one another—is thus something imposed according to our likes and dislikes, our values.

Buddhist metaphysics (if the term is not oxymoronic) is thus not grounded on ontology, but rather axiology. It is what might be termed a metaphysics of ambiguity in the context of which the teaching of nonduality—so important in the later Mahayana traditions and especially in Ch'an and Zen—is not a claim that things *are* fundamentally one as opposed to many, but rather that their original natures should be *seen as* indeterminacy or ambiguity as such. Again, it must be stressed that things are not taken to be originally 'this' or 'that' and only seen as ambiguous because of some epistemic shortcoming on our part. To the contrary, 'this' and 'that'—like 'is' and 'is not'—arise only through our own, value-driven activities of disambiguation, conditioned by our own intentions, likes, and dislikes. The world we live in and the things we identify in it are not discovered, but rather a function of our own doing. That is, all experience arises as a function of our karma—our irreducibly dramatic interdependence.

The Buddhist teaching of karma directs us toward admitting the impossibility of dissociating ourselves from responsibility for our situation. The world in which we live should be seen as a narration—a meaningfully ordered pattern of interrelationship—structured by our own values and intentions. The complexion of things we encounter moment-by-moment is thus a precise index of who we are and have been. We cannot claim, as Heidegger might for instance, that we were simply "thrown" into our current existential situation at birth. If we did not have some karmic connection to the world we witness around us, we would have been born into a substantially different one. It is by way of attending to things in an unwholesome way that we come to live in an unwholesome world, an unwholesome or fragmented narration.

As I'll use the term, "unwholesome" conduct or narrative movement pivots on the making and maintaining of fixed distinctions like those between 'self' and 'other', 'mind' and 'body', 'independence' and 'dependence', 'good' and 'evil', and 'facts' and 'values'. It is, therefore, attention conducive to conflict—to conduct qualified by an ongoing ignorance of the horizonless interdependence and emptiness of all things. Unwholesome attention denies our boundless intimacy with all things and thus depletes our responsive or dramatic resources. In practice, unwholesome attention is conducive to suffering (*dukkha*)—being subject to and not the master of our karma, and so living in a severely disadvantaged world. Unwholesome attention jeopardizes our health.

As exemplified by the teaching of the three marks, Buddhist practice conspires toward a radical dislocation of the self, bringing about a "Copernican revolution" whereby both 'self' as subject and 'other' or 'world' as experienced object are effectively decentered. As I've argued elsewhere (1996), this revolution amounts to seeing ourselves not as a center or lineage of individual thoughts, speech, actions, and their experiential corollaries, but as conduct or the movement of our mutually constituted narration as such. That is, our original nature is neither bodily nor psychic, neither material nor spiritual, but narrative. Indeed, it could be said that our true bodies are not fundamentally compositions of flesh and bone, but stories.

As with the Copernican revolution in astrophysics which did not change our daily observance of the sun "coming up" in the east and "going down" in the west, under mundane circumstances, the difference between living in a karmic or a scientifically realistic world is at best only marginally obvious. But in situations of crisis, when the bounds of normality are thrown into potentially disastrous stress, the differences are considerable. In astrophysics, this happens in plotting the course of an interplanetary or interstellar journey. In our lived experience, it is what happens when we suffer—when we find ourselves driven far from psychophysical equilibrium and narrative continuity by unusual somatic, economic, political, intellectual, or emotional conditions. At such points of disjuncture, we find it necessary to either negotiate a viable path back to our normal way of life or improvise a wholly new narrative out of the conserved elements of our previous lifeways. As might be imagined, the nature of this path—the path of healing—differs dramatically depending on the compass and techniques according to which we orient ourselves in a 'healthy' direction.

One of the central images of Buddhism is that of crossing the ocean of samsara and arriving at the "other shore" of nirvana or enlightenment—that is, a journey from the troubling world to the world as buddha-land. It is openly admitted to be a dangerous crossing—one for which there are no guarantees of completion. Not only do we soon lose the landmarks we've grown accustomed to using as the cardinal points of our life stories, the ocean on which we find ourselves is vast beyond measure and wracked with waves of every size and winds from every direction. According to the Buddhist view, the causes of this turbulence are not rooted in either chance or a fate transcendently dictated by parents, politicians, societal institutions, culture, or god(s). To the contrary, they are understood to be an intimate function of our own intentions—the drama or karma we create through actions motivated by our liking and disliking, our own most tenaciously held values. The topography of our troubles unfailingly mirrors the manner in which we have been constituting the gestalt of our lives—the pattern of our disambiguations.

Since trouble is seen as a function of our own doing, so must its undoing. Buddhist salvation is not about breaking away from the world, but about freeing all things by undoing the dualistic knot of our karma, the stranglehold of our habitually held likes and dislikes. And—especially in the Mahayana Buddhist tradition—since the teaching of no-self entails seeing interdependence as "basic," this undoing cannot be attained or enjoyed individually. Instead, since being is seen as subordinate to value, and things as subordinate to relationships, freedom (like trouble) is never just 'mine' or 'yours,' but only and irreducibly ours.

RESPONDING TO TROUBLE: THE CHARACTER OF BUDDHIST TECHNOLOGIES

Buddhists are no less interested in easing their pain and suffering, their difficulties and traumas, than anyone else. And while the Middle Path taught by the Buddha does recommend that we eschew overindulgence, it also insists on our forfeiting the 'pleasures' of extreme asceticism or privation. In short, it is a path of maintaining balance. No less so than members of any other cultural tradition, then, Buddhists have a need for techniques that will temper the experience of extremity. But, because the turbulence around us—the circumstantial condition of our discontent—is ultimately part of our own doing, Buddhist technologies have tended to resemble those of our most archaic forebears. That is, they have been predominantly social technologies rooted in the training of awareness, the perfecting of attention.

Instead of stressing increased control over our circumstances, Buddhist technology has aimed at opening up our capacity for improvising with and appreciatively contributing to those very circumstances. Rather than focusing on explicitly altering our situation, techniques like sitting meditation, the use of mantra, bowing, and guided visualization are part of a system for reconfiguring the value complexes that implicitly condition the topography of our experience. A fairly close and familiar analogue for this reconfiguration is the "gestalt shift" by means of which what we had taken to be a drawing of a vase reveals itself as two women in conversation. It is not by redrawing the picture that we bring the women into view, but by shifting our way of seeing—by reorienting the values configuring our perception.

For the Buddhist, living in samsara means that more often than not we find ourselves at a dead end from which we cannot exit and yet beyond which we seem incapable of proceeding. Samsara means circling, being locked in or blocked. One way of dealing with this is to try "redrawing the picture"—explicitly altering our circumstances to break through whatever has interrupted our smooth progress. That is the path of societal technology—technology oriented toward regulation and control. But blazing such a trail often takes a great deal of energy and becomes a kind of end-in-itself. Creating a situation that is unambiguously 'good'—however we happen to define that—means configuring it in such a way that alternative constructions or appreciations are maximally attenuated. In the case of the vase and two women picture, we might have to erase certain lines and add others that would make the "vase view" impossible to maintain. In other words, we have to break down certain relationships in our circumstances in order to restrict our attention and the attention of others to the perceptual and narrative movements we prefer.

As with the isolation and subsequent breaking down of, for example, natural forms like coal or wood, this process of isolating and breaking down possible courses for the flow of attention does "release" a certain amount of energy. When we can so conclusively define a situation that it can be seen only in the way we prefer, the attention of everyone involved is focused very nearly as if it were our own. This can work virtual wonders. A classic example is the way the energy and will of an entire people can be galvanized by an external threat. Differences of value and opinion that had previously caused the people's energy to be dispersed in both open and covert conflict are suddenly perceived as petty. United under a single set of shared values, even the impossible can be brought within the reach of such a people.

Such control comes at a great cost, however. Unlike 'things', values—and so our efforts at explicit control—do not remain neatly localized. They operate in concert with all our other values in all our circumstances, often with results we have rendered ourselves incapable of anticipating. For example, values we feel confident in using to guide our conduct in the marketplace do not stay put there. To the contrary, they are more or less rapidly infused into our neighborhoods and our homes. Think of the way parks are now spoken of in terms of their cost-effectiveness or the way our schools embody the economy of mass production.

Perhaps more importantly, the less we consciously attend to the disambiguating effect of our values—that is, the more transparent these values become—the less likely we are to exercise our ability to creatively shift our orientation to work with others and our situation. In a word, success at controlling things is conducive to an attenuation of our capacity for creative adaptation. As long as things go our way, we're fine. But as soon as something—or more likely, someone—behaves in a way that "doesn't fit," we are likely to be lost. Having been rendered apparently unnecessary by our various technologies of ostensive control, we have forfeited much of our capacity to improvise. As evidenced in our public and private lives, when confronted by trouble, our first reaction is to do more of what we've already been doing—effecting greater control, developing and acquiring more tools, more institutions, more laws. In short, when things don't quite go our way, we either add more technical "levers" or apply more force to those we already possess.

In sharp contrast, the ideal Buddhist person—the bodhisattva or "enlightening being"—is said to have an unlimited capacity for skill-in-means (*upāya*). Such a person is able to improvise with any situation to orient it (with a minimum expenditure of force or energy) away from the samsaric toward the nirvanic—away from blockage, stalemate, rigidity, and frustration toward freedom, harmony, flexibility, and joy. The bodhisattva is a virtuoso able to make unprecedented, creative, and aesthetically rich use of what others would deem "mistakes" or "problems." He or she does this not by forcing the situation to change, but by appreciating its unique qualities and drawing them out in an appropriate direction. Thus, the extensive teachings of Ch'an (Zen) Buddhism can all be summarized in four simple characters—*sui shih ying yung*, "accord with the situation, respond as needed."

Crucially, enlightening does not consist of asserting control over the situation, but of discerning what is needed to realize harmony and offering precisely that. For this reason, echoing the *Diamond Sutra*, Hui-neng (the sixth ancestor in the Ch'an lineage) said that a bodhisattva must have "a mind that relies on nothing." Not knowing what will be needed at any time, a bodhisattva must always be able to make do with whatever is present. Relying on anything—on any tool or on any particular view—means opening up the possibility of situations where you will be unable to "respond as needed." Hence the Ch'an Buddhist adoption of the Taoist term *wu-wei*. Often translated as "nonaction," and popularly taken as just "going with the flow," *wu-wei* is more accurately and literally rendered as "[conduct] without precedent." Far from connoting a submission to circumstance, it refers to the kind of spontaneous conduct or virtuosic improvisation that removes all blockages to the natural course of things (*tao*).

We might be inclined to read this as a type of control. Skill, we think, means being able to execute some chosen action both consistently and at will. That is not the Buddhist or Taoist understanding. Tremendous emphasis is in fact placed on not-thinking (*wu-nian*) and not intending—on realizing our own emptiness. From our perspective, improvisation implies ego—some central vantage from which options for movement or response are weighed and selected. Choice remains basic. But in both Taoist and Buddhist contexts, *wu-wei* is explicitly associated with the free circulation of energy or *ch'i*—that is, with a situation in which we need not control a thing because all things are able to take care of themselves. There is order in such situations, but one that is quite literally anarchic—centerless, without any overarching principles or precedents.

The order of the Indo-European cosmos is predicated on the existence of eternal laws or supreme beings. That is, global or cosmic order is conceived as possible only when there is a singular principle or will under which all things and events are gathered. Order implies for us both universality and regularity. In contradistinction, the ordered wholeness of the Chinese cosmos—as delineated in the text and use of the *I Ching*—pivots on the irruption of the unexpected (Hershock, 1991). That is, although it might be formally coherent, a cosmos lacking the unexpected could evidence only limited families of interdependence, with the consequence that meaningful change would eventually be blocked and our situation realized as intractable.

With this understanding of order as background, Chinese Buddhists found it quite natural to actually cultivate uncertainty and valorize improvisational brilliance. Especially in situations of extreme blockage, indeterminacy and improvisational virtuosity constitute indispensable techniques for realizing the interpenetration and harmonization of all things. We are inclined to think that any given trouble can be resolved in only one of two ways: through consistently precedented action, or luck. *Wu-wei* implies neither control nor coincidence.

For most of us, it is natural to think that resolving particularly difficult situations will entail passing through a potentially infinite number of intervening "states" or "stages." Not only is it easy to "get lost" along the way, it is clear to us that crossing such great "distances" requires the marshaling of great amounts of energy. We need power to effect certain transformations. But insofar as power means a concentration of energy, it also means a blocking of the free circulation of that same energy. From a Chinese Buddhist perspective, such a strategy for solving our troubles is not only conducive to our own arrogance and needlessly aggressive in nature, it is doomed from the start. The more power we amass, the less freely energy circulates, the less things take care of themselves, the more we are obligated to act on them, and so on in an endless spiraling that effectively seals us off from simply "according with the situation, responding as needed." By such a strategy, we will ultimately only succeed in crossing every threshold of utility with what is finally self-destructive vengeance.

Buddhist technology, then, is not about manipulating things in order to alter our circumstances. The early Buddhist doctrine that desire be extinguished is actually an injunction to resist segregating who we are and what we want by projecting 'aims' and 'goals'—the objects of our desiring. Ch'an master Lin-chi's suggestion that we should "kill the 'Buddha'" if we meet him on the road is a purposely iconoclastic way of saying that we should refrain from establishing any horizon between ourselves and enlightenment, our world and the buddha-land. Once such horizons are established—once we take enlightenment to be a state (of consciousness, bliss, liberation, etc.) to be attained—the free circulation of energy is blocked. Things begin running down, stagnating, decaying, no longer capable of "taking care of themselves." Buddhist enlightenment is not a state, but an orientation.

Instead of concentrating on building a perfectly predictable or orderly world, Buddhist technology emphasizes training ourselves to creatively appreciate—literally impart value to—whatever is present. It is concerned not with 'things' or 'situations', but the direction in which our narration is moving. Practically speaking, this means opening up an unprecedented and "distanceless" path between any present trouble and the harmonious interpenetration of all things. Indeed, if there can be said to be a basic principle of Buddhist technology, it is that of healing—returning every thing or situation that has become blocked or separated into intimate community with everything else.

And so, while technologies of control impoverish the world by systematically decreasing its ambiguity and capacity for spawning the unexpected, the inverse, social orientation of Buddhist technologies is world-enriching. They are productive of an order that is organic rather than mathematical, improvised rather than regulative, intimate rather than universal. Whereas our technologies have disposed us toward taking the world to be a system of things over which we exercise dominion or willful control through the concentration of power, Buddhist technologies represent a commitment to responding—or perhaps better yet, corresponding—with all things. They open up the way of uninhibited, unhesitating offering. Instead of freedom being identified with an absence of restrictions on our ability to choose this or that, Buddhist freedom is understood in terms of virtuosity as such—virtuosity in the art of contributing.

TECHNOLOGICAL DIFFERENCE: THE CASE OF HEALING

At this point, I would like to become somewhat more concrete by looking very broadly at the way our technological lineage biases health care and to sketch out a Buddhist alternative. Today, the most commonly invoked understanding of health refers us to the state of an organism with respect to its functioning, disease, and abnormality at any given time. More positively, health consists of the optimal state or functioning of an organism. According to this understanding, health can be effectively measured by taking vital signs, running tests on various body fluids, mapping the interior organs through one or another scanning technology, and so on. Disease and abnormality are seen as irregularities and as disturbances of (perhaps threats to) the continued balance and integrity of the organic system. While it is recognized as possible to prevent excessive exposure to disease agents like germs or carcinogens and so minimize the risk of illness, the onset of a disease is seen as an "accidental" or purely "circumstantial" invasion.

By contrast, a generally Buddhist understanding of health refers us directly to the quality of the relationships interweaving an organism and its environments, and the role of karma—the active expression of dramatic values—in their co-origination. If who we are is not precisely located—one of the implications of the new "Copernican revolution" outlined above—then there is no real precedent for thinking of health as the property of an individual organism in isolation from its customary environments. To the contrary, granted the interdependence and emptiness of all things, *health should not be seen as a condition or status of any individual body or mind, but rather as the orientation of an entire situation.* That is, health obtains in our conduct as such—in the movement of our narration or dramatic interrelatedness. To speak of a healthy person is thus to speak about conduct exhibiting a virtuosic capacity for responding to challenges in a meaningfully appropriate way.

Consider what happens when a child goes to the playground on a hot summer day. If the day is hot enough and the game interesting enough, she may well suffer from some degree of dehydration. From the prevailing medical perspective, this is a health risk defined by the state of the body when its loss of fluid in the cooling process outpaces the reserves and intake of fluid in a degree severe enough to involve overheating the body. Taken to an extreme, this can mean a fainting collapse or even an entire systemic breakdown resulting in death.

From a Buddhist perspective, this familiar explanation is at best only partial. Dehydration is not fundamentally a state of the body, but rather a particular quality of relationship "between" the child and her situation— one characterized by the absence of thirst-quenching conduct. Dehydration marks a breakdown of communication and understanding such that the child is attentively isolated from her environment—that is, the fruition of unwholesome relationship. The possible reasons for this absence and break- down are virtually limitless. It might be that she knew she was getting hot and thirsty but didn't want to stop because she was on the verge of beating a long-standing rival. Perhaps she didn't notice her need for water because she was thinking of an argument with her father and "unconsciously" pun- ishing her body as a way of punishing him.

Whereas the current medical view sees these "circumstantial" condi- tions as incidental to the direct causes of dehydration and treats the child ac- cordingly, a Buddhist perspective insists on taking them fully into account, especially the roles played by attention and intentionality. We are not bodies *and* minds, or individuals *in* environments, but rather patterns of dramatic interdependence out of which it is possible to abstract mindful bodies and their surrounding environments. What must be cared for are not separate 'somatic' or 'psychic' conditions, but the narrative out of which these are ab- stracted only as a matter of convenience and convention.

Again, it must be stressed that Buddhist teachers—not unlike the prag- matist G. H. Mead—have always insisted on seeing consciousness as given directly in conduct or meaningful interrelatedness and not as a faculty of an organism as such. That is, consciousness is not located in our individual brains or bodies, but rather in the relationship out of which 'brain', 'body', and 'environment' have for this or that reason been more or less abstracted. Thus, identifying ourselves with some ostensibly 'private' stream of experi- ence that we individually manage to the best of our ability is a root form of unwholesome attention and so health-compromising conduct—a willful ig- norance of our irreducible interdependence and intimacy with all things.

As a capacity for responding to challenges or crises—a quality of atten- tion—health cannot be any more specifically or essentially located than our selves. For this reason, it is impossible to disentangle karma for fouling or stressing our environment, from karma for fouling or stressing our selves. Ig- noring our environment—whether out of simple inattentiveness or out of the belief that we can control matters if they get out of hand—is indistinguish- able from ignoring or neglecting ourselves.

An immediate implication of such a view of health is that no illness can be seen as purely accidental—a matter of dumb, bad luck. In fact, what we call "accidents"—whether slipping on an icy walk, or catching a cold, or be- ing hit by a car running a red light—should be seen as evidence of patterns of unwholesome attention conducive to a dangerously unresponsive relationship with the situations in which we find ourselves. By ignoring ourselves or our environment, we are in fact compromising *both* our capacity for responsive virtuosity *and* the capacity of our environment to meet our immediate and ongoing needs. Moreover, any treatment that does not enhance our responsive virtuosity is finally counterproductive since it legitimates our continued ignorance.

Medicine Kings and Lords of Healing in the Buddhist Canon

In the Buddhist canon, there are numerous occasions where buddhas and bodhisattvas are spoken of as "physicians" or even "medicine kings." Typically, such enlightened or enlightening beings are not engaged in recognizably medical practices. To the contrary, their capacities as healers seem to stem most directly not from specifically medical knowledge or techniques, but from a profound vow or offering of healing attention. According to the sutras, simply hearing the names of these buddhas or bodhisattvas and treasuring the sutras in which they are mentioned is to be already freed from all difficulty and suffering.

A classic example is the *Bhaishajyaguru Vaiḍūryaprabhā Tathāgata Sūtra* (BVTS): The Sutra of the Azure Radiance Tathagata or Lord of Healing. The overall form of the sutra is a common one. The historical Buddha relates the compassionate intentions and deeds of the Azure Radiance Tathagata for the benefit of a particular audience, focusing on the miraculous power of his vows "to tear off from beings . . . the fetters of the karma which bind them . . . and to make them happy" (BVTS, p. 2). A description of the Lord of Healing's buddha-realm is given in sensuous detail and a further recounting of the healing effects of even just hearing this buddha's name.

To the contemporary reader, it is difficult to not view both the content and claims made about such sutras as simply fantastic. And, indeed, the worlds into which such sutras introduce us are very unfamiliar. The advent of a buddha or bodhisattva is accompanied by a total transformation of the world experienced in terms of 'birth' and 'death', 'subjects' and 'objects', 'is' and 'is-not'. Flowers rain down on perfumed breezes. The sky itself is a great opal in which pearl-like clouds drift and take on shapes of mythic beauty. The dust kicked up by walking there glistens with diamond light; jeweled fruit trees shade one's path; cool streams of ambrosial wine gurgle down resonant mountainsides in orchestral harmonies at once seen and felt.

This is not a slow, steady transformation in which first the earth and then its creatures and then the sky under which they move are successively redeemed, but a total gestalt shift from *saṃsāra* to *nirvāṇa*, from the world of pain, illness, old age, and death to a paradise in which all things do the great buddha-work of enlightenment. The advent of a buddha or bodhisattva is the birth of a new kind of place, the realization of horizonless harmony, the absence of unresolved conflict or ill, the healing of an entire world.

It is tempting, but unfair, to dismiss such accounts as metaphoric flights of fantasy, as simple fictions aimed at the production of faith. The bodhisattva stories help bring about a sensory anticipation of the perfection of offering and commitment—a realization of what it *means* to live as a bodhisattva or buddha. The injunction to continually reflect on, cherish, and hand down the sutras in which these stories figure is an encouragement to reconfigure one's attention and ceaselessly express the *meaning* or truth of enlightenment—to fully embody one's buddha-nature. In effect, this means a radical reorientation of one's karma based not on a belief in something greater or more powerful, but a believing that such a truly wholesome world can be realized: an enlightening and compassionate resolve. This is the arising of *bodhicitta*, the advent of a truly healing regard for all things.

What we must question is not whether such tales *are* true, but what it would mean to see them *as* such, what transformation of attention must occur for such tales to become a part of our own narration, and how such a transformation figures into the healing process. Entering into the narrative space of a bodhisattva or buddha-realm constitutes a very real reorientation of perception and so a way of establishing—no matter how subtly—a new karma, and thus the seeds of a new way of being human, a discarding of habitual modes of attention in which 'good' and 'bad', 'food' and 'poison', 'friend' and 'enemy' have been held rigidly apart. As the lay bodhisattva Vimalakirti insists, in a true buddha-realm even feces, urine and noxious odors do the enlightening work of a buddha. This means realizing that every problem, seen from some other perspective, is already a solution to yet other problems. Taking the tale of the Azure Radiance Tathagata *as true* is to move in the direction, not of changing one's factual situation directly, but of realizing the depths of its dramatic resources and negotiating a meaningful resolution of any difficulties therein. Most generally, it means reconfiguring the patterns of our interdependence in such a way that what was intractable and productive of suffering is so no longer—the realization of truly wholesome attention.

The Disparate Karma of Factual and Dramatic Healing

We have taken a very different route. Compared to ages past, even the most humble members of our society are marvelously capable of getting what they want. Technology has made it possible for us to manipulate everything from the climate in which we live to the structure of our genes. Through television and the Internet, we're able to virtually experience different worlds and peoples on demand. Compared to the latest product of the Hollywood film industry, the Sutra of the Lord of Healing is repetitive and boring, and we have become expert in banishing not only boredom, but an unimaginably wide array of illnesses and afflictions. Still, we are *not* free of boredom, suffering, and sickness. We do not live in a buddha-realm. Given the almost limitless and constant control we routinely exert over our circumstances and experience, this should be surprising. That it is not borders on tragedy.

While it is arguably foolish to blindly regret or forfeit the control we have earned over the factual dimensions of health and healing, from a Buddhist perspective, it is just as patently foolish to ignore the possibility that the brilliance of our "success" might also constitute a kind of blindness. Karmically, the dilemma is this: *the better we get at getting what we want, the better we get at wanting; and the better we get at wanting, the better we get at getting what we want, though we won't want what we get.* Gambling, drug addiction, and sexual obsessions are classic cases of short-term—and thus relatively visible—karmic complexes of this type. But at a different scale, the same sort of thing takes place with the advance of any control-biased technology. Carried out consistently enough, solving problems through exerting control is conducive to sedimenting karmic cycles that include a phase of generating further, slightly different problems. Thus, societies with the highest average speed of transportation are those in which the greatest amount of time is spent traveling, and those with the most advanced medical care are those in which the average person receives the most medical attention. For better or worse, skillfully wanting control means not only that there will never be a dearth of things to control, but that control itself as a guiding value of conduct will become increasingly ambient. The "cyclic" nature of karma thus virtually guarantees that phases of being in control will be matched by phases of being controlled.

As the reference to addictions and obsessions suggests, such karmic cycles are not at all foreign to our experience. But the idea that a parallel can be established between the underlying principle of addiction and that of technological progress is intellectually and mythically repugnant. Addiction, after all, is commonly understood as a sickness that distorts reality and erodes the individual will and sense of responsibility. If the same were true of our relationship with technology, we would be forced into questioning both the myth that through science and technology we are "zeroing-in" on the way things really are and the dream that they will eventually free us from all harm and suffering. Nevertheless, sufficient empirical evidence obtains to make such questions imperative.

For example, in *Limits to Medicine: Medical Nemesis: The Expropriation of Health*, Ivan Illich builds a strong case to the effect that while it is true that the average life expectancy has risen steadily over the past century and the mortal dangers of infectious diseases have diminished in similar degree, there is no evidence for significantly attributing these changes to widespread institutionalized medical diagnosis and treatment. To the contrary, it would seem that these gains in general public health are most strongly correlated with simple sanitation practices, not sophisticated medical ones. Illich goes much further, however, to detail the specific counterproductivity of current medical practice and the rise of an epidemic of iatrogenic—or "physician-originated"—illness. Having crossed over its particular threshold of utility, current medical technology has begun to produce, not alleviate, illness. "The medical establishment," he concludes, "has become a major threat to health" (p. 11).

Karmically, there is nothing surprising about this. The more deeply we invest in a pattern of conduct—motorized transportation, for instance—the more successful it will become in its own terms and the more likely it is that we will keep moving in the resulting narrative ruts. Illich's work, however, suggests that we must be meticulous in discerning the particular values or intentions being karmically compounded. Ostensibly, medical practices aim at producing (or perhaps, reproducing) health, but judging by the karmic cycle they induce, it would be more accurate to say that they aim at treating the symptoms and proximate material causes of illness. The difference is crucial. In actuality, modern medicine has not given rise to unprecedentedly healthy populations, but rather populations that expect (even demand) to be cured.

Without pushing the analogy too far, the difference between curing and healing can be illustrated by reviewing what happens when animal skins are cured and turned into leather. First, the skin must be identified as a separate feature of the animal and abstracted from it. It must then undergo a process that renders it an inappropriate host for any kind of parasite, germ, or bacteria. Finally, it can be shaped according to need. Fully cured, the animal skin has become leather. As such, it can be repaired, but can no longer repair itself. It can be used to absorb shocks, but is no longer capable of playing a role in avoiding them. Substituting "body" or "mind" for "skin," an uncannily accurate picture emerges of what it means to be "cured" by institutionalized medicine.

Instead of bringing about greater self-reliance and so a greater ability to cope with internal and environmental challenges, institutionalized medicine actually precipitates a recession of responsive resources throughout a served population. We become accustomed to saying "yes" or "no" to various care options for achieving the goal of "normal" psychophysical functioning, but not to attending our own, always unique circumstances in a more virtuosic and responsive manner. In short, we are training ourselves to be ignorant and—at least from a Buddhist perspective—unhealthy.

Karmically, illness marks at once a breakdown in our narration and an opportunity to discern and revise the conditions of its arising. Granted this, health and healing necessarily take place in a fully dramatic context. The counterproductivity of institutionalized medical care detailed by Illich is a measure, not just of the general and paradoxical inefficiency of technological solutions at a purely factual level, but of the degree to which that "care" has succeeded in diverting attention from our dramatic interdependence to our merely factual coexistence. We may be living longer, but most of the time cannot figure out why we bother.

Healing as Unprecedented Conduct

Sutras like that of the Azure Radiance Tathagata map out an alternative. Whereas the medical expert employs a wide variety of techniques to directly control and normalize somatic and psychic functioning, the Lord of Healing vows to perfect an exceptional and contributory mode of awareness, in this way freeing all beings from the karma for affliction. That is, it is by dedicating all attention to being of service to others that the bodhisattva develops limitless *upāya* or responsive virtuosity—the capacity for bringing any crisis to liberating resolution. True healing, then, begins with the vow for realizing conduct in which we are always *sui-shih-ying-yung* or "according with the situation, responding as needed."

This, however, cannot be a matter of either wishful thinking or will-power. Responsive virtuosity and spontaneity, whether going under the name of *wu-wei* or *upāya* or beginner's mind, are not realized directly. In fact, there is no greater impediment to responsive spontaneity than trying to be spontaneous. Instead, the bodhisattva diligently and systematically dissolves his or her karma for thinking, speaking, feeling, perceiving, and acting in unsurprising ways. Only in this way can all things—that is, all relationships—be oriented toward a truly liberating intimacy.

According to the early Buddhist tradition, our karma is not understood as being carried or transmitted by an essential and eternal self, but by dispositional complexes or *saṃskāra*. These consist of habitual configurations of attention-energy that, unless dissolved or otherwise countered, determine the course of our thoughts, emotions, speech, perceptions, and deeds—our relationships. On the one hand, our *saṃskāra* are quite useful—we would be unable, for example, to drive a car and carry on a conversation at the same time if the patterns of attention involved in safe driving had not been reliably formed into abiding dispositions. On the other hand, it is also a *saṃskāra* to become defensive in the face of criticism, and that can lead to both very slow learning curves and a great deal of unproductive and unnecessary interpersonal conflict. It follows, then, that if we are to accord with any and all situations and respond as needed, our attention-energy must be able to circulate freely. We must become aware of and capable of dissolving our *saṃskāra*.

This is the root function of meditation training—not to precipitate *experiences* of liberation, but to bring about the possibility of truly liberating *conduct*. By systematically diverting attention-energy from its accustomed pathways or *saṃskāra*, meditative training brings about the atrophy and eventual dissolution of our "natural/habitual" patterns of thinking, feeling, speaking, and acting. Responsive and healing virtuosity—like bodily flexibility—thus arises as the "surprising" result of discipline and not through deciding to "go with the flow" or doing whatever one feels like at any given time.

At the very least, then, the bodhisattva path of health and healing is a strenuous one of releasing attention-energy bound up in existing dispositional patterns through disciplined training. But since we live in an irreducibly dramatic cosmos, it is not enough that attention simply be released at random. This, quite clearly, would not be necessarily conducive to developing a karma for meaningful and healing virtuosity. The bodhisattva heals by both according with the situation *and* responding as needed, and this implies unconstrained attentiveness to the meaning and not merely the facts of one's circumstances. The bodhisattva's vow to compassionately meet the needs of others should be seen, then, as the practice of unlimited offering or appreciation.

Appreciative Contribution and the Karma of Dramatic Healing

The teaching of karma, enjoins us to see the topography of our (largely shared) experience as a function of our combined and continuing values and intentions. We do not live in a world of purely objective and so essentially independent facts, but rather in an infinitely meaningful and ever-dynamic world. For this reason, "according with the situation" necessarily involves not only understanding one's own karma—the specific nature of one's own desires and responsibilities—but the karma of all those gathered in the narrative present. Doing so is to become apprised of both the present sense of things, their axiological or karmic precedents, and their still-articulating meaning or ramifications. Granted this, "responding as needed" or freely improvising the resolution of any troubled situation or set of relationships must consist of negotiating meaningful paths around any narrative or dramatic blockages and breaks.

Such a horizonless capacity for turning all things to enlightening and liberating advantage depends on attending to and releasing their dramatically healing potential. Keeping the bodhisattva vow thus pivots on a limitless commitment to appreciating the present situation—seeing it as the *bodhi-maṇḍala* or place of enlightenment, the "place" from which the interdependence of all things is dramatically liberating. This kind of appreciation—far from being a passive recognition of the embedded values in a given, karmically configured, situation—is referred to as *dānapāramitā* or the perfection of contribution or offering. It is to at once discern and draw out the value of a situation, immediately recognizing and increasing its worth—an offering of attention through which the enlightening potential or buddha-nature of all things is confirmed and enhanced.

For appreciation/offering to be perfected or unlimited is thus already the co-arising of a buddha-realm, a realm of limitless value and significance. It is for this reason that Hui-neng insisted that "it is precisely Buddhist conduct (*hsing*) which is Buddha." (*Platform Sutra*, 42) The Chinese term *hsing*, translated here as "conduct," is used to refer to both the dispositional complexes (*saṃskāra*) that "transmit" our karma from situation to situation and Buddhist practice (*bhavana*)—the relinquishing of our horizons for relevance, responsibility, and readiness. A buddha, therefore, consists of the entire narrative movement encompassing the stable configurations of attention-energy that condition the topography of our individual and shared experience and the liberating transformation of this karmically constituted world from *saṃsāra* to *nirvāṇa*. In Hui-neng's terms, this is our *pen-hsing* or original nature.

Appreciation can be seen, therefore, as the bodhisattva path of unprecedented creativity and healing. It is a path that differs profoundly from those—like our technologically informed path of performing medical cures—that are biased toward control rather than contribution. To begin with, control excludes the possibility of true sharing—perhaps nowhere more clearly exemplified than in the hospital operating room where one's ability to control one's own body must be anesthetically interrupted for the surgeon to effect a "cure." Rather than promoting a recognition of our interdependence with all things, it promotes the dissociation of the controlling subject, the (often resistant) attention leveraged in the interest of control, and that which is controlled (one's body, one's child, one's situation). At bottom, control is conducive to fixing the boundary conditions of 'advantage' and 'disadvantage'—an unwholesome biasing of attention toward enforcing the disparity of wealth and poverty, the valuable and the valueless.

Because an increasing perception of the value of a situation is already to be more and more valuably situated, appreciation can be seen as reflexive, tending to dissolve rather than sediment boundaries. While you and I cannot both control what is done with a given painting—whether it's hung in my house or yours—there are no limits to how much we can both appreciate it. Indeed, far from my appreciation detracting from yours, they are mutually enhancing. The bodhisattva's contributory virtuosity thus occasions a space for mutual furtherance. The more adept one becomes at responsive and appreciative contribution, the more responsive and appreciative things will become, the more rewarding one's situation. As wholesome or healing attention, appreciation is inseparable from a wholesome and healing environment.

In sharp contrast with the karmic complexion of control-biased modes of healing, the bodhisattva establishes a karma for unlimited and meaningful contribution or offering and so the increasing opportunity for appreciation. It is not just the act of successfully responding as needed that is karmically intensified by appreciation, but the opportunities for so offering our attention. Thus, the perfection of offering (*dānapāramitā*) in Mahayana Buddhism is invariably associated with the practice of emptiness (*śūnyata*) or maintaining a mode of attention conducive to realizing both the openness and meaningful interdependence of all things. The bodhisattva vow is able to bring about a liberating intimacy of all things—the advent of a buddha-realm—precisely because it means relinquishing all horizons for relevance, responsibility, and readiness, having no blockages to the free circulation of attention-energy, no perceptions that do not naturally and spontaneously result in an appropriate and appreciative response. Even when it is not immediately possible to alter a situation's factual complexion in any significant degree, a bodhisattva is always able to negotiate a dramatic path around what would otherwise constitute both factual and meaningful interruptions or impediments. That is, a bodhisattva lives in a world of unlimited dramatic resources. The jeweled fruit trees, the opalescent sky, and the omnipresent flowers and incense characteristic of a buddha-realm denote a wealthy or wholesome attention—a way of being human by means of which the world itself becomes a dramatic treasury.

UNLOCKING THE TREASURY: A MATTER OF WILL OR THE FRUIT OF OFFERING?

For those of us not native to a Buddhist culture, the claims of such a "technology" are likely to seem either a sophisticated kind of superstition or so just so much self-deluding New Age idealism. Buddhist rhetoric may provide an interesting intellectual counterpart to our own tradition, but crassly put—you can't go to the bank with that. As far as we are concerned, changing how we see things—no matter how much it alters the way we feel—cannot actually change *what* we see. If anything, our conviction is that how we see things is usually the single greatest impediment to our finding out what something really is.

For the past twenty-five hundred years, the dominant tradition of Western philosophy has assumed the crucial importance of distinguishing appearance and reality—what we see things *as* and what they actually *are*. For us, values don't actually condition, but rather stand between us and the world. They obscure or color our view. At least since the time of Descartes, the ideal knower in the West is not someone fully and passionately in and of the world, but an observer enjoying a kind of "view from nowhere." Our belief is that only such an observer is able to know things for what they are; and only on the basis of such knowledge can we develop the science and technology needed to leverage the world to our advantage. Developing the appreciative subtlety of our attention may be aesthetically rewarding, but that is hardly practical. It won't put food on the table or mitigate the vagaries of the weather or conquer disease.

In an immediate sense, this is a legitimate criticism. There is no question that simply changing our perspective or values will turn a presently empty table into a Thanksgiving Day feast. But while it's true that no "gestalt shift" can directly put food on an empty table, an appropriate re-orientation might well be crucial to insuring that this "emptiness" doesn't become chronic. Altering our mode of attending things may not cure us of diseases we have already contracted, but what if the ways in which we now cure ourselves is eroding our capacity for resisting "infection" and sedimenting in its place patterns of conduct that render us increasingly vulnerable to illness? From the typically modern point of view, any unexpected and unwanted occurrences are seen as a function of either blind chance or an unfortunate conspiracy of some initial conditions and the operation of universal laws. Our ignorance may be admitted as one of the most typical of such "initial conditions," but in general, the causes of the straits into which we have fallen are understood as being external or other—the world's resistance to our wills. It is this resistance that our technologies are intended to master.

The Buddhist teaching of karma subverts the appearance-reality distinction and the epistemological and technical problematics it engenders. Far from being a function of some inherent recalcitrance on its behalf, the world's resistance to our will reflects conflicts among our own choices and the values they express. Consistently projected and adamantly maintained through the investment of our attention and energy, it is our own values that are coming back to haunt us. Indeed, the world's resistance must be seen as arising in interdependence with our will. In the absence of will, where is there resistance? As mentioned earlier, the very impermanence of all things guarantees that there are no ultimate blockages or patterns of resistance to things getting better. Will and the technologies by means of which we concentrate it are not crucial to freedom, but only to the creation and maintenance of impediments to things freely taking care of themselves—to the institutionalization of our own importance.

None of this is to say that Buddhism recommends leaving things as they are and observing a radically quietist form of existence. That view of matters derives from our presupposition of Being, of individual existence and the possibility and valorization of autonomy. From a Buddhist perspective, doing nothing is simply not an option. Since there is no way that things *are*, but only tendencies for ongoing transformation, there are no excuses for not directing things away from chronic troubles and conflict and toward increasingly intimate harmony. The simple fact that our technological "success" in controlling the effects of catastrophe has been accompanied by an increase of chronic problems is evidence of building karma for unwholesome ways of being human.

Control fascination disposes us to fill our empty table by planting more; storing more during times of surplus; developing fertilizers to increase our yields; undertaking selective breeding to produce pest, drought, or heat-resistant strains of desired plants and animals. If things get bad enough, we will simply resort to stealing from our neighbors or our neighbors' neighbors. In short, we attempt to treat the absence of food by developing techniques that allow us to create a more will-susceptible environment. At every step and at every scale, our belief is that something in our circumstances is out of place and that if we can identify what this is, we can change it or eliminate it. In this way we are convinced we'll not only treat the symptoms of our disease—be it hunger, cancer, inner-city violence, or what have you—but its causes.

Experience should have proven otherwise. We live in a day and time when basic, material poverty is at the highest point—both in sheer numbers and in percentages of the human population—that it has ever been. Contrary to the prejudices and overt propaganda of our technology, the research of Sahlins and others is unanimous in indicting not vernacular, subsistence cultures when it comes to meeting basic human needs for food and shelter, but ours. It is hard for us to believe, for example, that Stone Age peoples worried less about making daily ends meet than we do. We have been indoctrinated to believe that they lived in constant hunger and fear—that the uncertainty of life was overwhelming. In actuality, the uncertainty of life only became overwhelming when circumstantial control became central to our communal lives—when large-scale agriculture and husbandry made enemies of drought, spring storms, "predatory" or "pestilential" species, and so on.

The project of technically mediated control of the environment amounts to bringing about a disjunction of our preferred circumstances from the natural and often unpredictable patterns of things. As we've seen, any measure of success in this project comes at a quantifiable energy-cost. Indeed, we can only "perfect" our situation by creating as impervious a membrane as possible around it—that is, by rendering our circumstances complete. From the perspective of, for example, the Taoist-informed Ch'an Buddhist tradition, such completion means the creation of an ideally closed system of *ch'i* or energy. But as we've already seen, that means an interruption of the free circulation of *ch'i* upon which depends the capacity of all things to "take care of themselves." We, then, will have to take over. Our self-importance will grow. Sooner or later, this cannot but eventuate some form of illness, some dysfunction or degeneration. If blocked *ch'i* is the problem, exerting regulative control will only make matters worse. Any apparent successes will in the end turn out to have been merely complications that locked up even more of the energy needed to realize an actual solution.

Ecology—the most Buddhist of our scientific disciplines—has come to a similar realization through a consideration of the long-range effects of decreased biodiversity. The human "management" of ecosystems is not truly viable. If we do not see a species as a collective of individual plants or animals defined in terms of some genetic essence, but particular way of focusing, circulating, and returning *ch'i*, the function of a new species is to open up a novel pathway (*tao*) for the circulation and offering of *ch'i*, thereby rendering the ecosystems into which it plays both more flexible or responsive to change and more resilient. This latter characteristic obtains because species not only divert the flow of *ch'i* in a unique manner, they "store" and "amplify" *ch'i* in ways useful to other species. The viability of a species is thus not only a function of the unique structural characteristics of its member individuals, but the way in which its nature (*hsing*) or disposing of the movement of *ch'i* plays into the conduct or overall narration of the ecosystem. If a species cooperates with and nurtures the vitality of other species, it will not only survive, but thrive. If one species depletes rather than nurtures the others with which it enters into conduct, it will eventually face starvation. We might say that 'enough' is a basic species value—something control techniques induce us to forget.

Working to create a perfect situation—a situation in which our will or choice finds no final resistance—means that nothing will ever be "enough." It means that everything that remains must be drawn up into or overcome by our assertions. Living becomes an all or nothing proposition. Quite literally, "perfecting" control has the structure of an ultimatum. Thus, the classical Chinese term for arrogance—*tseng-shang-man*—literally means "adding on slowness." Arrogance is being a drag. It is retarding *tao*, hoarding *ch'i* so that it no longer circulates freely.

The kind of gestalt shift proper to Buddhist techniques for ending *dukkha*—for creatively responding to trouble—means resisting our habits of perception, feeling, cognition, and intuition. In shifting from the "vase" to the "two women" view, we are not further defining or limiting the picture— perfecting it—but rather opening up its possibilities. In the most direct way possible, we are promoting a return to the free circulation of energy. Going one step further and trying to sediment or guarantee the persistence of the "two women" would then be going one step too far—leaving the middle path in favor of one extreme over all others. Or in the words of Ch'an, it would be like adding legs to a snake—a difficult and entirely unnecessary labor.

PRACTICING THE DISSOLUTION OF WANTING

This bears reiteration. Creating a private world—a world perfectly responsive to our wills—is to establish the conditions of privation. The more private our situation, the more tightly and exclusively focused the flow of energy becomes, the greater our impoverishment. Increasing control over vicissitude or the irregular patterning of natural energy, to the extent that it is successful, leads to increasing the disjunction of both our world and our selves from their capacity for unprecedentedly "taking care of themselves." That, in fact, is one way of explaining the quantitative disparity between the time and energy expended in vernacular and contemporary industrial-technical subsistence. What we are maintaining is the variety and depth of our technically assisted discriminations—the boundary conditions that attempt to ensure the inviolability of our values.

Because the (at least Chinese) Buddhist understanding of order is one that includes rather than excludes the unexpected, one of the eventual concomitants of private security is a cataleptic *disordering* of the world at large—a decrease in its potential for responsive spontaneity and creative wholeness. That is, exclusively individual gains and control over circumstance promote communal disharmony and inflexibility. In a word, they mean trouble. At the level of our individual narratives, this is practically common sense. The anger and hurt that come from manipulating others for our own ends is no less familiar than the destructiveness that arises with selfishly articulated security and the jealousy it provokes. Our difficulty in seeing that the same principle applies globally is a function of our metaphysics of being and our relegation of relationship to a purely secondary and contingent status.

Presupposing that being is fundamental, it seems obvious that independence or at least integrity is as well. Informed by these basic concepts, we can happily assume that our individual gains are not necessarily someone else's losses. Where that does happen to be apparently the case, we are nevertheless confident that their loss is not our own. We are separate beings with finally incommensurable origins and ends. In the world of the practicing Buddhist, the presupposition of being is systematically extirpated and with it the assumption that privation is a local phenomenon and not something shared in by all. If all things are interdependent, the suffering of any one being is intimate with the lives and fortunes of all beings. The bodhisattva's commitment to liberating all beings is not, in this sense, a form of altruism—an act of conscious self-effacement for the good of others. To the contrary, it arises out of the realization that in actuality there are no 'others'. Thus, Ch'an master Huang-po insists that "wriggling beings and all the buddhas and bodhisattvas are a single body and do not differ." As one who has realized true nonduality, a buddha realizes that all troubles and privations are truly his or her own. A buddha can thus be seen as living in horizonless intimacy—an intimacy liberated from any implication of privacy.

Relinquishing our obsession with objective control and practicing instead the art of seeing things as enlightening and worthy of limitless appreciation directly orients us away from 'things' toward the originally ambiguous narration of which they are but conceptual, emotional, or perceptual abstractions. Things are what they *are* only because our attention has circumscribed them, established at least relatively fixed horizons for their definition. Shifting our attention by relinquishing these horizons is thus our most immediate way of releasing the energy bound up in form. Practicing emptiness—relinquishing our horizons for what is admitted as relevant—is liberating not because we get anything, but because we are removing blockages to the spontaneous and creative circulation of energy by freeing our attention from its customs, habits, and obsessions. Freeing all beings means releasing them from the boundary conditions imposed on them by our values. Thus, in the *Diamond Sutra* (DS, 3) it is said that even though a bodhisattva is dedicated to the liberation of all beings, he or she realizes that not a single being will be liberated. How is this? Because it is the condition of being itself—the condition of having been made to exist or stand apart from intimate interrelationship—that is relinquished.

Relinquishing our horizons for responsibility means, likewise, continually refraining from segregating what I wanted from what is, or what I've done from what chance or fate or the laws of nature have wrought. The teaching of karma insists that ultimately, we cannot "wash our hands" of any aspect of our experience. Ch'an master Hui-neng put it this way: "A true cultivator of the Tao does not see any errors in the world. If you see wrongs in the world, it is your own wrongs that are affirmed. We are to blame for the wrongs of others just as we are to blame for our own" (*Platform Sutra of Hui-neng*, 36) As mentioned above, the teaching of impermanence enjoins us to see that no situation is intractable, not only because change is always possible, but because we are karmically or dramatically intimate with every situation. There are no limits to the reach of our intentions because it is precisely they that have created limitation. Divesting ourselves of limits to responsibility means opening up our situation through the practice of nonduality—on the one hand avoiding any indulgence in the divisiveness of blame and on the other hand responding spontaneously as needed.

Because all things are in constant flux, realizing and maintaining a truly liberating intimacy also entails relinquishing our horizons for readiness—in effect, setting no boundary conditions for service, for our willingness to appreciate others and simply respond as needed. The so-called "sudden enlightenment" school of Ch'an Buddhism initiated by Hui-neng was founded on the realization that complicated techniques are needed only by those incapable of relinquishing their limits to readiness, their reluctance to spontaneously and yet sensitively respond to need. As the public records of encounters between Ch'an masters and their students make quite clear, limitless readiness is incompatible with hesitation and deliberation. In short, relinquishing our horizons for readiness means responding without precedents or calculation, realizing conduct that is truly *wu-wei*.

Together, the relinquishing of our predisposed limits to relevance, responsibility, and readiness constitutes a system out of which arises the true conduct/practice (*hsing*) of Ch'an Buddhism. It is that practice about which Hui-neng remarked that "it is precisely Buddhist conduct/practice that is the Buddha." It is not a practice initiated and carried out for the good of the 'self', but in order to realize the absence of both 'self' and selfishness. Hence the Buddha's declaration that in attaining ultimate enlightenment he did not attain "one single thing" (DS, 22). In actuality, enlightenment consists of conduct in which nothing is held onto, nothing is grasped, and yet through which no one is finally left wanting.

This practice and the various techniques useful in bringing about its realization mark a radical alternative to control-oriented technologies. Even countenancing the possibility of such an alternative means already having undergone a massive paradigm shift—a profound reordering of the way we see the world. More specifically, it means accepting the premise that values precede all definition, all limitation, and hence all being. Making an effort to realize such a technology means at the very least a willingness to put down the current configuration of our likes and dislikes and release the creativity locked up within the horizons they constitute—both in terms of our own attention and of the *ch'i* or energy that they contain or block. Potentially, it means realizing a buddha-land—a realm in which all things do the work of enlightenment or liberation. And because the relinquishing of our horizons for relevance, responsibility, and readiness is a way of realizing our intimacy with all things, it is also to relinquish our selfish association of freedom with independence.

Contrary to the biases of our own presuppositions, the relinquishing of control does not lead to either dependence or wanton activity. Dependence implies subjection to conditions beyond one's direct control and so includes within it the values of 'independence' and 'control'. It is not alternative to, but rather included within them. What we might be inclined to call "random activity" is from Buddhist perspective, always seen as a function of prejudicial values embedded below the threshold of consciousness and so as finally binding rather than liberating. That is, random actions are a function of unacknowledged, past karma. In this sense, randomness is not the opposite of control, but its inversion—a control that has become blind, concealed, and thus wholly imperceptive and unresponsive.

If 'freedom' can be rehabilitated and understood as virtuosic skill in improvising meaningful interdependence, desire need not be seen solely as a cause of frustration—a prime condition for realizing the resistance of the world to our will. To the contrary, to the extent that we travel the path (*tao*) of offering, desire need not connote self-centered attachment or craving. To the contrary, it is a crucial factor in our immediate realization of an unprecedented responsiveness to our situation. Such an understanding of desire is not at all foreign to us. It is that form of emotional engagement by means of which we are led to so fully attend to the desired that we entirely forget ourselves. Holding onto nothing, offering ourselves without reservation, things may freely come and go and there is nothing that is not conducive. For some, this is realized in sublime moments of improvisational music-making or dance. But for most of us, the most familiar and profound site of such liberating desire is in parenthood and truly erotic involvement. It is then that our attention is offered with unconditional freedom and our desiring nurtures rather than announces a need for nurture. Desiring like this, because it elides all the various horizons segregating 'self' and 'other', is not conducive to having (*yu-wei*), but rather not-having (*wu-wei*) or releasing all things. It is the way of ending all wanting.

What does such poetic, even romantic hyperbole have to do with technology? A partial answer is that Buddhism offers us a viable ethics of resistance to the societal dictates of control-biased technology. By emphasizing virtuosic appreciation rather than manipulative discrimination, Buddhist practice does not lead to the extraction of value but its restoration. Instead of breaking down natural relationships to create artificial 'beings' of one sort or another, it conserves those relationships even while deepening them, opening up new dimensions for their meaning. Whereas an orientation toward control seems invariably to lead to a propensity for deliberate or calculated activity and quantitative evaluation, a bias toward appreciation subordinates quantity to quality and deliberation to improvisation. This means at the very least placing working together before what works for either 'me' or 'you'. That is, Buddhist technology is concerned less with measurable results than with shared meaning and purpose.

The doctrine of karma explains our present situation—with all its institutions, accidents, trends, and personalities—as a function of our intention, what we have meant by our actions. When a community loses a sense of shared meaning, the karma binding it together begins dissolving. That is not always bad. Much good can come of breaking down institutions or modes of conduct—narrative movement—that constrain our ability to flexibly and sensitively respond to changing conditions around us. But when control and independence reign as penultimate values, community itself dissolves into generic co-presence. Instead of being characterized by meaningful and mutual contribution, our narratives tend to become increasingly similar and yet insular. Instead of living among neighbors, we find ourselves living beside strangers.

Karmically, it is imperative that we look critically at our biases and see to what extent further inculcating them will make matters better or worse. If the correlation between control and privation is as I've suggested, increasing our control over our internal and external environments will provide us with more and more things, more and more tools, more and more ways of leveraging the world into a more 'pleasing' configuration. What it will not do is improve the quality of our narration. For that, we must jettison our bias for taking things to be objects to be possessed (known) and controlled and move instead toward enhancing the value of all things by attending to and appreciating the infinitely extensive and deep network of interdependence that they uniquely express. Doing so not only liberates these 'things' from the horizons of our private (and privatizing) concerns, but liberates us from those very horizons as well. Otherwise, as the old saying goes, if we continue planting ice, we'll only harvest wind.

Part Three

The Wheel of Dramatic Impoverishment: The Crisis of Community in the Information Age

Chapter 8

Concentrating Power

Are Technologies of Control
Ever Truly Democratic?

Having introduced to our conversation a distinction between the karma proper to technologies oriented toward control and those oriented toward appreciative contribution, I would here like to consider the political ramifications of our technological lineage, asking once again whether it is saving or enslaving us. That is, do our control-biased technologies promote truly democratic equality—something being claimed with great fervor, for example, by zealots of the Internet—or do they help to generically sediment the conditions of political disenfranchisement?

In our earlier questioning of the salvific role of technology, we determined that our control-biased technological lineage has not lived up to its practical promises. Far from freeing us from the need to commit huge blocks of our time and labor for the simple purpose of making ends meet, it has actually managed to radically increase the necessary time and effort involved in satisfying our basic subsistence needs. Moreover, while one of the great selling points of modern, control-biased technologies has been their purported neutrality with respect to prevailing religious, ethnic, political, or social complexions—a benefit to all equally—the development-driven proliferation of such technologies has in actuality been correlated with the exacerbation, not the elimination, of gross economic and political inequality.

If economic status and political influence can be taken as a workable index of power within any given society, the relationship between increasing technological sophistication and the equitable distribution of power would seem to be an inverse one. That is, the more technically "advanced" a society becomes—the more profoundly conduct is shaped by technologies of control—the greater the disparity between the rich and the poor, the powerful and those subject to their technically augmented wills. Thus, the United States not only boasts the highest level of general technical development in the world, but the widest gap between its most and least advantaged citizens. Granted the karmic understanding of all experienced conflict as a reflection of contradictions among our most consistently held values, it does no good to explain these "paradoxes" away by saying that our standards for subsistence have changed or that our "capital investment" in development has simply not yet paid off for everyone. Our much-celebrated ideal of "progress" is itself quite literally a product of our technical tradition, and the unequal distribution of wealth serves as a primary psychological and political force in the race for technological research and development. Neither will it do to appeal to the moral transparency argument and claim that these "paradoxes" are rooted in the greed of particular individuals. The fact that computing technology can be used by large corporations to monitor and direct consumer tastes or by individuals to freely circulate virtual works of art for the appreciation of others does not prove that the technology is morally transparent, but rather that—like each one of us—it is morally complex. Finally, our technological lineage as a whole can be considered neutral in respect of the disparities it apparently occasions in our narration only if the selfish advantages it brings to a select few are not unfailing and faithful reflections of its own deep structure and narrative orientation.

If there were no basic contradiction between promoting control and promoting truly democratic equality, we might do well to continue investing our "capital"—our time, attention, and natural resources—in the venture of realizing technotopia. But there is. If our technological lineage is conducive to the success of those bent on the inequitable concentration and use of power, it can only be because the root values of that lineage tacitly endorse steeply pitched hierarchies of advantage. When the basic value in which we're investing our life-energies and dramatic potentials is the same value that informs the means of our colonization, and when this value is control and this means of colonization involves the strip-mining of our attention, we may be encouraged to dream of democracy and meaningful equality, but that is as far as we will ever get in realizing them.

CONTROL AND THE CONFLICTS OF ADVANTAGE

Appreciation marries us with the focus of our concern, establishing the grounds for a continuing and nonexclusive intimacy. That is, appreciation not only opens up a caring and deeply edifying relationship between us and what we appreciate, it encourages a sense of community with others sharing our sensitivity and concern. Appreciation is not jealous or possessive. To the contrary, it is at root a sophisticated—that is, knowledgeable—mode of contribution. It is an offering of our attention in a way that is conducive to having our expectations surpassed without us getting or coming to possess anything tangible in result. Appreciation opens up our conduct for the circulation of energy and so is deepened by a diversity of viewpoints. Meeting someone whose appreciation runs deeper or more subtly than ours, we are not jealous but gratified. If we so desire, he or she can guide us toward greater intimacy with things by helping us relinquish the customary horizons of our ability and willingness to offer our attention. Appreciation loves company.

By contrast, control not only promotes a deep segregation of actor and acted upon, it polarizes those for whom the reality of control means the fulfilling of want and those whom it simply leaves wanting. Control is in this sense decisive. It implies an intentional and advantage-taking subversion of our interdependence, a severing of our patterns of experienced reciprocity. Mass media have not become pervasive in our lives, for example, because the technologies of which they are a part dispose us to offer our attention in appreciative contribution. To the contrary, it is because they are conducive to the capture of our attention, its colonial redirection, and a radical compromise of our potential for true intimacy.

Control is a kind of possession. At the very least, it means being in command of a grammar enabling us to dictate the narrative future of what we want and assert our own autonomy. Taken to an extreme, it means being possessed by a need to transform all other potentially decisive subjects into disposable objects—a structure of relationship very thoroughly explored in Sartre's writings on existential freedom. At once implied in and expressive of both independence and autonomous choosing, control and the technologies it engenders set up the world as a stage for a contest or contradiction of wills. This potentially violent tension may play out at the level of private versus public interest or more directly between distinct individuals vying for power over some other person or object, some share of available resources, or the movements and so meaning of some state of affairs. Since whomever or whatever I can truly claim to control cannot at the same time be subject to your will, control necessarily entails exclusion.

Naturally enough, we will want to argue with this claim. It announces the basic selfishness of control-biased technology, and while there are signs that selfishness is being increasingly "groomed" for acceptance as a legitimate personal value, it is still a relatively negative value in our society. We may object that control can in a very real sense be shared. For example, my control of humidity and air temperature by use of a heater or air conditioner does not directly contravene your own. At least, not so long as we are in separate rooms, houses, automobiles, and so on. That is, as long as the benefits of control are experienced in relative isolation, a technical bias toward it need not automatically trigger conflict.

This logic has become so much a part of our day-to-day lives that it is wholly unremarkable. Using separate "Walkman" radios or cassette players, we can listen to whatever we like without disturbing each other. Cocooned in our "freely chosen" media, we can be comfortably alone together. But this is really only to say that the conflicted nature of control can be rendered invisible as long as we are able to ignore one another. Simply stated, the logic of our "shared" control involves a radical exclusion of the middle ground of intimate relationship—not a Buddhist logic of emptiness whereby all things are seen as relevant, but a logic of mutual and assertive irrelevance.

That this is not simply a social fact, but a deeply political one, is neatly illustrated by a U.S. Supreme Court Justice's remark that our most basic human right is the right to be left alone (cited in Garfield 1995, 8). Being left alone to pursue our private ends and interests—as long as these do not conflict with similar pursuits by others—is a touchstone of what we mean by living in a democracy. Familiar though it is to most of us, however, the sentiment behind this claim is shocking to members of cultures and societies where human being is irreducibly relational. There, the desire to be left alone is tantamount to a rejection of both community and humanity: a statement of disdain and a refusal to either contribute to our shared narration or accept and appreciate the contributions of others. The right to be left alone is a right to not matter, a right to cultivate literally meaningless difference from those among whom we live and work. Such a right guarantees our freedom from coercion by others, but also a freedom from the responsibilities of caring about and for them. That we perceive this as a political necessity says a great deal about the extent to which what we mean by democratic governance pivots on the management of control and the protection of privacy. It also raises very serious questions about the capacity of a control-biased society to support meaningfully intimate community.

Whenever a control-biased technology seems to sponsor a fully shared power, it does so by isolating our wills—by promoting our universal autonomy and a basic ignorance or turning aside from our dramatic and unique interdependence. That is, such technologies are conducive to ignoring the middle ground in which both conflicts and their meaningful resolution take place. In such conduct, what is focused is not our felt community, but the predominantly factual relationship between our selves, a specific tool, and that aspect of our world that it has been designed to leverage.

As discussed earlier, it is the nature of tools such as televisions and computer terminals that they accomplish what we individually want or we abandon them. Arguing that a technical bias for control does not inevitably produce conflict—and so distinct winners and losers—on the basis of such tool-mediated cases of nonexclusive control is thus to commit a kind of category mistake. Since using a tool takes place along an individually determined vector of intentionality, it can never provide evidence for a *necessary*, and not merely contingent, contradiction of wills. Focusing on tools virtually begs us to appeal to the moral transparency argument, making it impossible to generate a viable critique of any given technology and invisibly obscuring the interdependence of control and conflict. Sadly, if our mediation by tools is ubiquitous enough, we may never even be aware of others with sufficient intimacy for the experience of a contradiction of interests to be possible.

We are perilously close to this point and still flirting. An evening stroll through any of the millions of residential neighborhoods in the country will be the same in one respect—the practically ubiquitous reflection on ceilings and in closed windows of the flickering blue light of television. It is a light of controlled relaxation—a light that fills the terrible and silent void where our intimacies once took place, a place we can scarcely even remember. At the same time as it fills in the space of lost intimacy, however, the television opens a great new space in our lives, a mediated and mediating space without which the pressures of our competition with and control of each other would long ago have resulted in an explosion—a cataclysmic rupture in the movement of our narration. The world to which we are given access via the media—whether uniformly broadcast like television and radio or standing ready and waiting like the Internet, twenty-four hours a day—is a world that allows us to matter as little to one another as we do by raising the volume of our wants to a point that ignoring one another becomes quite unconscious or natural. But this increased volume—the spaces that we visit by way of our favorite sitcoms, soap operas, sports programs, news channels, cartoons, movies, documentaries, and how-to shows—also serves as a "release" for the kind of randomly moving and yet highly compressed attention that results in a society where consciousness itself is being deeply colonized. In short, the media make our kind of 'democracy' possible by sufficiently expanding our present into a fifth dimension of virtuality—the cybernetic space of information—that we can tolerate the meaningless or "Brownian" motion of our attention and the tragicomic karma of being at once in possession of and possessed by control.

In this, we are all equal. Indeed, the rhetoric of equality (or at least "equal opportunity") that characterizes political discourse in the most technically "advanced" societies is perhaps best seen as compelled by and compelling technological development, not as any kind of truly social emancipation. Far from reflecting our increasingly meaningful contribution to each other's lives in distinct appreciation of our differences, equality summarizes what is practically and politically meant by technically achieving the right both to be left alone and leave others alone. That is, equality becomes a political ideal only when our mutual irrelevance has been successfully institutionalized and regulated. In an apparent paradox, political 'equality' functions as a finally discursive value prompted by and promoting the further valorization of control, not as a concursive value alternative to it.

As suggested by the history of rights discourse in the West over the past three centuries and more recently worldwide, 'equality' is quite literally a product of technological development, but one that is destined to remain necessarily and merely virtual. To be sure, the rhetoric of equality can and has been biased along competing communist or capitalist lines, but either way equality itself is held up as a prize won only by excelling in the development and proliferation of technologies enabling our increasing mastery over our personal and societal circumstances. As long as we continue evaluating technologies in terms of the tools they provide us, the duplicitous nature of equality—its function as a mask for the necessarily hierarchic distribution of power in a society technically governed by the valorization of control—will remain quite obviously non-evident.

Control cannot be both universally and privately realized except virtually—by way of technologies like those heralding the much-celebrated Information Age. Control establishes a current—a kind and direction of movement in our narration—that speeds some of us to our desired ends and against which others of us will either vainly struggle or capitulate. The popular incantation that "you can't fight progress" is a wonderfully subversive truism pointing out the nondemocratic nature of control-mediated notions of development. Progress has made it possible for us to be virtually equal and free, but is itself irresistible—the most poignant, perhaps, of the many ironies of the modern and postmodern worlds: an "offer" we could not refuse.

MEDIATED CONTROL AND THE "DEMOCRATIC" PROCESS

Bluntly stated, were it not for the artificially high volume of our wants, we would be poised to see that the valorization of technical control always means an uneven distribution of power. We have already noted the way in which this dramatic relationship plays out in the interdependence of corporate economic success and the creation and maintenance of intense gradients for energy and attention. But it also factors into the "democratic" distribution of political power. Many commentators on American politics have worried about the relationship between the media and the electoral process and many more about the role of lobbying by major corporations in the decisions made on Capitol Hill. Amassing political power—like the corporate massing of wealth and economic power—has everything to do with the attracting and directing of attention. The parallels are worth investigating.

In the marketplace, wealth and power can be accumulated most rapidly when the market is furthest from equilibrium or financial entropy. That is, when the market is most volatile, there is plenty of economic energy and attention to be selectively diverted. Indeed, in the absence of sharp distribution gradients, the movement of attention-energy is so languid that it is virtually impossible to effectively harness—whether for economic or political purposes. One of the reasons fads are so profitable for the corporate world is that they produce remarkably intense singularities of wanting throughout a population—curvatures of social and economic space that greatly accelerate the flow of wealth and thus afford significantly increased "handling" ability for those in a position to direct the resulting current.

Likewise in politics, power can be acquired and consolidated most rapidly when the state or society is furthest from equilibrium—when conflicts are most open and dangerous. Nothing is more disastrous for the growth of political power than peace—whether that enforced by an authoritarian regime or brought about through legally abolishing discrimination. The history of empire and nation-building provides ample evidence of the principle: there is nothing like conflict and crisis for opening up the opportunity to either shift or deepen political power. Entirely without historical precedent, however, is our current capacity for manufacturing conflicts and crises on a "need" basis.

To be sure, there has been a great deal of debate in the last several decades regarding the effect of communications technology on the political process. The use of mass media like newspapers, radio, film, and the first television broadcasts by Hitler's Third Reich at the dawn of the Information Age made all too clear just how well suited the media can be to both attracting and skewing public opinion for quite narrow and selfish ends. More recently, the importance of television both in U.S. presidential elections and in the articulation of a national disposition toward current events has been well documented, and there is no longer any doubt that the public is increasingly receptive to an incisive use of the media in even the most "democratic" nations. Proponents of the trend toward media-concentrated politicking laud the previously impossible "intimacy" of television campaigning—the ability to enter the living rooms of the voting public. Detractors vociferously lament the propagandistic effect (if not intent) of such methods of informing the nation.

At present, most speculation about the relationship between the media and the political process centers on the potential role of the Internet in the democratic process. For the most part this has been exceedingly hopeful. As the argument goes, the Internet opens up for the first time in history the possibility of direct, participatory democracy for all citizens. It not only makes direct, real-time referendum voting and polling feasible, it affords citizens the means of effectively researching the voting records, fund-raising activities, policy statements, and campaign platforms of political candidates. Of course, the same technical advance makes it possible for political aspirants to much more effectively and precisely tailor their campaign discourses. The information-gathering potential that would come with a fully "wired" nation would make it possible for politicians not only to much more effectively monitor, but also to control the national pulse. According to critics of the new medium, the Internet is no different from any other technology in providing special advantage to those with the money (and so time) to make maximum use of it.

Chilling though it is, I believe that the future of "democratic" politics in the Information Age can be clearly discerned in precedents now being set in the market use of geographic information systems (GIS). Briefly stated, geodemographic tools enable marketers to predict consumer behavior based on statistical models of identity and residential location—a highly sophisticated way of uncovering and exploiting new markets (Weinstein, 1987). More specifically, through the compilation of staggeringly large databases of information about consumer behavior linked to actual names and addresses, it is possible to target extremely well-defined markets. One corporation providing geodemographic services maintains a database that includes information on 100 million American households from census records, purchasing surveys, car-ownership banks, credit bureau files, credit card purchase records, and so on. Such databases now regularly include over a million information fields. If what power needs is a mass of information that its strategic placement allows it to exploit (Foucault, 1980, 75), then GIS technologies are not only deeply political weapons, they establish a much more than analogical connection between the interests of big government and big business. Contrary to skeptics who dismissed George Orwell's predictions in *1984* as wholly unrealized, "Big Brother" is not only watching, but keeping very meticulous records of what he sees.

The promotion of a fully wired nation by both politicians and corporations has been praised as an example of how cooperation between government and the marketplace can in fact benefit everyone. But in the same way that businesses are now targeting markets with great accuracy through GIS technologies, politicians are realizing that it is also possible not only to do precisely targeted campaigning, but a good deal more. For example, software like the "cookie" files attached to all Internet servers are ostensibly designed to speed user access to sites they have previously visited or to related sites. This not only provides a record of where a user has "surfed" on the Internet, it disposes search engines to follow what amount to habitual search paths. Just as knowing the feeding routes of game animals makes it possible for hunters to lie readily in wait for them, software like this in combination with geodemographic databases quite practically enables politicians to "place" politically useful information in the way of users who believe they are freely researching candidate platforms. Trails in cyberspace, like those that once crisscrossed the fields lying between the families in a community and that later became roads and highways lined with business institutions of every type and description, will not go underutilized for long. Granted our mass-mediated isolation from one another, the potentials for an abusive direction of public attention are effectively unlimited.

At this point, all the various parties either lauding and lamenting the marriage of "technology" and politics take it for granted that the outcome of this union will be more control. By whom, for whom, for how long, and to what extent are up for grabs, but not the axis along which this confluence will move our narration. That is, the debate concentrates on who wins rather than what we mean by winning. There is absolutely no doubt that each new tool and technique in our growing arsenal of control-mediating inventions will enable us to more "efficiently" achieve our individual aims and so further inculcate our established patterns of reliance and desire. What they have not done and cannot do is encourage our stopping to question and critically assess those patterns. Unless we do so, and without ever even noting the moment, we will simply pass a point of no return beyond which the democratic process will only be able to be characterized as "designer politics."

The current marriage of ostensibly democratic politics and our control-biased technological lineage is thus particularly worrisome. It promises a society in which each individual gets, to the greatest extent possible, to do and have what he or she wants. We have already seen the karmic dangers of taking this as a personal, much less a political ideal or end in itself. At the very least, such a union practically guarantees that the individual freedoms mediated by the government—like the "freedoms" of technically mediated control—will erode the grounds on which truly critical attention might develop. That is, such a marriage is capable of producing tautological political ideals and governments—ideals and governments that are beyond belief because they cannot be rationally contested.

Such is our belief in the moral transparency of technology that we are inclined to think that if such a dire scenario were ever to be realized, it could only be attributed to a "misuse" of the media. But in actuality, there is no one standing behind the promises of equality and autonomy to be directing any kind of misuse or abuse. An open evaluation of our political conduct makes it evident that—quite contrary to our "pre-Copernican" expectations—it is not some individual politicians, corporations, or governments that uniquely stand to gain by the circulation of unrealizable ideals of technologically supported and protected equality and autonomy, but rather an entire way of life, a narrative authored by no one of us in particular and yet into which we find ourselves almost ineluctably drawn.

THE SOCIETAL NATURE OF
A CONTROLLING ADVANTAGE

It is often presumed that the modern age is the age of the individual. In both the economic and political spheres, the "self-made" businessperson or politician is valorized as an ideal each and every one of us can take inspiration from and strive to emulate. And, of course, the individual genius in the arts and letters is no less familiar to us. In sum, the technologies of modernization, and the political ideals with which they are most consonant, claim a special relationship to promoting universal and yet fully individual welfare.

I'd like to contest that claim. While it is true that certain individuals do inevitably and greatly benefit from the ways in which a technical bias toward control plays out—whether politically or economically—this is not because of who they are as unique persons, but simply because of their membership in a particular class. Although the political rhetoric of control is that each and every one of us will attain real power to exercise as we see fit, the evolution of technologies of control has never promoted the dramatic fortunes of unique persons but the development of privileged *classes comprising finally generic individuals.*

It is quite clear that the evolution of increasingly precise and powerful systems for controlling our various environments necessitates a class of technical mediators able to discern when and how to apply and maintain the appropriate tools and techniques. Exactly who becomes a member of this mediating class is no more relevant than which molecules in an electrically charged volume of gas are nearest the electrode and so in a position to conduct the electrical current into the general population. Certainly, not all of us will or could be so positioned. What is essential is not which one of us fills any of the given and necessary sites of privilege, but only whether someone or anyone does.

It is an ongoing myth, for example, that medical diagnostics provide us all with relatively equal control over disease. In actuality, not only is the availability of medical services a function of wealth or position, but the authority to diagnose and treat disease has been concentrated in the hands of a very few. Who exactly become doctors is not in any apparent way related to their attainments as unique human beings, but simply their having been positioned to excel in school, pass certain exams, and aspire toward a certain station in society. In other words, the important characteristics of who becomes a doctor are not dramatic or meaningful, but rather factual. Although they are our "healers," doctors need not be healthy in even the most minimal sense. In the end, while it's true that doctors have clearly benefited from the increasingly technological management of health—having realized an 800 percent increase in real earnings over the past twenty-five years while the average American worker's real earnings dropped by nearly an eighth—they have not done so because of the personal qualities they have, the depth of their understanding of humanity and the meaning of a good life, but because they adequately fill an institutional void. In a word, they are not rewarded for social virtuosity but for societal competence. This is true in all modern technologies of control.

This should raise questions about whether the advantages afforded by technologies of control have ever really been *ours* or if they are advantages that we have on loan only so long as we pay the required interest or attention. Is there, in other words, a pattern in the distribution of benefits related to our changing individual fortunes that finally has nothing uniquely to do with who we are as persons? And if we are only benefited generically and not in any truly personal way by our technological mediation, to what extent can we really expect our cultural, religious, and aesthetic diversity (and not mere variety) to matter enough for them to be conserved in the course of things? More to the point politically, is there some necessary relationship between high and even accelerating rates of technological growth and the realization of classes of relatively generic individuals arrayed in ever steeper hierarchies of advantage?

The recent demise of both the Soviet and Maoist models of communism provides, I think, a basis for affirmatively answering the latter and for worrying very seriously about the compatibility of technological proliferation and truly democratic society. To be sure, the failures of communism as practiced in the former Soviet Union and in Maoist China can be attributed to a great many conditions. But one of the central facts to be explained is why these countries, in spite of enormous investment of both human and material resources, were able to accomplish so little in developing the basic technical and institutional infrastructure of a modern nation-state—why they failed to become competitors on the world market and why their internal standards of living remained so "pitifully behind" those of developed nations in "the West."

As an opening gambit, explanatory appeals are often made to the ways in which Soviet and Maoist society stifled individual creativity and initiative by practically eliminating immediate incentives for innovation and efficiency. The accepted cant is that cooperative business and research simply could not begin to stimulate the kind of genius that competition does, and in result, real scientific, technical, and industrial advances were both slow in coming and fitfully applied at best. But a closer look suggests that matters were not so simple. In fact, individuals with special talents were routinely given quite special treatment and training. The performance of Soviet athletes, ballet dancers, and chess masters is legendary, and while that of Soviet artists and academics is less well known, it was in many ways no less formidable. In a word, opportunities for individual excellence were far from being eradicated in the Soviet Union, and in those areas of international competition where individual efforts counted the most, the Soviets did very well indeed. Why not in the advancement of technology, business, and political power?

I would argue that the problem was not the subjugation of the individual, but the ideal of a classless society that stunted the growth of both Soviet and Maoist societies. What they lacked was not a commitment to nurturing individual genius, but for creating sharply differentiated classes of advantage within society—classes without which the root conditions of a technological bias for control would be at best only partially constituted. That is, internal inequities within these societies were simply not developed well enough to generate the kinds of energy and attention movement needed to galvanize a widespread technological and industrial revolution. If the failure of the Soviet and Maoist experiments is to be attributed to a lack of sufficient numbers, it was not brilliant individuals who were in short supply, but "brilliant" classes.

A successful bias for control means not just the concentration of skills, but their rationalization or strategic division. While a flint knife can be made and kept sharp by just about anyone, the making, distributing, and use of stainless steel knives necessarily exports control from the majority of us to some specialized others. This externalization of responsibility—like the externalization of costs so crucial to the growth of the global free market—is essential to the realization of both societally regulated independence and dependence. These, in turn, are essential for the continual, ever wider, and yet ever more focused circulation of energy, power, and wealth. A bias for control leads to classes benefited in increasingly differentiated ways just as inevitably as it does to concentrations of decision-making authority and capital. That is, it is the internal logic of control-oriented technologies to create classes of effectively generic individuals. In a word, it individuates without promoting dramatic uniqueness.

As class members, doctors are as bound by the structure of technical society as their patients. And as anyone with a knowledge of the inner workings of the corporate world can verify, CEOs retain control only as long as is corporately useful and not a moment longer. Officially, this is spoken of as proof of the pragmatism of corporate capitalism—its commitment to quality production at maximum profits. In actuality, it is simply evidence that it is not unique persons who are served by orienting our technical efforts toward increasing control, but the mechanisms and structure of that control itself.

To take this a step further: technologies of control force us into investing our time, attention, and energy in the maintenance of specialized forms of conduct over which we have no immediate influence. We must support not just ourselves, but our mechanics and medical technicians, our air-conditioning companies and waste disposal operators. That is, such technologies produce consumers. We are no longer qualified to grow our own food, make our own clothing, build our homes, educate our children, entertain or counsel or heal ourselves. Technologies of control advertise their role in promoting self-reliance but actually promote a breakdown of the relationships by means of which communities take meaningful care of themselves. Created instead are aggregates of ostensibly autonomous individuals who take their almost unbroken dependence on technical interventions and the expertise of largely invisible others as emblematic of their freedom and independence. In short, *we create the illusion of independence as a mask for a deepening dependency on others about and for whom we cannot care.* Because their work on our behalf is hidden by the tools we use in "controlling" our internal and external environments, not only can we afford to leave them alone, they are virtually compelled to leave us alone as well. Appreciation and compassion are strictly optional.

This is now almost invariably accepted as part of "the way things are." We have come to accept whatever benefits are trickling down to our level and hope someday to maneuver ourselves into a position where it is more directly our own wills (and not those of others) that determine the course of things. In a word, we tacitly believe that control itself is not a problem, but only our lack of it. We see no need or convincing reason to question its ubiquity as a technical/cultural value. And so, when Neil Postman—author of the book, *Technopoly*—traces out what he sees as the development from tool-using societies to technocracies and finally technopoly, he concludes that this final stage is a kind of humanistic dead end where we have unwittingly abdicated control of our lives, our ways of thinking, doing business, healing ourselves, and so on. According to Postman, the problem is that we have lost control of our technologies and become the controlled. His solution? A politics of resistance by means of which we wrest back control of our own lives.

As interesting as Postman's arguments often are, he fails to see that matters could never have turned out otherwise. It is not that our technologies have somehow stolen control away from us, but that the intensity of their development over that last hundred and fifty years have—for those with eyes to see—made plain the real cost of raising the value of control into highest eminence. Postman's critique implies that we must exercise more control if we are to regain a semblance of "the good life"—control of the engines of our mastery of nature and ourselves. From a karmically informed

Buddhist perspective, this could only make matters worse. Because technologies are patternings of conduct having no simple location, the values they promote are in a quite real sense ambient—part of the spaces in which our stories unfold. If we promote control through technical proliferation, it is inevitable that we find our lives being controlled, not because of who we are as persons, but by virtue of the classes to which we belong.

JUST SAYING NO: A CASE HISTORY
OF TECHNICAL DILEMMA

The concerns raised above are likely to seem quite abstract, pertaining as they do at the level of global politics and economics. As a way of moving our conversation in the direction of more personally and practically confronting the implications of a widespread technological bias toward control, I would like to address the "drug problem" in America. The discourse about drugs is political not only in the obvious sense of being engaged in by politicians at every level of government, but also by virtue of the fact that it has come to define our society and its generations, becoming practically inseparable from the complexion of our cities. By teasing apart the narrative threads knotted together in our problem with drugs, we will hopefully begin seeing that our prime social and political nemesis is not chaos or the unexpected, but rather our means and hope of vanquishing it.

Raising the question of substance abuse in the present context might initially seem incongruous. We tend to think of the nonmedical use of drugs as aberrant behavior induced by a combination of societal pressures, low self-esteem, and a self-destructive indulgence in potentially toxic escapism. Since not everyone in similar circumstances ends up addicted to or obsessed with substance abuse, however, the line of final resistance to its lures is understood to be that of each individual's will. The Reagan administration's "Just Say No" campaign most succinctly reflected the belief that the problem with drugs pivots on making right and wrong choices. It is a moral dilemma centered—as is true of all such dilemmas in our tradition—on the often arcane interplay of freedom and responsibility. The locus of this interplay, of course, is the supposedly autonomous individual—one of the "thousand points of light" the media so capably reminded us it was our national mission to help make shine most brightly.

According to this view, the drug problem is partly epistemological. People, especially our "impressionable youth," get hooked before they know any better, before they realize what's really at stake, before they have had time to understand what activities and so what values deserve their attention and energy. Granted this premise, it's perfectly logical to address the problem by "educating" young people about the dangers of drugs. At least in theory, once they are able to see what drug abuse really means in the long run, they will be inclined to resist its comparatively ephemeral and minor lures. If at the same time, we are able to exercise a reasonable amount of control over the availability of drugs, not only should the campaign be a triumphant success, a great moral victory will have been won—we will have salvaged the will of a generation.

This is not what has happened. In fact, over the last twenty-five years substance abuse has worked its way not only into the junior high and elementary schools, it has spread out of our inner-city ghettos and counterculture enclaves into mainstream, suburban America. In the last decade, the halcyon days of the New Republican era, the virulence of this spread has— if anything—only intensified. As is so often the case when our best laid plans go awry, this is not because we haven't implemented our solutions to the problem aggressively enough. To the contrary, *it is because our proposed solutions are of a piece with the problem itself*. Bluntly stated, our strategies are self-defeating. Our so-called solutions feed back into and, in fact, amplify the problem. In the case of drug abuse, not only will more controls not help matters, they will only make them worse. The substance abuse epidemic is not a fundamentally psychological, or sociological, or even epistemological crisis. It is technological.

This is perhaps obviously true at a superficial and, for that reason, not very damaging level. After all, the crack cocaine being smoked in American junior high schools is flown in from South America, the heroin shot into a young musician's veins is smuggled in from Thailand, the profits made by drug cartels are managed and laundered by the use of computers. Cellular phones and pagers are crucial to the day-to-day operations of those who deal drugs to the end-consumer.

Less obviously, the information technologies on which the media depend are instrumental in spreading awareness about and interest in drugs. Print publications, movies, television programming, music discs, and music videos all pose drug use or nonuse as a potent matter of individual choice. By connecting substance abusers to naive nonusers in such a way that the latter are obliged to at least indirectly contribute attention and energy to the former's patterns of abuse, the media provide a narrative linkage between minority patterns of abuse and the population at large. That the attention given is largely negative is less important than that the narrative connection is established and attention directed toward patterns of substance abuse. Rather than substance abusers forming a distinct and yet very peripheral element in our society, they are placed in our very living rooms. From that moment on, there is no denying that it is not merely the behavior of some fringe group that can be characterized as abusive, but *our* conduct. News of the drug problem changes the character of our narration. Like it or not, it alters the way we fashion our selves. In a very real way—even if for the most part only generically—it empowers the proponents of abuse, affording "them" some measure of control, however small, over what the rest of us think about, what we fear, and how well we sleep at night.

Aside from all the very real political implications involved, this need not be a calamity in the making. If our responses to media portrayals of substance abuse did not simply feed back the same values already driving abusive behavior, it's possible that the quality of our attention would prove instrumental in reorienting the movement of our narrative—our individual and communal conduct. In this case, the incredible amounts of energy being invested in the illicit manufacture, sale, purchase, use, and abuse of drugs might well be released for other, more community-focused forms of conduct. Importantly, then, a large part of the reason why the drug problem strikes us as so troubling and apparently intractable is precisely because it focuses the conflict implicit in our technological bias toward control.

As I've been using the term, "drug" refers to any substance—whether naturally occurring or artificially produced—that has pronounced and characteristic effects on our experience. Drugs alter the patterns of our bodily, emotional, mental, and spiritual awareness. Since they have relatively well-defined effects on those patterns, drugs can serve as remarkably effective tools in controlling the gestalt-generating functions of consciousness. That can be very useful. Whereas technologies of ostensive control work to change the "picture"—our world—by redrawing or decisively altering it, drugs work on the matrix of experience to change our view from the "inside out." Drug use thus constitutes an alternative technology for controlling the character of our narration. And in this sense, drugs can be seen as subversive of the institutions of control prevailing in a society.

The "war" on drugs is not waged because drugs are bad for business. To the contrary, they are part of an incredibly profitable industry dedicated to the control of mood and the modality of awareness. The war is not waged because drugs threaten national security by stealing valuable resources like coal or oil or by threatening our borders with armed attacks. The "war" is really civil in nature—a war within the horizons of our own most deeply held and cherished values. Drugs are literally revolutionary techniques— techniques that bring us full circle from frustrated immersion in stories (lives) in which we lack the power to determine our own courses, and back into a semblance of immediate, willed control. They give many people what all our other technologies cannot—the means to experience a preferable world, a less anxious and despairing existence. Drugs allow users to cut themselves out of the normal loop, to direct all their efforts not to profiting some rich business owner or influential politician or religious capitalist, but to directly transforming their own experience. Drugs enable us to control the chaos of experience made possible and necessary by political, economic, and societal systems that do not know who we are or why we exist.

There is no mystery to the appeal of such a technology for those disadvantaged by a lack of access to the kind of power needed for ostensive, world-altering control. Teenagers and racial/ethnic minorities are not genetically, but technically disposed to substance abuse. It is not that they are unclear about what values they should invest in or that they are duped by the false claims of drug euphoria. To the contrary, such disadvantaged members of our society—disadvantaged by race, age, economic inheritance, educational opportunity, "looks," primary mode of reasoning, or gender persuasion—are entirely lucid in their perception that drugs afford them a chance to personally taste the benefits of investing their attention in the technical realization of control. They might not be able to say this. But they know very well that the frustration they experience at being powerless to decisively alter or control the "way things are" is directly mitigated through drug use. By choosing appropriate doses, users are able to decide what level of risk they feel comfortable flirting with and managing. By choosing properly from among the pharmacological offerings available on the street, they are also able to determine the state they will enjoy and for how long. It is often claimed that drugs rob people of control over their lives, but that is not true. Drugs amplify the user's ability to control the state of their minds and bodies in so powerful a way that pain and poverty can both be made to vanish.

This is not so different from the role television plays in shaping our conduct or the role virtual reality is likely to have in the near future. Television programming also provides us with alternative realities we can invest with our attention and energy, and that we can and do weave into the narrative fabric of our lives in order to alter its pattern. But the television is "over there" on the wall opposite our couch or our bed. Even if we've paid a thousand dollars for it, the image it provides is not life-size or three-dimensional. It is a framed picture, not a horizonless world. When we stand up to get something to drink from the kitchen, we are not likely to enter a room replete with Corian countertops, spotless wood-laminate floors, and all the latest appliances like the kitchen we've just seen on *This Old House*. Our bathroom is not big enough to sleep four. It's worn and even a bit tawdry. Our family members are not as good-looking or as clever as our television friends. Their smiles are not as white, their clothes not as hip, and their planets not so well aligned. In a word, television may allow us to forget where we are for a time, but once we turn it off or walk outside the room there is no denying the quality of our circumstances and the lack of control they so manifestly evidence.

Drugs are not framed presentations of alternative worlds. When we leave the house to see what's going on down at the corner, there is no break in the continuity of our altered experience. It is not something in our world that has changed, but the very way our world feels and appears. All our senses are to one extent or another involved and transformed. And while the nature of this transformation depends on the characteristics of the 'high' any given drug provides, it is a thorough transformation in the sense that there is no "backstage"—nothing that is unaffected. By taking the right drugs in the right doses, we can practically dictate the tenor of our states of consciousness and so the contours of our experience. And we can do so to a degree otherwise quite unlikely if not impossible. Drug addiction is not escapism—an attempt at self-abandonment—but a toxic addiction to control.

This is the real crux of our dilemma about substance abuse. On the one hand, our technical effort and energy has for centuries been almost exclusively directed toward control and regulation. This societal bias, however, has—whether through historical accident or uncertain design—been married to an equally strong bias for seeing freedom as pivoting on individual freedom of choice. Drugs—and soon enough the combination of them with effective, full-sensorium virtual reality—provide an opportunity to cheat on the very laws that provide our control-biased technologies with the fulcrums needed to ostensively leverage the world in accordance with our wants. The problem with drugs is not that they do something inconsistent with our overall technical values and dispositions, but that they are "too good" at what they do.

The drug problem reveals the darkness—the blindness regarding the interdependence of all things—lying at the heart of our technical bias and the primary values it articulates. Like all tools and techniques, drugs epitomize some general mode and orientation of our narration, some aspect of the complex character of our lived and always dramatic interdependence or karma. That is, drugs must be seen as irreducibly value-laden. It should be noted that this is not, however, to say that all drugs—or even any particular drugs—are by nature productive of ignorance. That is precisely the kind of conclusion our "being"-focused, essentialist metaphysics would incline us to draw. But it is not, for all its naturalness, a necessary or even particularly useful line of reasoning. Indeed, it may be that the problem of drug abuse is soluble only if we adopt a radically alternative form of reasoning—one that stresses relationships rather than states, responsivity rather than stability, improvised contribution rather than certain results and secure rewards.

According to the Buddhist view, no drug is essentially a substance of abuse. Like all other things, no drug has a self-same nature. To the contrary, the "same" plant or chemical compound can figure into the conduct of a community in radically different, even incommensurable ways. There have been many societies, for example, in which psychoactive plants have been used with regularity and without the disruption of community evident in our own use of botanically "identical" plants and their laboratory-isolated derivatives.

In such societies—and in deep contrast with our own—the technology of chemically altering consciousness is not oriented toward controlled states as ends in themselves, but rather toward establishing a more fruitful relationship between the community and its environment. That is, the persons undergoing catalytically triggered alterations of awareness do not do so to achieve and possess a particular state within a context of individual control, but in order to augment their ability to perform their communal function— as shamans, as hunters or healers, as seers or artists. Typically, such technologies have been embedded within a set of elaborate ritual practices that initiate the user into the new narrative bridges the plant makes available— the unprecedented ligations of previously disparate forms or aspects of our conduct. For example, a hunter-shaman might use a particular plant to establish an intuitive (as opposed to a merely deductive or rational) link between his awareness and that of his prey. By doing so, his conduct blends with that of the animal he is stalking and the two become complementary poles of a singular dance movement expressing the cooperation of their respective species. But perhaps more importantly, such rituals also guide the initiate toward realizing these novel, narrative possibilities in the service of benefiting the entire community. The locus of benefit is relational rather than individual.

American teenagers, of course, also use drugs in a nominally ritual manner. But instead of cultivating a disposition toward contribution, these rituals express and tend to strengthen our biases toward independence, individualism, and freedom through control. Instead of aiming at better serving their community through their use of drugs, American teenagers enter into a predominantly adversarial relationship with that community. Drugs enable them to assert their right to determine the contents and quality of their awareness—doing so on the basis of their own, uncoerced choosing, and in contrast with the needs and desires of their various environments. In our society, drugs are used to radically individuate awareness, to ignore rather than intensify our interdependence. Rather than being used to better appreciate our world, they are used to subjectively alter it.

Solving the drug problem cannot, for these very reasons, mean further stressing independence and will-power. Instead, it means an axiological conversion—a shift in our basic technical orientation from regularity and security to improvisational virtuosity, from the defining and possessive bias toward control to the priority of contribution or appreciation. That is, if drugs are not inherently destructive of either our personal or communal health, and if they are currently playing a decidedly destructive role in our narration, we are obliged not to eradicate them, but rather invest them with new values.

The failure of the U.S. government's campaign to undercut drug use by promoting higher self-esteem finally lies in the impossibility of competitively delivering its stated goods. The local drug dealer does much better. In our society, self-esteem is inextricably bound up with the values of independence, freedom of choice, and control. What the dealer offers at a relatively low cost—both in terms of money and personal training—is exactly what the government promises at a much higher premium: the ability to willfully control the content and context of one's experience. Objections that drugs afford only an illusory control and a basically attenuated or impoverished range of experience are beside the point as long as control remains the prime technical value. Like all tools, drugs do what they are designed to do and do it well. Arguing with a crack addict about the "debilitating" and "communally destructive" effects of crack use is like arguing with a television addict or Internet junkie about the dangers of mediated experience. They are getting exactly what they were promised and what they want. The only hope of winning such an argument comes with shifting the locus of concern—both from the individual to our narration as such and from control to contributory appreciation.

THE MEANINGLESS POLITICS OF GENERIC DEMOCRACY

Democracy is often defined as government by and for the people. Under the logic of a bias for control, "people" necessarily refers to the maximum aggregation of fundamentally autonomous individuals. In the context of conduct primarily oriented toward the societal attainment of control, "people" cannot refer to a community of persons linked in fundamentally dramatic and hence inherently meaningful ways—a harmonious play of unique characters mutually contributing to and benefiting from their differences. A community in this sense refers to a neighborhood—a complex folding together of relationships in which the primary mode of attunement is closeness or care. That is a far cry indeed from the typical voting district or even the typical "town hall" meeting. And the democratic process as defined by the wants of any such aggregation of individuals is a process that systematically elides the humane qualities we associate with true community. The needs of the "people" may indeed be promoted, but not their liberation from the calculative and so essentially decisive rationality of control-mediated freedom.

I have no doubt that conceiving of democracy as pivoting on the right to vote is quite "natural"—perhaps even unavoidable—where the primary technical value is that of control and the prevailing belief is that freedom is necessarily identified with individual choice. Voting is a perfectly logical way of insuring our ability to individually promote and protect our interests. But when voting takes place in the context of powerful mass mediation, the likelihood is that the interests promoted are those of classes and not persons. Moreover, the right to vote also grounds a belief in our right to assert our will—not to appreciatively contribute to our situation in whatever way we can, but to lodge demands that our conditions better comply with the structure and intensity of our wants. There is, to be sure, the tyranny of the single-minded dictator, but also the dictatorship of a mass-educated and power-informed majority—a tyranny that may undermine true community to an extent unmatched by even the most virulent autocracy.

If we live in a karmic world where all things are dramatically interdependent, electing to ground political process on a legitimization of rights to assertive control will deeply incline us toward the realization of a public sphere in which greater assertiveness and less responsiveness is increasingly expedient and toward a form of governance in which prescription and proscription become paramount. That is, the technologically supported understanding of democratic process as one based on individual rights to assert control over our circumstances is conducive to a government primarily involved in defining what can and cannot be done—the institution of the rule of law. Guaranteeing freedom—the ostensive aim of all democratic governance—thus becomes a profoundly ironic process of setting up boundaries for our conduct, a process of establishing constraining horizons for both attention and meaning.

Such a form of governance cannot but be hopelessly conflicted. According to it, the freedom of the people can only be accomplished through consistency and clarity in their regulation. Individual rights can only be guaranteed on the basis of collectively prescribed limits for legitimate wants or desires. The efficacy of assertion can only be warranted through ensuring that its weight or gravity is essentially generic—that every vote or opinion is as good as every other. The quality of our lives can be safeguarded, but only if it is at first translated into quantifiable standards liable to universal application. As with all control-oriented technologies, such a system of governance promotes individualism, not dramatic personalism. It benefits classes of people, but not irreducibly unique persons of character and the communities—or relationships of intimate care—that they creatively and unaccountably express.

According to this line of analysis, there is a shared technical origin of the most profound social, economic, and political crises facing those of us living in the world's "most advanced" democracies. And they will elude adequate and lasting solution as long as the axiological priority of control remains unchallenged. As with the drug problem, the direction in which we should focus our attention is no longer intuitively obvious. To the contrary, it requires a conscious re-orientation of our concern from the discursive logic of possession and control to the concursive aesthetic of appreciative contribution.

The meaning of such a re-orientation includes at the very least a new vision of democracy—a commitment to seeing it as less a matter of securing individual rights than of cultivating character. What I have in mind is *not* the institution of a kind of "moral society" in which our primary focus is the acquisition or demonstration of classic virtues such as honesty, courage, and integrity, much less narrowly defined, and the conservative indoctrination of specific sexual and political mores. Too often, such virtues and mores have done little more than identify those traits our prevailing technologies have been capable of consistently nurturing. To the contrary, what I mean by the "cultivation of character," is not the intensification of some quality of our being, but the awakening of each of our unique capacities for harmonizing with others—what is formalized in Ch'an Buddhism as "according with our situation and responding as needed." In this sense, cultivating character is not cultivating virtues, but virtuosity.

Recommending a shift away from the politics of control toward a politics of appreciation is not, then, to forward some program—a "ten-point plan" for political and social salvation. Programmatic solutions all ultimately depend on an understanding of causality as linear—a model that does nothing more than replicate the intention-biased logic of control. The recommended shift toward appreciation is thus a way of stressing that the democratic process does not amount to some complex structure of objectively maintained behaviors, but to a particular kind of *awareness*. As such, democracy is not something limited to any particular organizational structure. It does not depend on the existence of any particular laws or legal protocols. Instead, democracy is best seen as that type of political awareness most suited to the realization of always improvised harmony. In a word, it is awareness boundlessly skilled in the resolution of conflict or trouble.

Embracing appreciation thus implies a belief that creative solutions to our troubled narration will emerge spontaneously—or *tzu jan*—if we can properly attune ourselves, if we can liberate our attention from its obsessions and aversions. That is, appreciation entails what Ch'an refers to as "letting go with both hands"—holding onto nothing so as to be able to respond in any direction, at any time as needed. This is the relinquishing not only of our horizons for what we might otherwise be inclined to think mark the limits of relevance for solving our problems, but our horizons for responsibility and readiness as well. Fully realized, a politics of appreciation involves freeing our awareness from all habitually set horizons.

This is a radical proposal. But if technologies are patterns of our conduct and if a bias for control thus means that some of us will always be served and others will inevitably be drafted into unwilling service, it represents the only consistent and philosophically cogent response to the erosion of our communal health and freedom. What stands in the way of such a revolution are not the material or social circumstances in which we find ourselves. To the contrary, what stands between us and the resolution of our very evident suffering is no more substantial than the quality of our day-to-day experience—the gestalts according to which our awareness configures the world. More specifically, it is the iconic nature of our technically trained and media-informed experience that most forcibly blocks our world from appropriately and creatively taking care of itself.

Chapter 9

Narcissism and Nihilism

*The Atrophy of Dramatic Attention
and the End of Authentic Materialism*

Technology influences not just our present modes of activity, but also the way we understand our world and the material changes it will likely undergo in the future. Automotive and air transportation, for example, have not only altered our practices for moving people and things from place to place, but have led to significantly new ways of construing "place" and "distance." Likewise, while telephone and computer technologies have clearly transformed our offices and urban centers, the tempo of business transactions, our "pace of life," and our average cardiovascular condition, they have also led to drastic revisions of what we mean by "work," "knowledge," and "communication."

Yet, if we accept as valid the Buddhist insight that 'outer world' and 'inner experience' are not finally separable but should be seen as dramatically interdependent poles of our narrative movement, such objective influences of technology clearly cannot tell the whole story. There must be as well a sense in which technologies alter the shape of our present and future selves just as much as they do the present and future layout of our communities or our practices for storing and transmitting information.

To the extent that we identify ourselves with a central, experiencing ego and our technologies with the tools they produce, it is easy to think we are not essentially altered by our technological biases. Even in the case of artificial heart valves or joints where we quite literally incorporate technological produce, we see ourselves as remaining fundamentally who we have always been. But if, instead, we see ourselves and our technologies as given directly in conduct, the dividing lines between them become increasingly horizontal— a function of perspective rather than simply objective, ontological features of the way things are. Situated completely in our midst, the values promoted by our technologies are thus in a very real sense integral to the form and direction of our irreducibly dynamic interrelationship. They revise the narrative structure of our stories—our true bodies—and, like gods, make us over in new images.

Since it is part of the Buddhist worldview that consciousness should not be seen as a private possession—an intrinsic faculty of an organism—but rather as a relationship from which both 'organism' and 'environment' can be relatively abstracted, the ways in which technological bias structures and directs our conduct must also be seen as ways in which it transforms the nature of awareness as such. That is, in addition to their objective or factual shaping of our world, technologies at once express and influence the form and formation of subjectivity. They affect not just what we want and do, but who we are, by altering the quality and meaning—not just the explicit content—of our experience. Granted that our world is irreducibly karmic—that is, intentionally and yet interdependently configured—understanding the interdependence of technological systems and the structure of awareness as such is crucial to exposing and explaining both the apparent 'invisibility' and epidemic spread of the colonization of consciousness.

RATIONALIZING SUBJECTIVITY: THE IMPERATIVE SPLITTING OF THE NUCLEAR SELF

We have already noted that the success of material colonization depended on efficiently extracting and transporting useful physical resources from a colonized locale. Often, this entailed defining the colony as a predominantly diamond- or coal- or lumber-producing land—a practice that unfailingly and severely disrupted the richly delicate balance of native ecosystems and patterns of subsistence. Since culture arises in interdependence with an environing nature, such changes inevitably altered the local means and meaning of community, and this led in turn to the appearance of a "humanitarian" need for exercising further interventive control on behalf of the colonized. Peoples that had for centuries lived in and through interdependent balance with their surroundings suddenly found themselves vitally dependent on foreign ideologies and expertise. With the replacement of openly colonial intentions and market ideals by those of the development imperative, this process of ecological and communal disruption underwent an intense phase of escalation, rendering truly local economies and ecosystems impractical to the point that they are now practically extinct.

The colonization of consciousness kicks things up yet another notch. Flourishing on the basis of a breakdown and selective biasing of our "attentive ecology," the new colonialism quite literally reconstitutes who we are. It has already been suggested that the development imperative that grew out of material colonialism involved, first, the rationalization of clans and "extended families" into separate, nuclear family units, and then the further rationalization of these nuclear units into single-parent households. The colonization of consciousness parasitically carries on this process by rationalizing the nuclear self—the individual family member—into the autonomous and yet manifestly incomplete self. Characteristic of this new self is the splitting of subjectivity in such a way that it becomes its own object. Living devolves into a subject choosing one or more lifestyles, and those virtues by means of which character is constituted—the narrative force of personhood—migrate into the increasingly iconic, extrapersonal dimension of a continuously and fashionably changing objective world. Engaged in the karmically recursive project of "making itself" however it chooses, the more successful such a rationalized self is, the more ill at ease it becomes.

As in the case of colonized lands and economies, this process of rationalization is initially effected through and primarily plays out as our systematic impoverishment—the systematic disruption of our indigenous patterns of emotional, intellectual, and spiritual subsistence as holistic characters in meaningful interdependence, and our subsequent redefinition as individuals in want. Only instead of an exploitative extraction of massive quantities of coal or rubber or manufactured goods, what the new colonialism mines and exports are forms of attention useful in the accelerated proliferation and maintenance of control-biased technologies. The circular consequences are no less disastrous for the colonized consciousness than they were for the colonized land.

Many native peoples have decried the rationalization of the land—it's reduction to a source of "natural" resources for the industrial and commercial development. Mining activities, logging, clear-cutting of forest for mechanized agriculture, and the building of roads and railways all mark a dramatically impoverished relationship of a people with the land. To the extent that the Buddhist understanding of consciousness as relationship is granted, this is also an impoverishment of awareness as such. A fully rationalized terrain is not listened to, but driven over, reformed, and ultimately ignored. Land ceases to be a source of meaning and is seen instead as tabula rasa awaiting inscription. So, too, for the rationalized self—the self in need of help.

In his visionary and poetic novel, *The Famished Road*, Nigerian-born Ben Okri describes what happens in a community when the forest trails and footpaths used by villagers and the animals who live and work with them are replaced by asphalt roads and automobiles. Unlike draft animals, automobiles seem uninterested in understanding the ways of men, women, and children. Unlike the forest trails and footpaths of old, and like a hard strip of night laid down on the land, the paved road absorbs the blood and sweat of the men and animals who build it, but offers nothing back in return. On its margins, the only things that seem able to grow are shanties and loading docks, roadhouses with electrified music and imported alcohol. The main character of the book, a spirit-child named Azaro, watches in amazement as the minds of the people change—his parents and friends and neighbors. Dedicated to the ideal of unabated growth, the road to development is always hungry.

In much the same way that the imperatives of free market capitalism are conducive to global economic monoculture and the voraciously local seeking of competitive advantage through productive specialization, the colonization of consciousness at once promotes the ideals of universal equality and individuality and the recognition that our self-interest is best secured by accepting our specific incompleteness as human beings and competing as best we can to satisfy our wants. Much as entry into the global free market means the demise of subsistence economies—and so the destruction of those pathways by means of which a community ritually and regularly confirmed its constitutive relationships—the colonization of consciousness means that our increasing autonomy will be correlated with an increasing inability to meaningfully take care of ourselves. Compassion may become optional to what it means to be a person, but not consumption. The result is that the successfully colonized postmodern personality is at once narcissistic and nihilistic—both proud and afflicted with low self-esteem. We are who we can afford to be.

That such a personality is an artifact of a dramatically destructive bias for control and not a natural condition of being human has been poignantly illustrated in the recently published transcript of a roundtable discussion of emotion and healing by the Dalai Lama and a number of Western scientists, psychologists, psychiatrists, medical doctors, and social workers (Goleman, 1997, 184ff). At the point that one of the discussants began speaking about techniques for improving self-esteem, the translator signaled for a stop in mid-sentence, entered a long exchange in Tibetan with the Dalai Lama, and then informed the group that there is simply no way of translating "low self-esteem" into the Tibetan language. Those gathered were so taken aback by this realization that speculation ensued as to whether this proved that at least some emotions are not universally human, but rather cultural artifacts. The Dalai Lama himself was astounded that an emotion like "self-loathing" is even possible. Never once in all his dealings with Westerners had he considered "poor self-esteem" as a condition they might be suffering and that Buddhism therefore needed to address. Informed that low self-esteem is not only compatible with great pride, but most often occurs in conjunction with it, his surprise turned to amazement.

And yet this is precisely what we would expect if the postmodern self is the result of perfecting the karma of control—the radical polarization of being simultaneously satisfied and dissatisfied, getting exactly what is wanted and finding ourselves immediately and so chronically in want. None of this is to suggest, of course, that low self-esteem and pride are new phenomena. The intentional and consistent biasing of conduct toward control is nothing new and narcissism and nihilism have existed in various cultures for a very long time. But it is important, I think, that their combined prevalence is at its strongest in America today—arguably the most technologically advanced nation on the planet—and historically absent in Tibet, where Buddhist technologies of appreciation were traditionally more important culturally, economically, and politically than those oriented toward control. Perhaps even more tellingly, Helena Norberg-Hodge (1991) has observed that in the three decades since Ladakh was first opened up to the forces of modernization in 1962, not only has there been a rapid deterioration of traditional Ladakhi culture, but the first and ever-increasing incidence of a sense of profound impoverishment and disadvantage among especially young Ladakhis. The colonization of consciousness has managed to make even the high desert of Ladakh bloom with rationalized selves in just a single generation.

In the colonization of consciousness, generically low self-esteem serves as an insurance that we do not practice the equivalent of "import substitution"—an absolute anathema to the goals of free market globalism. In much the same way that an appetite for foreign goods arises with the redirection of labor away from holistic and yet local subsistence practices, low self-esteem arises as a natural consequence of the efficient and continuous export of energy-attention from locally meaningful cultural and interpersonal modes of conduct—at once a cause and result of our dramatic impoverishment, our realization of personal insufficiency.

NOTHING REALLY MATTERS ANYMORE, NOT EVEN MATTER

The extent to which the Earth's resources have been and continue to be shamelessly and destructively exploited in the service of realizing our dream of ubiquitous, technically mediated control is now widely, if not always well, publicized. But with the explosive success of electronic mass mediation and the emergence of a worldwide, commodity-driven fashion culture, it has become a dream cut off from its original ties to the veritable or authentic materialism that necessarily undergirds any caring and careful interdependence with our place. Processes of reciprocal contribution that were literally consciousness-expanding have collapsed into fleeting moments of consumption, and with this collapse our concern for matter as such—for what constrains but also qualifies our point of view—has all but disappeared. In its place we have rampant consumerism, an obsession with acts of taking possession that strips things of their histories and makes them essentially disposable, insignificant. And so the Marxist focus on capital and labor has for all intents and purposes been rendered a quaint anachronism. In the Information Age, what is crucial is not extracting coal or exploiting the physical labor of a working class, but attracting and directing attention.

The extent to which we—like all colonized people—have become materially and culturally dependent on the values and tools by means of which we have been colonized can be gauged by the phenomenal success of the entertainment and travel industries—industries that market experiences and memories as such in a worldwide "war on boredom." We are no longer capable of entertaining ourselves. And this is not due to any lack of material opportunities or a diversity of environments, but to our growing inability to sufficiently appreciate our situation and enter into creative correspondence with it. In other words, it is not our immediate situation that is poverty stricken, but our attention as such—our capacities for attending, for being wholly present and caring. In a very real sense, we no longer fully own our attention and have forgotten how to be truly interested.

Concisely stated, the new colonialism necessarily and for ostensibly benign reasons promotes increasingly iconic awareness—an awareness attuned almost exclusively to the symbolic rather than the sensory, to use-function rather than aesthetic interplay. Like all things, exported attention, uprooted from its originally dramatic context, has no inherent nature. It can and indeed must be directed. Since the health of the information economy depends on attention circulating at usefully high rates along pathways of corporate advantage, situations that produce a sense of contentment—a willingness to appreciatively come to rest—are anathema. From this, it follows that the reduction of things to signs is the essence of good business in the Information Age, a new and postmodern development imperative. For the fully colonized and impoverished consciousness, the world is manifestly a system of interpretations. Things are attractive or repulsive, to be sure. They continue to direct attention. But in a very real sense they no longer matter. They have been flattened into mere signs devoid of any intrinsic value. What remains in such a "world" are only 'travelers', 'destinations', and the signs pointing toward them.

ICONOGRAPHY AND THE END OF MATERIALISM

In a world composed almost entirely of signs or icons, there is a preponderance of places to arrive and a great paucity of sustained directions. The very apparent wedding of narcissism and nihilism in the advanced guards and manifestos of the information elite is in the end not at all a matter of simple accident. The contraction of the horizons of our caring and concern to the limits of our individual and ostensibly autonomous selves is of a piece with the retraction of our interest in and appreciation of the uniqueness of our dramas, the dramas of our families and communities. But this also signals a disregard, an absence of true care, for the materiality of our various environments. Because we have been trained to disregard all but the most blatantly iconic dimensions of things, nothing outside of us can really matter. We simply don't sustain enough interest in either the people or things we live with for them to flower and bear dramatic fruit. In short, since we don't enrich them with deep and abiding appreciation, they also fail to enrich us.

Not surprisingly, to the precise extent that we have come to live in what we can call the significant universe, it is our subjectivity—that which invests attention in and so founds the meaningfulness of signs—that is of ultimate concern. Increasingly, we have no more feeling for the material of our musical instruments or our clothing or our furniture than we do for the pages on which are printed our defining texts. Signs are, after all replaceable and exchangeable. They exist for *our* benefit, not their own. In the end, we seldom have feelings except for the one thing we staunchly—and, perhaps, must—refuse to divest of its depths: our own 'self'.

'Selfishness' is a function of not caring for and about others. A trait we denounce in our children, our workmates, and our colleagues, it is at the same time a way of living wholly consistent with both our technical bias for control and the Information Age encouragement to disengage the meaning of texts from both their authors and their historical contexts. What this ultimately amounts to is a radical segregation or discourse ("flowing apart") of form and material—a segregation that devalues both by robbing materials of their uniqueness and forms of their sensible depth. It is a nontranscendent Platonism that denies all superordination while at the same time negating the actuality of uniqueness.

Grass is not just "something green" that covers the space between our front door and the street, but with shocking regularity, that is all we perceive. Especially if we have a "lawn care" service contract, we can completely ignore the way our yard grows, what it responds to with exuberance and what it suffers. When we cut and prune and weed, we establish a familial, caring relationship with our yard. We begin listening to what it can tell us of its needs and desires and also to what it can tell us about the quality of our listening, the depth of our virtuosity in responding to unexpected changes in its presence. At its deepest levels, caring for our yard can be a healing communication, a wholesome respite from our mediated isolation.

If speech is a modulation of conduct, it is clear that all things in some sense have voices and contribute to our narration. The joy of running barefoot through a verdant field is part of an always unique singing out of which we should only with great caution abstract 'humans beings' and 'grass'. But with increasing pride at being liberated from the tyranny of particular things, we perform just such a dazzling and dualism-producing reduction of our world to a complex of signifiers and signs. Nihilism and narcissism are two poles of a circular movement by means of which we at once triumph over irregularity and the unexpected and erode any clear remembrance of how and why this control, this ability to order, was first desired and then deemed necessary.

If consciousness is seen as a relationship given directly in the movement of our narration or conduct and not as our private possession, then any alteration of conduct is already an alteration of attention or awareness. Silencing things through exerting unmitigated control over them is to decisively limit their capacity for unexpected and creative contribution both to the rate and orientation of our dramatic interdependence. It is also to silence part of ourselves. Being able to decisively control or order our materials and the things fabricated out of them occasions an otherwise impossible security. But realizing security in this way is also to be secured. With the ability to control our environments and the myriad things populating them comes as well a loss of vulnerability and, with that, a loss of intimacy.

Because we no longer have to worry about the ability of things to resist our wills, we no longer have to pay close attention to them. Our perception of things tends, then, in the direction of dismissing rather than searching. We stop learning from things anything that we have not already placed in them. The blatant narcissism of postmodern epistemologies that assert the irreducibility of interpretation has for the most part not been critically assessed because signs do not speak for themselves and so cannot converse with us. Seen as signs, things can only tell us what we want. Unfortunately, in the absence of even the possibility of alternative voices, there is no erotic alternative to narcissistic self-absorption.

So prevalent is this silencing of things and the consequent impoverishment of the dramatic possibilities of our narration that an entire industry has developed around the notion of "self-help." Its basic premise is that the dissatisfactoriness of our lives need not be tolerated. To the contrary, most of our troubles can be overcome or controlled without recourse to professional help by attending more fully to our own needs and learning to better express these—both to ourselves and to others. In some ways, this endorsement of self-reliance is quite appropriate. At the very least, encouraging people to forego professional mediation can be a way of encouraging them to take full responsibility for their circumstances. Unfortunately, it seldom turns out that self-help leads to responding more fully and sensitively with our total circumstances. To the contrary, what typically occurs is a further discourse or controlled flowing-apart of "self" and its surroundings, not the conversational flowing-together of improvised concourse.

In fact, the futile circularity of the contemporary call for self-help makes itself evident in the now canonical assertion that we must first learn to "love ourselves" before we can go on to "authentically loving others." While it is true that some of us do manage this first lesson, very few manage to proceed from there to the second. In practice, we get trapped between the obdurate world of mute signs and an inner vacuity that—quite unlike the absence of defining essence endorsed by Buddhism—does not place us into more intimate connection with the world. Instead, it reinforces our conviction that at bottom not just all things, but we, too, are meaningless. That is, even when most successful, our narcissism confronts us with a dual nihility—the 'outer' nothingness of an increasingly iconic world and the 'inner' nothingness of an identity defined by our individuality and independence. Nihilistic narcissism is the natural product of our technological denial of interdependence and the consequent impoverishing of our biographical resources. Iconographic density means biographic vacuity.

LOSING OUR DIRECTION: THE ICONIC ROOTS OF BOREDOM

From a Buddhist perspective, it is not just our technically mediated experience, but *all* experience—at least all experience accompanied by an experiencer—that is to some extent iconic. To paraphrase the *Diamond Sutra*, 'things'—the objects of interdependence denying discriminations—are not things, we only refer to them as "things." More than just a presaging of the Whorfian insight that the map is not the terrain, the *Diamond Sutra* alerts us to the fact that the comprehensibility of things—their presence to our awareness as objects we're able to grasp—says more about our intentions than it does about any original nature of these 'objects'. In the same way that all icons are images or representations that quite explicitly point away from themselves, the objects of our awareness invariably refer back to us as knowing subjects, mirroring our values. Every instance of perception is an act of self-referential definition, a way of controlling the horizons and meaning of both things and our selves.

Now, the function of icons—no matter how skillfully realized—is *not* that of attracting and holding attention, but rather *directing* it elsewhere. Accordingly, icons cannot be either so complex or alluring that they become perceptual ends in themselves. Icons are not meant to be appreciatively lingered over or lovingly attended. In fact, if they should ever succeed in capturing our attention, they are sooner or later transformed into idols.

Iconoclasm—whether religious, political, or cultural, and wherever it oc-curs—is a violent revolution against such a reification of our icons and the forgetful subversion it entails.

In sociobiological terms, the largely iconic nature of day-to-day experi-ence is an evolutionary advantage. Being able to identify at a glance which plants are 'food' and which are 'poison,' which cries mean 'danger' and which mean 'pleasure', is crucial to being able to respond with certainty and rapidity. The iconic nature of mundane experience ensures that we do not become fascinated by our experience as such—something that might well compromise our capacity for survival. But the efficient exclusiveness of all perceptions also ensures that our experience is relevant to what we want and need, what is useful or harmful for us. Because we don't typically devote any attention to our experience as such or to the full sensory possibilities of any item of our experience, our attention is "freed" for continual scanning of our circumstances, enabling us to extend the range of our attention.

Of course, there is a fine balancing act here. We can extend the range of our attention through the transformation of things into icons or signs only by reducing the depth of our encounters with them. The same efficiency that insures our perception of what we can use and what we want so flattens our relationships with things that they are no longer capable of surprising us. We can become enslaved by the success of our experiential habits.

Those of us who have either had children of our own or who have spent significant amounts of time caring for infants know that while their atten-tion is relatively easy to distract, they are also liable to falling into deep fas-cination with things we dismiss almost immediately from conscious awareness. The world they live in is still populated by things that have no fixed meanings. Theirs is a world of unlimited possibilities, of fluidly shift-ing gestalts and open-ended meanings. As children age, we witness the grad-ual replacement of this world of true things by a world that is predominantly iconic. The crucial point of transition can be identified with great precision, though it varies from child to child. It is the moment at which they first an-nounce their boredom—the moment when they have lost enough of their in-nate capacity for appreciatively attending to the world about them that they feel "there isn't anything to do." Boredom announces biographic vacuity—the onset of nihilistic narcissism.

As might be expected given their disparate presuppositions about the na-ture of the world, a Buddhist understanding of the advent of boredom is in-terestingly in variance with that common among parents and educators in the contemporary West. We typically assume that boredom arises because our children aren't motivated, because they haven't developed a taste for achieve-ment and so an ability to direct themselves. With a great sense of mission, we embark on a process giving them the tools to do so, exposing them to the joys of reading or Internet exploration or organized (parent-mediated) sports. We teach them to vary their environment to keep themselves interested.

From what I've been referring to as "the Buddhist perspective," boredom is similarly seen as arising from a lack of directedness, but the solution is neither varying our environment nor developing a craving for achievement. These, in fact, are seen as leading to an even greater susceptibility to boredom and the sense of being "at loose ends." Children become bored because they are not able to spontaneously and suitably direct their attention. But treating this malaise must take into account the fact that their disability does not arise out of any environmental lack. To the contrary, it arises where their awareness is so profoundly restructured through sufficiently constant immersion in iconic modes of experience—modes in which there is an experiencing subject and an experienced object, and in which the value of the latter refers more or less explicitly back to the former—that they are incapable of breaking the circle of their expectations. Boredom arises when we have exhausted the dramatic possibilities of our present situation. And this can happen only when we have come to so ignore our interdependence with things that the only "voices" we can hear are those of our own individual and yet culturally constituted egos.

The problem with "curing" boredom by immersing children (or ourselves) in an explicitly and predominantly iconic world—like the world of plastic toys, video games, "children's" books, soap operas, media sports, or news broadcasts—is that it accustoms us to having our attention directed back toward what we want. This means that our egos become disproportionately prominent—something that no doubt underlies much of the explicitly selfish behavior to which we are more and more subject. But perhaps more importantly, such a "treatment" necessarily cultivates the disposition to treat our sense of biographic vacuity "directly." When a stimulus begins to bore us, we simply switch to another. And by this simple attempt to use what is iconically available to ease our discomfort, we begin training ourselves to consume.

Now, since it is the function of all icons to efficiently direct attention, this training will also eventuate an atrophy of our readiness for and ability to direct our own attention. We slide into depending, for example, on the media to supply us with sufficient differences to keep us interested in our own lives—even if not always in our actual (and not merely iconic) circumstances. Needless to say, learning how to shift our iconic context enough to keep our attention moving only makes matters worse, not better. Rather than learning to lose our egos by thoroughly offering our attention to our situation, we learn to indulge our wants.

The difference between consummate gratification and appreciative offering or contribution is crucial—a difference exemplified in the contrariety of watching TV or cruising the Internet and, for example, the horizonless eroticism of artistic creation. Instead of trying to recapture our ability to attend fully to the things around us *as* things, we surround ourselves with new icons, new representations. Shifting from appreciating things to controlling the content of our experience, we forfeit our beginner's mind and with it the root conditions for non-narcissistic affection. The initial bout of boredom suffered by each of our children is the pain of a mind newly addicted to the world of signs and the egos to which they refer, but not yet expert in obtaining a relieving fix for their attention. It is the pain of realizing that when nothing is interesting, neither are we.

Teenagers and adults living in "highly developed" nations are now almost fully immersed in mass-mediated entertainment and news, almost constantly subject to the dictates of a commodity-driven system of commerce. A normal day begins with the radio or television coming on and ends when it goes off for the night. In between are newspapers, magazines, televised news and entertainment, radio in the car, muzak in the office and on the phone when placed on hold, computerized mail, multimedia merchandising, and "down time" exploring the Internet or playing video games. In sum, the majority of our waking hours are spent paying attention to icons.

But this means as well that our awareness is being almost continuously directed. The colonization of consciousness is about selectively moved attention—legal and indeed much-approved mind control. And because we are mostly getting what we want, few of us are revolting. To do so is to be branded "irrational" and "anachronistic"—a modern-day Luddite fighting progress. Choosing to not own a television, to not include television programming as part of our day-to-day life, is very nearly unthinkable—as bizarre as choosing to not live in a building of some sort. In the near future, the same dismay will greet the suggestion that we resist subscribing to an Internet server and elect to live outside of the comprehensive and lightning-fast information environment it affords us.

The prevalence of boredom and the readiness with which we treat it by recourse to ever more extensive, mass mediation is a reliable index of the extent to which the world of our experience is—and has for a long time been—both self-referential and iconic. Nevertheless, as strong as the parallels might be between iconic existence and the type of existence enjoyed by most of the objects of our experience, except for those rare occasions when we suspect our senses of deceiving us, we do not think of all our experiences as being representational, as guiding our attention toward something unsensed. To the contrary, we are quite convinced that the world is more or less as we experience it. Ignorant we may be of certain of its details. Whole ranges or even continents of possible experience may have until now eluded us. But what we have seen and heard, tasted, touched, smelled, and pondered—that, we are convinced, is the world. Figuratively put, the senses are our windows onto the world, and if from time to time they have led us into error, it is because we have not thrown them open widely enough or because we have been too distracted by the billowing of the curtains (the presuppositions) we have hung in them.

And yet, it is a commonplace that people who pursue experiences without reservation are the fastest to become jaded, admitting that no matter how many "memorable" events and possessions they've accumulated, nothing makes any more sense than it ever did. If anything, things make less sense. These are people whose consciousness has, perhaps, been too successfully colonized, their attention so thoroughly mined that their biography has stretched to a breaking point. Such members of our society are often liable to thoughts of suicide on the one hand and on the other to dreams of a "normal life"—a life that may make no more ultimate sense than their own but that has the merit of presenting itself as less complicated, less stressful, and somehow more solid, more real. They are often those among us who are most ripe for political or religious conversion.

Such turnings about in the seat of consciousness mark the incursion of a new and encompassing narrative—a reconfiguration of experience according to an overarching and transcendent point of reference. That is, having realized the nihility of the things they've experienced—the absence of anything meaningful being pointed toward by the play of signs upon signs that we've come to accept as daily life—such people find themselves suddenly confronted with the opportunity to get everything to make sense, to have everything fall finally and sensibly into place. All that is required is unswerving belief, an unmitigated sacrifice of their attention-energy to a particular value or set of values. By this means, the vacuity yawning just beyond the sheer film of our daily experience can be dispelled and replaced by a universally valid and transcendent principle or principles that brings to order the Babel-like, unbroken clamor of signs and significations.

Importantly, such conversions occasion as well the possibility of reclaiming some readily grasped meaning for our impoverished biographies. The universal grammars of "socialist revolution," "evangelism," "scientism," or "New Age" spirituality all allow a *necessarily meaningful* extension of our life stories into an ever more fulfilling future. This is indeed a kind of salvation—the saving of the ego-self from "inadvertent" colonial extinction. But the necessity of the deliverance afforded by each of these belief systems (or the many others like them) suggests that they are in fact more of the same bill of goods sold us by our technical tradition and its bias for control. What such apparently disparate systems save is precisely that part of us that is supposed able to sublimate at once the narcissism of control and the nihilism of iconically impoverished attention. This it accomplishes by helping us dedicate ourselves to the "selfless" realization of the "one true world order." We should exercise extreme caution. It's not my intention here to disparage every form of religious and political conviction. But I do want to call attention to the likelihood that such convictions can indirectly and unintentionally sponsor our further colonization. By naively projecting our bias toward individuality onto the world as a whole—transforming it thereby from a centerlessly self-articulating cosmos into a transcendently ordered universe—such convictions have the structure of dictation even if they ostensibly demand our utter modesty, our submission to higher powers or principles. It need not be that the principles of any particular religious or political orientation are necessarily false or misleading, but only that the univocity and universality they typically promote effectively prohibit true conversation. We may all end up agreeing, but what is lost—the same thing lost with the dawning ubiquity of technologies of control—is the possibility of *surprisingly* harmonious narration. Since harmony is impossible in the absence of difference, we should be deeply wary of any system of belief advocating the elimination of the latter in the service of some "higher good." Creativity is simply not compatible with monotony, no matter how "agreeable" it is.

In the largely uncontrolled world of our forebears—a world prior to supermarkets, automobiles, multimedia computers, and worldwide information/advertising coverage—the view that the world we experience is the one-true-world was no more valid than it is today. To reiterate, *all* individually experienced events are to some extent iconographic. But in the Buddha's India, for example, a journey of even a few dozen miles could place a traveler in a world where not only one's familiar notions of "proper" or "normal" food and clothing, but one's "natural" language, religious rituals, and narrative traditions were manifestly absent. So important and unavoidable were such differences in prevailing modes of conduct that the Buddha explicitly instructed his students to adjust their teaching methods and vocabulary to suit the local cultural context. That is, the effective spread of the Buddha-dharma or teaching was seen as predicated on responsiveness to the symbolic and significant as well as more material, cultural needs of the local community.

The advent of practically ubiquitous mass media and the information technologies supporting them make it possible to directly affect the content of people's lived experiences virtually simultaneously, worldwide. That is, it is now possible to establish worldwide constellations of icons by means of which our personal identities and dramatic possibilities are largely defined. But more importantly, the local acceptance of these technologies and the consequent re-orientation of a people's conduct makes possible a profound conditioning of the structure of their experience and ideation apart from any "imported" content. Increasingly, locality no longer matters—and not in the sense that the Buddhist practice of emptiness means a realization of the irreducibility and horizonlessness of our interdependence. To the contrary, locality is rendered superfluous because the generic nature of mass-mediated experience makes it possible to effectively and almost entirely ignore both our uniqueness and interdependence. Thus, from a radically Buddhist perspective, our present conviction that the world we experience is basically the world as it is amounts to a virulent form of idolatry—the deification of our mediating and so segregating representations.

A good many of us are at least intellectually willing to assent to this kind of claim. After all, there is little disputing the claim that perception is highly selective—a function of either evaluation or envaluation, either the drawing out or projecting of values. As pragmatists like Richard Rorty persuasively and popularly insist, the idea that the human mind is a "mirror of nature" has been "proven" untenable, and along with it the naive supposition that perception literally presents the world rather than re-presenting it in accordance with our consciously and unconsciously held values.

As a corrective to various forms of conceptual or symbolic absolutism, this acceptance of the relativity and variety of our significations is arguably quite laudable. And yet, in the same way that we are warned by the Buddhist sage, Nagarjuna, not to make emptiness into an end in itself, we must beware that relativism, taken as a description of the way things *are*, is liable to encourage rather than discourage the further colonization of consciousness. This follows from the simple fact that relativism argues for the (at least ideal) equivalence of all standpoints or views. Whereas the Buddha taught the relinquishing of all views, relativism insists on their survival rights and individual validity. In short, relativism amounts to a fragmentation of absolutist universalism. It insures our right to individually define and so control our worlds and our experiences in them. From the ubiquitous and absolute "one," we move to endorsing the infinite absolutions of an irreproachable "many."

On the face of it, relativism narrows the locus of concern to the individual (nation, community, person, etc.). But in order to secure an abeyance of the worst kinds of conflict, it necessarily promotes at the same time an ideal of universal rights—to self-expression, self-governance, equal access to information and so on. In practice, relativism makes the ostensive "best" of both worlds, uniting the cultural themes of individuality and universality in a single, sensible system. The potential complicity of such a disposition with the dictates of the new colonialism—and so with the triumph of iconography—should be apparent. Relativism insists that, in the end, interpretation is basic. In response to the question about what the world rests on, postmodern relativists update the old adage that it's "turtles all the way down" and insist that, like it or not, it's just signs all the way down. No matter how deeply we look into "nature," we see our own reflections, more or less consciously. The "world," our "gender," our lifestyles and their meaning—all are constructions subject to no other necessities than those we establish.

FROM PERCEPTION TO CONCEPTION: DEEPENING THE NEW, LOCK GROOVE

The explicitly iconic nature of mass-mediated experience contributes to a thinning of our biographical resources, doing so in part through a leveling down of local differences. With the appropriate technologies in place, any given location is as good as any other. This means at once a radical individuation of point of view—an abstracting of our ability to know from the degree to which we are fully and locally present—and an equally radical tendency for all vantages to become progressively generic. Mass mediation is, in other words, conducive to a programmatic reduction of the uniqueness of our moment-to-moment experience, a reduction of its nonrepeatable, site-specific content. Such a reduction, persistently enough endured, conditions an attenuation of the virtuosity of our attentions—the degree to which we remain responsively and meaningfully alert to truly unanticipated and exceptional occurrences.

Leveling down the uniqueness of experiential content in combination with the homogenization of our modes of attentiveness effects a restructuring of subjectivity fully consonant with the dictates of a commodity-driven system of commerce. Granted that such a system enjoys reasonable security, this is a "viable" restructuring. As long as we can get our food out of grocery stores and regain our health in doctor's offices and hospitals, the sacrifice of our capacity for attentive diversity is not life-threatening even if it does constrain the depth of our personal narratives, our biographies. We can "get by" just fine.

Or can we? The transformation of subjectivity now well underway worldwide proceeds on the basis of an ignorance of immediate connections or relations—an ignorance of things as dramatically historical focuses of horizonless interdependence. For that reason alone, such a transformation signals a reduced capacity for responding as needed in situations beyond our (technically mediated) control. That should worry us. To make an analogy, our almost ubiquitous reliance on icon-driven assessments of our situation put us in a position not unlike someone committed to traveling only by automobile. The automobile surely increases our ability to travel quickly from place to place, but also limits the kinds (if not number) of places we can visit. In the end, we can go only where roads permit, and when there is an impending natural disaster on its way, that can be a great disadvantage.

By inculcating a "legitimate" ignorance of what we don't want, re-structuring our awareness according to the primary values of control and efficiency drastically compromises the relational resources needed to negotiate interruptions of our preferred courses of events. It makes us increasingly liable to suffering and the experience of not knowing what to do about it. In a word, a bias toward predominantly iconic experience is directly and yet "paradoxically" conducive to our being controlled. It marks a reduction of our capacity for sociality, for conduct that is spontaneous and improvised, and a parallel entrenchment of the societal biasing of our narration—our willingness to both regulate and be regulated.

One of the implications of seeing consciousness as a relationship we enjoy with our environments (and not as a property of our individuality) is that a reciprocity obtains among changes in our conduct and changes in what and how we perceive. The Buddhist claim that all experience is to some extent iconic is, at bottom, rooted largely in the recognition that far from simply passing on the world as it is, perceiving is an editorial activity—a weeding out of what is "useless" and a scaled and hierarchic foregrounding of "what matters." The anthropological and psychological literature is well stocked with the differences in perceptual content obtaining between, for example, urban-dwelling black Africans and their bush-dwelling counterparts. But anyone who has done trade work at a relatively advanced level or sold acoustic guitars in a music shop knows that while there are some common denominators in what various customers see and hear, there are remarkable differences as well—especially when it comes to the qualitative dimensions of things. Quite evidently, what we perceive are gestalts that emerge through a process of value-biased simplification. Whether—as empiricists of the eighteenth- and nineteenth-century British stamp maintained—there lies a basic level of pure sensation underneath this editorial activity we can leave for professional philosophers to dispute. The fact remains that our experience is by no means "pure."

Now, the editorial activity we refer to as "perception" partially, and only partially, warrants the claim that all experience is iconic. At least in a minimal sense, our perceptions establish the overall context of experience and refer us back to our own likes and dislikes, our own scales for utility and interest. We don't see in the infrared, for example, and when searching intently for something good to eat in the kitchen, we simply don't see the shape the cabinets are in or the half-emptied can of dog food on the second shelf of the fridge. But establishing the possibility that our experience can shift into an almost exclusively iconic mode and with it the structure of our awareness, we have to appeal to more than this editorial process.

This 'more' is what we can loosely refer to as "conception" or "thinking." If consciousness is not metaphysically disjunct from sensation, but emerges as the mutually responsive relationship of an 'organism' and its 'environment'—that is, as a function of the movement of their narration or conduct—then concepts cannot be held to be fundamentally private or internal, mental constructs *about* the world. To the contrary, they must be understood as equally psychic and somatic expressions *of* that world and its movements. More specifically, concepts are ambient—originating as and then further promoting regularities in conduct.

Conception is not, then, something limited to human beings. In fact, all sentient beings extend into the conceptual dimension. This doesn't mean, of course, that all sentient beings are equally conceptual any more than the fact that all beings enjoy some measure of spatial and temporal extension indicates that they're all the same size and evidence the same kind of topological complexity. At any rate, the salient point at present is that concepts are given in conduct. Our concept of dog—or to use the convention introduced above, 'dog'—should be seen as arising through our particular, concrete activities of calling and petting, our emotional investment in these behaviors, the responses of the animals with whom we've entered into relationship, and so on. For a child, 'dog' is inextricably bound up with 'playmate' and 'friend'. It includes open displays of affection and even jealousies. It involves running and chasing, protective stances, and pining. For a lab worker in a university medical research center, 'dogs' includes the ranges of technical manipulations performed on the animals' bodies for the purpose of scientific investigation and so typically excludes the sociality of a child's emotional relationship with his or her animal friend. For a hunter, 'dog' includes those patterns of conduct or narrative movement related to the tracking, stalking, and killing of either edible or trophy game. The love and affection displayed by a pet dog is almost never seen in a lab animal, not because of a difference in the original nature of dogs, but in the narrative spaces opened up by the movement and orientation of these disparate forms of conduct. That is, the differences lie in the mode and direction of the narration of man and animal. The concept of dog is not originally located *in* us, but between us—in the space of dramatic interrelationship or conduct. To paraphrase the *Diamond Sutra*, 'dogs' are not dogs, we only refer to them as "dogs." In actuality, 'dogs' are our creations, and not just because of our techniques for breeding the appearance of certain characters. 'Dogs' are our creations because they come to be—they exist—only in and through our shared, regular conduct. But, then again, the same can be said of 'you' and 'I'.

As in perceptual activity, conceiving entails an abstraction of relevant aspects of our sensory situation. But whereas perception occurs in the context of a given present moment defined by the limit of our senses, conception also abstracts over time. That is, conception has to do with generalization as well as abstraction. It marks the orientation of our attention toward things that are not actually present. More than just an act of remembering, conception involves the identification of permanent or at least recurrent features of our conduct and experience. In thinking, we cut away all but the essential core of a situation—a process we have come to believe reveals the truest nature of things, their most pristine and distinct status.

In purposely simplistic terms, we don't think about what actually obtains, but about regularities in the patterns of our liking and disliking. Rooted in the editorial process of perceiving, conception is best seen as a second order abstraction or distillation, a kind of squaring of the axiological biases guiding our perceptual activity. While all perception is to some extent iconic, conception raises to the second power our tacit commitment to representation.

From a Buddhist perspective, conception thus marks a purposeful ignorance of impermanence. And in many ways, this is a valuable skill—a learned activity—and one particularly well-developed among human beings. But as Jorge Luis Borges—that incomparable inventor of literary alternatives to the mainstreams of Western philosophy and history—has said, every thought is the forgetting of a difference. Specifically, it means a cessation of moment-to-moment attention to the 'thing' we're conceiving, an ignorance of the large and small changes each and every thing is at some level and at all times undergoing. If, as the *Tao Te Ching* suggests, big problems are best solved when they are still small, this tendency to overlook subtle changes will only foster a felt need to exert more control in the furtherance of our continued security. Moreover, because conception is oriented toward the identification of permanent features or regularities, it also encourages a forgeting of the uniqueness of all things and so an ignorance of the very differences that establish the root conditions for truly harmonious interdependence. In short, conception entails a value-driven disregard of the emptiness of all things. Ch'an Buddhism's infamously antagonistic attitude toward thinking (*nian*), is based on precisely the sedimentary effect it has on our conduct. Conception promotes an inordinately societal orientation of our conduct—an orientation incompatible with improvisational virtuosity.

That conception is a powerfully effective strategy for initiating control over our circumstances (and, inevitably, one another) is indisputably manifest in the remarkable degree to which human beings have managed under its auspices to "harness" nature. The dominion we exercise over things is directly proportional to the extent that they have been relegated to the status of icons, largely under the technically leveraged pressure of our conceptual expertise. The ability to view the planets mathematically, for example, was crucial to landing men on the moon and laying claim to it "for all mankind."

And yet the miraculous nature of this feat and the control that it, like many others of its kind, evidences can blind us to the fact that we can only control what we can identify—what is both limited and relatively stable. The extent to which we are oriented toward control is thus an index of the degree to which we live in a world of largely generic icons. For the most part, we can't bring ourselves to worry about this. After all, doesn't our technical ability to control or regulate the world in fact "prove" that what we have identified is really there? Don't our technical triumphs assert the accuracy of the scientific, religious, political, and commercial ideologies that have so readily and thoroughly sponsored them?

Having assumed that the world is not directly a function of our intentions—something "empirically evident" to everyone who has ever tried and failed to get something they desperately wanted—it makes sense that any progress we make in forcing an unruly world into obedience indicates our having divined the secret laws of its inner and outer workings. But what if this assumption is simply wrong? What if the lack of immediate relationship between our intentions and the topology of our experience is a function of the limited, fragmented nature of our icon-driven temporality? What if the world is—as Buddhists claim—always and precisely conditioned by the patterns of our intentional activity or karma? What if the 'world' is simply a record of the consistencies in our disambiguations of the original, unfixed nature of things? And what if our increasing boredom with our circumstances must then be seen as a reflection of our becoming less and less interestingly human?

In the Buddhist cosmos, our technical successes only prove the remarkable degree to which we have remained consistently oriented in our thoughts, feelings, speech, and deeds. That is, our success doesn't reflect the accuracy with which we're "zeroing in" on reality, but our virtually exceptionless commitment to intensifying our own karma. In a wonderfully ironic twist, Buddhist metaphysics suggests that getting what we want as soon as and whenever we want it is manifest evidence of a long-standing investment of our attention and intentions in these very wants. In short, such control is not a sign of the richness of our experience, but the pervasiveness and resilience of our modes of poverty. The conceptual biases driving our technological progress do not serve, then, to free us from our lacks. To the contrary, by "squaring" the biases of our likes and dislikes, they work toward profoundly intensifying our karma.

The kind of regulatory power that sending a man to the moon marshals is indeed shocking. It means first a demystification of the world—a denial of the world's capacity to surprise us. This alone is bad enough. It is in the measureless spaces of mystery that new possibilities are engendered and new desires realized. It is only through the mysterious that things work out better than we ever could have expected. A perfectly regulated world would be a world without wilderness or spirit, a world bereft of dramatic depth.

Because conception or thinking moves us in the direction of 'useful' generality and even universality, it encourages us to cultivate regularity and establish standards. And the natural outcome of such conduct—institutions and efficient interchange—is perhaps exactly what our wants tell us we need. Treating deeply entrenched and often habitual wants requires secure and reliable "delivery systems." But if consciousness is directly given in conduct—the movement of our narration—these systems inevitably lead toward regulating and standardizing our selves. While control over our environment demystifies the world and renders it tiresomely predictable, it also marks the domestication of our own spirit. Quite simply, if our concept-conditioned bias for control becomes dominant enough, we lose the ability to surprise ourselves.

THE COMMODITY-DRIVEN TRANSLATION OF DESIRING INTO WANTING

At some point, the convenience and efficiency of our acts of taking possession crossed a threshold beyond which things in their full and mysterious materiality began rapidly receding into the oblivion of pure signification. In our headlong rush to acquire ever more and newer possessions, the unique energies of things—their *ch'i* or mana—cannot reach us. Or they reach us so fantastically diminished that they are no more able to warm us than the light of distant stars. The analogy is, I think, a good one in that it suggests that part of the problem is a compression of our shared temporality with things into an ideal moment—the moment of taking possession. In the same way that rapidly approaching a distant star will make light emanating from it shift into the blue or "hot" end of the energy spectrum, our lust for acquiring things raises them into a kind of prominence. If we were able to stop and fully appreciate these things, slowing down enough to enter into their orbit, they might indeed help nurture us and even bring us to unexpectedly luscious and unique fruition. But instead, we rush ever more rapidly past on our way to the next acquisition and their light or energy shifts so deeply into the red that they eventually become as interchangeable and unimportant as grains of sand on yesterday's beach.

An openness to creatively rich relationships of mutual contribution depends on shifting our awareness from an orientation toward control to that of appreciation. In the absence of such a shift, our relationship with things eventually comes down to equally momentary instances of use and (either permanent or temporary) dismissal. We simply don't come to rest with things long enough for a true conversation or "turning-together" to be possible. It isn't that we don't want things—we do, and often very intensely. But the velocity of our consumption is so great that—as with travel or commercial transactions more generally—we somehow don't seem to have time to do anything more than keep consuming.

Bluntly stated, we have all but lost the ability to desire. That we are almost incessantly assailed by wants, by experienced lack, is beyond contesting. But wanting is not the same as desiring. Wants are centripetal in that they ultimately refer us back to ourselves, the recipients of what was lacking. As implied in its etymological roots (*de* + *siderus*, "to the stars") desire is a predominantly centrifugal focusing of attention—an appreciative longing that aims at closeness, even union, without the collapse of difference. As might be expected granted its shared roots with the practice of consideration (*con* + *siderus*), desiring engenders intimate concern. Far from resulting in the gaining of a new possession or our arrival at some fixed and satisfying destination, desire brings about a crescendo of appreciative familiarity in which we find ourselves offered so fully that 'I', 'my', and 'me' fall completely away. True desires are thus quite rare, even celestial.

Distinguishing desiring and wanting in this way, it's clear that our economy is based on taking things with which we could enter into truly desirable relationship and translating them into commodities useful only in the satisfaction of wants. When a Dene hunter goes out onto the tundra, he intends to invite a bear to take his favorite spear into itself and then enter his home to warm his wife and children, literally becoming incorporated by them. Dene hunting does not aim at temporarily taking possession of a bear's life and then, once some set of wants have been satisfied, forgetting about it altogether. To the contrary, it aims at establishing a ritual relationship by means of which both human and bear prosper in mutual respect. Seen in this light, clan totemism is a sophisticated recognition of interdependence—a realization that to the extent that other species offer themselves to us, they are caring for us and so playing the role of parents and elders.

We may smile knowingly at the naiveté and mythically proportioned befuddlement of peoples who honor animals as relatives or the sky and earth as their original father and mother. According to our presuppositions, they've got at best a crude and merely intuitive model of natural, biological evolution—a model that we have nearly brought to perfection. But in affirming that sky and earth are our ancestors is not to commit ourselves to a simplistic and mistaken biological claim. It is to deeply acknowledge a felt relationship of mutual caring and contribution. When we disparage such feelings as "primitive" or "childish," we are not proving our sophistication, but the depth of our wanting, the extent to which sun and moon and all the creatures of this earth—constant partners in our narration without which we would not be alive at all—have been reduced to mere signs.

We are right in thinking that the life of the Dene or any people who continue to respect all things as members of their family is deeply romantic.

It is a life based on desirous relationships—relationships that involve such refined levels of consideration that they are capable of lasting not just a single lifetime, but for thousands of years. In such a truly romantic life it is possible to miss many things, but not to want them. It is instead our determined effort to control things that leads to our constant forgetfulness about our interdependence with them. In turn, this forgetfulness not only occasions our continued wanting, but the steady depletion and eventual extinction of those things we might otherwise have considered so intimately a part of ourselves that we could never imagine being at once fundamentally autonomous and incomplete.

If it were the case that our consumer practices were primarily motivated by a responsive and intimate commitment to things, the state of our attics and garages and closets would be inexplicable. But in actuality our consumption, driven by a need to satisfy our advertised wants, necessarily entails largely forgetting what we have gotten. Indeed, the sheer bulk of the almost entirely unnoticed "things" we possess testifies to the thinness of their presence in our lives, their essentially iconic mode of obtaining in our experienced world. Such incredibly various "goods" can only have come so profusely into our lives if the act of taking possession is at the same time an act of dismissal.

Of course, it is not just things that are commodified and then forgotten in the act of consumption. Wanting sex can be satisfied by a one-night stand or by a visit to a prostitute—acts that reduce lovemaking to a kind of commerce. In cases like that of a prostitute and her john, 'sex' is the 'thing' wanted and each member of the relationship quite explicitly perceives the other only as a commodity or sign. Names and histories, hopes and dreams, are strictly optional and largely perceived as detracting from the pure act of consumption. But such a reduction of persons first to things and then to mere signs is not restricted to such extreme cases. Our increasingly societal dealings with each other as only a 'bank-teller' and 'customer', or only a 'toll-taker' and 'commuter' amount to the same thing. Seen only in terms of their roles or classes, and not as friends and neighbors whose families have shared time and space for decades and generations, other people become existentially thin and eminently forgettable. In this process, it is not just others who are reduced, however, but our own selves as well—from full members of a vibrant community to relatively independent and yet unavoidably dependent egos. Since consciousness is given in conduct, wanting necessarily reduces or impoverishes both the thing wanted and the person who wants.

Granted this, the much deplored vacuity of the TV generation should not be surprising. Television—both in advertising and the representation of idealized life stories—teaches wanting, not desiring. And it is not even some deeply unpredictable and mysterious other that we find ourselves lacking, but a generic object—a thing or person experienced through only two of our senses and never immediately. Television does not present us with a full, six-dimensional experience—something seen, heard, tasted, touched, smelled, and considerately thought about. To the contrary, what we're presented are icons—symbols or signs of people and places and things, but *never* the people, places, or things signified. MTV and most current news programming take a still deeper cut into our attention and so amplify our wants by immersing us in a medium composed almost entirely of glimpses. Either way, what we attend does not need or respond to our caring and—like all fruitless activity—eventually atrophies and ceases.

It bears pausing at this point to consider what it means that the average American father spends less one-on-one time with his children in a week than he does watching a single half of Monday night football. Meanwhile, his children spend vastly more time playing video games or watching cartoons, MTV, and "children's programs and videos" than they do sharing time with him and their mother combined. The average American consumes and is dramatically consumed by four hours of television a day.

How can it be that television characters, sports figures, and newscasters deserve more of our undivided attention than our own flesh and blood? How can it be that we are satisfied by attending to people that are completely unmoved by our attentions? In part, I think, this is because the kind of attention the media require and promote in us is so easy to give—a giving for which we are prepared by our prevailing modes of commerce and mundane existence. But it's also in part because the media give us the illusion of being able to definitively control our experience—something our family members constantly remind us is impossible. While domestic violence is not something new, I suspect that its narrative or dramatic function is more than ever before a way of venting frustrations caused by people and things that refuse to be as we want.

Mediate experience is not just regulated—guided by statistical profiles of market viability and the exercise of corporate hegemony—but regulating. The passivity of television time is notorious, but in the end, so is time spent cruising the Internet. We can almost effortlessly seek out and selectively consume data. By just keying in a search command, we're presented as if by magic with a list of hundreds of likely destinations. With a convenience no less astounding and thorough than that of supermarket shopping, we are able to "access" information about practically any topic we can imagine. But in the process, knowledge is being commodified—transformed from a historically rich and so enduring relationship into a product consumed.

That the addictive appeal in "surfing" the Internet or in sampling the panoply of cable TV offerings does not lie in where we arrive but in the effortlessness with which we get there is readily evident to any uninvolved observer. While there is certainly a popular rhetoric about the incredible variety of program sites now available by cable and through multimedia computing, there is little to suggest that this variety has any function other than the capture of maximal amounts of short-term attention. If "channel surfing" is becoming increasingly common in our households, it is not because we are deepening our appreciation of each show by returning to it at random points with an awareness "freshened" by exposure to other programs. To the contrary, it is simply because we are getting everything we want from TV through little more than glimpses.

It is not the *content* of mediate experience that is addicting, but its *structure*—the manner in which it reconfigures our awareness. What feels good is skipping from scene to scene in rapid succession with no conscious attempt to relate these in any way, dramatically or otherwise. What we have done is to move "beyond" the need for history, for meaningful narration, and the responsibilities these entail. There is a deep incommensurability between jumping from radio station to radio station in search of something we want to hear and the role played by the "audience" in a traditional Nigerian village or at an "island style" graduation luau where 'performers' and 'audience' are only relative and finally irrelevant distinctions.

The quality of some performances, the meaning of some events, can only become apparent when a sufficiently responsive context has been realized. This usually means a continuous attention and readiness for appreciative contribution—the sharing of time without which meaning is reduced to something at once private and completed. Mass media discourage the kind of commitment needed for realizing true community—whether in our homes or beyond. As knowledge is increasingly reduced to information, knowing who we are and to what communities we belong becomes a merely significant and not a fully dramatic process. Already, our closest relationships are incredibly likely to become basically discursive objects—objects that encourage our verbal, bodily, and emotional segregation. If the rate at which we marry and divorce, couple and discouple, can be attributed to one major condition, it is that we are being trained to merely want, and not truly desire, our partners.

When the ignorance that is necessarily a part of wanting reaches a sufficient intensity, our entire narration—every aspect of our dramatic relatedness—is impoverished. Wanting finally means the emergence of a clear subject-object distinction—a distinction coextensive with the appearance of an identifiable, individual, and so basically abstract ego. To be sure, this is a so-called natural event. A similar, ideal isolation from our environment is understood as part of what happens to each of us in the transition from infancy to childhood, adolescence and adulthood. Establishing boundaries for 'self' and 'other' is part of what we call "growing up." The novelty in our current situation is that our technological bias for control and our practically incessant and willing subjection to predominantly iconic mediation is making alternatives to egoic existence or "standing-apart" from the things and people around us almost unimaginable.

Thus, while the word "healthy" originally meant wholeness and implied that we were in proper relationship with everything around us, health—particularly mental, but also physical—is now conceived in terms of degrees of independence. We are healthy when we don't need help from others, when we don't require their constant attention, when we have no dietary restrictions or particular requirements for exercise or rest or medication. In the same way, it is now "natural" for our awareness to be independent of where we are actually situated. Living in the here and now is something we typically have to work long and hard to accomplish. Witness the difficulty we have in simply watching our breath for even just a minute without being distracted by some thought of past or future. What is now "natural" is freely skipping from time to time and from view to view without ever feeling compelled to take root. As exemplified in our cable TV and Internet use, our nature is now to be ideally independent, to be able to jump from one situation to another with no intervening connections. We touch down without being touched. We move along without being moved. And we call this "the good life."

Chapter 10

The New Meaning of Biography
The Efficient Self in Calculated Crisis

Like all things, "the good life" has no fixed or essential nature. At the very least, it is clear that what it means to be living "the good life" depends on where we are in our lives—whether we have the needs, capabilities, and responsibilities of infants, children, adolescents, adults, or elders. But as comparative studies by anthropologists, sociologists, and psychologists have made undeniable, what it means to be an 'infant', a 'child', an 'adolescent', an 'adult', or an 'elder' is profoundly conditioned by both culture and politics. That is, the human life cycle is neither universal nor unchanging, but rather highly particularized and adaptive.

Still, within any given society, there is some general agreement about what is both factually and ideally involved in successfully negotiating the path from birth and infancy to old age and death. In most of the so-called developed world, the current version goes from being born as helpless and totally dependent creatures among health professionals in a hospital to retirement, increasing dependence on others, and a death among health care technicians in a nursing home or hospital. In between, it is understood that we will consolidate our particular mode of autonomy, establishing our identities and gaining increasing control of both our circumstances and ourselves up to an ill-defined point at which we will find ourselves suddenly "over the hill" and on the way rapidly down.

Some twenty-five hundred years ago, in what is perhaps the oldest recorded description of the human life cycle, Confucius relates how, "At fifteen, my heart-mind was set upon learning; at thirty I took my stance; at forty I was no longer of two minds; at fifty I realized *t'ien ming* (the "celestial directive" according to which the world is organized); at sixty my ear was attuned; and at seventy I could give my heart-mind free rein without overstepping the mark" (*Analects*, 2.4). For Confucius, the general movement in human development is from initially opening up to one's situation in an appreciative way to being able to freely improvise with and contribute to it.

The contrasts are striking. For example, in the contemporary world, the adolescent is notoriously self-absorbed, rebellious, and troubled; in the Confucian, the adolescent is intent on developing a core set of appropriate forms of conduct. At forty, we typically find ourselves in an identity crisis of major proportions, whereas the Confucian has earned full and straightforward confidence. At sixty, the Confucian person is at least ideally most attuned to his or her situation; in postmodern society, the sixty-year-old is thought of as falling out of touch—someone who can be effectively tuned out. And at seventy, while Confucius felt he was finally able to improvise freely with changing circumstances and never miss a beat, we are typically feeling out of step, stiff, and behind the times.

The general trajectory of the Confucian life cycle—as in so many subsistence and traditional cultures—is thus one of continual ascent and becoming increasingly valued as a member of society—a gradual easing of contributory constraints and the realization of ever more meaningful placement in the community. In the most highly "developed" nations today, the trajectory is explicitly finite and subject to gravity, reaching a zenith anywhere from age thirty-five to fifty-five and in a steady downward trend thereafter. Where Confucian elders are understood as worthy of reverence, our elderly are considered either irrelevant or burdensome.

Whether there are exceptions to these life cycles or whether they serve primarily as cultural fictions and not as "objective" phenomenologies, there is no denying their general validity and disparity as biographical frameworks. Nor is there any denying that the infusion of a society with technologies biased toward control is correlated with a rapid revision of the ways in which both children and the elderly are perceived and cared for— the institution of a biographical "bell curve" according to which we are most fully ourselves at precisely that point in our lives when we are most in control and least so during the "infirmities" of infancy and old age.

From this it follows that we can gain some understanding of the way in which our biographies are conditioned by an increasing technological bias for control by looking at the ways in which our most "productive" years are spent—those years in which we enjoy the greatest force of character and authority, the golden years of our work careers. In a very broad sense, critically assessing our work practices, what they mean to us, and the kind of mind cultivated through them provides us with a practical frame of reference for seeing who we are making ourselves into, the kinds of self we are actively fashioning in service of the new colonialism.

COMMERCE AND COMMODITY: THE NEW GRAMMAR AND VOCABULARY OF "I AM . . ."

We have already seen that the biases for control and efficiency that underlie our embrace of mass production and mass marketing are conducive to the commodification of everything from the food, clothing, and shelter involved in maintaining our daily existence to the most central values distinguishing our cultures. The result is that we now accumulate possessions at a completely unprecedented rate while receiving less and less in terms of experiential depth and dramatic complexity for our labor. Granted the Buddhist understanding of personhood as irreducibly relational, we would expect a similar destiny for our productive lives as workers.

Indeed, work is now so specialized that there are listed in the *Dictionary of Occupational Titles* well over a thousand distinct job categories. Much as clothing in traditional societies is of limited variety but highly individualized and clothing in postmodern societies almost infinitely variable but highly generic, jobs are becoming both highly specialized and yet impersonal. Contemporary workers know full well that if they do not want to perform as instructed and with satisfactory efficiency, there is always someone else standing just behind them who will. Apart from media stars who command the attention of millions, everyone is expendable.

While some specialization occurs in virtually all societies, this degree of fundamentally impersonal specialization strongly suggests that basic subsistence practices have been so thoroughly rationalized that they have themselves become mere commodities. Thus, while new classes of jobs are being created with great rapidity, full employment is seeming to be a less and less realizable goal—at least economically. As Jeremy Rifkin has suggested in his book *The End of Work* (1995), the economic pressure to automate work previously done by humans is so great that even service industries like banking are looking to total workforce reductions of 30–40 percent over just the next eight to ten years. That is, having been translated into a resource commodity, employment is becoming scarce enough that it may soon have to be legally conserved and protected. Otherwise, work is very likely to become purely semiotic.

A major consequence of this technologically conditioned shift in work and employment patterns has been the steady rise in temporary service agencies, mid-life career changes, job-hopping, and the substitution of horizontal for vertical mobility as a reasonable ideal. As work is commodified, it is virtually guaranteed that work histories—like records of other commodity purchases we make as a matter of course—will become increasingly varied, long, and subject to market fashion. It is not just our shoes and our homes that do not last the way they used to, but our skills and our jobs. And in the same way that technological mediation has led to a truly antimaterialist consumer society, it is leading as well to an ever greater tendency to ignore the intrinsic value of work and so its meaningful relationship to who we are as persons.

In the halcyon days of European industrialization, Marx already decried the subjection of labor to capital—its translation into a simple and quantifiable resource commodity and thus its dramatic deflation. But while his argument that wealth needed to be more rationally and equitably distributed evidenced admirable intentions, in the long run it did little more, having failed to adequately question whether the prevailing concept of wealth had not always been and still continued to be karmically impoverishing. Based on a faith in the salvific capacity of the Western technological lineage, the Marxist project was an oxymoronic one of equally distributing control. Full employment could be guaranteed in Marxist economies, but only at the cost of fearfully inefficient production and creativity-oppressing state monopoly. As long as control serves as a society's primary technical value, development can only mean increasing consumerism, the commodification of labor, and the proliferation—not elimination—of classes.

The efficiency rationale of development is such that we are permitted to identify ourselves with our work, but barred from taking it as a path of authentic self-development. Although there are exceptions, the average person in the most technologically advanced societies at once rues and avidly looks forward to the day of his or her retirement. On the one hand, life is empty enough that work is preferable to aimlessly passing day after day as an economically disadvantaged consumer; on the other hand, work is experienced as an imposition—an inhibition of freedom and not its most satisfying context. Much as the commodification of material resources and knowledge meant forfeiting the ability to grow our own foods, build our own homes, heal our own bodies, teach ourselves, or harmonize our own communities, every two steps toward factual wealth and freedom entails at least one step away from full and dramatically satisfying employment.

As the locus of business moves from the multigenerational, narrative complexity of the family courtyard or village bazaar to the efficient and convenient environs of corporate commerce, not only is business conduct transformed, so are we. For example, while the shift from face-to-face business relations to electronically mediated ones has had only a relatively minor impact on the length of the working day, it has made it possible to entirely recast huge blocks of time previously "wasted" on getting to know each other. In sharp contrast with the temporal and social modalities of business in rural Bali, for example, we no longer find ourselves sharing tea and fruit with various members of the family while negotiating the wholesale price of silver jewelry. We no longer happily weave portions of our life narratives into those of our business contacts as a joyfully natural matter of course, but only begrudgingly as a kind of economic necessity. And in our more mundane business dealings at the mall or in the convenience store or at the gas station on the corner, we are content to scarcely take notice of the clerks who handle our transactions. In fact, we are more and more inclined to simply bypass all human contact by using one of our credit cards to expedite the transaction.

There is no doubt of the efficiency of any individual transaction thus "purified" of personal narration. The consumption of mass-produced and mass-marketed commodities in generic shopping malls cannot be beaten for overall convenience. And yet, this efficiency and commercial ease have not come without cost—a cost exacted not only on our pocketbooks, but on our bodies and minds, the directions in which our narration moves, its drama, and with it the feel of our community.

Perhaps the most obvious result of this increased efficiency is that many more individual transactions or (more generally) productive activities can be fitted into "the same" eight-hour workday. As the received opinion would have it: with the remarkable technical advantages now widely available, we're "getting more done" in less time than ever before. That is supposed to be an unqualified good. But is it? There is, after all, a fallacy involved in proposing that if it's a good idea to carry out any individual transaction in less time, then it must be good to carry out *all* transactions in less time. It is the same fallacy underlying the confident proclamation that technically advancing control is ubiquitously good based on our happy, but admittedly individual use of the latest computers or power tools or "smart" missiles.

In fact, like the threshold of utility discovered by Illich in his study of transportation practices in different societies, there obtains a threshold for the velocity of business transactions up to which efficiency means less overall time spent in business activity (and so more real free time), and beyond which further increases in "efficiency" actually bring about an absolute increase in the amount of business being carried out. In the same way that widely available rail and automotive transportation led first to increasingly large amounts of time devoted to travel and then to travel being viewed as an end in itself, the technically driven acceleration of business practices threatens to elevate business as means into business as end. At such a point, businesses stop serving our interests because we have been fully drafted into serving theirs.

Thus, the workaholic is literally defined or bounded by his or her work. Instead of work being conducive to increasingly fruitful and intimate relationships with friends and family, the workaholic is notoriously absent where he or she would normally be most meaningfully and valuably situated. Seldom seen by his or her children and spouse, engaging "friends" and "associates" only in the "after hours" context that extends rather than ends the workday, the workaholic suffers from a radical contraction of the self—a dramatic attenuation of those relationships conducive to realizing virtuosic sociality and not simply societal expertise.

Ironically, but hardly surprising from a karmic perspective, while our technological progress manifestly allows us to do more work in less time than ever before, after a certain level of "advantage" we also find ourselves having less truly free time. Illich's own (1981) studies of the unacknowledged and yet pivotal role played by what he calls "shadow work" in our economies can be read as an objective introduction to the dishonesty of our evaluations of technically mediated and accelerated business. It is not the peasant farmer who works eighty hours a week year-round, but the high-tech entrepreneur. Somewhat later, we'll look in more detail at the ramifications of the postmodern temporality of the dawning information age, but even at this initial level of analysis, it should be clear that the recent history of our employment and business practices—like those for our entertainment and even our intimate relationships such as marriage—is a history of "hunters" being captured by their "game."

THE EFFICIENCY OF STRESS: CONTROLLING TIME AND MISGUIDING ATTENTION

This way of describing the situation is liable, however, to restrict our attention to the extrinsic (or behavioral) rather than the intrinsic (or attentive) dimensions of the relationship of technological progress and the quality of consciousness. Complaints about the pace of contemporary life are legion, but a consideration of the effects of pace on the dramatic tenor of our attention and experience is much less frequently remarked. We are aware, for example, that the pitch of our day-to-day activity is such that we often need a full two weeks of vacation before we can slow down enough to truly enjoy the sunrise or fully appreciate the silver play of moonlight on the ocean. If such periods of temporal detoxification were frequent and of conveniently short duration, perhaps this "need" wouldn't be particularly remarkable. But they are not. We simply do not have the time to appreciate things. Tragically, it is a rare day that we dwell in any moment long enough for it to blossom in a fully meaningful way.

Recourse to various drugs—including but by no means limited to nicotine, caffeine, and alcohol—has become endemic to our way of life as a means of either "getting up to speed" or "unwinding" enough to balance our energy and offset the effects of day-to-day life pressures. But finally they are manifestly insufficient to return a sense of meaning to our most common, daily affairs. Like our medical practices, they treat the symptoms, but not the originating conditions of our discomfort. For the most part, we now accept this. The mundane chores and duties we take care of as a matter of course are not supposed to be meaningful. That is one of the cold, hard facts of adulthood and self-sufficiency. But this fact, like all others, is deeply value-laden. Our control-biased and technologically accelerated pace of life is conducive to a reduction of both temporal depth and the quality of our attention and experience for the same reason that highway traffic signs are big and simple—at the speed we are passing them, they would not be able to effectively direct our attention otherwise. The faster we go, the less meaning any given sign can occasion.

Granted this, we might still object that the point, after all, is to get where we're going, not to take in sights along the way. That seems reasonable for some kinds of trips, but not for all, and almost certainly not for the one from birth to death. While some of us do better than others, we seldom clear our body-mind systems entirely of the toxically attenuated forms of temporality and experience characterizing especially our work-centered lives, but increasingly common in our patterns of entertainment as well. Our pace of life not only makes it difficult to enjoy meaningful relationships in our daily affairs, it subjects us to effects not unlike the g-forces we experience on carnival rides. Only the effects are not short-lived and exciting, but chronic. In result, we suffer a wide range of both organic and psychic distortions gathered together under the medical umbrella of "stress."

The basically unhealthy nature of temporal compression and the kind of iconic awareness it promotes are least controversially evident when we consider the epidemic rise of stress-related illness in the most technologically advanced societies. In subsistence societies, where so much of daily life is endowed with ritual meaning and where the pace of life is notoriously languid, such ailments are virtually unknown. In part, this can be attributed to the simple fact that persons are not understood as separate from, but rather constituted by what they do, the relationships of which they are a part. The rationalization of postmodern living involves a compartmentalization of life through which our time at work, at leisure, in chores, and with our loved ones are all effectively segregated. In result, we experience distinct boundaries between the different 'parts' of who we are—the different parts of our lives—and with them the increasing potential for debilitating friction as we hasten to make all our various ends meet.

More often than we are comfortable admitting, the harmonious functioning of both our communities and the human mind-body system is so regularly and deeply compromised by the rationalization of our conduct and the technically accelerated pace of our lives that even the most miraculous advances in medical technology are incapable of alleviating our distress. If anything, medical care often seems to compound the effects of stress—a typical case being the "side effects" of blood pressure medicines on heart function, digestion, sleep patterns, and overall sense of well-being.

As suggested earlier, from a Buddhist perspective, illness and distress ultimately hinge on inappropriate modes of attention or ignorance. From such a perspective, stress manifestly occurs as a function of compulsively or chronically misguided attention. And as this would lead us to expect, the most successful programs for stress reduction focus on learning to disengage from our habits of experience and attend to our bodies and minds in a more mindful or appreciative way. As first detailed in Herbert Benson's (1975) book, *The Relaxation Response*, the crucial element in stress reduction is not the particular technique used or the exact nature of what we mind, but our way of minding—the qualitatively open temporality of the attentive relationship.

Importantly, all such techniques make it clear that we cannot force ourselves to relax. Increasing our capacity for control does not alleviate the effects of temporal compression. To the contrary, it can only further amplify them. And that, finally, is why using drugs to treat stress so typically fails, whether we do so by doctor's prescription or illicitly. If we include deaths due to smoking, alcoholism, and exercise or diet-related hypertension and heart disease—all quite clearly dependent on chronically misguided forms of attention—stress is the number one killer in the most technologically advanced societies.

The physical and emotional distortions of "stress"—as dire as they sometimes are—do not, of course, exhaust the assault of a technological bias for control on the character of our subjectivity or personhood. Quite clearly, stress also deforms our familial relations, the tenor of our friendships, and the complexion of our communities. But the changes wrought by our technical orientations extend even deeper into our constitution as persons. For example, what we mean by "remembering" has been undergoing dramatic and consistently oriented changes over the last several hundred years. As evidenced in, for example, native Hawaiian genealogical chants, memory in oral cultures is typically associated with actively entering into and maintaining a network of relationships—an effort to insure the continued and meaningful wholeness of a community that includes not just humans, but plants and animals, minerals and climatic conditions. In this sense, recitation was not simply a primitive means to the end of storing information, but a way of continually and ritually embodying a felt interconnectedness with all things. It was through memory that the past was fully and practically personalized.

By contrast, today's generation speaks quite uncritically of "storing things in my memory" and "searching my memory banks" for answers. Remembering is no longer an enlivening of deeply sensed relations—an act of literal reunion or regained membership—but a matter of retrieving data. The very fact that a "photographic memory" is considered perfect or complete is ample testimony of the extent to which we have come to accept the impersonality of remembrance as ideal—an ideal that takes as exemplary a fully generic, camera-like subject who neither adds to nor subtracts from what is remembered. Standing apart from the recalled, we occupy an ideal space and like Leibnizian monads communicate only by transmissions across an imperceptible but implicitly sensed and tacitly accepted void. Memory has shifted from the dimensions of the sacred into those of the profane, and with it a significant portion of what we include in ourselves as persons. The result is a double alienation—from both the memorable world and the memorable (as opposed to the merely remembering) self.

THE INFERTILITY OF EXPERT MIND

While there is perhaps a legitimate sense in which we "get more done" now than ever before, in another and equally important sense, we are also becoming less. Because our work environment is geared toward efficiency, our responsibilities and so the kinds of attention we must exercise are markedly streamlined. On the job, we perform our duties with maximal professionalism—what we can refer to as an "expert mind." This type of mind already knows all there is to know about the task at hand or where to find out. Mistakes are few and if there isn't much room for real spontaneity, that seems a reasonable trade-off for the surgeon's skill or the arcane magic of our tax accountant.

The mind of the expert, however, is not just in control. If we situate mind in conduct rather than in the private interiors of our isolation from one another, it becomes clear that the very nature of expert mind is control. What this means is an orientation of our dramatic interdependence away from the unexpected and toward the predictable, from improvisational virtuosity toward regulating standards. Small wonder that we find ourselves craving novelty and paying well for convenient doses of it.

The expert mind is efficient because it no longer entertains truly searching questions. For any situation, the horizons of relevance are already fixed and so clear and distinct that there is no incentive for further—and so truly furthering—inquiry. This decisive definition of what is relevant and what is not—a definition that constitutes identity by purposeful exclusion—marks a kind of excellence. In particular, it announces skill in the translation of things into signs.

The "practical" benefits of such a translation are well advertised. For example, an expert surgeon is able to see in a glance what is organ and what is tumor, what is symptomatic of "health" and what is not. What is not always recognized is that this ability to see at a glance is at the very same time an ability to not-see as well. Thus, we typically see only the symbolic content of the stop sign at the corner without seeing the pits and scratches on its surface, the precision of its geometry, or the way it plays off sunlight filtering down through the branches arching over the road. Briefly put, we see the stop sign as a driver sees it, just as the surgeon sees the interior of the patient's body with a surgeon's—and not, for example, a husband's—eyes. While it's true that there is a sense in which all perception is editing, expert perception carries the editorial process to a logical extreme. It leaves no room for the irrelevant.

From a Buddhist perspective, this is not always an advisable move. When the efficiency of control is a paramount value, emotions, felt connection, dramatic depth, and intimacy are relegated to that indeterminate and unconscious place beyond the horizon of what is relevant. The not-seeing that is so crucial to realizing an expert mind is unavoidably an ignorance of the full interdependence of each thing and all others. For this reason, it is as well an ignoring of certain aspects of ourselves. More and more frequently, our emotions are sprung on us as if out of nowhere and our sense of the meaning of things as elusive as the contents of a dream we once had sometime long ago.

If who we are is not understood in terms of some essence or soul but as the full range of our narration, expert mind not only limits the 'objective' pole of our conduct, but the 'subjective' pole as well. And because all expert seeing and not-seeing are at root intentional and meticulously guided by our manifest 'success' and 'failure' in achieving our aims, this limitation very quickly becomes dispositional—a part of our karma. What is lost in result is not only the sensory depth and relational complexity of the 'things' in our world, the possibility of their articulating in wholly unexpected and yet creative ways, but also some degree of our own depth and complexity—our capacity for responding to trouble and crisis in a meaningful way.

It is no mystery, then, that it was Albert Einstein—a largely self-taught, scientific maverick—and not the chaired professors of the then current physics community who developed the presupposition-shattering theory of relativity. Nor is it any wonder that it was not the well-read head monk, Shen-hsiu, but rather Hui-neng—an illiterate and fatherless young firewood-collector—who was able to answer the challenge of Master Hung-jen and express the essence of Ch'an Buddhism. Indeed, as evidenced in Hui-neng's initial breakthrough while listening to chanted verses from the *Diamond Sutra*, a crucial part of his teaching is a continual injunction for us to realize the emptiness of all things through the practice of resisting the expert and yet karmically binding translation of things into signs.

Buddhist emptiness does not amount to a state of affairs—either a "peak experience" or some kind of ontological "ground zero"—but is realized as the process of continually and carefully relinquishing our horizons for relevance. This means not only an erasure of the dualistic distinction between 'is' and 'is not', but an erasure as well of our tendency to fix our own identities as subjects by fixing the objects of our attention and activity. In short, emptiness is practiced in order to free things from our instrumental limitation of them just as much as it is to free ourselves from attachment to the 'things' we have made.

It is for precisely this reason that the classic teaching stories of Ch'an Buddhism have unilaterally reviled the deliberative dualism implicit in self-control and praised instead the goal-less and so boundless resourcefulness of spontaneous virtuosity. To be able to accord with any situation and respond as needed—the simplest formulation of the direction of all Ch'an or Zen teaching—we do not need an expert-mind, but that of a true beginner. Only the beginner's mind is wholly free of both the 'known' and the 'unknown'—an absolutely unsullied and horizonless readiness.

Of course, in the interest of avoiding possible misunderstandings here, it must be stressed that beginner's mind is not incompatible with possessing the kinds of skill and tacit understanding that only come with a lifetime of dedication to a particular endeavor. In the sense that Ch'an uses the terms, a master craftsperson *is not* an expert. Indeed, his or her mastery consists of never having forfeited the freshly attentive lucidity of a beginner's mind. A master—whether in carpentry, midwifery, or Buddhist practice—is someone who quite diligently remains a student in every moment of his or her life. Expertness is therefore not a function of how much one knows how to do. It refers to a certain structure of knowing that is closed to revision. Beginner's mind means always improvising through the envelope of the known, and to this extent allows for having differing degrees of realization. A master's mind is not just open, but truly or appropriately virtuosic in its openness.

In the contemporary workplace, there is no time to cultivate a beginner's mind. Time is too precious to be "wasted" on non-instrumental engagement with either our work or each other. This doesn't mean, of course, that we never make friends at work or are never baffled and made painfully aware of how little we know and how much we have still to learn. But our friendships are taken to be strictly "extracurricular"—not a part of our work as such, but something we manage in spite of it—and our experience of being inexpert is not seen as a positive vein in our conduct but as an announcement of our lacks, our incompleteness, our separation from the things and situations around us. Unlike the manifestation of beginner's mind in the Buddhist sense, these experiences of nonexpertise do not evidence our unlimited readiness to offer ourselves as needed to our narration with others. To the contrary, they evidence our awareness of the ways in which we are blocked from responding freely. Unfortunately, we typically see the corrective as pivoting on an accumulation of information or experience. Rather than calling for a shift in our *mode* of awareness, we assume a need to alter its contents, adding to it new vocabularies and behavioral patterns. In other words, we suppose that we need to *get* something new, not offer ourselves in some new way.

When our bias toward control presses us into leaving behind the vulnerable readiness crucial to a beginner's mind, we leave behind as well those reaches of our sentience and sentiment where intimacy is first engendered—intimacy not only with those we work with and for, but with the materials on and through which we labor. For the vast majority of us, work has ceased to be that incomparable conduct through which we most deeply and widely discover and express who we are. We have jobs. We earn wages. But that alone will never lead to crafting truly meaningful relationships with the varied resources we avail ourselves of with such increasingly little appreciation and respect. And so, nothing is more common in discussions of our working lives, perhaps, than the admission that fulfillment eludes us. For the most part, our work is vacuous.

Though we are increasingly productive, more and more *we* are left wanting. This is not due to any kind of chance, material impoverishment. To the contrary, we consume more stuff in greater variety than ever before. We are left wanting not because of some prohibitive scarcity, but because our expertise has radically impoverished our materials. Our almost unilaterally praised ability to control our various environments has meant an explosion of readily available commodities and at the very same time a silencing of both those environments and the materials we extract from them. In a sense that is much more than merely metaphorical, fulfillment proves increasingly elusive for much the same reason that we find listening to ourselves speak for more than a few minutes incredibly pointless. Our relationship with the things around us has ceased to be a conversation—a turning together in creative reciprocity—and degenerated into the worst kind of monologue: the giving of orders.

THE VICTIMIZATION OF SUFFERING:
AN EXPERT INVERSION

The idealization of what we've referred to as "expert mind"—a mind thoroughly fascinated with and expressive of controlled efficiency—is not conducive to bringing any more of ourselves to the job than we need in order to fulfill *its* demands. Simply stated, because it "gets in the way" of efficiency and the quest for control, we bring into our work less of who we are, less of that essentially limitless narration from which 'you' and 'I' are only contingently abstracted, than the Balinese silversmith or the Italian grocer who ran the corner store forty years ago. In the same way that truly personal conversations are now mostly frowned upon in the workplace, so are truly personal attentions—those modes of subjectivity to which drama and meaning are native. This privatization of personal attentions—so crucial in an age of sexual harassment suits and corporate "right-sizing"—means a drastic reduction of the scope of our conduct that is oriented socially or toward the always improvised realization of intimacy. Indeed, we now tend to think of intimacies as primarily binding—rooted in conditions and commitments—and not as marvelously and fully liberating.

There are, needless to say, exceptions to the "rule" that the working world is one of personal inattention biased toward controlled and so invariably controlling relationships. Counselors and psychologists, for example, specialize in cultivating a therapeutic intimacy with the stories and storytelling of their clients. But even here, the point is not to become friends and family—to share in the realization of a living and open-ended community—but simply to help troubled individuals cope with their troubles and individuality. Rather than therapist and client weaving their originally disparate narratives into a single, more flexibly resilient new texture, they finally accentuate their integrity—their existential separateness.

In a word, the emphasis in our work practices on expert efficiency means that the dramatic dimension of our conduct is maximally attenuated. Unfortunately, this means as well that our jobs tend toward being personally irrelevant. They are just what we do for money, for the means of carrying on our consumer practices. And not surprisingly, because our work itself is dramatically impoverished, there is an intensification of "office politics," job-related rivalries, grudges, and suspicions. In part a function of our competitive ethos, but also in part a reaction to the dearth of intimate attentions in the workplace, it is increasingly common for us to engage in conduct oriented toward the distinction of our egos.

Our conviction, of course, is that none of this is a real problem. The roles we play at work are "only roles" and so not truly definitive of who we are. Erving Goffman's extensive work on role-playing and personal identity in his book, *The Presentation of Self in Everyday Life* (1959), argues otherwise. If we play a role well enough and long enough, we internalize the values expressed through its prescribed modes of conduct and—for the most part entirely unconsciously—adopt them as our own. This rubs us the wrong way. It suggests, contrary to our belief in individual autonomy, that our sense of who we are is deeply rooted in the patterns of our day-to-day conduct.

And so, while the vast majority of us who have jobs rather than careers or life vocations are certainly and conveniently convinced that we only "play" our roles, matters may well be very much other than we think. We think that for the most part we just "do our job" and keep our personal lives out of it. We believe we are still capable of intimacy when the situation is appropriate and that not doing so in our business or commercial dealings is hardly a galling infringement on our individual rights. But assessing our recent communal and personal histories with as unprejudiced an eye as possible casts serious doubt on the veracity of such beliefs. After all, in perfect keeping with the thrust of Goffman's analysis, it has to be admitted that the growing impersonality of most of our day-to-day interactions has been correlated with increasingly wanton crime, increasingly virulent substance abuse, and increasingly self-serving behavior not only in the workplace, but in our schools, on our playgrounds, and in our homes. That is, for all our convictions that we are surviving our roles basically intact, our conduct itself argues otherwise.

We have a long and at times quite venerable history of promoting the ideals of individuality, independence, and control. For the sake of better ensuring the extensive realization of these ideals, the orientation of our conduct has been increasingly societal—that is, our narration has increasingly stressed the importance of regularity and institutional guarantees. Our public hospitals and schools, our courts and stock exchanges, are evidence of the success of our promotional efforts. But so are the faces of the homeless and hopeless thousands who lead lives stripped of practically everything but their autonomy, and so is the remarkable proportion of our population that lives behind prison bars—in 1995, one out of every 166 people living in the United States. In the absence of direct and thorough causal explanations, our overwhelming disposition has been to see such failures of true community as unrelated to our institutional success at securing individual freedoms and prosperity. But if our interdependence is taken as basic, it is difficult to avoid admitting that in actuality we have been disposed to ignore the rapidity with which we are becoming institutionalized victims of the very means we have been using to prevent and end our own suffering. Efficiently expert and calculatedly factual solutions to what are at root axiological crises can only compound and resolve our troubles.

Although we all look forward to a good life, it is undeniable that who we are is most importantly conditioned by our bad times and suffering. Hence the remark by G. I. Gurdjieff that the very last thing we are willing to let go of is our suffering: it quite literally defines us. The karmic dilemma of calculatedly factual solutions to our suffering is that they do little or nothing to alter the dramatic conditions that gave rise to our suffering in the first place and simply establish more fertile conditions for its recurrence. That is, factual solutions are conducive to chronic suffering. But since these solutions involve our active control of our circumstances, they also tend to ever more precisely define us as victims of circumstances beyond our control. The better we get at factually resolving our problems—the more expert we are in dealing with the purported causes of suffering—the more selfishly we find ourselves being afflicted.

Among the verses attributed to early Buddhist nuns (the *Therīgāthā*, vv. 213–23), there is a story that I think is particularly relevant to our present concerns and that will help clarify the role of a bias toward calculated or efficient control in our biographic institutionalization of the 'victim'. At the beginning of the story, we encounter Kisagotami, the young wife of a wealthy man, wandering the streets of her village. Her hair is in tangles, her clothes torn and covered with filth. In her arms is the swelling corpse of her last born child. Now wailing in open and uncommon pain, now desperately pleading with passersby to give her medicine for her child, she has obviously lost her mind. And it is no wonder. Her first-born child had succumbed to famine some months ago and just as the grief of his passing was subsiding, her husband had fallen ill and died. These tragedies she had endured. But when her only remaining child had stopped eating and eventually died, she had broken.

At one point, a villager advised her that a great teacher was staying in a park not far away and suggested that perhaps he could help her. Kisagotami carried her dead baby to where the Buddha was teaching, threw herself at his feet, and begged him to help. He said that he would, but first she would need to bring him four or five mustard seeds from a house in which no father, son, mother, daughter, or slave had died. Kisagotami set out and went from one end of the village to the other, knocking on every door and asking if death had ever visited there. Of course, she reached the outskirts of the village without finding a single house that death had not visited. She returned to the Buddha and in his quiet presence, her mind cleared. From that day on, she was one of his most devoted students.

Most of us will have no problem stating the meaning of the story. Kisagotami finally sees that as great as her own tragedies are, they are ultimately nothing special. Death and suffering are universal. Her relief comes with knowing that she is not being particularly singled out and that everyone is to some extent affected by the same kind of suffering as she is. But from a thoroughly and deeply Buddhist standpoint—especially a Chinese Buddhist one—this way of understanding the story is, in fact, part of the problem it's intended to help solve. In short, our natural interpretation stresses the generic nature of both our troubles and who we are as troubled beings. Our pain may recede into the background as a result, but it is only attenuated, not transformed.

To be sure, part of the story's meaning is that Kisagotami realizes the absence of any free zone where suffering cannot reach us. This is not to say, however, that impermanence and suffering are everywhere the same, but only that there is no place in the world where we can avoid being confronted with troubles and crises. At a superficial level, this certainly means no happiness can last indefinitely and that no good circumstances will stay so forever. But it also means that no gridlock is intractable. Contrary to what we might be inclined to believe, all situations are negotiable.

More critically, however, Kisagotami also realizes that suffering is never really private, that it always occurs in the context of a communally articulated life story. When she goes from house to house in her village asking if death has ever visited its inhabitants, she is not answered with a brusque yes or no. To the contrary, she is reminded how the family's eldest son recently died as a result of a hunting accident or how Kisagomati's own cousin passed away just a year ago from the same illness as her husband. Hearing these stories, Kisagotami is drawn ineluctably back into the dramatic texture of her neighbor's lives, their hopes and fears, their sorrows and joys, their dreams. This is the beginning of her healing. By entering the homes of her neighbors one after another and asking them about the intimate fortunes of their families, Kisagotami effectively undermines the wall of grief-induced madness thrown up about herself in "protection" against further tragedy. The space she enters and opens herself to is the unlimited reciprocity and uniqueness of true community. It is in these moments of healing narration—the dramatic and careful intertwining of life story into life story—that the painful separation of 'self' and 'other', of 'fortunate' and 'unfortunate', is dissolved. This is Kisagotami's awakening. Unlike the biblical Job, Kisagotami's liberation is not private or internal, but fully social.

The biases of our technical expertise move us in the opposite direction. In today's world, Kisagotami would likely have been given sedatives as a first recourse. If these failed to sufficiently normalize her behavior, she might be committed to a hospital for "observation" and psychological/psychiatric counseling. Both the method and the aim of her treatment would emphasize her individuality and the dimensions of her malaise that are common—shared by other, similarly afflicted individuals. At a physical level, the treatment is aimed at restoring as nearly "normal" a balance of chemical constituents in the body-brain system as possible. At the psychic level, it would entail assessing her problems through appeal to one or another therapeutic model held to be widely, if not universally, applicable. While some effort might be made to "deal with" the specifics of her situation, Kisagotami is finally seen as "one of many" and not as part of who we are. We may try to stop the pain flowing through and out of her, but not by taking it into our own lives, incorporating it into our own stories. And yet, if the orientations of Buddhist practice are not entirely misplaced, it is just such a repairing or remembering of our narration that is most crucial. Troubles are never really mine or yours, but ours. Resolving them comes about not by reinforcing the impression that we are individuals—beings who stand alone and apart from others in some kind of essential independence—but by restoring awareness of our dramatic interdependence.

It might well be that if Kisagotami were living today in a major contemporary city, none of her loved ones would be taken away from her by famine or illness. Our technical development has created an unprecedentedly strong and thorough buffer against such contingencies. But in our world of electronically mediated commerce where our identities are largely articulated through commodity consumption and where the things we possess and use are so historically thin that they amount to various forms of litter, any major troubles that do come our way prove to be profoundly disturbing. In the same way that modern homes are more susceptible to *irreparable* damage by hurricane force winds than those built, for example, by indigenous peoples throughout the Pacific, the structure of our lives, the tenor of our consciousness is in many ways at much greater risk than that prevailing in Kisagotami's village.

Indeed, I would argue that there are two major consequences of living in the kind of icon-rich environment we are driven to realizing by our technical biases for control and efficiency. First, we are creating conditions under which it is difficult to either establish or cultivate the kind of dramatic depth required to keep our stories going under the most extreme circumstances. That is, "when the shit really hits the fan," we lack the narrative resources to improvise and cope with our situation in a creative fashion. The kind of relational complexity, flexibility, and redundancy required to do so has simply been too systematically undermined by the rationalization of our daily commerce and by the almost exclusively iconic nature of so many of our communication practices and possessions.

Secondly, the control-biased shift away from truly attending to the things and people in our lives so thoroughly silences our material and social situation that our own intuitions are forced into the egoic project of purely internal or private dialogue. By orienting our conduct toward collecting things rather than toward responsibly and responsively allowing them to become part of who we are, we end up valorizing a kind of attention insensitive to anything but our selfish (even if at times explicitly "altruistic") ends. In effect, the things around us are barred from providing us with unexpected clues for how we might creatively reorient our narration. So severe are the effects of this bias that we find it perfectly normal to assert that we are often alone—in the park or in the ocean, at work or the movies, even in our own homes.

In sum, the almost exclusively iconic environment that we are apparently committed to constructing is so distinction-rich and yet interdependence-poor that we more often than not greet trouble by either acting like it isn't there (avoidance through ignorance) or by increasing the rate and intensity of what we've already been doing. We simply cannot see any other options. At the same time that we are almost continuously in want, things are so densely packed and dramatically attenuated that our options seem quite limited. In Buddhist terms, we are unaware of the emptiness of all things, unaware of the infinite pathways by means of which each thing is constituted and sustained by all others. This sort of ignorance may not impede our ability to manipulate our circumstances with some measure of efficiency, but it does make it impossible for us to appreciate the diverse pathways out of our present and perhaps very troubled situation that are uniquely focused by each person and each thing we encounter. Walled in by the very distinctions by means of which we have been able to secure our control over things, we find it almost impossible to perceive the opportune and valuable nature of all things and meaningfully reconfigure our narration. That is, our very skill in expertly manipulating our circumstances stands between us and the capacity for opening up our lives by changing the narrative gestalts by means of which they're constituted.

Bluntly stated, our biographies have become painfully thin—so much so that we not only feel compelled to surround ourselves with an ever denser buffer of identity-defining and ego-securing possessions, we are almost obsessive in our willingness to immerse ourselves in surrogate dramas. Having become victims of our own capacity for control, and chronically misplaced our attention in the distillation of ourselves as autonomous individuals, we have rendered ourselves ripe for dramatic colonization.

THE COMMODIFICATION OF DRAMATIC MEANING

The immense popularity of professional sports and soap operas signals not just the dearth of drama and personal meaning in our own, immediate lives, but the successful commodification of both meaning and drama. While it's true that all cultures have developed narrative traditions comprising characters that serve as models for both exemplary and deficient personhood, these myths, legends, fairy tales, and heroic epics did not function as surrogates for fully lived relationships with the members of our families, neighborhoods, and communities. What is peculiar about our wildly prevalent obsessions with sports and soaps is not that they provide us with collectively attended dramatic narratives, but that they exercise such an inordinate influence on both the content and structure of our awareness.

To be sure, there are vast differences in the kinds of narrative substitutes offered by mass-mediated sports and soap operas. Sports emphasize on the one hand individual personalities in relative isolation from others, and on the other hand the fortunes of teams as groups of (largely generic) players and coaches. While there is some attention to the private lives of coaches and star athletes, for example, what captivates viewers are the performance personas revealed both on the field and in interviews. What matters is not how the players or coaches feel, but what they do, how well they execute their roles. One way of putting this is to say that sports coverage emphasizes plot over character development, actions over motivations.

That sports reporting has traditionally appealed primarily to men has less to do with how many males are "weekend warriors" than it does with the foregrounding of dramatically simple performance statistics and competition results. The clarity of winners and losers combined with the capricious machinations of luck resonates—in our society at least—with the typical constitution of masculine gender. Pennant races, playoff series, and the championships in which they eventually result are modeled after the dramatic structure and proclivities of male attention and activity. And not surprisingly, as women have familiarized themselves with the once "masculine" values of the workplace over the past three decades, their interest in sports media have undergone exponential increases as well.

As might be expected from these observations, soap operas have until quite recently been almost exclusively an obsession of women. The notoriously convoluted and "illogical" plots of soap operas contrast sharply and in gender-identifiable ways with the linearity of sports dramas. Instead of the often flamboyant and always highly independent sports personalities, soap operas are peopled by men and women deeply and apparently inextricably bound up in one another's lives. The emphasis is not on particular skills, but on complex coping strategies; not on a fully public movement toward a final, crowning achievement, but on the circuitously private navigation of interpersonal space. There is competition, but no clearly distinct winners and losers. In fact, it's often hard to tell who's doing well, who's blowing an episode, who's headed toward heaven, and who toward hell. In the end, it is not performances but passions and motivations that matter and prevail.

If the growing interest of women in sports has been correlated with their entry into the male worlds of business, politics, academics, and the military—their entry into active and aggressive patterns of conduct and hence technologies that previously had been almost exclusively the province of men—the demonstrated interest of males in both daytime and nighttime soap operas seems to be correlated with their absorption in passive and accepting forms of conduct stemming both from their immersion in the media and the changing characteristics of the workplace. The "sensitive male" is not so much the result of intentional self-cultivation on the part of individual men as the amount of time they spend in the passive forms of attention inculcated by consumption of various media and in discomforting awareness of their growing inability to guarantee the security of themselves and their families.

The point, of course, is not that these media products influence gender construction in ways good or ill. On the one hand, that would be to fall in the trap of seeing media content as having a linear causal relationship to the gendering of society rather than one of complex interdependence; on the other, it would be to make at least tacit judgments about the nature of such apparent trends in our society as the acceptance of polyandry, homosexuality, and bisexuality that might well embroil us in disputes about these judgments rather than helping to critically evaluate the kinds of power relations inherent to the process by means of which these values are being circulated. For our present conversation, what is most important is discerning how the mass-mediated worlds of sports and soap operas function as surrogate narratives and why they enjoy such immense and general popularity.

What it is about sports, soap operas, and evening sitcoms and dramas (especially dramas emphasizing mystery and the solution of crimes) that we spend more time watching, reading, and talking about them than we do the fortunes of our own family members? Why do they command so much of our attention? Why are we so obsessively hungry for the stories of our favorite athletes, soap characters, musicians, and actors? What deficiencies, in other words, are we making up in our own life narratives? What biographical poverty do we suffer that—while our children are turning to wanton sex, eating disorders, substance abuse, and violent crime—we spend on the average six hours a day consuming some form of mass-mediated news or entertainment?

There are, of course, no simple answers to these questions. Asked why we spend as much of our energy and attention as we do in consuming mass-mediated information and drama, we're likely to reply with questions of our own. "Why not?" for example, or, "What else is there to do?" For most of us, by the end of the day, we're "too tired" to do much more than watch some TV, cruise some Internet sites, or flip through some magazines. Translated into narrative terms, we are too dramatically depleted to exert ourselves in any more fully creative relationships with the people and things sharing our lives. We just feel like "zoning out" for a while.

It would be the height of naiveté to suppose that our fatigue, our deficit of creative attention, is somehow an "accident" of contemporary living. To the contrary, our biographical and creative poverty is a central feature of the world resulting from the new colonialism—a world in which attention has become a basic resource, a kind of "renewable" capital that fuels not only the economic and technical engine of mass-mediated news and entertainment, but the commodification of both culture and personal character. We can say that our weariness is a function of overwork and stress, but that is really to say the same thing: we are worn out by the systematic misdirection of our attention.

Anyone who has spent six or eight hours at a stretch working in a ceramic studio or on a personally meaningful building project knows well the difference between the satisfying and even energizing sense of exertion it brings and the debilitating lethargy of even an hour of office boredom. What wears us out is not the number of calories burned in an activity or the number of hours in concentration, but the tenor of our awareness. The legendary soporific effects of television are no accident—it cultivates passive and yet draining and restless habits of attention, the very opposite of dramatic creativity.

Just as the destruction of native forest makes it impossible for original peoples to reaffirm their own traditions and resist dependence on the "goods" offered in colonial barter, once the mining of our attention crosses a certain threshold, we no longer have enough left for engendering truly meaningful lives of our own. Instead of creating and maintaining dramas of our own, we are caught up in diligently attending the dramatic entanglements of people who are not part of our lives. Viewed dispassionately, this is structurally similar to what happens when a warehouse retailer moves into a new area. Like mom and pop stores, relationships and dramatic possibilities that are not attended will atrophy and finally dissolve. Compulsively consuming information about mass-mediated lives therefore means that our attention-energy—our dramatic capital—is effectively taken out of local circulation. To be sure, it benefits the corporations and individuals informing and entertaining us. But the dividend that cycles back to us is infinitesimal.

Not only are we constantly paying attention to dramas and lives entirely disconnected from our own, we are being trained to assess the status of our own lives in terms of both what we're provided via the media and how those provisions are consumed. That is, we're compelled both by the overt content and the technological structure of mass mediation to evaluate our lives in terms of our individual wants or 'desires'. Finally, we discover that we have forfeited so much of our capacity for seeing the interdependence and historical depth of the relationships—the fathomless narration—constituting our world that we no longer know how to resolve our own troubles. We're simply incapable of marshaling the kind of attention-energy and relational flexibility needed to improvise in a virtuosic manner with whatever comes our way.

To put this in the starkest terms possible, the disintegration of our families, neighborhoods, and communities is a function of inattention. It is not external pressures that are causing the collapse of meaningful community. To the contrary, it is the evacuation of attention-energy from our personal and communal spaces that is bringing about their steady implosion. With the technically achieved export of attention, a dramatic vacuum is effected in our lives—a vacuum working against our conscious interdependence. And because the technologies and tools crucial to our colonization affirm and promote our individuality and ideal autonomy, our attempts to mitigate the effects of this implosion through further consumption of media dramas can only make matters worse.

We're being trained to be careless of our shared immediacy. The time we spend watching televised sports, reading the sports page, arguing about our team's latest draft picks, cruising the Internet for virtual franchises to manage or for behind-the-scenes news—this is all time or attention that we are not offering our own life dramas and the partners we have in them, both living and inanimate. A family seated in front of a TV is not doing something together *as* a family, but as individuals. We can argue that this need not be the case. Parents can force children to watch critically and discuss what they've seen and heard, making TV a focus for an edifying relationship of parent and child. To be sure, this seems possible. But it is not what happens. The focus of the relationship mediated by television is never really "us," but always and exclusively what is televised.

This is not to say, however, that there is something "wrong" with TV sports, with soap operas, talk shows, sitcoms and hour-long dramas. The problem is not the explicit program material—although some of this is rather deadening from anything but the most aesthetically and morally bankrupt perspective. No, the problem is the *technology* of mass mediation, the way it structures our conduct and consciousness and captures our attention-energy.

Surfing every dawn at the same beach with the same "dirty dozen," participating in community theater either on stage or in back, working in a neighborhood garden and "talking story"—these promote some feeling of shared purpose, some meaningful interrelatedness. They evidence our shared commitments, our willingness to remain focused together. When we attend to a fellow surfer's presence in the line-up day in and day out, occasionally hooting our approval, maybe making up a nickname for him or her, either teasing or remaining serious as his or her character suggests, our energy is establishing the conditions in which friendships take root and out of which random acts of kindness emerge with perfect naturalness. In a word, our energy stays local without remaining private and so conducive to privation. We can welcome newcomers and introduce them to the familiarity that makes surfing together more uniquely rewarding—more uniquely meaningful—than just surfing alone.

There are two problems with mass media—they are generically massive and they mediate us in an apparently transparent fashion. The "good" of the media is that they connect us with one another in a more or less indirect and so "responsibility-free" way. The "bad" is that the media stand between us, holding us apart by attracting our time and energy to maintaining their dramas rather than our own. And we pay to be held apart. We pay directly with our purchases of advertised commodities—purchases that translate our time at work into some profit-generating product we come to possess. But more importantly, we pay with the reduced quality of our community with one another, our true familiarity. We are being charged twice for the "service" of being mediated and are so blind to what this means that we blame our dramatic exhaustion on our diet, or on the time we have to wake up, or the sound of the neighbor's barking dog. Because we view the technologies that mediate us in terms of the tools we use—our TVs, computers, radios, and print resources—we simply don't see that the dramatic poverty of our lives, their lack of meaning and profoundly sensed interdependence, is a result of our caring so much and so often about characters that don't care for us in return. The interest we pay media dramas is never reciprocated except in the most generic sense—giving us, the public, what we popularly want. The time we spend attending to the lives of people for whom we're at best a single digit in some statistic—that time, that energy, is simply lost.

Of course, it could be argued that media dramas of all sorts, from the best feature films to the news reporting of the rescue efforts on behalf of a child stranded at the bottom of an abandoned well, stand as evidence of the fact that we still care—and not only for ourselves and those closest to us, but for members of our extended community as well. Such a view, however, proves untenable. Caring for media-transmitted profiles of strangers is not on a qualitative par with the conduct that emerges from our truly intimate narration. In both our work and our entertainment we've agreed to forfeit our dramatic interrelatedness. With the colonization of our consciousness, we have so well come to accept the precedence of symbols over realities that we do not even blink at the declaration that the world is a text. We allow this assertion, not because we believe the world to be authoritatively scripted—a work of manifest genius—but because our experience has become so seamlessly symbolic that the madness of our isolation from one another strikes us as merely ironic. We may "care" about the plight of young mothers in Bosnia whose husbands have never seen their children and probably never will. But what do we do? Do we invite such a war-casualty into our lives to share our kitchen and our bathroom, our own sadness and joy, or do we simply change the station or put a light-hearted comedy in the VCR?

CONSUMING AND BEING CONSUMED: THE LAW OF THE POSTMODERN JUNGLE

A generically dramatic world needs structural supports of a type and to a degree unnecessary when our narration is locally and uniquely invested with meaningful attention. To begin with, the substitution of generic for unique dramas encourages an absence of felt responsibility for the things and people around us. Typically experienced as a nonspecific loneliness or isolation, our irresponsibility is mirrored by our situation as unresponsiveness—a tendency for things and people not to directly resist our will, but rather to seem impervious to or unaffected by it. Certainly, the mass-mediated dramas we spend so much of our time attending are not altered by our feelings, thoughts, speech, and deeds. And as the kind of attention appropriate to media consumption becomes more and more habitual, it quite naturally also becomes more general. Thus trained not to expect responses from the narrative situation we attend, we gradually lose the capacity for appreciating our situation and discerning the unique ways in which it corresponds to our needs. Finally, to the precise extent that we are not actively and meaningfully supporting others, they in turn are in no position to actively and meaningfully support us.

This sense of being situated in a dramatically unresponsive world conditions in turn a felt imperative to acquire "goods" serving to connect or attach us to our circumstances. It is as if our dramatically depleted biographies are in need of a material superstructure to keep from falling in on themselves. But our consumption of mass-produced goods that obtain in a predominantly iconic fashion is only marginally effective in this capacity. Consumer-good patterns of commerce condition a divorce from our material context in such a way that we have very nearly lost the ability to perceive things in terms of their intrinsic values. Lost almost entirely are the networks of interrelatedness—the dramatically social relationships—that used to be involved in introducing a new acquisition into our lives.

For example, it is possible today to walk into a music store in any major American city and choose among hundreds of drums—from components comprised in the Western trap set to "ethnic" drums like the conga, the dumbek, or the tabla. Catalogs are available from which it is possible to order virtually any percussion instrument made anywhere in the world. There is, no doubt, something intoxicating about the convenience of such stores— a convenience that is increasing exponentially with the advent of web-malls and on-line shopping. But as with most forms of intoxication, some kind of attention must be sacrificed for this convenience.

In traditional societies, musicians are typically part of the entire process of making music—a process that "begins" with gathering the materials used in making their instruments and that "culminates" in the singing and dancing of their communities. While the aspiring percussionist in New York need only scrounge up enough money to buy a drum or two—money that they can as well have gotten in the course of a drug deal or theft as by working at the local fast food restaurant—a traditional drummer from, say, Nigeria must select and cut down a mahogany tree in which there is already living the "drum" they will one day play. Using a stone ax under the guidance of a mentor, the future drummer chops out hunks of living tree-flesh one by one. With each whistling swing of the ax, more mahogany falls to the turf on which the drummer stands. More sap—the golden, sunlight-infused blood of the tree—wells up in the almost vaginal opening the drummer is carving into the tree. Once the tree is felled, it is dressed to the proper length, again with just bare hands and stone or crude metal tools. There are no chainsaws or power lathes, but lots of sweat and muscular effort. With help from a master, the drummer goes over every inch of the drum as it takes shape, learning how to go keenly over those same inches again and again as the drum is brought into the world. Later, an antelope is hunted and slain from whose skin the drum's head will be made and from whose sinews will be fashioned the straps that allow the drum to be pitched and its voice kept taut and resonant.

Unlike a typical New York teenager who may well want nothing more than to vent his feelings through drumming and maybe "pick up some chicks" in the process, the Nigerian musician is intent on giving a new voice to the forest—a voice that unites the speaking of the mahogany with the speaking of the antelope with the speaking of human beings. The rhythms and feelings that play through this new voice are not just human and certainly not just those of the individual drummer alone. They are the timing and sentiments of the forest itself—that great, living web of relationships out of which appear and into which disappear the spirits of all things. Drums are not just instruments—commodities put to use—but revered members of the community that have names and voices and lives just as its human members have names and voices and lives.

In contemporary America, the great majority of musical instruments sold very quickly find themselves relegated to a silent existence in dark and dusty closets or attics. They are not members of the family, but largely forgotten and unappreciated possessions. The aspiring New York teenager will undoubtedly play his or her drums and may want to deliver relevant and musically captivating messages to his or her community. He or she may even develop a personal attachment to the instruments by means of which this message is eventually conveyed to a listening public. But the focus here is almost invariably selfish. Without a lived history, without a family and a name, the drums may speak, but only what they are told to say.

In even deeper contrast with traditional Nigerian drums and drumming is the contemporary use of digital drum machines. Here, the instrument has been technically "improved" to the point that it ceases to be something the musician plays, but only something he or she *orders to play*. The resulting rhythmic patterns are perfectly controlled, the volume infinitely adjustable. The drum machine has a practically unlimited range of voices the musician can call on, but no voice that is truly its own. In fact, this transparency is considered the drum machine's most important feature. Not itself an instrument in the traditional sense, a drum machine is a means of programming the sonic representation of percussion instruments. That is, the digital drum interface is a tool for selecting among and programming the display of instrumental and rhythmic icons.

Initially, electronic percussion was used to augment natural, acoustic drumming. But in very short order, it has come in many instances to entirely supplant both drum and drummer. In techno-rave music—the music of choice among many of those most deeply immersed in the information revolution—there is no "live" drumming. The music is heavily, almost brutally percussive, and entirely programmed. Especially in dance mixes, the single most important consideration is how many beats per minute are programmed into a given track. The ideal is typically considered to be in the neighborhood of 135 bpm—a frequency associated with the induction of trance or the disjunction of dancers and their normal states of consciousness, their customary relationships. In such music, and by extension in the lives of those immersed in it, rhythm has been reduced to a formula, a calculation, a matter of efficiency.

Whereas traditional drumming is always at least dialogical, a co-implication of drum and drummer in which neither is in the position of simply ordering the other, the contemporary use of sampling technology makes possible a fundamentally monological approach to the making of music and (more generally) the making of sense. The shift from handmade, acoustic drums to factory-produced instruments and finally to drum machines marks a shift from hearing and performing rhythms as unique expressions of a widespread, interspecies community to a situation where music and meaning have themselves become iconic. Learning to play music as an initiation into the conversation obtaining among trees, wildlife, and humans has—practically speaking—been rendered extinct.

Similar fates have befallen nearly everything that once meaningfully augmented our basic patterns of subsistence. And as these relationships have been forfeited, so have whole ranges of our own modalities for attention and care. The consumer ideal threatens the possibility of truly global community—one comprising not just we humans but our full, material context in all its diversity and depth. But that is not all. Compulsive consumption, by divorcing us from our ability to perceive things in terms of their intrinsic values, also divorces us from the ability to perceive our own worth and intrinsic value.

The rapid loss of felt importance that things undergo once we acquire them thus discloses a great deal. It signals not just our inability to fully and creatively appreciate what we've bought, but a dematerialization of our personal narrative. No longer caring about things as things, but only as icons—in terms of the profiles of our possession of them—we also begin caring for ourselves in the same way. No longer intimately related to the things we live among and use, they can no longer maintain our intimacy with either others or ourselves. By accumulating things bereft of their histories and so of any inherent meaning, we are increasingly inclined to deny our own dramatic historicity. We stop living as such and instead find ourselves merely having this or that lifestyle.

THE RATIONALITY OF LITTER: CONSUMING SELF, CONSUMED COMMUNITY

Granted the interdependence of all things, the fate of the things around us necessarily reflects at least some portion of our own. For this reason, prior to looking more closely at the biographical function of lifestyles, it is useful to address in somewhat greater detail the dematerialization of things—their postmodern translation into icons or signs.

It appears given that the Information Age will mean the semiotic triumph of mass marketing and mass production—the realization of a global virtual economy. In part this is because the primary commodities will increasingly be almost completely immaterial signs. New software or multimedia products, for example, don't look or feel anything like what they finally provide us. Buying a CD-ROM disk is buying not just the information stored on it, but the streams of computer-generated experience toward which the disk directs us. With the institution of fiber-optic linkages or their equivalent worldwide, we will no longer need to purchase disks or physically handle the items for which we're shopping. They will simply be transferred to us instantly, opening up new windows on continually upgraded worlds that can be ordered at will. And with sufficiently sophisticated virtual reality technology, these worlds will in no way be individually experienced as inferior to the one we currently enjoy.

Of course, the argument can be made that for any immediately foreseeable future, we will still be obliged to purchase food, furniture, clothing, automobiles, sports equipment, and entertainment-information electronics more or less as we do now. Virtual reality will, in short, be a supplement to—not a replacement for—our current mode of sensory experience. Moreover, the much advertised fashion for collecting and even using unique, handmade items might be taken as suggesting that a fully mass-produced world is not something we are disposed toward allowing. But the plausibility of these objections would itself seem likely to be indebted to our mass-mediated misperception of the world we actually live in. If our primary avenues of information about the world and one another are news and entertainment media, how likely are we to understand just how profoundly homogenized and effectively virtual our lives are becoming? It being the business of the media to attract and hold our attention, are they not structurally obliged to virtually present us with attractive differences, the nonordinary, and the extramundane?

Although we might obsessively document our existence with photographs and videotapes, we do not turn on the TV to watch transmissions from a stationary camera positioned above our own neighborhood. What we want—and what we are given—is something new, something we didn't see yesterday, something we can't find in our own living rooms or subdivisions or apartment blocks. It is no wonder that the world as perceived through the media is inordinately full of signs of uniqueness and novelty—a represented world full of things and events that announce themselves as one-of-a-kind. By contrast, the world we actually live and work in is a world of Walmarts and McDonalds. Mass-produced and mass-marketed, our world and our lives are already overwhelmingly generic and—in spite of our fascination with things unique—are becoming more so every day.

This is not to say, however, that our world isn't geared to satisfy our individual wants. Forgetting for the moment that the origins of many of our "individual" wants can be traced directly to the effects of our colonization by the media and the values their various technologies promote, it is nevertheless true that the Information Age has made it possible to combine mass production and what we might call micro-marketing. For example, even in the world of shopping mall consumerism, there is a revolution underway that presages a world of ideally individuated and efficient access to goods and services. The clothing industry is already beginning to use the Internet as a medium for direct, real-time inventory stocking and distribution. This enables stores carrying a particular line of clothing to stock only a few of each size and style. As purchases are made, a real-time, central computer orders the shipment of purchased items directly to the store. This means less overall shipping charges—from manufacturer to wholesaler to retail chain warehouse to individual retail shop—and more flexibility in display options. Clearly, if you don't need to carry massive backstock, you can display more variety and so capture more attention. This marketing and inventory strategy has already proven remarkably profitable, but will only become truly revolutionary when enough of the population is on-line to make direct marketing through Internet stores or malls the norm.

The controlling advantages are manifold. For the manufacturer, it means cutting out some of the "middlemen" in the marketing chain. That immediately means a greater share of the consuming public's currency. It means as well being able to lower both costs and selling price and so the realization of greater sales volume, which further lowers costs and on again through the next cycle. But in addition, it allows the supplier (either manufacturer or wholesale consortium) to manage the marketing process with previously undreamed-of precision. Once the computer linkages are established and powerful enough, it is possible to respond literally at the speed of light to even the most minor changes in market interests. If a particular jacket is generating intense interest in McPherson, Kansas, this week—and perhaps this week only because of a concert at the local college where a singer wore one just like it—the interest will be able to be captured and translated into profit with an almost magical immediacy.

More "goods" for less, when we want them, as we want them. This seems like a dream come true. After all, cheaper, more readily available commodities means economic "growth," more jobs, and so a bigger slice of a bigger pie for everyone. But making things cheaper also and inevitably devalues the materials they comprise, and this is the root condition of the market transition from things to signs. Briefly put, if I can purchase two computers for the price that I paid last year for one of roughly equivalent or even slightly less power, the physicality of computers recedes from attention, and their functional aspects or forms intensify and are foregrounded. It may well be that the hydraulics of consumer-driven economies are such that increased demand objectively yields higher production and so lower unit costs. But this is more than an "objective" transformation of some parameters of the production-consumption cycle. It also marks a change in consciousness.

Quite simply, the steady decline in what a given item costs is subjectively experienced as getting more for less. What we get more of is features, uses, flexibility, interactivity, or even just flair. At the same time, we get less size, mass, matter, material. If I can buy two computers for the price of one, it only makes "sense" that their value is not primarily a function of the plastics, metals, and labor that figure into their manufacture. To the contrary, it is the way these materials are configured that constitutes the real value of the computer. And while value is shifting its residence from things as full and deeply sensory and emotional foci to 'things' as forms or signs, our attention is at the same time shifting from interrelatedness and co-implication to the end result of satisfying our wants.

In such a light, the parallel and complementary trend toward miniaturization is quite revealing. Miniature electronic components, for example, are much harder to build, fix, and maintain than their full-sized siblings. Not surprisingly, a notebook computer is much more costly than a desktop system of equal power and flexibility. To be sure, part of what makes the trend toward miniaturization market-viable is the fact that we live in increasingly limited spaces. If there's going to be room for all the things we can't live without, they had better be as small and compact as possible. But at a deeper level, miniaturization is about idealization—purifying "things" of their material component and so translating them ever more fully into signs. Because signs as such have an absolutely minimal intrinsic worth, we feel little if any compunction about disposing of them when they become worn or even just out of fashion. Miniaturization steps up the velocity at which things we use regularly will turn into litter.

Granted this explanation, our typical disregard for things leased or rented takes on a new cast. Leasing means knowing that we don't have to care—or be finally responsible for—the materiality of our home or automobile. Our relationship with them is based almost entirely on our use of them. Like things understood to be disposable, things rented or leased do not have the power to call us into caring relationship. They can make no demands on us, can evoke no necessary level of consideration or contribution, and so never become parts of who we are. If we don't give a thing any more of us than is needed to satisfy our individual wants, the relationship is finally masturbatory.

If nanotechnology ever succeeds in making it possible to assemble—from the atomic level up—any product out of any available matter, the "signification of the world" will have triumphed completely. At such a point, form will have been disengaged from virtually every nonartificial system of relationship. If we are able to simply order a molecular assembler to turn our lawn cuttings into steak this week and a new telephone next week, the cut tips of the grasses and shrubbery surrounding our homes will have completely lost their own, organically crucial meaning. Not only will they not compost and so replenish the soil out of which they once grew, all memory of their past will be erased. Molecular assemblers will mean the complete silencing of material. Sticks and stones will no longer speak for themselves and as themselves. We will have gained the ability to order matter at will. And with that, the Manichean struggle between spirit and matter will have ended.

It might be objected that such a liberation from the restrictions of available material will never be realized. The world of nanological genies is still just a technical dream based on a few small successes in building atomic-size machines. But whether such a dream is ever fully realized or not doesn't really matter. The fact that the vast majority of us would "do almost anything" to have such a genie at our disposal means that the dream has its roots very deeply buried in our cultural ground and our individual patterns of priority. And at any rate, the worldwide credit system is a reasonable substitute. Today, it's possible to insert a plastic card in an electronic reader and receive in return just about any good or service you want.

Again, what is most astounding and important about the promises of nanotechnology and the services of the credit industry is that they are viewed positively. Imagining the ability to make anything we want out of any other thing we have already announces the extent to which we no longer even know, for instance, what wood or metal are. In examining a koa-wood coffee table, we no longer perceive anything even remotely like the practically unlimited range and depth of fully interdependent conditions without which a koa tree can never have sprouted and grown to maturity. Indeed, it could be said that compared to our ancestors living five or ten millennia ago, we no longer even know what it means to eat. Eating has become a consumption of food commodities. Buying a loaf of bread at the grocery store, spreading some butter on it, and taking three or four bites before dropping the crust in the garbage is not eating, but consuming.

What is lost in the translation is the entire cycle of which this is but the most symbolically convenient aspect, the aspect most individually rooted. The whole process of selecting grain, planting it, nurturing it, harvesting it, and milling it into flour is lost. The maintenance of yeast cultures, the collection of salt, the building of an oven and then a fire—these too are neatly excised from our experience and potential appreciation of bread. Homemade bread tastes so good not only because it's freshly baked or because the recipe is so well conceived, but because eating it is the culmination of a process that includes love and care and intimate attention. What our immersion in consumer-culture has accomplished is an almost unmitigated censorship of things. They are simply no longer in the position to contribute to our stories, our drama, in anything but the most incidental fashion.

Nowadays, we eat without knowing where our food comes from. We defecate and urinate without knowing how our wastes are disposed. We live, in short, in a bubble of signifiers that ostensibly matter to us, but all the while are surrounded on all sides by a realm we don't even suspect. Only if our power to control things runs out, if the electricity or the water quits running, will we be forced to confront that emptiness—that realm of intricate interdependencies—about which our expertise in consuming ready-made commodities tells us absolutely nothing.

We can see our future by looking closely today at what is purchased in the extreme upper echelons of our information-based virtual economy. There, purchases are not of actual things or resources, they are essentially symbolic transactions. In the so-called "commodities market," this is taken to the point that people are trading pork and cotton futures. That is, they are trading on the likelihood of future production, wants, and demands. In such circles, there is an almost ideal dislocation of sign and signified, and commerce is primarily about the movements of the former. If sales are evidence of captured attention, the transactions taking place at the highest levels of our commercial endeavors are mappings of the actual and anticipated, societywide movement of attention. Granted that our wants are so deeply informed by the media, these transactions also serve as an index of how much our role in directing our own attention has atrophied.

With the advent of electronic shopping, individual shoppers will be able to engage in the same practices as multinational, corporate giants. We are even now able to do almost all of our business at a keyboard or on the telephone, never once finding it necessary to dirty our hands or to enter face-to-face negotiations. With direct marketing over the Internet, resistance to the flow of our attention in the direction of mass-produced commodities—whether material, cultural, artistic, or intellectual—is practically eliminated. The superconductivity of the dawning information economy can be extrapolated from the already astounding extent to which credit-card convenience has been able to liberate our attention from satisfyingly intimate relationships with the things in our lives and make it readily available for commercial capture. Credit convenience reduces the material drag of our consumer activity to the point that the things we acquire come without any history at all, stripped of all sensory, temporal, and relational depth. In result, we are unaware of even the network of societal interdependencies that go into the manufacture and distribution of the things we own, much less the natural webs of interrelatedness that constitute the materiality of those same things.

At the same time, having been reduced to the unidimensionality of signs, the things we buy do not hold our attention for long. We are accordingly and in short order left wanting. That is, the incredible speed and ease of purchasing in an information economy translates into a felt readiness or need for more purchasing. No doubt, this is a simple way of putting things. But a karmic analysis—like that of Illich regarding transportation practice—suggests that it is not simplistic or mistaken. Asking who really directs and so owns our attention can be given a particularly practical imperative by noting the readiness with which we quite "willingly" place ourselves in debt. In fact, credit convenience is so effective in strip-mining our attention that in the United States alone, the 1996 consumer credit debt (not including mortgages and automobile or bank loans) was in excess of $450 billion. At an average interest rate of between 15 and 18 percent, that is an incredible burden we are collectively shouldering for the sake of "convenient" consumption. Granted the equation of sales with captured attention or realized wants, this figure represents a remarkable and saddening testimony to the efficacy of advertising and the direct marketing of lifestyles in the colonization of our conduct as such.

We can thus identify two sides to the patterns of consumption in an information economy. On one side, we find ourselves busily articulating our differences—establishing our individuality—by consuming generic commodities. Deciding what we consume, and when, does not sum up all of who we are, but it is a primary process in defining who we are—a primary element in the fashioning of our identities. The fashion industry, then, is not really about conspicuous consumption for its own sake, but rather about developing and perfecting our personas. Putting together an appropriate "wardrobe" is a way of refining our character and casting it in a relationship of generic belonging. It means having the right clothes, the right car, the right address, the right kind of spouse. Not surprisingly, when most artfully arranged, our possessions fit together as an ensemble and giving up one— the suits of a trial attorney, say, for the ripcord baggies of a surfer—will mean giving up the Mercedes and the "high-maintenance" lover as well.

In addition, consumerism is most conducive to merely collecting things—not gathering them in true systems—and this points to a less obvious side of our constitution as consumers. In the sense used here, and first forwarded in general systems theory, a system generates order in unexpected ways. Thus, the combination of two atoms of hydrogen with one of oxygen yields water—a substance that exhibits properties that neither hydrogen nor oxygen possesses. A living being manifests qualities that the molecules it incorporates, taken individually, never do. The standard generalization is that systems are always something other than the sum of their parts.

By contrast, collections are nothing more than aggregates that behave in at least statistically predictable fashions. Unlike water molecules or ecosystems, piles of sand, sets of rare coins, and closets full of shoes do not exhibit unexpected properties. They do not adjust to changes in their context and do not engender novel responses to challenges of their structure. Aggregates can persist, but there is a sense in which they do so ahistorically, without meaning. They get bigger or smaller, but they do not develop or mature. Whatever order a collection has is strictly imposed.

Open systems not only improvise their own types of order, they take care of themselves. The more complex a system is, the greater its intrinsic diversity, the more vulnerable it is to challenge. At the same time, however, this diversity means greater adaptability, an increased capacity for unprecedented conduct. Systems theorists place great emphasis on the fact that an open system is in dynamic energy exchange—a relationship of mutual contribution—with its environment. Should this exchange break down, the system is most likely to disintegrate into constituent subsystems.

While not precise, there is a strong analogy to the traditional Chinese claim that "when *ch'i* circulates freely, the ten thousand things take care of themselves." While the open nature of systems encourages a free flow of energy through an environment, collections tend to simply absorb and so block energy. That is, because collections evidence the absence of a mutually contributory relationship with their environment, neither responding to nor creatively corresponding with changes in it, they can be seen as conducive to the conditions of disease. Collections are a form of pollution.

This can be made more concrete by considering the difference between a collection of rainforest animals in a zoo and in their natural habitat. While the animals in a zoo collection require a constant input of attention and energy in order to be kept relatively healthy, the same animals in the wild—that is, in their natural, systemic relationships with one another and with the earth, water, and sky—have for millions of years been taking quite good care of themselves as individual species and as contributing members of a large ecosystem. Put somewhat differently, while animals in the wild are useful to the ecosystem of which they are a part and so imbued with value, zoo animals have only extrinsic value—their utility as occasions for human entertainment or education. Because they are no longer disposed toward their environment in a meaningful and contributory way, the animals we have collected in a zoo are ours to dispose as we see fit.

Bluntly stated, collecting things is a way of producing waste. Because the stuff we collect in satisfaction of our consumer wants are not organically or systemically related, they will never take care of themselves. Nor will they nurture us. Because our own purpose—the structural reinforcement of our ego identities—is a function of acquiring and not maintaining commodities, this stuff we accumulate eventually lapses into disuse and disrepair. Simply put, the "goods" we collect don't continue to hold our attention and so cannot but turn into one or another form of pollution. Establishing our individuality in a world of ultimately generic and conveniently available commodities is—apart from truly exceptional cases—a process of littering.

The vast market for collectibles—everything from plates to ceramic figurines to coins, rocks, insects, books, art, and even experiences—points toward a peculiar fascination we have with the detritus of our patterns of commerce, a "fetish" for the things that have fallen out of circulation or usefulness. We may scorn garbage-pickers—people who sort through and faithfully secure incredible amounts of the refuse that is constantly sifting out of the network of our possessions—but their passion for acquiring "junk" is not structurally different from the behavior of a music collector who devotes great amounts of time and money amassing a fortune of recordings he seldom listens to or a collector of books that neither he nor anyone else ever reads. And if we're honest, it is a passion different only in degree—not kind—from our own ego-reinforcing patterns of consumption and collection. We may not indulge any particular commodity fetishes, but we do establish our identities largely through what we consume, through what we take out of circulation. Consuming is at bottom the final phase in a sometimes shorter and sometimes longer process of producing waste. Beyond the consumer, there is only the sewage plant, the incinerator, the landfill, or the toxic waste dump.

The entire pattern of conduct linking acts of control-biased production, marketing, consumption, and littering thus serves as a kind of centrifuge that reasons our world into 'self' and 'non-self', that which orders and that which is ordered. And yet, each of us must admit that our existence as consumers can be painful. As the popular clichés about millionaires without any friends aptly illustrates, surrounding ourselves with collected 'goods' defines us both in the sense of establishing our identities and that of limiting or isolating us.

It is ironic, but entirely predictable, then that when a lover finally decides to cut us off completely from his or her time and attention, we often go shopping (for new 'things', a new haircut, a good bout of drinking, etc.) to overcome our depression and frustration. Consumption is therapeutic in such cases largely because it shores up the boundaries we relaxed in the hope of long-term intimacies. In short, our depression is forced out of awareness by either repairing damages to the wall of our identity or (in extreme cases) actually building up an entirely new one. By adding possessions, we increase the size and security of those aggregations we refer to as our "selves." But we also render ourselves incapable of living in a world that takes care of itself, where meaning emerges spontaneously, where order grows rather than being imposed, and where we gather as true communities rather than merely coexisting in one or another form of collectivity.

Consuming is essentially something we do alone even if in the company of others. It fixes our boundaries, defining us through the concreteness of our mediating possessions. By consuming, we effectively express and safeguard our independence. But the "therapeutic" effect of acquiring new possessions—even if as temporarily as we do in eating half a pound of chocolate—is also tied to the fact that it is through consumption that we articulate our identity as somehow belonging with one another. In the absence of an intimate commitment to mutual contribution and appreciation, our togetherness largely obtains through coparticipating in the collective and public display of our individuality. Shopping at a mall along with thousands of others is a celebration of shared purpose. Listening to all the best-selling artists of our generation, watching the most popular shows on TV, and avidly following the fortunes of our favorite professional sports franchises all serve to "unite" us with similar others, even if only mediately or virtually. Although we are typically only being alone together, linked by wanting the same team to win or the same generically available articles of clothing to wear, that no longer bothers us. If the truth be told, anything more would force us into an uncomfortable self-consciousness, a realization that there is no one other than us who is responsible for the quality of our narration. As consumers, we do not need to concern ourselves with who actually sews the clothing we buy or under what conditions they labor or for what compensation. We can consume and enjoy the "fruits" of our colonization with a happily clear conscience.

Unfortunately, in the same way that a collection of animals in a zoo cannot truly take care of themselves, our independence is a form of bondage. As our patterns of consumption increasingly embroil us in collecting not just clothes and kitchen utensils, but friends and lovers and memories and knowledge, we find that we are no longer taking care of ourselves. And with the breakdown of the extended family into the nuclear family and now the single-parent family, we are seeing quite directly the effect of unbridled control in getting what we want by way of a commodity-based economy. It is not just us as individuals, but our families that can no longer fully care for themselves, requiring a host of institutions to maintain their viability—day-care centers, insurance companies, and counseling services, not to mention the delivery systems for our food, clothing, and shelter. Fully in keeping with the imperatives of global development and the colonization of consciousness, communities are as well being reduced from dramatically self-sustaining and improvisation-rich systems to mere collections of individuals united for the most part only through their institutionally secured and generic autonomy. Our neighborhoods are no longer neighborly. Felt community is almost a thing of the past. And so, although we talk about living together in democratic freedom, more often than not we are only sharing a common lifestyle.

THE PRODUCTION OF BIOGRAPHICAL LITTER: CHANGING MINDS IN AN AGE OF LIFESTYLE CHOICES

As consumers, our compulsion to collect is heavily conditioned by the direct advertising of new fashions, new tools, and new ways of filling our "leisure" time. But direct advertising, as extensive as it is, accounts for only a relatively superficial level of the range of wants cultivated by and through the media. Below and supporting this level are the 'desires' created by entertainment programming for new forms of daily life and new rates and styles of sensation.

The media now make us constantly aware of a range of choices regarding lifestyle that would boggle the minds of inhabitants of even the most cosmopolitan cities just a generation ago. The economic advantages of marketing lifestyles rather than particular products or commodities should be clear enough. A lifestyle defines not just a "personal" identity, but a dynamic and integrated pattern of consumption that can be adjusted for different levels of income, geographical location, age, family and marital status, cultural and political exigencies, and so on. A "green" lifestyle thus manages to link together vegetarian eating habits, ecotourism, "save the whale" T-shirts, hemp clothing, alternative music, activist publications, handmade imports, and CFC-free air conditioners. On one hand, a lifestyle packages sets of values and on the other sets up relatively open-ended aggregates of products and services the purchases of which are mutually reinforcing. In most developed nations, there are now a wide array of lifestyles pivoting on our customary decisions in matters sexual, religious, political, dietary, and intellectual as well as those that are more obviously material. Lifestyles link us up with others of like mind through distinctive patterns of commerce.

As we transit from the era of development into the postmodern era of colonized consciousness, the defining focus of a lifestyle is shifting from the more public and circumstantial to the more private and apparently essential. It is no longer merely our neighborhood, hobbies, and clothes we are encouraged to consistently coordinate, but the nature of our politics, sexuality, and religiosity—the nature not only of what we do, but who we are as members of a community and as individuals. At least from a Buddhist perspective, the distinctive horizons established for our conduct by any given lifestyle also condition the structure and tenor of our awareness. In selecting among a variety of those available, we are choosing our customary modes of subjectivity and interrelatedness.

Since much of our knowledge of lifestyle alternatives comes through direct and indirect media advertising, and since entry into a lifestyle means adopting a particular pattern of commerce and commodity consumption, there is a strong sense in which lifestyle discourse brings about a propensity for seeing attention as liable to the dictates of fashion. That is, certain forms of awareness will be seen as in fashion and others as out. The most obvious evidence of this is given in the alternative fashions for illicit drug use within and between lifestyle communities. The lifestyle of the forty-something, urban cowboy includes consuming major market beers; that of the thirty-something, upwardly mobile Manhattan stockbroker, a proclivity for cocaine; that of the twenty-something student and waiter in the grunge scene, a taste for heroin. But by no means is the lifestyle-specific marketing and consumption of "states of consciousness" restricted to the use of licit or illicit drugs.

It's easy to either ridicule or downplay overt fashion-consciousness, and most of us have done so with a pleasure and self-righteousness that should perhaps have given us considerable and not altogether comfortable cause for self-reflection. But even if we leave the issue of inadvertent hypocrisy to be sorted out by each of us on our own, it remains that the idea of having selves and forms of subjectivity that we effectively fashion is an idea that we embrace wholeheartedly. It is an idea that dovetails perfectly with the dominant Western tradition of construing persons as autonomous individuals—as independent knowers and creators whose freedom pivots precisely on their ability to choose their lives and choose them with a minimum of constraint. Most to the point, it is also an idea that seems increasingly plausible and appealing the more deeply we enter the burgeoning Information Age.

For example, granted the absence of physical constraints in Internet-mediated relationships, it's possible to undergo 'gender' change at will. I have heard of a man well into his sixties who has for a couple of years "been" a thirteen-year-old girl acting like a thirty-three-year-old in various Internet chat-rooms. His (her?) preferred partners are men attracted to just barely pubescent girls—men who enjoy acting out the kind of sexually ambiguous relationship he had forced on his own daughters. Whether this fantasy "life" is morally or spiritually advisable or not is debatable to say the least. But the lifestyle of which it is a part is as acceptable on its own terms as any other. It is simply one choice among a million others.

And yet, lifestyles are a fairly recent invention, and the seemingly innocuous, even positive expansion of the imagined possibilities for our being human has a rather dark and still largely unacknowledged shadow. A strong analogy obtains, for example, between the way our understanding of music has been transformed by recording technologies and the way we understand living has been conditioned by lifestyle marketing and discourse. A glance over the past hundred years of music in the United States makes it quite clear that the development of music recording and playback technologies brought about both the progressive atrophy of a decisively communal dimension in music performance and music appreciation—an atrophy of truly folk music traditions—and a growing tendency to perceive music as a willfully ordered product, not a full body-mind practice. In the same way, the intense marketing of lifestyles has been correlated with a narcissistic tendency to see our lives as significant and yet ultimately signifying products rather than dramatically intimate processes.

In a word, the shift from simply living to "having a life" or "pursuing a lifestyle" marks our emigration into a predominantly iconic world. It means separating more distinctly than ever before ourselves as natural subjects and ourselves as fashionable objects—a bifurcation that has considerable impact not only on our construing of authenticity and responsibility, but our dispositions regarding interdependence. Clearly, if I can willfully exchange one lifestyle for another without suffering any essential harm, and while realizing substantial gains both subjective and objective, the people around me—my friends and workmates, the clerks in the banks and stores I frequent, the teachers of my children, my doctor and psychoanalyst, and all the rest—are at bottom inessential. My ability to move freely from lifestyle to lifestyle, from one circle of acquaintances and values to another, means ultimately that I am not fundamentally dependent on anyone else. Much less am I obviously and irreducibly interdependent with them. They can be replaced or done without. According to the popular rhetoric, you can do whatever you like as long as it doesn't get in the way of my doing the same.

Because lifestyle discourse promotes the independence of the individual, under its influence, the course of our lives becomes a record of our decisions—a record not just of what we have chosen, but what we have cut off and left behind. Turning away or turning apart becomes basic to who we are even when—as in the case of a family move—we think we are doing our best to consider the needs of everyone involved. At bottom, lifestyle discourse sediments our alienation from the actual, felt processes of growth and maturation. Through its iconic transformation of living into having-a-life, the colonization of consciousness marks a reevaluation of our given-togetherness whereby it is much, much easier to simply adopt a new lifestyle than it is to practice the perfection of our present way of living.

And because these lifestyles are marketed as individually chosen and articulated, we have the impression that they exist independently of one another, that no lifestyle really or necessarily conditions any other. Lifestyles are free-floating options and any ripples we might notice propagating from one to another—from the suburban dream to the inner-city nightmare, for example—are passed off as incidental or accidental. Even though the present climate of political correctness constrains our expression of it, we have been trained to believe in the innocence, even the benign potentials of mutual exclusion.

At the level of perceptual attention, the situation is no less complex and dire. Our contemporary fascination with alternative lifestyles also signifies a departure from orienting our narration based on immediately present, maximally unique, and interdependent cues to generic and ostensibly independent, media-transmitted prompts. In Buddhist terms, this amounts to turning away from the most subtle and for us most directly useful expressions of our karma—the embodiment of our values—and attending instead to their greatly weakened reflection in the mediately transmitted world of universal icons. That is like ignoring the trail in front of us, the surrounding terrain, and even the maps our friend drew for us and hiking instead solely under the guidance of such tried-and-true rules of thumb as "the shortest distance between two points is a straight line."

Under the force of advertised novelty, we may have the impression that these mass-mediated prompts act as catalysts in realizing our own individuality, that they quicken our refusals to live by any fixed and constraining norms. But precisely because these prompts are not actual, but merely virtual, they cannot in fact serve as anything more than effectively universalizing signposts in the imagination of our possible futures and our decisions among them. In other words, the shortest distance between here and our desired lifestyle may well deposit us on the edge of an impassable abyss, but we shall at least be guaranteed company when we arrive. That our company will, like any other collection, prove incapable of doing anything to help itself or its situation may be noted with rueful irony and a shrug of our shoulders, but that is about all. The safety net of our institutional infrastructure will insure our continued coexistence.

Just as digital instruments allow us to compose with musical samples and effectively bypass the learning processes involved in generating them acoustically, the marketing of lifestyles via mass media drives us in the direction of seeing our lives in terms of experiences accumulated rather than attentions offered. Instead of promoting a balanced sensorium with all six senses maximally attuned to our various and ever-changing environments, mass mediation endorses an abbreviation of awareness. And so, rather than appreciating the unrepeatable and irreversible currents of our present situations and effectively coevolving with them, under the guidance of the media we have found it increasingly natural to think of difficulties as things we can shut off or discard. In effect, we lose the distinction between growth and change as something accomplished instantaneously and at will—like the placement in a hip-hop track of a digital sample from Coltrane's solo in "A Love Supreme."

Not surprisingly, the iconic existence characterized by having and changing lifestyles darkly mirrors our projections regarding the lives of traditional peoples. As the contemporary refrain goes, traditional societies were and continue to be so rigidly a product of ritual interactions that there obtains in them an appalling lack of opportunity for individual freedom and creativity. The range of choices we now possess in how we behave both privately and publicly signifies for us an uncontaminated advance. Our choices, our options, announce our hard-won freedom from traditional roles and the goals they support. We may have lost along the way some sense of deep community, but that, we surmise, can be rebuilt on a new foundation stressing each of our rights to pursue the life we want.

There are, of course, reasons to mistrust even the qualified simplicity of this refrain's conclusions. For instance, those of us who have taken the time to successfully undergo training in, for example, Zen meditation or one of the traditional arts of Japan would claim that our denunciation of ritual needs mitigation. In at least some cases, rituals act as pivots for unique self-expression, and what is being perfected in ritual training is not behavioral form, but the *kind of awareness* conducive to harmonizing—to mutually nurturing one another in the spirit of appreciated differences. Initially, there is indeed a rejection of individualism, but this in the end proves conducive to the cultivation of a more mature creativity and a more fully realized personal uniqueness. We are forced to restrain our own habits of preference and rejection and, by working through them, eventually attain a (hopefully virtuosic) ability to disregard our own dispositions and freely contribute as needed in whatever situation we find ourselves. Here, freedom is not a matter of selecting this or that prefabricated and purposely alluring alternative, but one of responding in the absence of habit. And as anyone knows who has taken the time to observe herself closely, it is precisely in our likes and dislikes that we are most predictable, most habitual. It may well be that in accepting the promises of lifestyle discourse we have simply traded a local set of prescriptions for universal, but no less, constraining ones. In the end, while we may choose which particular fashion we will adopt in making our selves, we do not determine which fashion statements—which cultural icons—will be made available for choosing.

As unique individuals, we are largely powerless with respect to the orientations provided us via media prompting. The media present us with perspectives that we can adopt or reject, but not transform in a truly improvised way. Even in interactive games and multimedia packages, the perspectives available to us are set in advance and are thus effectively impervious to our responses. What we are being trained to do in such relationships is to ignore the vast middle ground lying between acceptance and rejection. In a Buddhist sense, this is a recipe for disaster not because we are likely to make bad choices—we may in fact get rather adept at receiving exactly what we want—but because it fails to stimulate our capacity for skillful and subtle responsivity. Indulged long enough, this almost invariably leads to a concern for changing our lives and ourselves from the outside in—by replacing ourselves, by moving from some unsatisfying 'here' to a generically represented and yet appealing 'there'. With this, we have stopped seeing our flowering as human beings in terms of real growth—a process in which change is at once global and characterized by practiced movements circulating what is ostensibly interior and what is exterior, a kind of kneading of our selves and our environs through the improvised resolution of crisis or suffering. Instead, the fruition of our lives comes to be seen under the rubric of mere aggregation.

In fact, as time under mediation lengthens, our concerns are directed less to the achievement of new ways of living than to the infinitely less challenging satisfaction of particular desires for sensations as such—that is, for stimulation abstracted from the potency of unabridged interdependence and mutual responsivity. We can argue that this is not so, but the invasion of the home by television and mass-mediated music has led us to a point where our time is focused almost exclusively on media imagery. There is nothing surprising or apparently amiss in an evening that finds mother reading and father dozing, both in front of their television, while one child watches his or her own shows and the other listens to a million-selling CD on headphones. Even if all four members are miraculously gathered in the same room, they are likely not looking at, speaking with, or caring for one another. Their attention—at least between commercial or programming breaks—is directed at the television, the computer game, the multimedia learning environment.

Increasingly, it suffices that we are exposed to and perhaps enter vicariously into virtually presented realities. And so, the Internet has become the current rage as a "place" to meet new people. More so than ever before, many of us find affairs preferable in a slightly delicious way to the struggles and joys of a lifelong marriage. A good affair, after all, is profoundly sensual, intense with satisfied 'desires,' and yet clearly episodic. If it becomes too difficult, it can simply be ended, hopefully without hard feelings. After almost forty years of intense exposure to mass media, most of us prefer or at least feel most comfortable in situations where we can observe and perhaps even be observed without being touched. And this aversion to touch is not restricted simply to the matter of bodily contact, but extends to the tender and yet necessarily dangerous spaces of deeply aesthetic and emotional experience as well.

Chapter 11

The Digital Age and the Defeat of Chaos

*Attentive Modality, the Media, and the
Loss of Narrative Wilderness*

Roughly twenty-five hundred years ago, the Taoist sage Chuang-tzu re-
counted the story of the King of the North and the King of the South,
great friends who frequently visited one another by traveling through the intervening lands of Hun-tun or Chaos (*Chuang-tzu*, chapter 7). One day, the
King of the South remarked on the limitless hospitality of Chaos and suggested that they do some favor for him. The King of the North agreed and
came up with a brilliant idea. "Have you ever noticed," he asked, "that
Hun-tun doesn't have the same kind of senses we do?" The King of the
South nodded. "Well, then, let's make holes for him so he can see and smell
and taste and hear just as we do." So on the first day, they drilled one hole
into the body of Chaos, and on the second day another, and so on until they
drilled the seventh hole and Chaos died.

The Jesuit gloss on this during their tenure in China was that it was
surely a good thing that Chaos was vanquished and order—in our likeness
and so in the likeness of God—enabled to reign supreme. After all, how else
than through the triumph of regularity over chance are we to enjoy a secure
and happy life? How else can we insure the requisite conditions for an end
to our own sufferings and those of others? But in traditional China, Hun-
tun's fate was not understood in terms of triumph, but tragedy. In Can-
tonese, the written characters for *hun-tun* are pronounced "won ton"—a
term that is by now familiar to every Chinese restaurant patron around the
world. In China, Chaos is not an archetypal adversary, but a roiling
dumpling soup in which you never know when something good will pop
up—a continuous circulation of elements, a harmonious blending of com-
plementing and ultimately nourishing differences. For the Chinese, the death

229

of Chaos marks the end of a spontaneously open-ended cosmos and the institution in its place of a transcendently principled universe. The "senseless" world of Hun-tun is replaced by the sensible one of human artifice—the world answering to our wants and values.

From the narrative perspective of the traditional Chinese worldview, Hun-tun's demise means the end of dynamically self-articulating, global harmony. It means the settling of the ten thousand things between Heaven and Earth into fixed positions reflecting the sedimentation of our own importances. And to the exact extent that we are in a position to control where and when things fall into place, it will mean that what we like will always come out on top and near to hand. That may be good, at least in the short run. But it also means sacrificing the always unexpected ways in which what looks like a bad or even impossible situation turns out fabulously well. It means making the kinds of fixed distinctions that not only encourage an ignorance of the interrelatedness of all things, but that set up a precedent for taking a callously dismissive attitude toward people and things assumed to be "not me," "not mine," and "not my responsibility"— people and things that simply don't fit into our plans. The end of Chaos means perfecting the kind of order we want, and each step in that direction marks a step away from virtuosity in realizing a horizonless and liberating intimacy with all things.

Chuang-tzu's tale about the fate of Lord Hun-tun asks us to consider that good but naive intentions can have effects quite the opposite of what we imagine ahead of time. It also asks us to consider that a truly commodious and richly welcoming world, like that of Hun-tun, cannot be made-to-order but can only arise spontaneously or *tzu jan*. For Chuang-tzu, the best of all possible worlds is not one in which we get exactly what we want, but one in which we are pleasantly surprised by things we never could have imagined wanting.

Our technical bias for control disposes us to smirk at such a "dreamily sentimental view." We are sold on the association of order and control, of reality and predictability, of calculative accuracy and satisfactory returns on our efforts and interest. And to be sure, it may well be that in an abstract sense—for *any* individual, in *any* place, at *any* time—'freedom' and 'independence' have to do with getting things to turn out as we want, being able to live in a world that is effectively made-to-order. The question is whether becoming such universal or generic 'individuals' and living in such a world is really desirable. The sadly compulsive quality of so much of our mass-mediated lives—that portion of our time when we are most clearly capable of ordering what we want and getting it—suggests not. Our almost insatiable appetite for media dramas, for increasingly graphic and yet iconic violence and greed, for mere representations of love and tenderness—these testify in a way theory cannot, both to the growing poverty of our own narratives and the shallow monotony of what we want. Far from being inordinately meaningful, our lives and lifestyles are all too often only predictably and generically demeaning.

A REASON TO BE NAÏVE: DISPARITIES IN THE METAPHYSICS OF MEANING

It is explicit in the dominant scientific and religious traditions of the Indo-European West that what is most real and true is what is most regular and lasting: for example, universal "laws of nature," the elements of the periodic table, God. The faculty for apprehending these—the part of us most capable of grasping the (universal) truths underlying the play of phenomena—is, of course, reason. In an originally quite literal sense, reason consists of taking the accurate and reliable measure of things. And it is no accident that the technically mediated regulation of our various natural and human environments is commonly referred to as the "rationalization" of our life-world. Our technical successes are part of a larger cultural project of reclaiming the world from the changeable and chaotic—the realization of a universally ordered existence.

In the context of this project, our efforts to weed out chance and control our circumstances manifestly represent a reality-enhancing concentration of what is truly valuable in things and in the world as a whole. By promoting regular and predictable experience, we effectively promote the 'real' and 'true', the 'useful' and the 'good', lifting them out of obscurity in what William James so famously referred to as the "big, blooming, buzzing confusion" of the world. The ultimate aim, of course, has always and (in spite of a change of preferred vocabularies) continues to be perfection—the achievement of immutable completeness, an elimination of the vagrant tensions of wanting.

A world that is fundamentally predictable—that is, regular and neither chaotic nor ambiguous in its essence—is a world that can be captured and dedicated to our satisfaction. Even if the causal details elude all but a statistical grasp, the lawlike playing out of initial conditions is a process we can turn quite decidedly to our advantage. The Cartesian declaration that the world and its constituent (material) parts are best seen as a vast clockwork was thus intended to stress both the ultimate rationality of the world's movements and our ability to read and eventually control its various states. In short, within and thanks to the limits of the laws of nature, we can leverage the world into conformity with our wants and imagination.

This, however, is as much as to say that the world can be made over in our image, relegated to the status of a mirror. This is at once a thrilling and frightening proposition. Indeed, part of the controversy surrounding Richard Rorty's (1979) denial that the mind is a "mirror of nature" is that—like Heisenberg's Uncertainty Principle—it begs the question of the extent to which objectivity is even possible. If we cannot factor ourselves out of the equation of the world, it may be that things ultimately tell us much less about themselves than they do about us. But regardless of where we situate ourselves on the problem of relativism, it remains the case that cultivating an ability to control what will happen, when, and where also involves eradicating the conditions under which the world is manifestly both surprising and dramatically meaningful. That is, a control-biased rationality inevitably brings us to the realization of a dilemma: the more successful we are in domesticating wilderness and identifying "the way things really are," the less meaningful everything becomes. Reason, at least as understood in the dominant Indo-European traditions, has the structure of a dilemma.

In these traditions—especially those in the West—meaning has most often and in roughly chronological order been identified either as a function of "authorial" intent, as a finite and inherent content of a text or a situation, or as something constituted in or through our individual interpretations of texts or situations. Thus, in explaining the spreading sentiment in the second half of the nineteenth century that the world was no longer meaningful, Nietzsche announced the "death of God," the metaphorical demise of the world's author. In retrospect, it is clear that Nietzsche's radical coming to existential grips with the absence of meaning pivoted not on an awareness of any galling recalcitrance on the part of reality, but rather its shocking malleability. The "death of God" signified a recognition that the "book of the world" had all along been a collection of blank pages on which we'd been keeping a careful diary of our own fears and vanities. The world had never really resisted our intentions and designs because it had never had any of its own. Nietzsche's claim amounts to saying that our error has been in telling a story in which *we* were not the authors, but rather some transcendent Being who in the end turns out to have been an untenable fiction. His famous response to this revelation? Accepting the task of becoming "supermen"—accepting once and for all the role of true creators.

By the mid-twentieth century, this no longer seemed a blasphemy. The meaninglessness of things was already being taken less as a distressing absence than a kind of perversely favorable characteristic of things—their absurdity. The world as a "work" might not be going anywhere, but that wasn't necessarily so bad as long as where we are and what we have are as we wish. If the world has no tale of its own, if it consists of a collection of brute and so mute facts, we are free to tell whatever "versions" we please—at least, that is, within the limits of humanly established horizons for taste and propriety.

As demonstrated by the postmodern declaration of the infinite possibilities for interpreting any sign, we have more recently come to celebrate the rootless and fruitless nature of our situation for what it is—an opportunity to make whatever we like, to get whatever we want out of the materials available, be these conceptual, material, or even spiritual. We have been freed from history. There is no world drama. There are only facts and states of affairs. And in the absence of a transcendent author, we are free to compose these more or less as we wish. Meaning is no longer something transcendent to our own interpretations and reasons—something we can grasp only on the pain of paying close and careful enough attention. To the contrary, whatever we grasp is the meaning of things. The equation of the world need not be divined. To the contrary, it is most efficiently arrived at by simply "reading backward" from the results before us.

From the death of the world's author, to the denial of irreducibly dramatic connections among its manifest 'facts' and 'states', to the celebratory nihilism and narcissism of postmodernity, what has remained common in our views about meaning is a disposition for taking it to be something belonging to or possessed by either a subject or an object. By contrast, the Buddhist understanding is that meaning consists of the middle way between subject and object—something that is given directly in conduct or the dramatic unfolding of our interrelatedness. Meaning is not something we can take possession of or grasp, but a continual and always underdetermined burgeoning or ramifying—the open-ended tending of things that we can only understand through attending to them in an irreducibly appreciative way.

Thus, while Buddhist hermeneutics allows the importance of authorial intent, of coherence analysis, and comparative criticism in determining what a problematic text or event means, the final resort is always and explicitly practice or conduct itself. The meaning of the *Heart Sutra* is given in how our conduct is reoriented and modulated by familiarity with it. The meaning of a Ch'an *kung-an* or "public case"—like the meaning of our lives or the world we are continuously articulating—is not something we arrive at, some destination, but how things are going, our dramatic direction. In short, meaning is the expression or evolution of appreciative attention—not something gotten, but offered.

At a superficial level, this may not sound too dissimilar from the postmodern construction of meaning. But instead of associating meaning with interpretation (with subjective and essentially individual "readings" of things) or with dissemination (the broadcast of these readings), the Buddhist view entails seeing meaning as the irreducibly dramatic quality of our interdependence or interplay. The difference may be slight, but just as crucial as that between the pre-Copernican and post-Copernican views of the solar system.

While postmodernism—the hallmark philosophical movement of the Information Age—prides itself on announcing our freedom from the tyranny of objective being and thus bears a superficial similarity to the Buddhist metaphysics of ambiguity, it does so by claiming meaning as an individual (and also corporate) right. We are entitled to say what something is or is not. We "write" the equations that ultimately order and make rational sense of the world's myriad variables. Meaning is not offered, but willed. The postmodern location of meaning in the interpretative act thus places the deliberating and deliberate self in the position of calculating not just what is possible and preferred, but what is irrelevant—the rational exclusion of the unknown as immaterial.

Buddhist hermeneutics runs in the opposite direction—the practice of seeing all things as interdependent and thus realizing the erasure, not sedimentation or fusion, of horizons for relevance. In this sense, meaning in a Buddhist world is seen in narrative rather than calculative terms. That is, it consists of possibilities opening up rather than closing off, with eliding the subject-object, self-other, and meaning-text dichotomies. Meaning and order are not imposed or asserted, but improvised. From such a perspective, the technical valorization of control establishes and maintains the conditions for a meaningless life—one in which we enjoy considerable and calculated accuracy in getting what we want through the depletion of those narrative resources needed to meaningfully and not just factually resolve our troubles.

Granted this, the postmodern malaise of realizing the need to "write" our own stories and make up our own meanings for things, announces we have been thrown back into the shell of our subjectivity and placed ourselves in very real want of narrative or dramatic depth. That we feel this need to construct or reclaim our own narratives does not just announce a realization that there is no transcendent author of the world, no inherent meaning in individual things or events, and so no world drama, but our profound ignorance of and even aversion to the possibility that the world's drama is simply authorless. In short, the postmodern fascination with "personal narratives" indicates the extent to which our basic mode of attention is one that discounts the possibility that a meaningful world drama or narration can be autopoetic. That we satisfy our want of dramatic depth almost exclusively by recourse to generic, mass-mediated tales further announces that this mode of attention orients our conduct away from improvisational and contributory virtuosity and the realization of dramatic diversity toward simply choosing among various and regularly available narrative commodities.

The world understood as narration is continually emerging as a spontaneous whole of interweaving relationships, each part of which is dramatically interdependent with all the rest. By denying the inherent drama of things, both postmodernity and scientism legitimize the political, economic, and cultural sponsoring of individually authored meaning. That is, they sponsor the kind of evaluative methodology that has us seeing technologies in terms of tools and assessing benefits and risks from within the most constrained horizons possible. This is good, but only for those in a position to gather power and wealth through taking advantage of our blindness to all but selected icons, our ignorance of the limitless interdependence of all things. For all their apparent antipathy, postmodernism and science end up equally stressing the centrality of decision rather than responsive virtuosity in the realization of freedom and constitution of meaning. And the world they bring about is not one of harmoniously "coming together" in surprising and dramatic narration, but one of assertively "cutting away" what is irrelevant to the calculated satisfaction of our individual and yet generic 'desires'. The triumph of regularity and certainty—so basic to a calculatively realized life and the technological translation of all things into signs—marks the reduction of our world as drama to a kind of synopsis.

CALCULATION AND NARRATION: DISPARATE MODES OF WORLD-MAKING

An icon-rich world, while relatively abbreviated, is still open to individual interpretation. Signs can be ambiguous. But once the transition is made to fully endorsing a calculative regard for the world—albeit only in specified contexts—even this personal component of interpretative uniqueness becomes superfluous if not suspect. There is, after all, nothing negotiable about the result of adding 'two' and 'three'. 'Five' is unequivocally the only meaning of their summing—a meaning that is, for all its clarity and distinctness, dramatically stillborn or sterile. It has no tendencies toward otherness and so elicits nothing spontaneous in or from our attention. It makes no difference who carries out the summation, and in the end this amounts to the process making no difference to whoever does carry it out. The calculative mind is a mind that in very definite ways limits the range of its concerns and care. It practices ignorance, but an ignorance that is expert in arriving at unambiguous ends. Being able to calculate drastically alters both how and why we tend things, how and why we care at all.

The original Latin root of the word "calculation" is *calcus*—a term that literally means "pebble" and that refers to the small stones used to stand for items being counted. Calculation entails both abstraction (removing an event or thing from the relational continuum of nature) and representation (accepting a standard, iconic substitute for the unique things under consideration). In calculating, we move away from concerns for things as irreplaceable focuses of relationships to seeing them as integers or units in an orderly scheme of universals (classes) and particulars (instances). Counting, giving an account, forwarding a rationale, weighing risks, and gauging returns—all depend on our discrimination of what *is* relevant and what *is not*. In the absence of such an act—an act that practically subverts the emptiness or interdependence of all things—we would simply be incapable of achieving closure with respect to our concerns. Our calculations would remain incomplete. In short, we would be doomed to an 'irrational' situation—a situation we cannot grasp because it eludes orderly discrimination or limitation.

The translation of things into integers is thus part of a larger cultural project of securing regularity—the rationalizing of existence. The play on words here is entirely intended. Calculation is a means of justifying our "standing apart" from all things because they, too, are taken to be units that in essential ways stand apart from one another. Appealing to an earlier distinction between the social and the societal—between the orientation of conduct toward improvised relations or toward regulated and regulative institutions—we can say that numeration is a primitive (or first-level) technique for both fostering and maintaining societality. For any calculation, there is only a single right answer and many wrong ones—a clarity that has, at least for the last five hundred years in the West been held up as a standard for all valid knowledge. There is no equivocation in mathematical operations. Arrived at in an orderly fashion, calculated results are not negotiable. Unlike the capricious ambiguities of narration and needing no further explanation, calculations stand on their own as fixed accomplishments. Through them, we are able to peel away what merely seems and reveal what "actually exists."

The so-called digital revolution is but the most recent and technically sophisticated phase of this project. If everything from poems to symphonies, and from landscapes to the logical structure of thought or the topography of our genes can be translated into a digital architecture of simple, electronic ons and offs, are we not zeroing in on being able finally to map and eventually manipulate everything around us? When everything can be reduced to numbers—to those elements of our life-world that are most radically immutable and fixed in value—won't this signal a kind of world-purification? an end to all ambiguity and chaos?

Certainly, the ultimate promise of biological computing and nanotechnology is achieving on the one hand a practical omniscience regarding the structured existence and statistically defined natures of all things and, on the other, an equally practical omnipotence in being able to call into either virtual or literal existence absolutely anything we want. We may be limited by the "laws of nature" and whatever transcendent deity there may be, but aside from these potential horizons for our expert control of things, we may one day have complete freedom to have, and perhaps even be, whatever we want. Whether this promise is ever fully realized or not is less relevant than the fact that we have been willing to take it up as a collective dream. In a fully digitalized world, nothing need be left to chance.

As implied above, calculation and narration are best seen as contrary modes of disambiguating the originally unfixed nature of all things—contrary organizations of awareness as such. Calculation is that mode through which are established discrete and fundamentally interchangeable objects and equally distinct, discriminating subjects. Practically speaking, this allows a truly astounding capacity for direct and indirect exertion of control. By breaking down the inherent interconnectedness of all things and radically focusing on their individual statuses or identities, calculation divests things of the dramatic dimension of their histories and so of their own meaning. Indeed, this dramatic thinning-down of things is precisely what makes them incapable of resisting our will in any but the most crudely material fashion. Calculative meaning is never intrinsic to the way things are going, but obtains if at all only in respect to some extrinsic frame of reference. Far from being a paradox, the evacuation of meaning from things themselves is an unavoidable consequence of their radical individuation. Without an externally imposed frame of reference, an equation is just a string of ciphers, a gathering of people in the park is just a crowd.

By contrast, narration is a path of nondiscrimination—a mode of world-making conducive to realizing uniquely dramatic interdependence. Narration marks the orientation of awareness away from the general, the purely abstract or conceptual, and mere "facts" shorn of all inherent value and meaning. To the contrary, it proceeds by foregrounding through analogy, deepening and extending and not analyzing relationships. Narration weaves apparently disparate units or elements into complex wholes in such a way that the result is always something not already present in the things dramatically gathered. Thus, while calculation establishes universal order—an order "good" for everyone even if individually articulated and legitimized—narration remains steadfastly personal and elicits orders that are always unique and often very surprising indeed. Whereas calculation orients us toward efficiently discriminating between what is and is not, narration orients us toward meaningful ways of seeing the characters of things or what they are functioning as.

Just as a "Cliff Notes" version of *Hamlet* leaves us wondering what all the fuss over Shakespeare is about, an icon-rich, calculation-focused environment is one we find hard to fully appreciate—an environment the greatness of which simply eludes us. But apart from such very real aesthetic ramifications, the translation of things into signs or icons markedly raises the stakes of the control and security purchased thereby. In effect, it "paradoxically" renders us more vulnerable than ever, glossing over our intimate relatedness with all things about us and so curtailing the responsive capacity and flexibility such intimacies afford us. If our fingers had no joints, they would be capable of virtually none of the kinds of work they now perform. In the same way, iconically articulated dramas and relationships are incomparably less rich and fruitful than those into which we uniquely and wholly enter. More importantly, if persons are not fundamentally individuals, but systems of relationship, to deplete the world's narrative and dramatic resources is to deplete ourselves. In effect, the iconic reduction of our world to a collection of generic signifiers is to reduce ourselves to exactly the same state of oddly satisfying want. We become shining, happy people for whom there is always something new even though everything—to quote a Talking Heads lyric—is at the same time, "the same as it ever was."

Narration involves improvising with ambiguity, but never its conquest. If the topography of our life experience is seen in karmic terms, the ambiguity of what any event or situation means is the only warrant we ultimately have of our freedom. Likewise, the creative maintenance of ambiguity—the practice of nonthinking or *wu-nian* in the Ch'an tradition—functions as a primary and effective method for liberating all beings. And by contrast, the ideal of absolute clarity and distinctness—so prized from a calculative standpoint—means the end of freedom, the triumph of our self-bondage. It means we (and so our worlds) are so thoroughly sedimented by our own karma—our own intentional activities—that nothing can surprise us. That is, the cycle of wanting and getting is no longer open, no longer indeterminate. The room for failure, for resistance to our wants, has been eliminated. Under such circumstances, it is impossible to truly suffer. But, according to the Buddha, this means it is just as impossible to realize enlightenment.

THE DIGITAL DEFEAT OF ANALOGY:
THE NUMEROLOGY OF RATIONAL VALUES

In comparison with the societies of most indigenous peoples, we are remarkably, almost overwhelmingly, preoccupied with quantities. One of the first things we teach our children is how to count—their own fingers and toes, their toys, their siblings. In spite of evidence that all the mathematical skills so painfully acquired by schoolchildren between the ages of five and eleven can be easily learned in a single year around age ten or eleven, we insist on their being subjected to mathematics instruction during every single day from the time they enter school until the day they graduate or drop out. There are, of course, rational accounts for doing so. For instance, children are handling money at an early age and need some sort of foundation in the basics of addition and subtraction in order to do so. But the truth of the matter is that we no longer question why we are so insistent on mathematics—it is so "natural" to teach our children "their numbers" and how to manipulate them that we never pause to question the underlying values of this disposition.

In contrast with monetary economies, those centered on the practice of bartering are decidedly more conducive to attending first and foremost to quality, not quantity. Without being reduced to a common monetary denominator, a new litter of sheepdogs is not necessarily worth either more or less than a newborn calf. Any trading of sheepdogs and calves has to take into account the health of both, their roles in the overall way of life in the local community, their specific genealogies, and so on. In short, what is essential to the practice of barter is a familiarity with the extended relational histories that the things being bartered have with everything else—the way in which they weave both into our communal narration and our personal (not to mention, often peculiar) understandings of it.

Basic to more vernacular cultures, then, is a rationality based on complex analogies rather than a reduction of things to represented essences. In such cultures, value is not a quantitative concept, but a qualitatively analogic one—a function of interrelationships in process. When dogs and cows are reduced to 'animals' worth 'X' dollars per head, the dramatic depth of analogic value is entirely sublimated in the service of rational clarity. Assigning a monetary worth to a thing or service is a way of rendering its history irrelevant precisely because money—in spite of being subject to the pressures of "inflation" and "deflation"—is essentially ahistorical and nondramatic. And so, while it's "true" that the $100 I'm willing to pay for your sheepdog stands for the degree to which I want your dog, it's also true that your litter of four pups represents $400, at least potentially. When it comes to doing business, 'sheepdog' and '$100' are fully interchangeable signs. For $100 I can get a dog; with a dog, you can get $100. This makes a kind of sense. But what kind? What are we really doing when we file a lawsuit seeking "damages" for the death of a son? What does it mean that the owners of a trucking company can "compensate" us for the tragedy caused by the company's negligent vehicle maintenance program by handing over a court-specified sum of money and not—as might have been the case several hundred years ago—one of their own next-born sons? How can money ever fill the dramatic, relational vacuum with which our family is now afflicted?

These kinds of calculations—determinations of value—happen all the time. Uncommonly useful in the promotion of efficiency and control, they are priceless techniques for sedimenting a way of life to which we have, consciously or not, decided to give ourselves both body and soul. Teaching our children to be both numerate and literate is a symbolic act of initiating them into this life. What is important about numeracy is not making sure they can tell if the sales clerk gives them the correct change when paying for candy after school. What is important is providing them with a method of seeing any given thing, any complex of qualities, as a simple, general integer—a thing that *is* unequivocally. The puppy is one of four that are basically "the same" and so each worth the same $100. And if none of these four is acceptable for its "accidental" qualities of, for instance, body markings, there are dozens and dozens "just like them"—each one for $100. But at a deeper level, we are also teaching our children that the *value* of a thing can be expressed numerically. Entering into the kind of relationship with a thing that allows it to be counted is to decisively constrain or bracket not just its qualitative dimensions but its dramatic meaning. Counting things is at bottom a denial of intimacy with them, their unique place in our narration, in who we are.

When we say that a beginner's guitar, a sheepdog puppy, and a tennis racquet are all worth $100, we are asserting their *equivalence*. This isn't to say that we play tennis with a guitar or make music with a puppy. We don't. But there is a very real sense in which putting a price on things encourages seeing them as only extrinsically related to us through the mediums of our exchange—whether currency, credit cards, electronic accounting, or what have you. At an axiological level, teaching our children how to count is giving them a strategy for establishing standard limits for the things in our lives—things that partially constitute who we are even as we partially constitute them. What numeracy provides is a sure method for abstracting our selves from the things around us. In some ways, this frees us from them by making it possible for us to count things as possessions rather than truly owning them. There is an almost visceral sensation of having more room to move when we realize that the things and people around us have no necessary claim on who we are. If we can count things, we can also discount them. We need not care for, nurture, or even just maintain them. We can simply and always just remove them from the equation.

This is, in fact, what we do when we think of an enemy encampment as 153 soldiers rather than as 153 men like ourselves with pictures of their wives and children in their packs, with aging parents and dreams of peace. Reducing the enemy to simple numbers is essential to any kind of warfare, but especially the kind now practiced where it is possible—as it was for the U.S. military using only "conventional weapons" for the three days of the Gulf War—to kill between 300,000 and 500,000 people without any American soldier ever having to look into the eyes of his or her Iraqi counterparts. The same ability to consider situations in purely statistical terms is essential to much of our current economic, political, and educational practices. And we can justify each move we make because we are already convinced that in and of themselves "the numbers don't lie." People may be able to select statistics in such a way as to support their own conclusions, but that—we are convinced—is a problem with these people and the immorality or selfishness of their motives, not a problem with statistics as such. In other words, we revert to the same cant we typically spout when the merits of any of our other technologies are called into question. It's not the technology itself, but the way people use it that is to blame for any ills with which it's associated.

But statistics can only make sense (of, say, data we've collected) if we first identify some things in some definitely specified degrees or ways as *the same*. That is, statistical analysis is carried out only on the basis of ignoring differences as such. In effect, we set horizons for relevance and assert that for our purposes—for the sake of bringing our karma to fruition—the things under consideration differ only numerically, as one integer differs from any other. If this dog dies or this forest is destroyed, what of it? There are always *more* dogs and *more* forests. What this means is an erasure or severe toning down of the tensions, the *diversity*, needed both for harmony and for dramatic development. Diversity implies a systemic complementarity, a responsive turning apart or dynamic adaptivity. The world viewed statistically is bereft of such meaningful differences. In place of diversity, we have simple variety. There is no whole presumed as original and so no grounds established for an order that is at once fitting and altogether surprising.

In short, we are apparently committed to teaching our children that individuality and generality are basic and rational, not interdependence and uniqueness. Indeed, it is no accident that "reason" is cognate with words like "rate," "ratio," "ration," and "rationality"—all of which derive from root words in Latin and French meaning "counting" or "calculating." To be reasonable is to be able to provide a universally valid account for what we do. It is being able to rate things, to determine their value in some standard fashion. And it should not be particularly hard to see why this connection might hold—the connection, that is, between calculation and acquiring true and ordered knowledge of the way things are. Ultimately, we can control only what we can identify. There is no possibility of controlling something that has no horizons, that is perceptually and conceptually unlimited. Nor is there any way of truly controlling things that are essentially constitutive of who we are since that would entail controlling the controller—something we do only on the pain of dividing the self.

This works well enough in theory. Freud's splitting of the human "atom" into ego, id, and superego is no less elegant than the physicist's initial division of atoms—once thought to be indivisible—into protons, electrons, and neutrons. But in practice, a divided self is either a self in internal torment and conflict or acting this out in manifestly "schizophrenic" behavior. In short, a divided self is no longer in control. Thus, the first step in successfully brainwashing someone is to break them down, to induce a profound sense of doubt or "two-mindedness." The same realization informs the Islamic injunction against images of Allah—the "pious" urge to construct icons or representations of the gods or God is really a haphazardly disguised element of the attempt to exert control over the divine. Idolatry is not evil because it indicates a lapse into naive and wrong beliefs, but because it represents an attempt to influence and eventually usurp divine power. The old military and political truism of "divide and conquer" is just another way of saying the same thing—reasoning or establishing the limits and identity of things, if not the only way to exceed or overcome them, is at least the best.

Enumerating things is the "logical limit" toward which we are encouraged to conduct ourselves by the iconic biases of perception and conception. Taking enumeration one step further and performing the kinds of manipulations possible through algebra, geometry, and calculus, for example, is to fund the rational development of techniques for ever more effectively and efficiently leveraging our power to control our situation. Each new technical level we attain lengthens our "levers," not only making it possible to influence a greater proportion of the situations in which we find ourselves, but distancing us ever more conclusively from dramatic intimacy with the objects of our control.

Part of the difference between the shepherd and his relationship to his flock and a modern livestock corporation supplying lamb worldwide is a difference in how sheep are counted—whether personally or impersonally. The shepherd sees his flock as a community of dominant and subdominant males, of females capable of bearing offspring and those beyond the age of reproduction, of immature sheep both male and female, and all the relationships, genealogical, emotional, and temperamental that obtain among them. Unlike the corporate employee who oversees the management of a veal-producing farm, the shepherd is personally involved with the lives of the sheep he tends. He lives among them and through them. At a very fundamental, emotionally and dramatically sophisticated level, their stories are indistinguishable from his own.

It was suggested above that numeracy provides us with a method of abstracting ourselves from dramatic involvement with the world of which we are parts, but it is equally true to say that abstracting ourselves from the world—say, through a Cartesian/Christian division of body and mind—is precisely what makes numeracy attractive. In most of the cultures in which persons are understood as complexes of relations rather than as autonomous individuals, the idea that everything, and not just a few things immediately at hand, could be broken down into units and quantified was simply not entertained or considered particularly useful and important. What this indicates, however, is not a "fuzziness" in the intellectual and perceptual capabilities of such peoples, but the extent to which the unique and sensuous characteristics of things outweigh their abstracted, common features. While numerical sophistication provides us with an index of the extent to which the calculation-biased reduction of things to icons has been undertaken, and in spite of the fact that this reduction has been undertaken with increasing frequency and commitment worldwide, it does not provide us with a general means of "objectively" ranking the cognitive development of all societies. All it warrants is a method for ranking the progress of societies committed to articulating and promoting the values of individuality and control.

Peoples not disposed toward numerical sophistication can thus be seen as innocent and even childlike in only one fully legitimate sense—like children, they tend to live more fully in and through their senses than in and through their representations. That they are typically more likely to talk about being involved with their environments in relationships of reciprocal caring than one of dominance or even stewardship is not particularly surprising. Nor should it be seen as necessarily unrealistic—a phase of development best left far behind. The ecological disasters that we have already triggered through blind commitment to our calculative and controlling biases stand as ample testament to the need for exploring the meaning of alternate forms of sophistication—forms we can no longer afford to disparage as "primitive."

An analogical understanding of our world disallows taking a "view from nowhere" as ideal. To the contrary, such a view is seen as one from which nothing could (at least analogically) be understood at all. By removing ourselves to a purely objective distance and securing there a fully independent subjectivity, we would effectively isolate ourselves from precisely the kinds of open-ended and nonreductive relationship toward which analogies direct our attention. To be sure, doing so brings about an almost miraculous ability to leverage things to our individual advantage. But it also excludes from consideration that domain of inherently meaningful possibilities for relationship in which things can present themselves as surprisingly relevant to our own needs.

As so trenchantly described by Descartes, the numeric rationality that now underwrites the digital revolution is perfectly suited to bringing about clarity and distinctness—the elimination of irrelevancies or distortion. Those of us old enough to have made the transition from listening to vinyl records to magnetic tapes to digitally encoded compact discs have immediate experience of the numerological eradication of distortion. Compact discs have none of the surface noise, tape hiss, or compression of dynamic range associated with earlier recording technologies. Although a few diehards claim that analog recordings sound warmer and fuller than the best digital ones, most of us cannot tell the difference. But were we to eliminate all the harmonic and intermodular distortion present in a recording session, we would immediately notice the difference: a piano would be indistinguishable from a harpsichord, a guitar, or a saxophone. The unique voices of these instruments are a function of harmonic and intermodular distortions determined by the particular materials used in their construction and the shape and size of reverberating spaces they enclose. Stripped of all harmonic and intermodular distortion, notes played by a piano, a guitar, or an electronic tone generator are indistinguishable and—to most of our ears—completely sterile and unmusical. Truly digital sounds—and not digital samples of acoustically produced tones—are entirely generic. While making no particular claims on our attention, they also do not guide it in any characteristic ways. Such tones are, in an immediate sense, bereft of drama, meaningless.

Whereas valorizing our dramatic and familial relationships with the things around us is conducive to feelings of kinship and cooperative appreciation, our historically dominant tendency to see things in calculative terms has amounted to an assertion of our superiority over them and their reduction to significations for present and future utility. Contrary to the modalities of a shepherd's concerns, what matters for corporate investors are not the characters and relationships being articulated in a flock of sheep, but only how many pounds of meat or yards of wool can be harvested from it, and what it will cost to transport these "products" to the markets where they will bring the highest unit price. Big business is a numbers game, a game of calculated risks.

In the case of the futures market, what is calculated is not so much the "produce" as such, but fluctuations in the conditions of our wanting them. Simply put, even though the grains and metals being traded have not yet been harvested or mined, speculators are able to make money by assuming control of shares of future produce and then "betting" on the direction and degree of market tides. That is, in the futures market, money can be made whether the tide of market interest is going out (unit commodity prices falling) or coming in (prices rising). The point is keying into the (presumably unpredictable) flow of market wants and staying one step ahead of the changes. This is business at the most abstract level possible. Things—and here are included even national currencies—are reduced to the purest of signs: numeric indexes of future wants. Corn that has not even but put in the ground may be bought and sold a dozen times. In actuality, these commodities are purely abstract signifiers of how much attention is being captured and at what rate of return. Not so differently from power plants that harness the energy of oceanic tides and convert it into electricity, the futures market converts the energy or power inherent to the movements of consumer attention into a readily useable form—a volatile combination of cash and credit. The only limit on how much power can be drawn is the limit of how much attention can be attached to the commodity-icons being traded.

Ironically, and yet tellingly, it is at this most abstract level of buying and selling that the most money can be made in the shortest time. The independent farmer raising feed corn can lose everything with a season of bad weather while futures traders who have never set eyes on a live corn plant can double their money many times over in the course of the same season.

The further away from fully material and so sensuous things we move, the more completely we are able to divorce ourselves from full intimacy with them, the more we are able use them to our advantage. That is, maximal power and control come with minimal attention to dramatic uniqueness and narrative complexity. The digitally assisted conversion of things into calculable signs is essential to international, corporate business precisely because it (at least virtually) frees them from all but the most generic and dramatically tenuous systems of natural interdependence.

Just as ore must be separated from the rock in which it naturally occurs before it can be worked into tools, the translation of things—including everything from cultural values to national currencies—into freely tradable commodities is a process of transforming relational systems into usefully autonomous existents. The calculative enumeration that makes futures trading possible takes this transformative process to the logical extreme of constituting practically frictionless entities—entities that can be traded at will by using digital computers and fiber-optic or satellite-relayed transmission lines because they do not truly belong anywhere at all.

By remarking that 'is' and 'is not' are the twin barbs on which all mankind is impaled, the Buddha invited us to attend to our suffering, not as the result of purely objective or external conditions befalling us, but as a function of our making and maintaining distinctions. Distinctions create rents in the fabric of our interdependence, tears in our mutual narration, and this cannot but compromise our wholeness and lead to distress. Much like the mathematician Kurt Godel—the author of the famous "incompleteness theorem"—Buddhists have long been aware that no self-referential system of calculations can ever be complete and that the "minimum" cost of a consistently calculative regard of things is our segregation from them. In short, we cannot be part of the equation if we expect to achieve a final and rational solution for it. Nor can we consistently maintain a calculative frame of mind and avoid a sense of the incompleteness of our world. The digital reduction of things (including plants, animals, and humans) to statistical entities explicitly involves ignoring their unique possibilities for dramatic contribution, their narrative depth. And to the precise extent that it makes our lives more efficient, such a reduction cannot but lead to feeling that we live in a basically interrupted world—a world of unmitigated suffering.

THE MEDIA AND DIGITAL TROUBLE:
SUFFERING ALONE TOGETHER

Written and filmed stories, while open to multiple interpretations, nevertheless restrict the domain of dramatic meaning to the scope of the individual audience member. We can make of the story what we will, taking away from it something of value to us. But this is very different from entering into a healing relationship with the people, places, and events narrated through the story. We can listen intently to the story of Kisagotami and perhaps change our thinking about the nature of suffering and its resolution as a result, but we do not help her, do not become members of her extended family. Neither can she help us or become a member of ours.

This is such an obvious fact that we tend to overlook the significance of spending so much of our time so incompletely engaged with commodified dramas. For example, we have all found ourselves in the situation of doing something that we "know" we shouldn't do. We normally pass this off as a result of the relative weakness of our wills or some conflict among our values. But, in actuality, this failure to do what we "know" we should reveals more about the profoundly attenuated circumstances under which we came upon this knowledge than the state of our present intentions. Knowledge that is superficially grasped in ultimately superfluous circumstances is of no help whatsoever when we are pushed to our limits. It is one thing to hear on dry land that you should remain calm if you wipe out in big surf. It's another thing altogether when you're spinning uncontrollably in the black and blue water exploding off the reef at Laniakea on Oahu's north shore, low on air and unsure of which way is up.

While we are made aware of the suffering of others often and graphically through the media, we are in no position to do anything about it. Bluntly stated, mediated suffering is inherently intractable. We may become aware of a fantastic number of details concerning a situation. We may hear various expert opinions on how to construct and deal with the "facts" of the case in question. We may even see how the situation is brought to an end. What we do not and cannot manage at any point from our initial introduction to mass-mediated suffering to our witnessing of its "resolution" is to exert ourselves on behalf of and in cooperation with the people directly affected. That is, our knowledge is purely theoretical—a view we acquire. It is not practical—the realization of a resolution in our conduct.

Seen in karmic terms, media presentations of suffering may well help assuage our need for dramatic involvement by augmenting our personally impoverished narrative resources. This will encourage our wanting more access to such presentations—both more frequently and more intensely. But because these presentations of suffering are passive objects for consumption, we are not learning how to actively respond to either our own troubles and crises or anyone else's. To the contrary, we are making karma for simply "looking on" and trusting that someone else, somewhere else, is taking responsibility for bringing things to conclusion. In short, by consuming mass-mediated dramas, we are training ourselves *not to respond* to situations as needed. As we know it through the media, suffering is essentially meaningless.

The Buddhist objection to the media- and commodity-driven intensification of the iconic aspects of our world is thus soteriological. It is not the media's various contents that are particularly problematic, but the patterns of conduct inculcated by participating in the technologies involved. When perception is more than minimally editorial—certainly when our experience is overwhelmingly iconic and the dramatically unexpected therefore held maximally at bay—our ability to relinquish our horizons for relevance is limited and, consequently, so is our ability to respond to our situation as needed. Under such circumstances, our troubles necessarily and yet needlessly drift into apparent intractability because while generic panaceas may solve equally generic problems, they can do nothing to resolve the irreducibly unique crises in which we are actually—if often unconsciously—embroiled.

We do not suffer because we are in pain. We suffer because something has gone wrong in our story—wrong enough that it threatens to collapse the structure of our narration. At least in the Buddhist sense, suffering (*dukkha*) arises as a falling apart of our dramatic interdependence, a severe enough breach or interruption of our interrelatedness that things are manifestly incapable of righting themselves. When a family member is diagnosed with cancer, our suffering is not a function of the illness itself, but how well or ill our story is able to accommodate the challenge cancer delivers. The coping pattern of depression-denial-anger-acceptance reflects one of the most common trajectories of such accommodation—a trajectory that carries us from abject blockage through emotional combat with the threat to our life narrative, and finally to the emergence of a new direction for that complex of relationships we refer to as our family.

Sadly, there are increasingly large numbers of people who cannot navigate this transition in even the most mundane circumstances. Referred to nowadays as "clinically depressed," they are people who are at a crippling, narrative impasse. They cannot return to the life they once and more or less contentedly led; nor can they muster the kind of vitality required to engender a new life. In the terms we've been playing with in our conversation, they are people whose conduct has become so dominantly societal that while they possess a detailed and often obsessive awareness of their wants, they have no true desires. They simply cannot see the point in going on, cannot improvise a meaningful reconfiguration of their circumstances.

While such severe clinical depression is an extreme case, it graphically illustrates the structural elements of all persistent suffering. At bottom, all of our troubles depend much less on our material circumstances as such than on our own failures in improvising a dramatic resolution for the interruptions they occasion. What conditions the persistence of our suffering is the poverty of our narrative resources—our relational depth and diversity—and so our ability to creatively incorporate or appropriate the 'mistakes', 'bad luck', 'accidents', 'prejudices', and 'tragedies' that afflict us.

To be sure, the difficulties we have in resolving our own troubles are exacerbated by the complexities of our economic, political, and cultural contexts. In comparison with times past, we can perhaps quite legitimately claim that we have to deal with a lot more (potentially troubling) "stuff" than our parents or grandparents. But there is a sense in which this complexity itself is symptomatic of the same lack of dramatic depth and narrative resources that condition our inability to meaningfully improvise either around or with the interruptions to which our personal and communal stories are increasingly subject. The connecting factor is our technology-driven disposition for inadvertent, habitual, misguided, or simply excessive editing. That is, trouble comes when—for the sake of perceptual or behavioral efficiency and the exercise of control—we indulge the translation of things into mere icons or signs. Turning aside from or denying the emptiness or infinite interrelatedness of things, we turn away from precisely that treasury of dramatic possibilities through the opening of which the harmoniousness of our narration would have naturally (*tzu jan*) arisen.

No doubt, the structure of iconically attuned awareness is compatible with rapid decision-making. And in a world profusely stocked with every manner of commodity, efficient judgment can indeed be seen as a kind of virtue. But quickly choosing among alternatives is not the same as the kind of critical and yet unhesitatingly careful regard that comes from practicing the appreciation of intimate relationship. Decisions invariably narrow the field of narrative possibilities by effectively closing off the extension of awareness in certain directions or dimensions. In this sense, the rapid-fire reactions of a video-game expert have almost nothing to do with Buddhist spontaneity—the realization of a horizonless capacity for unprecedented and yet meaningful resolutions of actual, and not merely virtual, suffering.

MEDIATION AND MEDIOCRITY

We can scarcely turn on the television without being inundated with news from around the world about this or that tragedy, this or that war or terrorist attack, this or that murder or outrage. But our basically iconic exposure to the suffering of others neither encourages feelings of personal responsibility nor serves as a catalyst for spontaneous response. In those relatively rare cases when public contributions are sought for disaster relief or the performance of a particularly expensive medical procedure (typically on a child), what we are asked to give are not time, effort, and creativity, but money—that most generically 'useful' of icons. It may be that we imagine ourselves to be acting out of compassion when signing a check over to some relief agency or charity. But in the absence of direct, fully responsive community with those we aim to 'help', such acts are not only deprived of physical, sensory depth, but emotional and spiritual depth as well.

This is not to say we should categorically refrain from contributing our economic resources to charities and relief funds. But, we should realize that the compassion we manifest in this way is almost exclusively iconic. We know only what the media have represented for us and can enter into only that kind of conduct that the media can support. For the most part, we are almost entirely blind to the network of conditions that have actually given rise to the suffering we hope to alleviate and are reacting merely to the results as presented. Unaware of the complex systems of interdependence that actually constitute the situation with which we find ourselves concerned, the 'troubles' we are responding to are themselves merely iconic. Because of this, we really have no means of even ascertaining, much less guaranteeing, that our 'compassionate' acts actually help the situation rather than simply making it worse. And so, even aside from the publicized cases of fraudulent and grossly inefficient charities, the fact of the matter is that our altruism treats only symptoms—often in such a way as to insure their continuation.

The tragic consequences of the "green revolution" during the 1960s is a classic example of this with explicitly technical overtones. With entirely "altruistic" motives, Western agricultural specialists imported the best of scientific farming techniques to South Asia in an attempt to overcome the hunger afflicting so many hundreds of millions of the peasant-folk living in the region. Using the latest machinery and the most advanced strains of "engineered" grain, the initial effects of the "revolution" were indeed green. The yields of bushels of grain per acre markedly, even remarkably, increased.

But as soon as U.S. economic aid to the region was reduced in an effort to balance the increasing cost of the Vietnam War, the yields began plummeting. Gasoline for farm machinery was in short supply and prohibitively expensive. Grain engineered for maximum yield proved susceptible to local insect and bacterial populations. For as long as it could be supported, pesticide use rose toward epidemic levels. Because they were most affordable and in spite of their association with birth defects in both livestock and humans, pesticides like DDT were employed long after being banned in the United States. Since entire villages had pooled resources to incorporate the new miracle techniques, the failure of the revolution not only had a minimal—and in some places, a negative—effect on hunger, it destroyed the basis of indigenous patterns of cultivating, harvesting, and distributing crops. With no possibility of going back to the "old ways," massive sellouts of arable land to corporate investors was followed by an exodus of rural peasants into urban areas where their skills were irrelevant and their social support systems nonfunctional. In short, like so many of our other attempts to help others, the green revolution paved a steep road to hell with the best of intentions.

Media-stimulated awareness of suffering seldom manifests in a horizonless readiness to respond as needed. Faced with a child covered with sores and the signs of malnutrition, few of us are so heartless as to not share our table with her. Presented with televised images of thousands of such children, we for the most part just feel hopeless, convinced that there is nothing much we can personally do. Our material and narrative resources, impoverished as they may be, can be offered to an actual child before us. We can place ourselves at her disposal, offering precisely and often spontaneously what is most appropriate. But there is no means of doing so with those whose suffering affects us only through the generic conduit of mass media. And for this reason, there is also little meaning in our acts of 'compassion' other than that which *we* assign to them. In the world of mass mediation, altruism, too, can be almost exclusively narcissistic.

The question we must grapple with is how we can ease the suffering of others when the iconic structuring of our awareness undermines the very relations—the modes of dramatic interdependence or narration—that must be knit back together for healing to occur. Confirmed by the media in the opinion that we and everyone else are fundamentally discrete individuals—even if often caught up in times and histories essentially beyond our control—what basis is there resisting the societal inclination toward greater regulation and hence an increasing privatization of all but the most mundane dimensions of our commonality? With the commodity-driven privation of our ability to truly desire and not merely want, what dramatic resources can we draw on in finding meaningful and not merely factual connections between our fortunes—whether 'good' or 'ill'—and those of others? If we accept as incontestable the association of freedom and (technically mediated) control, why should we embrace an ideal of improvisational virtuosity? After all, for most of us, any petition for sociality in this sense is tantamount to a call for anarchy, for the end of all order, for a lapse into chaos.

Even granting that it has been our own efforts and values that have placed our communities at the risk that they now are in, as long as the manner in which we learn of these risks is the primary vehicle of their intensification, how likely is it that we will undertake the kind of critique needed in order to alter the patterns of valorization that fund our present courses of conduct? If we know that we are a community only through the mass media, how can we ever come close enough that we can truly matter to one another, spontaneously contributing who we are to the realization of a liberating intimacy?

Mass-mediated exposure to the life stories and suffering of others provides us with both extremely varied information about "them" and equally restricted opportunities for offering ourselves in appropriate response. If who we are is in fact given in the movement of our narration—our conduct—this restriction inevitably conditions an atrophy of our character, an attenuation of the depth and range of our attentiveness. Persistently enough indulged, a diet of mass-mediated narratives is highly conducive to increasingly mediocre and narcissistic forms of subjectivity. Granted the truth of Ch'an Master Pai-chang's teaching that enlightenment is just the perfection of offering, ubiquitous access and exposure to mass mediation amounts to a structural occlusion of our buddha-nature—the same kind of destructive limitation suffered by our natural environments with the triumph of urbanity and a way of life dedicated to the technical proliferation of control.

Ecologists have long claimed that diversity constitutes a singularly important value in any natural system. And in consonance with both Buddhist thought and the holistic pragmatism of George Herbert Mead, some have even gone so far as to insist that if consciousness is not a 'thing' or 'state' but a continually burgeoning relationship between an organism and its environment, then the quality and complexity of our own awareness can be seen as dependent on the diversity of our lived environment. That is, the complexity of the human mind quite literally has its roots in the diversity and complexity of the natural world. Pressing this insight to its logical conclusion, it has been argued that any significant reduction in biological diversity on the planet would necessarily be correlated with a similar reduction in the complexity and creative potentiality of consciousness. Biodiversity in this case is not merely good for aesthetic reasons or for the sake of preserving a high level of ecosystem adaptivity—a kind of responsive virtuosity that, after all, we might well imagine our technologies make irrelevant—but to the preservation of characteristically human levels of sentience and sensibility.

Arguments that the media have been instrumental in promoting the multicultural ideal and so the advancement of axiological diversity are finally invalid because they assume that diversity amounts to just another way of saying variety. All of the cultural transformations in which the media have played crucial roles have also involved the commodification of values—the reduction of cultural ideals and practices to things that can be "chosen" independently of the whole systems of which they were originally parts. What is lost in this translation are those features of the whole that differ from and are irreducible to the qualities of its parts—in actuality, precisely that which we cannot control or plan. The diversity of a natural ecosystem does not consist of the mere co-presence of a large number of plant and animal species, but in the patterns of interdependence that allow each part of the system to both prosper in its own right and contribute in uniquely appropriate fashions to the system it helps constitute. Ecological diversity should be seen, in other words, as the achievement of a qualitatively distinct narration of all the elements of an environment—a narration that is, moment by moment, at once whole and open, both meaningful and fully improvised.

While it's true that the media make readily available a historically unprecedented "wealth" of experiences, information, and dramatic vignettes, these are presented to us with the same absence of systemic wholeness that characterizes the aggregate of items-for-purchase we find in any suburban shopping mall. In sharp contrast with the diversity of a natural ecosystem or a spontaneously realized culture, the various 'things' collected together in a mall are not wed through patterns of always reciprocal nourishment, caring, and desire. Wandering through it, unlike attentively wandering through a rainforest or along an undeveloped seashore, can teach us nothing about these modes of contributory and appreciative interdependence.

Ecosystems—like Chuang-tzu's ten thousand things—can truly be said to "take care of themselves." By contrast, the commodified information and goods to which we have such miraculously variable access are effectively useless unless wanted. In and of themselves, the commodities that constitute the elements of so much of our life-world have no meaning, no direction. Far from taking care of themselves, they require our constant monitoring and maintenance. Whatever organization they collectively express is something we are responsible for—something we impose or order. Far from contributing in surprisingly creative ways to the furtherance of our narration, their sheer quantity as often as not simply overwhelms us. They are massed together but not growing. They persist without maturing. Stripped of any histories that might reveal their interdependence and intimacy not just with one another but with us as well, they are mute reminders of the disturbed condition of our own hearts and minds.

What shopping malls and the architecture of the World Wide Web really expose is the ordered and yet profoundly fragmented condition of our own natures. The absence of true diversity that is characteristic of the "postmodern" world reveals the precise extent to which we have fallen into ignorance of our own interdependence with all things—the extent to which we have, for the sake of controlling the satisfaction of our wants, forsaken true community with the things that ultimately engender our own possibility. At once, we have turned our backs on the dramatically new worlds to which they might open us and on who we might then become there.

The translation of things into mere icons or signs accomplishes much in clearing the paths between our wants and their satisfaction. But, to play out an analogy with Illich's analysis of transportation technologies, this translation encourages paving these paths to yet further increase the efficiency of the transitions from want to satisfaction *and back again*. Just as the development of railway and automobile transportation systems have ended up increasing the time we spend traveling, the commodification of things has resulted in our spending more and more time in acts of consumption. With the growing ubiquity of the media, we are witnessing a similar translation of narrativity, drama, knowledge, and even experience as such into commodities and with practically identical consequences: the acquisition of stories, dramas, knowledge, and experiences has become an end in itself apart from any creative role these might play in our lives.

The increasing appetite in the world's most developed nations for intensely varied and often violent lifestyles and forms of entertainment is often taken to be an atavistic phenomenon triggered by the pressures of technologically sophisticated, urban life. While there may be some merit to this view—it provides, after all, a fairly cogent rationale for consistencies in the content of these "new" lifestyles and forms of entertainment—it does not explain the structural dynamics of the changes we are witnessing. In addition, we must allow that axiological hegemony of the type that has accompanied the rising ubiquity of especially the information technologies closes rather than opens the field of cultural and so communal creativity. That is, in much the same way that monoculture cropping depletes our soil and effectively narrows the range of plants it can nourish without supplemental fertilizers, the universalization of values that goes along with mass mediation impoverishes the ground of narrative improvisation. In keeping with the calculative biases of our technical orientation for control, satisfying our increasingly extensive and various wants is undertaken by quantitative—and not qualitative—intensification. Because the new technologies make the transfer of information and iconic experiences so easy and efficient, we end up wanting more and still more. Because this "more" is provided to us individually—even if generically—and because it arrives bereft of the kinds of narrative connections that would deepen an awareness of our interdependence with all things, the long-range effect of mass-marketing culture and knowledge is a fragmentation of both our communities and our own wholeness as persons. In short, contrary to the claims of those profiting most from them and the protests of those most addicted to the artificial fertility they promote, mass mediation means our growing isolation and biographical sterility.

Now, it might be argued that if it were not for the media, we would have absolutely no inkling of the suffering going on in the world at large. If not for televised news and Internet discussion groups, what would we know of the political, social, and personal travails of people living in other American cities, much less on other continents? But it is important that we wonder why it is that while we are constantly being made aware of such suffering we are not constantly in tears or leaping up in ready and fully attentive response. A partial answer to this is that the human nervous system is such that constant stimulations of any sort and virtually any intensity will eventually be attenuated enough to fall below the threshold of conscious attention. On the one hand, this property of our nervous system underlies our ability to overcome the debilitating effects of pain, at least up to a certain threshold beyond which the nervous system is incapable of "turning down the volume" enough for us to do anything much more than attend to our distress. On the other hand, it also underlies the addiction cycle whereby regularly indulged and intensely pleasurable sensations or experiences eventually lose their edge and invite still more constant and intense indulgence. Quite clearly, the infiltration of practically every waking moment of our lives by one kind or another of media stimulation can be seen as driving us into a "need" for more and more intense stimulation if we are to continue deriving the kind of "pleasures" they afford.

This, however, is hardly helpful to the media's cause. It underscores the fact that while we are being exposed to an incredible variety of experiences via the media, they dull our attention. In short, the media actually undermine the diversity of our lived worlds. Otherwise, why would our liability to boredom be increasing? How could we explain the fact that the more we expose ourselves to the media, the less we are consciously aware of what we're being exposed to and why? The correlation of television and video-game playing, for example, with a passive perceptual state is commonly accepted. What is typically left out of this stated acceptance, however, is a critical appreciation of the disparity between the ostensive variety of media content and the striking monotony of the conduct and hence kinds of awareness the media are so instrumental in constituting. Contrary to the well-advertised claims of the media on their own behalf, more is leading to less and less.

The nature of the media is such that while there are multiple views of any given world event—dozens of locally available newspapers, magazines, cable channels, Internet servers, and so on—these views exist in the same kind of isolation from one another that they do from the events they represent. That is, they are not organically but only accidentally related to one another. In some circles, this disintegration of anything like a universal, monolithic worldview is held up as a great advance—a step in the direction of freeing ourselves as individuals from the dictatorial visions of the family, the clan, the nation, and so on. The fact that this liberation is accompanied by a birth of altogether new and intense strains of despair is considered one of the "prices" we pay for our freedom—a necessary and at any rate unavoidable sacrifice. And at a purely theoretical level, there is much to recommend this conclusion. There is, indeed, a very real kind of tyranny in every event falling into a predetermined place according to some "master plan," regardless of whether this plan is religious, political, economic, or cultural in nature.

But, assuming that our choices are between monolithic master plans and relativist fragmentation is simply another way of utterly devaluing our dramatic interdependence—the priority of our always changing and ambiguous narration. It is true that the world as represented through the media is a world capable of supporting a great variety of alternative constructions. The decisions of programmers, newswriters, broadcasters, cable service owners, government leaders, and so on all take up positions from which they divide the "same" world. And in keeping with our penchant for mathematical modeling, it appears to be a world that is infinitely divisible—like a sphere composed of an infinity of variously oriented, circular planes. But is this absence of any single story meaningfully uniting these profiles into a living whole a revelation of the world's nature or simply its representational lack of one? Is the absurdity of modern and now postmodern life a once-hidden universal of the human experience, or is it a vacuity imposed on our world—our narration—by the tightening isomorphism obtaining between our awareness and the structure of the media informing it?

MEDIA AND THE DECLINING NARRATIVITY
OF POPULAR CULTURE

Through a consistent dedication to promoting technologies biased toward control, we have waged an extremely effective campaign against chaos, against all that is unplanned and impossible to anticipate. Along the way—and so paradoxically to our way of thinking that we have come to regard it as a revelation—we have at the very same time been undercutting the roots of both meaning and necessity. That is, our success in being able to control our circumstances has cost us enough narrative depth that while things happen more predictably than ever before, we have less and less idea of what they are happening for. The twin demise of necessity and chance has rendered "what for?" an almost purely rhetorical question, even if we add "do I want it?" in the middle. Meaning has become "a problem."

The ancient Chinese who devised the heuristic system called the *I Ching* understood full well that a holistic, cosmic order cannot obtain in the absence of the unexpected. Lacking this insight, it has been our predominant belief that defeating chance would secure the orderliness of the world—a security from within which each one of us could at long last articulate a consistently meaningful existence. In fact, the opposite has been the case. Our almost miraculous power over both chance and nature has managed not only to strip things of inherent meaning—their capacity for redirecting our wills, our intentions for the future of our mutual narration—but to erode our sense of who we really are, what we truly mean. On some level we understand that the point of our existing cannot be only living *longer*, or gaining *more* influence or contacts, or *adding to* our material holdings. But these quantitative measures of who we are and why often seem to be all that remains. The reduction of the world to a collection of facts has worked wonders for our ability to control things and order our existence. But this silencing of things has meant as well a shouting down of their own tendencies, dispositions, and directions. In a word, our control over things is an index of the world's devaluation. Reduced to an increasingly dense collection of sites, the world simply cannot accommodate truly dramatic development. We can *get* practically anywhere we want, but find it nearly impossible to embark on a real journey. Journeys are not about destinations and itineraries. They are about the always deeply narrative process of opening up new continents of meaning—something that is impossible when time and space are so compressed that there is room only for departures and arrivals but no adventures.

It's not accidental that an acute awareness of the ultimate meaninglessness of things started circulating among philosophers and marginalized members of the cultural elite at about the same time as the invention and spread of the power loom and the locomotive. Nor is it mere coincidence that the absurdity of life so persuasively envisioned by European existentialists like Sartre and Camus reached a kind of apogee in the middle of this century at precisely the point when the transportation revolution was at its theoretical and commercial zenith. The ascendance of postmodernism marks the latest phase of this parabolic movement from a world that is spontaneously meaningful and so essentially uncontrollable to one that is eminently controllable and yet finally meaningless. While its origins can be traced back into "radio days" of the middle third of the century and its popular dissemination correlated with the spread of television, a maturely realized, postmodern world is only just now taking shape, at once aiding and abetted by the computer revolution and the dawn of the so-called Information Age. Twenty-five years ago, for example, the postmodern view of past, present, and future being mere signs that under the right circumstances could be meaningfully arranged in quite different orders was comprehensible only at a theoretical level. But with the advent of Internet chat rooms and discussion lists, the linear temporality of our communicative practices is being rapidly and quite practically deconstructed. The fragmented structure of postmodern literature with its emphasis on overlapping, inconsistent and yet not wholly exclusive viewpoints mirrors not just the kinds of monadic relationships characteristic of cyberspace interactions, but the kinds of often exceedingly intense and momentary interpersonal connections taking place among the participants at techno-raves.

As manifested in the generational transits of our philosophical and cultural elites, this parabolic movement is perhaps of little direct interest to most of us. We have likely had only the most passing acquaintance with them, and almost surely have no inclination to view that as any kind of shortcoming. But if concepts develop as regularities in our conduct, and if conduct is explicitly understood as our being led together (*com* + *ducere*)— the movement of *our* narration—then the proclamations of philosophers and critical aestheticians cannot have arisen in a vacuum of high-sounding abstraction. To the contrary, and as the examples above illustrate, they are often highly concentrated—perhaps even exaggerated—counterparts of regularities prevalent in the popular domain as well. In short, the parabolic movement toward individually well-ordered and yet increasingly meaningless (personal and communal) conduct cannot be restricted to the realms of philosophy and literary criticism, but necessarily shows through in the changing contents and complexions of our popular cultures as well. Whether any particular conceptual movement is expressed as well in the mainstream of a culture or only at its margins is a function of all the conditions present and so almost always open to debate. But the point stands that no final divorce is possible between consistent dispositions in how we think about our lives and continuing patterns in how we live them.

This is not to suggest, of course, that popular culture dictates the content or direction of philosophical discourse or, for that matter, the reverse. The patterns of our entertainment preferences and what they reveal about our karma and the structure of our subjectivity are related to the prevailing conceptual landscape in the same manner as the proverbial chicken and egg. In actuality, neither could ever have come "first" since they have never really been distinct or discrete. What is basic is conduct or narrative movement as such and not either our conceptualization of it or some statistically derived composite of its trajectories.

The importance of making this point is not to secure the claim that philosophical speculation has some inherent practical value. At least at this phase of our conversation, what is crucial is the manner in which it establishes grounds for denying that the popular appeal of, for example, graphically violent action-adventure films is a function of their "pure, entertainment value." To the contrary, if interdependence is taken as basic, this appeal actually displays in almost blatant full-relief a very widespread and profound disposition in our conduct—that is, in the topography of our ongoing and dramatic interrelatedness. In a word, popular appeal is an expression of our karma—an index of the regular and regulative intentions we have and are continuing to make regarding the nature and direction of our experience.

According to the Buddhist perspective, arguments raised in support of or opposition to the claim that "media violence" causes or is caused by "real life" violence are of a piece with the discourse about 'chickens' and 'eggs'—a flowing-apart that canonizes our ignorance of both the priority of relationality and our own responsibility for what is happening all around us. What such discourse circularly invokes are the central values—control and individuality—of the very technologies we hope to bring into question. We end up back at the same moral impasse at which we are deposited by the "guns don't kill, people do" argument. If we argue against the technologies and the tools resulting from them, we argue against our preferred vision of ourselves as autonomous individuals. But seen without the bifurcating lenses of linear causation, both "media" and "actual" violence are manifestly constitutive of our conduct, of who we are and where we are headed, both communally and personally. Taking a closer look at trends in the mode and content of our mass mediation is thus a practically useful means of seeing how successful the colonization of consciousness has been and in what direction not just 'you' and 'I', but the whole of which 'we' are merely abstractions is being perhaps irreversibly perverted.

THE MEDIATED WILDERNESS

One of the most notable trends in the news and entertainment industry over the past four or five decades—roughly since the entry of television into a majority of American homes—has been a growing realism or literalism in dramatic program content paralleled by an increasing fragmentation or deconstruction of the traditional story line. For example, the *Leave it to Beaver*-style '50s family with its deeply suburban setting and values— earnest parents; well-meaning, somewhat innocent children; prankish rather than vicious antagonists—gave way in a series of waves to families with sometimes insoluble problems, families with pregnant teenagers and alcoholic mothers and two-timing, sarcastic fathers. The evening news has gone from a kind of pinstriped, talking-head reportage characterized by a continuous narrative line to a flashy, "magazine"-style presentation where the "pages" have come apart and been hastily reassembled. In postmodern news programming, political, economic, sports, entertainment, and human interest stories overlap or break into one another in a format most closely resembling the video fashions pioneered on MTV.

Of course, increasingly realistic media programming can be partly explained by the technical underwriting provided by improved camera and broadcast/viewing equipment, as well as by eye-catching, computer-generated special effects. That is, programs have become more realistic because realism has become technically possible. This "climb the mountain because it's there" account, however, is clearly incomplete. The shift toward realism and literalism also reflects changing market tastes. The last decades have seen a growing dissatisfaction among the viewing public for "sanitized" entertainment and news content that evidences more than anything else a need or want of contact with something like the "real world." With the kind of dramatic isolation promoted by a technologically sedimented valorization of control and individuality, the media have gradually come to be seen as our "eyes to the world"—an absolutely crucial extension of our sense organs and sensibility. Program content has naturally modulated in such a way as to provide access to the world around us with a variety and intensity that stand in direct proportion to the attenuated diversity and depth of our day-to-day lives.

At a still more basic level, however, "real world" programming vastly increases the capacity of media-transmitted drama to be experienced as personally relevant and to serve, therefore, as a replacement for our immediate narration. In particular, realistically portrayed narrative tensions are conducive to a degree of audience identification with mass-mediated characters and dramas—participation that is compatible with a significant experience of risk in the absence of any felt imperative to act upon it. Such programming thus satisfies the need for dramatic consumption—the need for explicitly meaningful experience—while doing nothing to encourage actual dramatic involvement. That is, "real world" programming serves as a kind of experiential "sugar" that alleviates our dramatic hunger without in any way nourishing us. To the contrary, it brings about an addictive ignorance of precisely what might actually and not just virtually satisfy our need for meaning.

Of course, the experience of dramatic tension and release, even if only virtually, is not always desirable. And as might be expected, the trend toward realism is noticeably absent in comedy programming where people and situations are presented in quite clearly unrealistic worlds at sufficient distance from those we live and toil within that we are quite comfortable laughing at them. The agenda of especially mass-mediated comedy—in sharp distinction from the best of stand-up comedy, for instance—is never to laugh at ourselves in moments of meaningful catharsis, but rather to induce a cataleptic escape from our immediate circumstances. Bringing the absurdity of our lives too close to home would almost ensure crossing over from the comedic to the tragic and a collapse of the distinctive space within which humor takes place.

The fragmentation of the story line in Information Age media follows similar principles as the trend toward dramatic realism. Computer-assisted editing allows for rapid cuts, segues, image overlays, and a degree of overall compositional complexity that was simply impossible twenty or thirty years ago. But the capacity for effectively deconstructing the movement of mediated narration cannot explain the rapidity with which such techniques have become virtually ubiquitous. Most generally speaking, rapid-fire editing creates a mediascape comprising only "temporal plateaus" and nothing in-between. We jump instantaneously from plateau to plateau in an essentially directionless and uncommitted fashion. Scenes are thus long enough to allow the audience to grasp as 'scenes', but short enough not to invite their attention to linger. In a word, the typical mediascape is almost purely iconic.

For first-time viewers, dropping into the midst of such an experiential space can be disconcerting. Like running down a steep set of stairs, once you get started it's much easier to simply keep going than it is to stop. Rapid editing creates temporal momentum, a sense of dynamism that nevertheless decreases the viewer's proactive attentiveness. Individual scenes or experiential plateaus are of such minimal duration that there is no incentive to "look for" meaning. One simply keeps leaping from mediascape to mediascape, not in order to arrive anywhere, but simply to keep moving. In this sense, postmodern media evidence a radical departure from the modern and premodern conception of meaning as something either arrived at or first possessed and then imposed. But in contrast with the Buddhist conception of meaning as given directly in the *direction* of our narrative movement, postmodern meaning consists of a purely disseminating motion as such. Clear and careful directions, no less than destinations, are effectively deconstructed by the instantaneous nature of the changes between scenes. What we are left with is a motion that cannot be defined or formulated according to any known calculus—not quite random and yet not quite disambiguating either. But in the end, such motion amounts to committing ourselves to a nondramatic path as debilitating as that blazed by Buddhists who wrongly take emptiness to be "the way things are" and not a liberating method or practice. Quite simply, the fragmented time of postmodern narrative mirrors our growing inclination not to make differences that really matter, that commit us to a particular dramatic course. In a beautifully ironic twist, the attention of mass-mediated viewers is most effectively kept from wandering by simply not allowing it to settle.

It is important that, unlike radio dramas or news broadcasts, interest in video-mediated programming can be maintained and intensified without recourse to sophisticated vocabulary, grammatical complexity, or locutionary brilliance and the kinds of attention these require. Single pictures being "worth a thousand words," movies and television programs have immense quantitative advantages over spoken word or print mediation when it comes to presenting a given amount of information in a short period of time and carrying out an increasingly global colonization of consciousness. While spoken-word and print media deliver information at a relatively fixed and limited linear rate, video is capable not only of rapid-fire, cut-and-paste editing, but of presenting simultaneous messages in complex and yet comprehensible images. Thus, while a traditionally constructed spoken or written narrative develops an image over time, only gradually providing us with a sense of wholeness or completion, video imaging allows apparent wholes to be presented at a glance and then deconstructed or analyzed for meaning content at virtually any rate and from any number of vantages. This seems not only more objective, but more egalitarian. The linear biases of verbal grammar can be more or less dispensed with and along with them the impression that meaning depends on attending to "what follows." Unfortunately, the deconstructed grammar of visual media is also conducive to either monologic presentations of information in which contribution is kept to a minimum or to "participatory" presentations in which contribution occurs in essentially random and so meaningless fashions.

In most spoken languages, the sense of a term depends at least in part on what has preceded and comes after it. In languages like Sanskrit and Latin, this meaning-fixing context is contracted in prefixes and suffixes. Word order is not absolutely essential. But in languages like Chinese, there is so much phonetic repetition that it is only extended, phrase-level contexts that allow sense to be made of any given utterance. There is no equivalent to this grammatical stress on continuity and context in video imaging. The rapid cuts we find in everything from news to cartoon programs can work only because the sense—and finally the meaning—of each scene or video byte is not dependent on what surrounds it. Ultimately, "seeing is believing" not because vision is somehow more reliable than our other senses, but because seeing represents or serves as a metaphor for comprehensively grasping our situation.

But these advantages, while going some distance in explaining the media shift toward more literal program contents and less continuous forms of temporality still don't tell the whole story. In the same way that the Chinese invented gunpowder but never developed sophisticated firearms and bombs, we might have invented video devices without ever realizing a television and film industry as we know it today. We have still to wonder, in other words, what it means that a discontinuous stream of literal glances caught from a variety of vantages has become our normal mode of informing and entertaining ourselves.

The flow of our conversation thus far would encourage answering that this shift in the structure of media narratives is conditioned by and in turn conditions a similar shift in the most common modes of our personal and communal narration—the movement and orientation of our conduct and so of who we have been and are coming to be. More briefly still, this shift is simply dictated by what we want. But some caution is required in understanding and drawing conclusions from this statement. For example, it is now almost a cliché that media portrayals of outlaws and rebels became important in America during the 1950s and 1960s as a substitute for the ordered regularity of everyday life. According to such a view, cinematic and television westerns, for example, appealed to the viewing public as strongly as they did not because of a nostalgia for things past or a fascination with the exotic, but because the characters involved lived in such immediate and dangerous interplay with wilderness—especially the wilderness of maverick human nature. The explicitly rugged individualism idealized in most westerns and embodied so archetypally by actors like James Dean and the early Marlon Brando can be seen, at bottom, less as a celebration of some realized national identity than as a counterweight to the prevalent fear of being swallowed whole by modern living—dissolved by our successes in managing our own existence.

What this position fails to explain, however, is how media-presented adventures and outlaws can substitute for actually lived or experienced adventure and wilderness. After all, a recipe cannot substitute for a meal even if it comes complete with detailed and appropriately scented photographs. If mass-mediated adventure can somehow stand in for actual, personally undertaken adventure, either our lives have become essentially iconic—the equivalent of having a diet comprising mostly recipes and a few actual food items—so that "actual" and "media" adventures are effectively equivalent, or the latter serve not as substitutes, but rather as compensation for a lack of the former. In other words, it may be that mediated 'wilderness' compensates us for a loss of the real thing in much the same way that a particular sum of money can compensate us for a meal we missed due to a late plane.

In the first case, there is an implied confusion of merely represented and actually lived adventure and wilderness. This is, in fact, something that happens. Especially among young children, cinematic tragedies are often experienced as real events—meaning, they fail to establish appropriate horizons between their own life drama and that which plays out on the movie or television screen. But such a confusion does not seem to last into adulthood or hold generally true even among children. In the latter case, the relationship between the represented and actual is more complex. Cinematic dramas are understood to be different in kind from lived dramas and yet accepted as a kind of symbolic currency that allows the viewer to gain some "purchase" on the kinds of surprises, emotional states, and sense of purpose that are wanting in their day-to-day lives. The products of mass-mediated imagination thus constitute a medium of exchange, the elements of which function as icons of our individual emotional and dramatic experiences. This being so—and as would be expected due to the individuating bias of the technologies that make mass media possible—watching films and television, cruising the Internet in search of new "discoveries," and "exploring" the worlds to which we have access via CD-ROM are all basically narcissistic.

While the analogy is liable to be interpreted as unnecessarily crude, our practices for entertaining and informing ourselves have become both desireless and private in much the same way that masturbation is. The climaxes of masturbation are factually equivalent to those that occur in lovemaking; there is the same emission of bodily fluids, the same increase of heart-rate and respiration. But masturbation never leads to the kind of tenderness that true lovemaking engenders. It never results in those intimate conversations in which we discover, perhaps for the first time, both our own true voices and the incomparable vastness of becoming close. Likewise, the satisfactions of watching television or cruising the Internet—even when publicly indulged—are expressly one way. Far from bringing about a sense of closeness—the harmonic interplaying of all difference and distance—our consumption of media programming and the offerings of the World Wide Web at once obliterates our differences and distance while holding us still separate. The iconic "intimacy" we enjoy with our media "partners"—our favorite web sites, television characters, sports heroes, and movie stars—no doubt expands our horizons. But even infinitely expanded horizons are still *our* horizons. Far from realizing horizonless creativity, the media simply extend the ranges of what is 'me' and 'mine' or 'you' and 'yours'—the horizons of our selfishness.

Faced with objections about the morally problematic nature of much of what it produces, the motion picture industry typically justifies the variety and intensity of cinematic content by stating that it simply answers to the public's taste and appetite. In other words, what the industry produces and at what levels of intensity are driven by what the market wants. As long as wants and their satisfaction are seen as essentially separate, as long as experience and behavior are seen as distinct, as long as subjective and objective views are taken to be incommensurable, there is nothing much to question in this reply. But if we see interdependence and not independence as basic—or, better yet, conduct and not either the abstraction we call "experience" or the abstraction we call "behavior"—then patterns in the evolution of these wants, in the tastes and appetites of the consuming public, mirror patterns in the evolution of both our subjective experience and our objective behavior. Refusing to admit the fundamental nature of individuality means admitting that the film industry and its market—like chicken and egg—are mutually entailing. Producing "what the public wants" is just another way of saying "sedimenting what we are becoming"—in this case, beings who want generic representations of wilderness, rebellion, sex, violence, horror, and crass, off-color humor.

It could be argued, of course, that the media-driven valorization of outsiders and wilderness underwrote much of the popular literary and musical revolution that began with Beat poetics and produced such unique forms of countercultural genius as that manifested by the Rolling Stones and the Grateful Dead in the musical world and political revolutionaries like the Students for a Democratic Society and the Black Panthers. Certainly, the media's coverage of the counterculture was crucial in promoting some awareness at least of the movement's ideals and values. But what it spread were ultimately only commodifications or icons of the actual and unique revolutions taking place at the time—revolutions that were smothered by the insensitive attentions to which they were subsequently subjected.

The media-promoted spread of countercultural ideals did open up new ground for the national imagination—new ground that was crucial in compensating for the growing predictability of our day-to-day lives. The value of alternatives made itself quite spectacularly evident. But the resulting efflorescence of new lifestyles, new types of characters, new modes of dramatic interaction, and new genres of entertainment was from the start doomed to collapse in on itself. The miraculous speed and ubiquity of mass mediation was such that the truly personal and inherently unique relationships that fund the emergence of a viable culture—a culture that not only thrives in the moment but responds creatively to challenge and crisis—were rapidly overshadowed by the loose connection of membership in "a generation." As the counterculture was transformed from an unprecedented grassroots phenomenon into a resource for marketable commodities, and the interdependence of its various ideals and values obscured by the rhetoric of "free will" and "free choice," the diversity it originally manifested degraded into mere variety. The so-called me generation that came into existence by the mid-1970s came by its narcissistic preoccupations rather honestly—as a function of the very media through which it articulated and celebrated its awareness of itself.

Part of what happened in consequence of the commodification of popular culture that began taking place with such virulence in the 1960s was a curious partnering of high-minded idealism and gut-level cynicism. Rapidly spinning, media-orchestrated cycles of enchantment and disenchantment, of hopeful illusions and disillusionment, worked out in broad societal strokes the same kind of pairing of narcissism and nihilism that control-biased technologies inculcate at the level of user-individuals. At this juncture, an era of gritty realism replaced the idealized portraiture so common in 1960s cinema. The punk generation thumbed its collective nose at the undeniable hypocrisies of its predecessors, asserting in no uncertain terms that not only was everything basically "fucked up," but that the best thing you could do under the circumstances was to perfect "getting fucked up." This idealization of the "way things are," the transformation of current fact into present value, marks the onset of an extremely tight feedback loop whereby our wants (our lacks) are mirrored back in our thoughts, speech, and deeds as satisfactions. Narcissism turns masochistic. Sex becomes a game of domination and submission. Painful disengagement and social marginality becomes a badge of personal, if only iconic, honor.

In effect, the commodification of culture and the attendant celebration of alternative lifestyles as choices led to the mundane being thrown violently and unexpectedly back into the face of the mediated public. Tracking this movement in film, we witness a shift from novel characters like the societally unacceptable and yet somehow endearing Brando in *The Wild One*, to Robert DeNiro's very ordinary and very painfully imbalanced *Taxi Driver*, to Anthony Hopkins' Hannibal Lecter in *The Silence of the Lambs*. Today, on any given weekday in any American town, it is possible to rent dozens of children's classics and a wide assortment of "Disney" movies, a few dozen subtitled foreign "art" movies, and a good selection of music and game videos. A row or two away are hundreds of action-adventure movies featuring every imaginable kind of explosion and weapon attack, a heavy handful of relatively current slasher movies, dozens of soft porn films, hundreds of cinematic treatments of rape and murder in a virtually unlimited range of degrees of explicitness. What the public has wanted is more of everything, and the resulting variety of choices it is being offered is almost nauseating.

Both the graphic intensity and the sheer number of films (or web sites, compact discs, or "bestsellers") to which we are subjected as consumers says something very important about the quality of our awareness: we do not pay very subtle attention to things and we have come to prefer the ignorance this implies. The iconic nature of so much of what we expose ourselves to in the course of a day has conditioned an atrophy of our perceptual acuity—our capacity for noting surprising details, for listening to the voices of the natural world, for appreciating what is understated or not stated at all. Having accepted a variety of choices as reasonable compensation for the sacrifice of lived diversification, we have—through immersion in our technologies of control, our control-biased patterns of conduct—set ourselves up for a calculated focus on monadic intensities rather than relational qualities.

THE DENSITY OF POSTMODERN TIME AND SPACE AND THE CRAVING FOR VOLUME

A world composed of generic sites and signs, while bereft of inherent meaning and thus dramatically impoverished, also suffers from an almost unlimited density. Mass production, mass mediation, mass communication—these modes of societally biased conduct all greatly increase the availability of the commodities with which we have replaced fully historical, dramatically significant things. They ensure that we will have as many opportunities for consumption as we want—everything from exotic foods to foreign films, from dream vacations to practically infinite amounts and varieties of data.

So far, we have been saying, so good. With cable television and a computer-modem, we are even now able to "be" practically anywhere we want, when we want. And once the planet is fully cocooned in fiber-optic cables, current and nagging limitations on video and multimedia linkages will become a thing of the past and distance—both temporal and spatial—will have been virtually overcome. By greatly reducing both the temporal and spatial depth of what we perceive and experience—the richly manifest network of interdependencies that constitute all naturally occurring and handmade things—our technical translation of both things and distances into icons has shrunken the world to the point that it seems entirely within our reach.

This, for better or worse, is simply an illusion and not an altogether pleasant one. For example, having almost instantaneously available a practically unlimited variety of sites for our attention effects an extreme compression of the perceived dimensions of our world. Positively welcomed—as in the longtime Disney World attraction, "It's a Small, Small World"—this compression promises to bring us all closer together in mutual respect and enjoyment. When the entire world is practically at our fingertips, how can we continue indulging xenophobic prejudice? How can we continue hating people who in cybernetic terms are our "next door" neighbors? Aside from the naiveté such a welcome evidences regarding the axiological hegemony and commodification of cultural values that accompany the technical shrinking of the world, there is the simple fact that the reduction of the world's perceived size is accomplished by removing the interstitial spaces in which the unexpected always and invisibly resides. By removing the distances between any two places or any two people, we effectively remove the places where surprises lie in wait, where dramatic revolutions are fomented and first emerge. In the simplest and truest terms possible, the world and the human spirit lose their vastness.

In the compressed world of instantaneously satisfied wants, the surprising gives way to the shocking. That is, immediately unfolding, meaningful and yet unanticipatable reconfigurations of our narration give way to intrusive intensifications of experience. Shocks bring us up short. They intensify the present to the point that it breaks off from its surroundings and becomes a thing by itself. In a state of shock, there is no possibility of realizing truly dramatic interdependence. By contrast, and despite their sudden appearance in our lives, surprises play out over time, blossoming, opening new narrative possibilities and so new fields for the expression of who we are. When the world is vast, we have no problem finding a place for our offerings, no lack of room for truly expressing and not just defining ourselves.

Having the world at our fingertips means that nothing is necessarily closer or further away than anything else. The natural basis of priority is undermined. And this need not be tragic. It can ease some of the cruder forms of provincialism and selfishness to which we have been so apparently prone. But it can also lead to the impression that the limits of the world and the limits of our selves are one and the same; that others are an extension of us. In this sense, the cybernetic reduction of the world to an infinitely varied and dense collection of sites and signs is liable to encourage our narcissistic tendencies. When the importance of distance—of time and space—is virtually annulled, we find ourselves in a world that no longer manifestly and creatively orders itself. It is 'you' and 'I' who establish connections. It is on 'my' decisions or 'yours' that the order of things pivot.

The time of dramatic interdependence is basically genealogical. It is the unfolding of relationships that are irreducibly mutual and co-responsive without ever becoming either static or formulaic—an expressive gathering of what is past in caring and dramatic contribution to realizing what has never been. There are no generic family members and there are no finally generic moments in natural temporality. Narrative time is about growing—growing up and growing older. It is not about "getting" old—arriving at some destined state of being aged. That is a way of speaking proper only when moments are basically iconic—when time is associated with clocks more than with seasons, something you can be "on" or "out of."

The metaphor is not so far-fetched as it might at first appear. We should wonder, for example, why there is a correlation between modernity and postmodernity and the sedimentation of relatively stable and regulatory "generation gaps." Why is it that, as traditional cultures are brought "up" into the modern world through the infusion of our preferred technologies of control, they begin suffering a severe disintegration of familial values? Why is it that we now identify ourselves more commonly and comfortably as and with members of our "generation" than we do with the diverse roots and branches of our family trees?

Postmodernity interrupts the natural flow of familial time. If a child can download a computer file through the Internet in which sex is perhaps not explained, but graphically displayed, what incentive does he or she have for broaching the subject with his or her parents? If it is possible to read through a myriad of histories reputed to be the finest and foremost in the world by ordering copies from a web-bookstore, why approach grandma or grandpa for their personal reflections on the last six or eight decades? The disdain with which most teenagers now regard their elders—even their college-aged siblings with whom they're but a few years apart—is not a long-standing, universally human phenomenon. But in the context of a postmodern world, it makes perfectly good sense. "How much can my parents or my older brother or sister really know about what's going on in my life? They don't even live in the same world. We might live in the same house, but they might as well be on another planet!" We have all heard these kinds of remarks. And we have tacitly accepted their validity because we know ourselves how little the values we had as teenagers carried over into our college years and beyond. Today, the divisions between various generations have attained an almost Cartesian clarity and distinctness and it is only our acceptance of them as 'natural' or 'unavoidable' that keeps us from noting how tragically little meaningful commerce moves across these lines of demarcation.

Far from being an odd and abstract tangent, talking about differences in the way we now experience time and distance is critically relevant to seeing what our bias for control and regularity has purchased. The shift from family time to generational time is evident throughout our conduct, in the ways we identify who we are and why we're acting as we do. It is now quite natural for us *not* to think of the family primarily as a felt relationship extending limitlessly back in time—a complex, ever-evolving whole. To the contrary, "family" signifies a nuclear unit ideally comprising a mother, father, and children, but more commonly including just a single parent plus a (sometimes shared) child or two. Just as our time has become more societal—institutionally constituted, regulated, saved, and secured—so have our families and communities.

This contraction of the family, the loss of the world's vastness, generational strife, and the denial of natural order implied in the technical triumph over distance—are these coincidentally related or are they in actuality just different manifestations of a general reorienting of our conduct, the movement of our narration? Is there a linear, causal relationship between the violence on our streets and the violence we watch on television and in the movie theater? Or is it simply that both forms of violence answer—difficult as this is to admit—only to what we have led ourselves to want?

Looked at with as little prejudice as possible, it would seem obvious that the density of our day-to-day, media-dominated experience, when combined with the absence of natural order that accompanies the technical elimination of distance, would create conditions under which we would at some level suffer the effects of a kind of sensory claustrophobia. There is, in short, a profound lack of sensed (as opposed to interpreted) depth in the signs that constitute our primary objects of perception—a lack that translates into an experienced need for something "more," for some way out of or past the obdurate variety confronting us, some way of putting our things, experiences, and lives, into perspective. But because our calculative bias insures that this "more" is understood in quantitative rather than qualitative terms, our typical strategy has been to raise the volume of our current levels of experience.

There are kinds of music that must be experienced at "live volumes" in order to make sense. If the music isn't loud enough, the spatial and dynamic relationships among the instruments being played are lost to the extent that everything flattens out onto an impenetrable aural surface. Lacking this volume, we simply never get fully "into" the music, and so it ends up either being ignored or sounding like just so much noise. Adding more volume allows the music to expand enough to become listenable and open to appreciation. A similar process has been taking place—albeit unconsciously—in our society-wide craving for more intense entertainment experiences, for more graphically and realistically represented displays of violence. It is part of our attempt to make sense out of the craziness confronting us, the impenetrability and apparent intractability of so much of the context for our individual life narratives. But, the sense of catharsis or release is temporary. The more we raise the volume, the more commodities can be jammed in to vie for our attention, the denser becomes our symbolic universe, the more we feel stuck or trapped. The cycle not only repeats, but deepens.

The current fascinations among young people with metamphetamines like crack and ice, among adults for sensational reporting and bizarre forms of sexuality, among the disenfranchised members of our society for criminal violence, and among all of us for various kinds of addictive behavior—especially compulsive consumption—all function as methods for turning up the volume of experience. Unfortunately, being based on the satisfaction of wants, they lead eventually to an amplification of our wanting and our impatience. Most of us can't stand waiting in line for more than a minute or two. Heaven forbid that we should have to defer satisfying some want for a month or a year or a decade or two. We don't have the impression of there being enough time to wait and at the same time we feel deep down that there isn't ever enough happening. We need more stimulation, more volume. But more volume rapidly gets translated into a space filled by still more icons, more signs, more choices—in the end, even greater density, stronger gravity, and more likelihood that we will simply keep traveling in the orbits our karma dictates, wanting only to go faster and faster yet. And just as accelerating through a turn gives us more control, this process will in fact be felt to be proof of our success.

That we also have to attend more and more closely and exclusively to the road in front of us is typically overlooked. That we travel ever more and ever faster while seeing and caring about ever less along the way—well, that is so-called "progress." In fact, the very speeds at which we are moving and consuming allow us to simply not see the biographical litter we are creating and the material waste we are constantly generating. What we lose is the capacity for appreciating the diversity—the patterns of harmony-realizing uniqueness—in our surroundings. We lose the desire and capacity for truly growing old with one another, for liberating intimacy from the narrowness of our momentary cravings and their satisfaction. Sacrifices can be noble. But nobility can be quite futile—especially when we are sacrificing that readiness for surprise without which our narration becomes terminally anticlimactic.

Chapter 12

So What?

It would be easy, even after all the time spent coming to this point in our conversation, to simply say "so what?" So what if there are sizable trade-offs involved in our technical valorization of control? So what if mass mediation levels down some of our differences and uniqueness? or if traditional cultural values, the old familial structures, and some near mythological sense of community are rapidly being made obsolete? Who knows? These changes may turn out for the best. Maybe they are just growing pains. And maybe they are not.

The bald fact of the matter is, we are not going to give up our cars, our refrigerators, our air conditioners and heaters and electric lights. We are not going to dismantle our computers, televisions, and radios. Nor will we cancel all our subscriptions to newspapers and magazines or our telephone, cable, or Internet services. For better or worse, for richer or poorer, we're locked in. The lives we lead and call our own depend on the successes of our various technologies and the control they afford us. Our health, the birth of our children and their education, our entertainment and sense of purpose—none of these can be disentangled from the patterns of conduct that fund the steady stream of new tools into our lives, tools without which we would be incapable of holding chaos as effectively at bay as we do. There is no turning back—not for most of us and certainly not for every single one of us. The fact is, trying to jump off the technological juggernaut at this stage would be like jumping out of a car at highway speed.

Facts, of course, are always "theory-laden." But in the end, it makes no practical difference that the "bald facts" of our technological commitment enjoy that status only because we have for so long held 'control', 'individuality', and 'independence' in the highest possible esteem. The circularity may be logically repugnant, but as long as we're getting what we want, this will neither worry nor deter us. Admitting this, we already know the point from which we will move forward in a new direction if we're to do so at all. If we

271

are to resist the colonization of consciousness, if we are to overcome the narrative or dramatic poverty it induces, and if we're going to effectively counter both the reduction of cultural diversity into mere variety and the commodification of values on which it depends, we must free ourselves from the knot of our own wanting and satisfaction.

Of course, we would like to think otherwise. We would prefer our "enemy" to be somewhere "out there" and not within ourselves as constitutive values of who we have come to be and how—a function of our own karma. We would like to be able to blame someone or something objective for our dramatic impoverishment and the fragmentation of our communities— someone or something we could battle and defeat. But in a thoroughly dramatic and interdependent cosmos, matters can never be so clear-cut. As Hui-neng forcefully informs us, "If you see wrongs in the world, it is your own wronging that is affirmed. We are to blame for the wrongs of others just as we are to blame for our own" (*Platform Sutra*, chapter 36).

We are not in a position, then, to absolutely condemn our technological lineage. If the perspective we have been exploring on technology is accepted as a valid one, our dominant technical orientation has been wrong. It has disposed us to ignore interdependence in the promotion of individuality and independence, to forfeit our capacity for dramatically fruitful appreciation for the factual payoff of control. But precisely because all things are interdependent, our technological lineage can only be relatively wrong. While it may amplify the conflicts obtaining among our most cherished personal, political, cultural, economic, and religious values, our technological lineage does not create those conflicts. Where our technologies lead us astray, it is because we are in a very real and tragic sense simply chasing our own tails. As Hui-neng reminds us, the wrongs we identify "out there" also reside and originate "in here." Because it would quite literally be self-defeating, a general condemnation is not in order.

So what do we do? If we accept the need to realize meaningful solutions to our troubles and not merely factual ones, and if we accept the role of our current technical orientation in institutionalizing our incapacity for dramatically resolving our problems, how are we to proceed? We can begin formulating an answer to this question by clearly perceiving that neither of the two most popular strategies for technological reform are finally workable: first, the direct and often violent opposition to the spreading use of the tools generated by particular technologies and the practical capacities they afford us; and second, the attempt to redefine our purposes for using these tools and to promote the technologies of which they are a part on revised political, economic, and societal grounds.

According to the first strategy, the responsible technological revolutionary is obligated to overtly and even zealously attack the technological edifice our society has erected in celebration of its own core values. This can be as relatively benign as the "monkey wrench" sorties of environmentalists who spike trees to render them unsuitable for industrial logging or who repeatedly disable earth-moving equipment at dam or mining sites. At its most extreme, this strategy results in a Unabomber-style terrorism and all that goes along with it.

The other approach is to gradually "redirect" our technical tradition, adapting it to the needs of a truly multicultural world that endorses only the most neutral and universal human or even planetary values. This typically takes the shape of either a grassroots revolution—a "greening" of our technical tradition—or a purification process by means of which we collectively and consciously take control of our technical destiny. An example would be to promote the use of the World Wide Web as a means for virtually maintaining continuity within and between diasporic communities.

On the one hand, then, our approach has been to declare open warfare on our technological nemesis, and on the other to try our best to peacefully win it over to our side. Both approaches are self-defeating for the simple reason that they replicate rather than resist the basic values underlying our technological lineage as a whole. By confusing technologies with tools and the commercial systems that produce and distribute them, both strategies are conducive to a failure to realize that when we are most openly and deeply engaged in direct, technical revolt or reform, our attention is almost exclusively attached to and so promoting the very values we are ostensibly working against. In the same way that we can't fight fire with fire without getting hot, we can't "take on" or battle patterns of conduct or narrative movement oriented according to the values of 'control', 'independence', and 'individuality' without becoming literally involved with them. Granted the Buddhist understanding of consciousness as given directly in relationship and of personhood as narration, becoming involved with protesting our technological lineage is at once speaking out against and speaking out on behalf of it.

That is the irony of all nonconformity—a commitment to darkly mirroring that against which we ostensibly rebel. And so, it is not the "sold-out collaborator" who ends up most clearly evidencing this paradoxical conformity with "the enemy," but the single-minded terrorist. The tragedy of all terrorist movements is that a total and even profoundly visionary dedication to bringing some system of political, economic, social, or religious "oppression" to its knees amounts finally to an inverted form of worship. By spending all of his or her material, temporal, intellectual, emotional, and attentive resources on destroying some "nemesis," the terrorist not only keeps it constantly in mind but starves every other aspect of his or her narration. The true terrorist has no personal life—meaning a life devoid of intimacies, of aesthetic endeavor, of free and creative community—and cannot but live in isolation and anonymity. Dramatically impoverished to such an extent that their life has but a single purpose, a single focus, the terrorist suffers a tragic blindness to everything but what they aim to destroy and what might help in that mission. Terrorism is impossible without a practiced ignorance of interdependence.

Although it's often remarked in defense of violent and terrorist forms of resistance that we can—and sometimes, can only—fight fire with fire, it is seldom acknowledged that this tactic works only when very controlled burning is used to take fuel out of the path of an approaching blaze. If the fire cannot cross this "empty" space, if the availability of fuel can be limited, the blaze will be contained. Since the basic resource or fuel of the colonization of consciousness is attention as such, however, this is a tactic doomed to failure. Regardless of how things might at first appear, sacrificing all our attention to blocking the advance of the technological "firestorm" is only to be absorbed into it and make it burn that much more brightly.

Protesting a dam here and a microchip factory there might put some local "flames" out, but as long as the values of our social, political, economic, scientific, and religious traditions remain unchanged, the fire will not be eradicated. In the same way that we cannot say "where" a fire goes when it blows or burns out, but rest assured that it will reappear as soon as conditions permit, we should realize that though we can stop using certain tools and even undermine certain technologies, as soon as conditions ripen—most crucially the experiential condition of wanting—technologies aimed at increased control will flare back up.

Like the mythic knot of Gordius, the tangled karma of the control-mediated satisfaction of our wanting is in full public view, and yet, no matter how hard we try, we will never tease it apart directly. The very hope of mastering our situation and so controlling the network of intentions and actions that have conditioned its arising is in actuality just a deeper aspect of that same network. Far from loosening the knot, our "sincere" attempts to destroy our mechanisms and institutions for control only refine and intensify those very hungers and habits.

But trying instead to simply limit or "green" these mechanisms and institutions, while it may slow the rate at which our "Gordian" knot grows, is in the end no less self-defeating. Neil Postman's suggestion that we regain control of our technologies is a general statement of this strategy of "winning over or reforming the enemy." More practically formulated but no more productive of a true alternative to our technological lineage are Ivan Illich's various appeals for establishing vernacular versions of the technologies associated with economic and social development. For example, he has argued that developing countries should regulate vehicular design to insure that the means and rate of transportation remain conducive to local self-determination. By only building trucks or lorries capable of a maximum of twenty miles per hour, it is possible to ensure that as a society we will not cross the velocity threshold beyond which per capita, per day travel time increases with every increase in average vehicular speed. Doing so also ensures that transportation systems can be locally maintained by semiskilled workers. Because the tolerances of an engine designed for relatively low power output are so much more relaxed than those required for sophisticated, high-performance engines, it is possible to disintermediate parts brokers and factory repair shops through the on-site fabrication of replacement parts.

These are reasonable responses to a perceived need for placing brakes on our "technological juggernaut." They will not, however, result in a break in our technical orientation and so a break in the predominant direction of our personal and communal conduct. Indeed, such responses appeal to precisely the kind of rationality and prejudice against the unexpected that helped establish and maintain the prolific successes of our technological lineage as a whole. If we are to cut through the knot of our technology-driven conduct, we must resist the temptation to try teasing it apart and extracting whatever is still useful—the "safe" tools and "useful" patterns of behavior. Instead, we must direct our attention, our energy, somewhere else entirely.

I believe that Buddhist practice accomplishes exactly this. As succinctly phrased in the Ch'an (Zen) injunction to "accord with the situation, respond as needed" (*sui shih ying yung*), practicing Buddhism orients us toward contributory appreciation—what Pai-chang referred to as the "perfection of offering." Simply put, if we can place our attention-energy into appreciating rather than controlling our circumstances—and so the people and things sharing in our narration—our lives will be naturally and dramatically enriched.

For this, it is not necessary to actively endorse an explicitly "Buddhist" view of the world or a Buddhist approach to "salvation." To the contrary, we need only accept the priority of values over beings, of things over signs, of appreciation over control, and of interdependence over independence. That is already enough to shift our conduct from its present bearing on an increasingly fractured, generic, and dramatically impoverished narration. Given this axiological revolution, the movement of our narration—our personal and communal conduct—will naturally shift in the direction of articulating, not a world of universal agreement, but one that is truly harmonious—a world in which diversity is not merely preserved, but celebrated and deepened.

Granted the prejudices of our long-standing commitments to control, this will sound like so much wishful thinking—another warm and fuzzy dream of future utopia. When we think of changing the world, we think of rearranging things—moving resources or wealth for a more equitable or a

more personally advantageous distribution. We think of taking down old
political and social institutions and building new systems in their place. And
because we are committed to the idea of linear causation, we think this necessarily entails a kind of "chain reaction" whereby changes initiated at one
place at one time somehow manage to propagate worldwide. Given the
sheer numbers of human beings existing on the planet, we "know" better
than to expect any startling successes, certainly not by way of a "purely subjective" move from controlling to appreciating our circumstances. If for no
other reason than because there are so many people involved in so many
places and so many ways, we suspect that business will keep going on more
or less as usual. We may want some kind of revolution, may sense a need for
it if we're going to avoid the wholesale evaporation of meaning from our
lives, but we cannot see how it's possible.

Fortunately, a change of direction, unlike a change of state, need not
imply a miraculous and decisively total exit from one 'world' and arrival in
another. Some twenty-five hundred years ago, the Greek philosopher Zeno
argued that motion and so change is impossible. He reasoned that in moving from one place to another, we must cross half the distance first, a crossing that takes some finite amount of time. And in order to cross that
half-distance, we would first have had to cross half of that and so on ad in-
finitum. Because any distance can be infinitely divided, moving from any
one place to any other would take an infinite amount of time. Motion, Zeno
concluded, is illusory. Because they shared many of his presuppositions
about the nature of time and space, Zeno's contemporaries found that while
they could not deny the appearance of motion and change, neither could
they find a way to warrant its rationality.

We are no better off. It is precisely our presumptive commitments to the
reality and valorization of independence, individuality, and existential control that make it impossible for us to even imagine the world changing
"overnight." By definition, as individuals, persons are not meaningfully interdependent with all things—at least not in any practically important ways.
By definition, we cannot have the lives we want unless we can exert some
real control over contingency and crisis. And because we would—by definition—have to change one thing and then another and then yet another in
any attempt to fully "remake" the world, bringing about a wholly new
world, a wholly new narrative in which we all contribute in different and yet
equal ways . . . well, that is simply impossible. In fact, even hoping for such
a change is irrational, a stupid waste of time and energy.

But if we see changes as primarily orientational—as the playing out of
shifts in values and not the movement of individual beings—neither Zeno's
paradoxes nor the "rationality" of our current intellectual and technical
prejudices stand in the way of our expressing new worlds and realizing in

them a horizonless intimacy with all things. It is true that if we hope to "re-draw" the world in such a way that it is not only entirely unambiguous but an answer to our every want, we will be compelled to forcibly exercise almost infinitely extensive and detailed control. But "redrawing" is crucial only if we intend the world to be an answer to what we lack. The basic ambiguity of things can never warrant our being able to get whatever we want when we want it. But it does insure that no situation, no prevailing patterns in our conduct or narration, are closed to immediate change. Even if not one single thing is displaced or added to our present circumstances, it is possible to alter the entire gestalt or configuration of our world. We simply need to fully appreciate—caringly offer our attention energy—to our situation.

How things will change as a result—what new circumstances we shall arrive at—cannot be said in advance. The school of our choice may not accept us, the job we want may not appear, the person we're madly in love with may not return our affections. All that can be ensured is that the direction in which our narration carries us will be consonant with the orientation of our attention and appreciation. After all, the interdependence of all things means that there can be no real boundaries between our desires and their realization, between us and what we appreciate. 'Subjects' and 'objects', like 'selves' and 'others', are abstractions, not irreducible entities.

The critical importance of not confusing directions and destinations—like that between values and beings or desires and wants—is crucial to Hui-neng's teaching that enlightenment is not a state of consciousness or experiential release but rather a function of our readiness to awaken, to live a life fully committed to "according with the situation, responding as needed." Such a life does not have to be put off until we can appropriately change (and so control) our circumstances or our 'selves'. Enlightenment is not about "getting things right" or always "being correct," but about righting things that have gone awry and correcting the orientation of what has gone astray. In spite of the Buddhist claim that each moment of enlightenment is the birth of an entire buddha-realm, this is not some gargantuan undertaking that might well require marshaling an entire universe's worth of resources to realize. It is what naturally occurs when we simply but continually relinquish our horizons for what we see as relevant, what we see as our responsibility, and what we see as the extent of our readiness. In short, all that is required to change the world is an unwavering willingness to express a true beginner's mind.

Still, we want to know how this is to be done. How are we to resist the centripetal momentum of our Janus-faced tendency toward both narcissism and nihilism? How are we to free ourselves from the yoke of the new colonialism? And how do we feed ourselves in the meantime? Do we have to immediately burn our computers and televisions? Do we have to use our microwaves and our answering machines for landfill? Which institutions should we take immediate aim on and destroy, and which can we keep for a while longer—at least until our new modes of commerce and communication, our new patterns of entertainment and intimacy have fully taken root?

Questions like this cry out for answers. They are the frantic efforts of the controlling ego to retain its "charge," to remain central to the way things are and will come to be. And from a Buddhist perspective, it is precisely this expressed hope of "making things change for the better" that stands between us and a wholly unexpected and dramatically meaningful narration. Wanting answers to such questions is the last bastion of the valorization of control. Which is not to say we should leave things well enough alone. If single-minded confrontations with our technologies of control will not help, neither will letting things go on as usual. The "usual" is just the everyday face of our technical triumphs—our heroic, karmically binding conquest of the unexpected.

And so, we are finding ourselves in much the same position as Ch'an master Lin-chi when he was asked by the provincial governor to explain Buddhist enlightenment to an assembly of some five hundred monks, nuns, and lay people. As Lin-chi put it, "As soon as I open my mouth, I've made a mistake." At the same time, he admitted, "saying nothing at all is to withhold the social nexus, the drawstring of Ch'an." Without anything to go on, people will have no reason to change their direction. And that is as much as to condemn them to only deepening the ruts of their present karma, their already existing habits for conduct. Lin-chi invited someone from the assembly to engage him in "dharma combat"—to enter the uncharted domain in which every crisis, every challenge, is responded to as needed, without any hesitation whatsoever. The offering of our conversation is much more modest—an invitation to experiment with the meaning of appreciation.

Buddhist practice is not something 'you' or 'I' can do. To the contrary, it is the always unexpected and liberating renewal of our world that occurs when our horizons for relevance, responsibility, and readiness are continuously relinquished. Buddhist practice does not benefit us as egos, as autonomous individuals. It benefits our narration—our dramatic interrelatedness. For this reason, enlightenment cannot be seen as a release of the self, but a release from our various 'selves'. And so Lin-chi constantly exhorted his students to respond as a "true person of no rank"—someone without a fixed standing or position. Only then is boundless virtuosity possible.

Still, the practice of Ch'an was never understood as compatible with simply "doing whatever you feel like doing." That is not improvisation, an expression of true virtuosity, but mere indulgence—the playing out of our likes and dislikes, our karma. Moreover, the ideal of "according with the situation, responding as needed" not only implies cultivating maximal flexibility—maximal attenuation of our habits of thought, speech, and deed—it also implies having sufficient energy and focus to be able to realize in conduct that no situation, no crisis, is intractable. Traditionally, this flexibility and energetic resourcefulness were cultivated through the disciplines of daily meditation and psychospiritual exercise. At least in Ch'an, meditation does not serve as a way to solve our problems or bring about some special states of awareness necessary to "attaining" enlightenment. Rather, it functions as a way of removing blockages to the free circulation of *ch'i* or energy—blockages that may be physical, emotional, cognitive, or connative in nature. That is, a daily regimen of meditation is undertaken so that energy (and therefore attention) will flow freely enough through our narration that our problems will—like the ten thousand things—simply take care of themselves. Put in this way, it is clear that meditation is the key to our own, quite personal "perfection of offering"—our own commitment to truly appreciating and so continually adding value to and investing energy in the things and people on whom our lives intimately depend.

Meditating does not require any special equipment or tools. While some encouragement and initial direction is helpful, it does not depend on expert instruction or special circumstances. It is a simple—and yet for most of us incredibly challenging—process of fully attending only to what is present. One of the most commonly prescribed techniques is just sitting and watching our breathing without becoming either distracted, anxiously focused, or bored. That is, time spent meditating is directed toward realizing a beginner's mind that is as fresh now as one minute or ten minutes or a hundred minutes ago. It is realizing a mind that is so open to the circulation of present energies that it is not liable to either boredom or obsession.

Ironically, this is best accomplished by offering our attention to some chosen meditative technique every day, at the same time, in the same place. This removes the possibility of the ego continuing to assert itself through deciding when and finally if meditating is working or worthwhile or not. By engaging in disciplined, meditative training our attention is steadily directed away from the habits of thought, speech, feeling, and deed that normally maintain the identity or fixed horizons of our egos. Robbed of their normal diet of physical and psychic energy, these habitual systems naturally atrophy, freeing up energy for both deepening our meditative training and realizing new levels of improvisation in our conduct.

Skilled meditation should not, therefore, be seen as a process of controlling our attention. To the contrary, it arises only as the unreserved offering or contribution of our attention to the liberating movement of our own present and shared narration. As an offering, it is not something undertaken with received goods in mind, some expectation of things we will "get" in the end—whether knowledge, experiences, spiritual advancement, or what have you. In meditation we simply offer ourselves—all our attention-energy—to appreciating the moment in which we find ourselves. It is attending in the sense of vigilant caring—our most primordial mode of contribution, a way of transforming any locale into the *bodhimaṇḍala* or "place of enlightenment."

Meditation can be seen, then, as an alternative technology—an alternative to our technological bias toward control. Meditation breaks down the cycle of our wanting. In this way, it directly undermines the purposes, effects, and mechanisms of our control and being-controlled. When we break the cycle of our wanting, the compulsion to satisfy ourselves through decisive acts of consumption naturally eases. Like all compulsions, consuming thrives to the precise extent that we give it our energy, our attention. And since this diversion of attention from things to the consumption-mediated satisfaction of our wants is the basis of any technical translation of things into commodities or mere signs, meditation directly counters the tendency for our awareness to fall into a predominantly iconic mode. In meditation, we return to full presence with all things.

But this should not be confused with attaining some kind of omniscience—an infinitely crowded intelligence. Instead, it is realizing a mind that is as clear as space—a mind that is not only helpfully open, but open to help, a mind that is both welcome and welcoming. By contrast, whenever we're disposed predominantly toward control, our minds, our lives, are not only focused on attaining closure—for our wants, our deliberations, our intentions—they are effectively closed to what is not wanted or unplanned. Control silences the things and people sharing our world, making it impossible for them to spontaneously and dramatically contribute to our narration.

This closing off of the path of contribution that characterizes a bias for control is wonderfully summed up in the classical Chinese term for arrogance—*tseng-shang-man*. Literally translated, this means "adding on slowness." In contemporary slang, arrogance is "a drag." It inhibits the free circulation of energy and so the spontaneous resolution of crises—the natural and meaningful enhancement of our narration by all things and persons gathered within its dramatic realization. Technologies of control are patterns of institutional arrogance, given directly in conduct and thus in the moment-by-moment structure of our awareness. Meditative attention does not grant us omniscience, but it does enable us to listen to or accommodate the dramatic contributions being made by all beings. More importantly, it opens us to responsively incorporating these contributions in the expression of our own virtuosity. In a very real way, meditation frees us from the illusion and the pain of individuality and independence, of being dramatically "on our own." In short, it is a way of practically realizing our partnership with all things—a technological orientation toward fully realized humility and intimacy.

Meditative training establishes a movement in the direction of no longer needing to control or manage our circumstances. It directs us away from the necessity of securing our position or preserving the ideal integrity of our self-identities in the face of the unexpected. Meditation does not destroy factories or cut fiber-optic cables or spread computer viruses. But, as stated above, such aggressive approaches to limiting technological proliferation and the demise of cultural diversity in fact only feed further attention into and so promote the continued importance of control. Protest movements are like sparring partners for the systems they hope to destroy. The more committed they are, the harder they fight, the more they strengthen their opponents. Occasionally, the sparring partner will get in a good shot and bring the title-contender to the canvas, but not for long and—if the contender is any good at all—never in the same way again.

We can protest the "inhumanity" of computer systems and they will be made more "user-friendly." We can protest the inanity of television programming and the industry will adapt accordingly. Each one of our "victories" actually translates into a more transparent and clever opponent—an opponent so adept that in the end we don't even know who or what is hitting us. All we have is the pain, without any explanation or any idea of how to avoid its repetition. And because it is all we have, we will eventually start calling the pain by our own names and refuse to even think about giving it up or treating it because that would be the same as giving up ourselves. At that point, our colonization will be "complete."

Meditation undermines the value of control—not by fighting it, but by making it superfluous. Because they develop as coping strategies, technologies are abandoned only when the problems they addressed no longer obtain. This might make it seem possible for a technology to "put itself out of business." And indeed they might if problems were somehow independent of us—things that exist with full objectivity. But they are not, and we have no evidence of any technology making itself irrelevant. Technologies do adapt as our understanding of the problems they address is refined and deepened, but none have simply written themselves out of our narration. From a Buddhist perspective, we would not expect anything different. Technologies and the problems they address are equally a function of our values, our way of seeing things. To use the well-known cliché, the "same" glass can be either half-full or half-empty depending on how we look at it. Meditative training turns us away from taking our situation to be in need of more extensive and precise control and toward seeing it instead as an occasion for improvising new modes of cooperation and contribution.

In a very real sense, it is our problems that define us and so exhibit our limitations. But, as patterns of our conduct, our coping strategies—our technologies—are also part of who *we* are. Far from being something apart from us that influences or assists us as we permit, our technologies are inevitably part of the very texture of our interrelatedness—an expression of our intentions. And so, the irony of all technologies is that at the very moment they are overcoming a particular problem, they are necessarily giving birth to another of its kind. We normally think of this as "progress"—our ability to solve problems that we never even dreamed of solving before. What we fail to note is that these are problems we never would have dreamed of in the first place. They would simply never have occurred as problems had not cruder and less extensive versions of them been "solved" in the past. We—that is, our conduct—would have moved in some other direction.

Thus, technologies biased toward control produce problems requiring more detailed, precise, extensive, powerful, and incisive kinds of control. We "advance" from being able to control the movement of enemy troops by using the technical advantage of steel over bronze to using nuclear warheads and "smart" missiles. We move from paper and pencil accounting to using the latest expert system software on a computer that not only crunches our numbers for us but keeps track of our inventories and meeting schedules. We move from seeing accidents and illnesses as signals that something in our narration has been escaping our attention, our care, to seeing them as inconveniences or outright insults. Instead of learning *from* our falls from health, we invent new ways of repairing the damages to which chance has subjected us. We end up performing surgical and chemical "miracles" that extend our lives, our mobility, our independence. The geriatric ward of any hospital is filled with the fruits of this labor to get "more" out of life, to "increase" or "preserve" health.

By contrast, technologies biased toward contributory appreciation will lead just as inevitably toward problems requiring ever more subtle and far-reaching cooperation and contribution. Through such technologies, we not only come to live in increasingly valuable worlds—the buddha-realms so lushly invoked in Mahayana sutras—but as increasingly valuable persons. As someone with unlimited skill in appreciative contribution, the bodhisattva is dramatically invaluable.

But even short of this complete realization, the transformation is both evident and real. For example, in the context of a bias for control, the dimming eyes, faltering gait, and focusing on things past associated with old age are 'problems'. They evidence a loss of control and independence, a manifest compromise of personal integrity, and because of them we feel it necessary and natural to ghetto-ize the elderly. We build them safe and secure, closed communities within which they can pass their last days in relative peace and ease and with minimal strain on the still productive members of their families. But in other, more vernacular times and places, the elderly have been seen as crucial to the health of the family and the community. As the gaze of the elders shifted from the close and familiar things of daily life to things distant and remembered, they began the invaluable work of weaving the generations into a single, whole story. That is, it was the responsibility of the elderly to do the crucial work of dramatically and so meaningfully bridging past and future. A bias toward control not only compels us to "fix" the dim eyes and wandering minds of the aged, but to discount their stories, the value of their experiences, the meaning of their lives. A bias toward appreciative contribution moves us in the opposite direction of both attending the elderly in an appreciative way and soliciting their contribution to our lives. Cataract operations are wonderful, high-tech examples of the "good" that comes from a bias for control. But if we return clear sight to the elderly just so they can see how increasingly useless and burdensome they are, we should perhaps be asking if the patterns of conduct that make such operations possible are not leading us in the wrong direction. Granted that technologies are always ambient, controlling necessarily implicates us in being controlled while appreciation implicates us in being appreciated. The single most important question we must answer is which kind of people we really want to become.

Effectively halting our colonization means being able to stop seeing the problems "solved" by mass mediation and consumption-oriented commerce as problems in the first place. It means not reading our situation as announcing some want or lack that these technologies are designed to factually address. This need not entail rejecting all the fruits of our technological lineage out of hand. But it does mean being thoroughly skeptical about the long range and communal value of the kinds of purely factual solutions and problems toward which it disposes us. Between cataract operations and CD-ROMs of interactive pornography, there are great differences and no responsibly critical evaluation should erase these. For example, whereas cataract surgery restores a natural capacity for visual consciousness, interactive pornography offers a demeaning substitute for sensual awareness that reduces sexual gratification to solitary orgasm bereft of any connection to authentic modes of dramatic care. While both derive from a technical bias for control, they are quite differently related to our capacity for sociality and the cultivation of intimacy.

Still, such differences should not be seen as reason to think of our critical task as one of picking and choosing. That would be to lapse into the "greening" strategy of cultural commentators like Postman. Rather, we should first undertake a rigorous practice of opening ourselves to our present situation as an unlimited field of opportunities for developing more meaningful lives, for more dramatically realizing our interdependence and creative community. Meditative discipline allows us to initially establish such a heading for our conduct and we should be teaching our children to train their awareness through some meditative discipline *before* we teach them how to use a computer or watch television, before we subject them to the rigors of achieving literacy and numeracy. Given the massive amounts of time and money focused on inducing iconic awareness worldwide, the beginner's mind of our children is in danger of extinction. Unless it is actively conserved, the fresh and appreciative attentiveness we associate with children at their best will simply fade away into a past beyond recall, and in its place will be instituted very deep structures of resistance to movement in the direction of meaningful virtuosity.

But if meditative training is a necessary first step in reversing the colonization of consciousness, it is not sufficient. If our technological lineage is inseparable from the genealogy of our present selves, resisting the colonization of consciousness must also involve revising what we mean by personhood. For this reason, I believe that something like Ch'an Buddhist practice is necessary as well. Meditative training by itself will free up the energy reserves needed for revising who we are, but it will not necessarily bring about the realization of liberating virtuosity toward which Mahayana Buddhist practice orients us. After all, meditative training has been effectively used to promote skill in the martial arts and even in the realization of fully military ends and so the ideological institutions they protect. Meditation can free us from our habits of thought, speech, and deed and help prioritize the value of contributory appreciation. But dramatically orienting our entire narration toward fully enlightening virtuosity is, I believe, another matter. For that, we must manifest a character consonant with an unwavering orientation of conduct away from regulation and control toward caring improvisation and contribution. That is, we must move beyond the societal dictates of control, but also beyond a simple freedom from such inclinations and institutions. In a word, we must actively realize truly virtuous sociality.

By this, I don't mean we have to become "virtuous" in some prudishly Victorian or—for that matter—some ritually Confucian sense. After all, there are very important enlightenment stories in the Ch'an tradition where it is moving out of the safety of cultivating only societally approved virtues that marks the turn from living as a mere sentient being to living as a buddha. What I have in mind is instead a cultivation of the kind of personal character that is both resolutely caring and not susceptible to being stumped by any questions of relevance, responsibility, and readiness. Without cultivating this sense of who we are, we will inevitably end up in situations of crisis or suffering where we don't see what's relevant to a true resolution and simply adopt instead a "knowing" stance from which we can ignore or make light of the situation. Failing to accept responsibility for our role in the arising of each and every problem we're aware of, we will find ourselves having failed to act when it might have done some good. We will not be ready, moment to moment, for both according with our situation and caring enough to respond as needed to keep realizing an ever more liberating narration.

Contrary to the need for developing a resolutely caring character, the colonization of consciousness promotes nihilism and narcissism as legitimate modes of being human. As character traits, dispositions toward nihilism and narcissism entail the personal devaluation of all values and hence of all possibilities for who we might become. They announce the end of growth and so the meaninglessness of change. Like dietary deficiencies, such dispositions say something about the kind of conduct we have been indulging and the kinds of environments in which we have been living—in particular, conduct and environments that effectively starve us of the virtues or life-forces needed to remain fully caring, responsive, and creative. Unfortunately, the karma according to which we are dramatically impoverished is also a karma for being ignorant of our own role in starving ourselves of meaning—a technologically enhanced and blinding success in getting what we want.

Nihilism and narcissism are thus the ultimate fruit of selfishness and most brilliantly flourish when we have too little energy remaining to care about more than our own, individual existence. As both the final and efficient cause of our dramatic depletion as persons, selfishness arises when we have become so intensely involved in getting what we want (or wanting what we have not yet gotten) that we are no longer able or willing to appreciatively attend to the contributions of others in our meaningful interdependence. Taken to its extreme, selfishness amounts to a denial of any noniconic dimension to the things and people around us. Beyond selfishness, there is only the elision of all but the most purely anatomical dimensions of being human—the constitution of a sociopath.

We would like to think of the sociopath as someone who—whether for genetic or environmental reasons—has completely broken with humanity as we know it. But in fact, the sociopath is more accurately seen as the perfection of the controlled and controlling self—the realization of a character unhindered by appreciation and a concern for contribution. As such, the sociopath is not really an aberration, but a dark precursor of our own futures—futures that make us particularly uncomfortable because we cannot gauge their distance or the likely time of their arrival. And so, while we find the sociopath repulsive and frightening, as box office receipts for films like *Silence of the Lambs* and *Seven* evidence, we also find ourselves captivated by his evident independence and individuality in a world where he does exactly what he pleases.

We need to ask not only how our world is being transformed by our technological lineage, but how our characters are being formed and perhaps deformed. We need to ask what kind of persons we are becoming and whether that is what we most sincerely desire. We can maintain some ideal goal of living in a multicultural world, but if we do not express the kind of character compatible with improvising a truly harmonious narration at all times, that world will remain merely ideal. In addition to meditatively freeing our awareness from the iconic imperative of the new colonialism, we must embark on a path of contributory virtuosity—the development of a thoroughly appreciative way of being human. In short, we must begin healing the wound of selfishness—a wound that is not inflicted on our individual and factual bodies, but rather on the dramatic body of our interdependence.

On the face of it, there is nothing particularly startling about such an appeal. In seeming answer to the dramatic depletion occasioned by our mass-mediated lives, for the last several decades, there has been a tremendous interest in personal growth and spiritual development in the West. And along with this has come an interest in Asian contemplative traditions, shamanistic practices, and new forms of psychotherapy that open up the possibility of articulating wholly new modes of being human. But for the most part, the direction of these interests has remained steadfastly consistent with the centripetal momentum of our technical tradition. Even when meditation has been recommended as a kind of general tonic or panacea, it is advertised as a way of getting in touch with our inner nature, a way of creating a safe haven from the hectic pace of daily life, a way of embarking on a psychospiritual journey at the end of which we will have fully empowered and perhaps even perfected our selves.

In the same way that confusing technologies with tools makes it impossible to be critical of the truly personal and communal impact of the former, by focusing on either our experience or our behavior and not our conduct or narrative movement as such, we have failed to critically assess, much less alter the basic direction of that movement. Much of the "New Age" promotion of meditation and spiritual exercises has thus only reinforced our biases toward control and autonomous individuality. Rather than articulating truly alternative values and ways of being human, most "New Age" rhetoric calls for little more than integrating such shadow values as 'trust' and 'universality'. The more precisely defined such shadows become, the more refined must be those aspects of our selves blocking the free flow of energy by means of which all things might spontaneously take care of themselves.

New experiences and new ranges of acceptable behavior have indeed been won by our efforts along these lines, but not the kind of narrative reorientation and character needed for realizing an always surprising and harmonious interdependence with one another. We have not succeeded in "reinventing the wheel." To the contrary, our public and private life narratives have continued to exhibit the effects of profound fragmentation. We need only look around us the next time we are shopping, driving in rush-hour traffic, or picking up our teenager after school to see what our recent "personal growth" movements have really effected. And if that is not sobering enough, we can visit a homeless shelter or book a flight to Sarajevo or Bangkok.

It is easy to deny the connections or to say change comes slowly. But that is also to admit we have simply not developed the kind of character needed to relinquish our horizons for relevance, responsibility, and readiness. We have yet to realize a truly liberating intimacy, and what intimacies we do enjoy—if we are honest enough—can hardly be called liberating. As often as not, our most intimate relationships now end in the institutionalized conflict of estrangement or divorce—in the realization that we have somehow and yet again missed the point of it all.

But realizing, too, that attention is the basic commodity fueling the growth of the new colonialism and so our dramatic depletion as persons, we are far from helpless. Meditative training may not be able to directly provide us what we want, but it can directly and immediately help bring about a world that is truly desirable and not merely one we wanted. By taking something like the Buddhist notion of the bodhisattva as constitutive of exemplary human being, we can practically work toward relinquishing our horizons for relevance, responsibility, and readiness and move in the direction of realizing a narration that is dramatically meaningful and not just a series of so-called "facts" and "objective events" and our individual views of them. Thus oriented, our circumstances will be spontaneously seen as the root narrative conditions for the blossoming of a new kind of intimacy. Pursued in the spirit of expressing a truly liberating character—a character constituted not by the drawing of clear and controlled boundaries, but rather their erasure—our intimacy will naturally shift in the direction of increasingly virtuosic sociality, increasingly sensitive and mutual contribution.

Still, it must be insisted that there can be no recipes for success in this venture and no failsafe "programs" for resisting the colonization of consciousness, no predetermined path, no "how to" manuals, and no warranties of success. Improvisational and appreciative virtuosity cannot be a necessary and predictable consequence of some set of actions or intentions. Virtuosity is a trail we blaze only at high risk, by opening ourselves to maximal intimacy and so maximal vulnerability with and before the people and things sharing our narration. It entails a constant flirtation with failure, an almost stubborn willingness to lose everything. But, so what? The only alternative is more of what we have already come to expect, and what true freedom is there in only getting what we want?

It is tempting to dismiss the claim that we can reverse the effects of the colonization of consciousness by committing ourselves to "reinventing the wheel"—by forfeiting control for appreciation and foregoing greater skill in getting what we want for the cultivation of contributory virtuosity. A rational skeptic will want to argue that no matter how good such a reorientation of our basic values sounds on paper, in practice it is simply not realistic. Show me how appreciation will feed the starving millions, he is likely to demand, how it is going to cure the sick or house the homeless.

But such appeals to "reality" as the bottom line are in actuality an exercise in prejudice—an uncritical appeal to the essential values and problems posed and then answered by our technological lineage and its scientific, religious, economic, and political kin. We cannot use "reality" to determine the practicality of axiological resistance to the colonization of consciousness precisely because our hitherto preferred "reality" is what is most crucially at stake in the process. "Reality" does not finally refer to something given, but rather to the full range of what we consider possible. That is, "reality" arises with the relatively sharp recognition and fixing of our horizons for relevance, responsibility, and readiness. In this sense, Buddhist practice is necessarily unrealistic.

Quite clearly, reinventing the wheel is not possible. We cannot start technological history over again, and we cannot return the earth to a pristine state in one fell swoop. But far from being a conclusive argument against it, we should see the very "impossibility" of reinventing the wheel through a reorientation of the primary axis of our attention as our best assurance that such a process will at least not lead us into making the same mistakes yet again. That is something we can no longer afford doing. Indeed, an unprecedented accomplishment of the impossible is the only way to meaningfully break the cycle of our karma—our obsessive fascination with being in control and our determination to get what we want. Only thus will we be capable of seeing the world as a dramatic treasury and developing those ways of being human needed for realizing a liberating and dramatic intimacy with all things.

Bibliography

WORKS CITED

Benson, Herbert. 1975. *The Relaxation Response*. New York: Morrow.

Bhaishajyaguru Vaiḍūryaprabhasā Tathagāta Sūtra, translated by Walter Liebenthal as *The Sutra of the Lord of Healing*, Peiping: Society of Chinese Buddhists Press, 1936. (abbrev. BVTS)

Cobb, John B. Jr. and Ted Halstead. 1996. "The Need for New Measurements of Progress." In *The Case against the Global Economy and For a Turn Toward the Local*, ed. Mander and Goldsmith. San Francisco: Sierra Club Books.

Daly, Herman E. 1996. "Sustainable Growth? No Thank You." In *The Case against the Global Economy and For a Turn Toward the Local*, ed. Mander and Goldsmith. San Francisco: Sierra Club Books.

Daly, Herman E., and John B. Cobb Jr. 1994. *For the Common Good: Redirecting the Economy Toward Community, the Environment, and a Sustainable Future*. Boston: Beacon Press.

Diamond Sutra. *Chin-k'ang Pan-jo Po-lo-mi Ching*. In *Taisho shinshu daizokyu*, T8: 235 v.8, no. 235.

Fieldhouse, D. K. 1984. *Economics and Empire, 1830 to 1914*. London: Macmillan.

Foucault, Michel. 1980. *Power/Knowledge: Selected Interviews and Other Writings, 1972–1977*. Edited and translated by Colin Gordon et al. New York: Pantheon Books.

Garfield, Jay. 1995. "Human Rights and Compassion: Towards a Unified Moral Framework." Published online in the *Journal of Buddhist Ethics Online Conference on Buddhism and Human Rights*. URL: http://jbe.la.psu.edu/

Gauttari, Felix. 1992. "Regimes, Pathways, Subjects." In *Incorporations*, ed. Jonathan Crary and Sanford Kwinter. New York: Zone Books.

Goffman, Erving. 1959. *The Presentation of Self in Everyday Life*. Garden City, NY: Doubleday.

Goldsmith, Edward. 1996. "Development as Colonialism." In *The Case against the Global Economy and For a Turn Toward the Local*, ed. Mander and Goldsmith. San Francisco: Sierra Club Books.

Goleman, Daniel, ed. 1997. *Healing Emotions*. Boston: Shambhala.

Goodland, Robert. 1996. "Growth Has Reached Its Limit." In *The Case against the Global Economy and For a Turn Toward the Local*, ed. Mander and Goldsmith. San Francisco: Sierra Club Books.

Habermas, Jürgen. 1984, 1987. *The Theory of Communicative Action*. 2 vols. Translated by Joseph McCarthy. Boston: Beacon Press.

Hershock, Peter. 1991. "The Structure of Change in the *I Ching*." *Journal of Chinese Philosophy* 18.3 (September 1991).

———. 1996. *Liberating Intimacy: Enlightenment and Social Virtuosity in Ch'an Buddhism*. Albany: State University of New York Press.

Hsü Tsang Ching. 1967. (Photographic supplement to the Chinese Buddhist Canon) Hong Kong: Fo.ching Liu-T'ung Ch'u.

Huang-po. *Huang-po-shan Tuan-chi Chan-shih Hsin-fa-yao*. In *Taisho shinshu daizokyu*, Vol. 48, no. 2012a.

Hui-neng. *The Platform Sutra: Nan-tsung tun-chiao tsui-shang ta-ch'eng Mo-ho-pan-jo po-lo-mi ching: Liu-tsu Hui-neng ta-shih yu Shao-Chou Ta-fan ssu shih-fa t'an ching*. Edited by Philip Yampolsky from the Tun-huang MS. *Taisho shinshu daizokyu*, Vol. 48, no. 2007.

Illich, Ivan. 1973. *Tools for Conviviality*. London: Calder and Boyars.

———. 1977. *Limits to Medicine: Medical Nemesis: The Expropriation of Health*. New York: Penguin.

———. 1981. *Shadow Work*. Boston: Boyars.

Krebs, Al. 1992. *The Corporate Reapers: The Book of Agribusiness*. Washington, D.C.: Essential Books.

Lin-chi. *Chen-chou Lin-chi Hui-chao Chan-shih Yu-lu*. In *Taisho shinshu daizokyu*, Volume 47, no. 1985.

Ma-tsu. *Kiang-si Ma-tsu Tao-I Chan-shih Yu-Lu*. In *Hsü Tsang Ching*, vol. 119, pp. 405–408.

Mander, Jerry, with Edward Goldsmith, eds. 1996a. *The Case against the Global Economy and For a Turn Toward the Local*. San Francisco: Sierra Club Books.

———. 1996b. "The Rules of Corporate Behaviour." In *The Case against the Global Economy and For a Turn Toward the Local*, ed. Mander and Goldsmith. San Francisco: Sierra Club Books.

Nagarjuna. 1986. *Mūlamadhyamakakārikā*. Translated by David Kalupahana. In *Nagarjuna: The Philosophy of the Middle Way*. Albany: State University of New York Press.

Nagel, Thomas. 1987. *The View from Nowhere*. New York: Oxford University Press.

Needham, Joseph. 1954. *Science and Civilisation in China*. Cambridge: Cambridge University Press.

Norberg-Hodge, Helena. 1991. *Ancient Futures: Learning from Ladakh*. San Francisco: Sierra Club Books.

Okri, Ben. 1993. *The Famished Road*. New York: Anchor Books.

Pai-chang. *Tun-wu Ju-tao-yao-wen lun*. In *Hsü Tsang Ching*, Vol. 110, pp. 420–26.

Postman, Neil. 1992. *Technopoly: The Surrender of Culture to Technology*. New York: Knopf.

Rifkin, Jeremy. 1995. *The End of Work: The Decline of the Global Labor Force and the Dawn of the Post-Market Era*. New York: Putnam.

Rorty, Richard. 1979. *Philosophy and the Mirror of Nature*. Princeton: Princeton University Press.

Sahlins, Marshall David. 1972. *Stone Age Economics*. Chicago: Aldine-Atherton.

Saṃyutta Nikāya. 1942. Translated by Caroline A. F. Rhys Davids. 6 vols. London: Pali Text Society.

Taishō Shinshū Daizōkyō, The Chinese Buddhist Canon, edited by Takakusu Junjiro & Watanabe Kaikyoku. Tokyo: 1924–35. (abbrev. T).

Tenner, Edward. 1996. *Why Things Bite Back: Technology and the Revenge of Unintended Consequences*. New York: Knopf.

Therīgāthā, ed. H. Oldenber and R. Pischel London: Pali Text Society, 1966, trans. K.R. Norman, London: PTS, 1969, 1971.

Vimalakirti Sutra. *Wei-mo-ch'i So-shuo Ching*. In *Taisho shinshu daizokyu*, Vol. 14, no. 475.

Vitousek, Peter M. and Paul R. Ehrlich, Anne H. Ehrlich and Pamela A. Matson. "Human Appropriation of the Products of Photosynthesis." *BioScience* 36.6, June, 1986.

Weinstein, Art. 1987. *Market Segmentation: Using Demographics, Psychographic, and Other Segmentation Techniques to Uncover and Exploit New Markets*. Chicago: Probus.

SUPPLEMENTARY, COMPLEMENTARY, AND CONTRARY READINGS

Agassi, Joseph. 1985. *Technology: Philosophical and Social Aspects*. Boston: Reidel.

Basalla, George. 1988. *The Evolution of Technology*. New York: Cambridge University Press.

Bowers, C. A. 1993. *Education, Cultural Myths, and the Ecological Crisis: Toward Deep Changes*. Albany: State University of New York Press.

Casey, Timothy and Lester Embree, eds. 1990. *Lifeworld and Technology*. Lanham, Md.: University Press of America.

Chomsky, Noam. 1994. *World Orders Old and New*. New York: Columbia University Press.

Drucker, Peter. 1970. *Technology, Management, and Society*. New York: Harper & Row.

Eliade, Mircea. 1971. *The Forge and the Crucible: The Origins and Structures of Alchemy*. Translated by Stephen Corrin. New York: Harper & Row.

Ellul, Jacques. 1964. *The Technological Society*. Translated by John Williamson. New York: Vintage.

———. 1990. *The Technological Bluff*. Translated by Geoffrey W. Bromiley. Grand Rapids, Mich.: W. B. Eerdmans.

Gille, Bertrand, André Fel, Jean Parent, and François Russo. 1986. *The History of Techniques*. 2 vols.. Translated by P. Southgate and T. Williamson (vol. 1) and by J. Brainch, K. Butler, et al. (vol. 2). New York: Gordon and Breach.

Hall, David L. 1982. *The Uncertain Phoenix*. New York: Fordham University Press.

Heidegger, Martin. 1977. *The Question Concerning Technology and Other Essays*. Translated by William Lovitt, New York: Harper & Row.

Hickman, Larry A., ed. 1990. *Technology as a Human Affair*. New York: McGraw-Hill.

Ihde, Don. 1990. *Technology and the Lifeworld: From Garden to Earth*. Bloomington: Indiana University Press.

Magdoff, Harry. 1978. *Imperialism: From the Colonial Age to the Present*. New York: Monthly Review Press.

Mander, Jerry. 1977. *Four Arguments for the Elimination of Television*. New York: Morrow.

———. 1991. *In the Absence of the Sacred: The Failure of Technology and the Survival of the Indian Nations*. San Francisco: Sierra Club Books.

Marcuse, Herbert. 1964. *One-Dimensional Man: Studies in the Ideology of Advanced Industrial Society*. Boston: Beacon Press.

Mitcham, Carl. 1994. *Thinking through Technology*. Chicago: University of Chicago Press.

McLuhan, Marshall. 1964. *Understanding Media: The Extensions of Man*. New York: McGraw-Hill.

Newman, Jay. 1997. *Religion and Technology: A Study in the Philosophy of Culture*. Westport, Conn.: Praeger.

Norgaard, Richard B. 1994. *Development Betrayed: The End of Progress and a Coevolutionary Revisioning of the Future.* London: Routledge and Kegan Paul.

Raghavan, Chakravarthi. 1990. *Recolonization: GATT, the Uruguay Round and the Third World.* Malaysia: Third World Network.

Sclove, Richard. 1995. *Democracy and Technology.* New York: Guilford Press.

Shiva, Vandana. 1989. *The Violence of the Green Revolution: Ecological Degradation and Political Conflict in Punjab.* Dehra Dun, India: Natraj Publishers.

———. 1993. *Monocultures of the Mind: Perspectives on Biodiversity and Biotechnology.* Dehra Dun, India: Natraj Publishers.

———. 1995. *Captive Minds, Captive Lives: Essays on Ethical and Ecological Implications of Patents on Life.* Dehra Dun, India: Research Foundation for Science, Technology, and Natural Resource Policy.

———. 1997. *Biopiracy: The Plunder of Nature and Knowledge.* Boston: South End Press.

Shrader-Frechette, Kristin and Laura Westra, eds. 1997. *Technology and Values.* Lanham, Md.: Rowman & Littlefield.

Tierney, Thomas. 1993. *The Value of Convenience: A Genealogy of Technical Culture.* Albany: State University of New York Press.

Ulanowsky, Carole. 1995. *The Family in the Age of Biotechnology.* Aldershot, U.K.: Avebury.

Winner, Langdon. 1977. *Autonomous Technology: Technics-out-of-Control as a Theme in Political Thought.* Cambridge: MIT Press.

Index